The memoirs of a Polish
and resilience in surviving
to Siberia in

based on the me
of my Mother Alicja Góra
a story put together ove. ...e years,
piece by painful piece

A FAMILY
EXILED

TERESA RADOMSKA

Teresa Radomska 2023

dedicated to the Góral/Radomski family
and to all those Polish exiles who lie in unmarked graves
scattered across the Russian wilderness.

A scar that taints Russia

The sheer horrors of what they witnessed remained
burned into their memories, impossible to suppress.
'The excruciating hunger pangs and the piercing cold which
made our bones throb in the intense Siberian winters. The
family lived with the past, every day,
there would be reminders and the psychological
impact clung to us until the very end.' – *unknown survivor*

ISBN: 978-1-915889-05-8

CONTENTS

'To choose one's victims, to prepare one's plans minutely, to slake an implacable vengeance and then to go to bed ...... there is nothing sweeter in the world' – J. V. Stalin

Hitler, Stalin and Roosevelt

In September 1939, in the signing of the Molotov-Ribentrop pact, Stalin with Hitler partitioned Poland in two. I am concentrating mainly on the Russians in this memoir as Stalin was the guilty warmonger who caused huge misery and terror to my family. Millions of Poles, Kulaks, Cossacks, Ukrainians, Kazakhs, Soviet veterans and Orthodox Christians died or were executed and many others suffered similar fates. Stalin had seen an opportunity when signing the Pact with Hitler to take revenge on the Polish Military settlers of the Kresy whom he considered 'enemies of the state.'

I will call this action a Holocaust because it was, without doubt, the deliberate and systematic destruction of a group of people because of their ethnicity – and this Holocaust of the Polish people and their country is ignored by the West and neither of the perpetrators have made sufficient if any restitution to Poland.

They both inflicted horrors on the Polish people who in 1939 numbered 35 ml and by 1945 were 24 ml. As well as the two main protagonists there was the Ukrainian UPA an ally of Germany who murdered over 100,000 Poles, mostly women and children in Wołyn, Polesia, Galicia, Podilia and Carpathia. Poland had suffered the most awful barbarism inflicted on any nation and unlike the Jewish Holocaust which quite rightly has world wide support the Polish Holocaust appears to have none.

Stalin's hatred of the Poles was based on class and was the motivation for his first act on entering Poland in 1939 to focus on the bourgeoise of Poland, the elements of Polish society who would most likely oppose Communist rule and this included the military men who had settled the Kresy after the Polish - Russian war of 1920 – men like my grandfather Adam and Great Uncle Walery.

Stalin's aim was to crush the military families, there was no place for this 'clique' in the Soviet order, he had not forgotten the defeat of the 1920 war and he wasted no time in deporting them en masse to the frozen wastelands of Siberia. These Poles were damned in the eyes of the Soviets who hated them. Aristocrats, Military Officers, Judges, writers, teachers, forest workers, land owners, the bourgeoise of Poland, Stalin's reason for wanting to eliminate them as they posed a threat in being more likely to stand up to him.

Hitler's plan meanwhile was to establish the supremacy of the Aryan race which meant not just the elimination of Polish Jews but also of Polish Christians, who were referred to by Hitler as 'subhuman' (Untermenschen). His hatred for the Polish people in general, was so intense he intended to eliminate them from the face of the earth. One of his initial commands was 'to send to death mercilessly and without compassion men, women and children of Polish derivation and language.' His attitude towards the citizens of Warsaw was 'Every inhabitant of Warsaw has to be killed, including men, women and children and all traces of their existence have to be removed. Do not take any prisoners! Every building has to be razed, Warsaw must be levelled to the ground in order to set a terrifying example to the rest of Europe.' Adolf Hitler 1944. The Warsaw Uprising had infuriated the German leaders who decided to make an example of the city and its people.

The night time arrests by Stalin's Secret Police began in 1940 without explanation or warning when they arrested over 250,000 civilians, 'anti-Soviet elements' and took them to already waiting transport, – cattle wagons primed for the journey to exile. Without adequate clothing in the bitterly cold winter and very little food, it would lead to the starvation of hundreds of thousands who were faced with the ever present stench of death, gnawing hunger and oppression by the NKVD.

Poles were also to suffer the first of many deaths at Auschwitz for which the camp had initially been built in 1940, to hold Polish political prisoners, the first group arriving in June 1940. By October 1941 20,000 Polish Catholics and 10,000 Soviet prisoners of war had been 'processed' at Auschwitz. The Germans forcibly deported approximately 2.8 ml Polish gentiles into labour for the Third Reich and the Russians had deported almost 1.7 ml Poles to Siberia by June 1941. An innocent people terrorised by two tyrants who then suffered massacres at the hands of the UPA.

There is no argument that Hitler abhorred Jews and caused so many ruthless deaths, I do not wish to lessen the enormity of the murders in the Holocaust but there were others, non-Jewish victims who are forgotten from Remembrances. So many precious lives were lost, over 3,000,000 were Polish Christians.

Despite being under constant surveillance, many Poles risked their lives to help Jews during the occupations and many were murdered for helping Jews. Poland was the only country in Europe with the death penalty imposed ruthlessly by German death squads for helping their brother Poles. They were also terrorized into transporting Jews to the Concentration camps and not to comply would have meant death to them and their family. Many Polish railway workers were also forced into transporting their countrymen to the prison camps and gulags across the Soviet Union.

In June 1941 Hitler declared war on the USSR, in Operation Barbarossa and a Polish-Soviet agreement was signed, the Sikorski-Maiski, after the reinstatement of Polish-Soviet diplomatic relations. On the signing of that agreement in August 1941 Stalin had agreed to revoke the Poland related aspects of the Molotov-Ribbentrop pact of 1939 and an 'amnesty' was declared for the Polish citizens in the labour camps and gulags across Russia. This prompted a massive exodus of Poles fleeing the USSR to join the Polish Army in Iran.

Stories like this are unknown to many westerners and when told they find it difficult to comprehend the depravation of what 1.7 ml Polish deportees went through. Not many Western history books record this episode and few politicians honour these victims in speeches commemorating World War II. From a personal view accounts of the war are incomplete without this neglected historical tragedy which is also mostly unknown of in Poland's communist era, not taught in schools and forbidden to be spoken of.

There are many photographs in the public domain showing victims from German extermination camps and scenes of German atrocities but not a single photo of a Polish adult prisoner of the Soviet gulag! Or of a Polish Mother and child as they really looked after escaping out of Russia, starved, skeletal and in rags. The legacy of silence and disinformation and deception to which the Roosevelt administration went to during the war remains to this day unchallenged and is an affront to historical truth.

The US propaganda machine, the OWI, (Office of War Information) held back photos of skeletal Polish children, taken in August 1942 by Lieutenant Colonel Henry Szymanski of the US army, publishing instead those of healthy children. Szymanski's photograph's and report of his observations on the deplorable condition of the refugees was classified as 'secret' and not published until 1952. Such was Roosevelt's fear that Americans, especially Polish Americans would learn the truth about Stalin's crimes against Poland and her people, his brutality was ignored so as not to upset the alliance with him! – although this is hugely questionable.

Roosevelt hid the Soviet mass murder of Polish POWs in Katyn and supressed an official US Government report of it as well as ignoring a British report from Churchill. A Polish Officer, Intelligence agent & Resistance leader, Witold Pilecki presented his report on the mass murder of Jews in German occupied Poland to the Allies which was ignored. Jan Karski, a Polish Diplomat, Underground courier for the Polish Government in Exile and Resistance member, relayed his eyewitness evidence of the Holocaust to US Supreme Court Justice, Felix Frankfurter, it too was ignored. They both risked their lives gathering information in Auschwitz and the Warsaw Ghetto and were not believed by Roosevelt or Churchill.

The mistreatment of Polish deportees was ignored, there was a total blackout, instead, Soviet propaganda of these events was spread in radio broadcasts by the OWI and the VOA (Voice of America) agencies headed by Communist sympathisers. Roosevelt refused to admit one Polish orphan during the war despite official representatives from the British Government to take 30,000 of the Polish refugees left in Persia who were the dependants of the 44,000 Poles who had joined the Polish Army. Persia at that time had already taken in large numbers of Polish war refugees.

The State Department advised the British Government 'that the US would not accede to its request' but the British representatives asked a second time and in reply the State Department declared 'that the US immigration laws would not permit these people to enter the US' and furthermore the US State Department advised the British representatives 'to take the Polish refugees to South Africa' a country that had already taken in large numbers.

The State Department then informed the British representatives that if they could find some country to take the Polish refugees then the US Government and the American Red Cross would help with aid. General Sikorski met with Mexican President Manual Camacho who in December 1942 agreed to take 28,000 refugees on quite restrictive conditions and Roosevelt agreed to make $3ml available for the transportation of the Poles to Mexico and for their first year there.

The whole episode was shrouded in secrecy, the refugees were kept in internment camps with Japanese Americans and travelled from Los Angeles to Santa Rosa in Mexico in a sealed train guarded by US army officials. Some of these refugees and orphans were on the Windrush with the West Indians after the war, hidden from view and not allowed to mix freely.

The end of the war brought about the complete betrayal of Poland to Russian oppression at the Yalta meeting on 11th February 1945 between Roosevelt, Churchill, and Stalin. It was a most unexpected blow to the many Poles dispersed throughout the world, who had fought, bled and died for the Allied cause. An agreement had been reached, with no resistance from Roosevelt or Churchill and no representation from the Polish Government, that Poland would fall into the Soviet sphere post WW2. The matter of returning home suddenly ceased to be taken for granted. How could my grandparents return to a communist Poland, a dictatorship? Unless you were a communist there was no future in Poland

and my Dziadek abhorred Communism.

Or as Witold Gombrowicz Polish novelist and dramatist put it, 'The end of the war did not bring liberation to the Polish people, in the battlegrounds of central Europe it just meant swapping one form of evil for another, Hitler's henchmen for Stalin's. While sycophants cheered and rejoiced at the 'emancipation of the Polish people from the feudal yoke' the same lit cigarette was simply passed from hand to hand in Poland and continued to burn the skin of the people'. I think Dziadek would have agreed with those sentiments.

Poland had become a forgotten backwater trapped behind the Iron Curtain and largely ignored by the world until the rise of Solidarność in the late 1970's and early 1980's. My grandparents died in 1983 and 1984 and lived to see the beginnings of revolution but not the eventual outcome.

The Germans destroyed 43% of Poland's educational, scientific and research institutions, over 50% of transportation and telecommunication infrastructure, 55% of the health infrastructure (352 hospitals) 60% of industry and nearly 1 ml acres of forest. They destroyed 40% of Poland's cultural goods (25 museums). They looted and transported to Germany, 2,800 European School paintings, 11,000 paintings by Polish masters, 1,400 sculptures, 172,000 old manuscripts, maps and gravures, 300,000 graphic art items, 15,000 rare books, 22 ml books from library collections and many other rare and valuable objects including priceless furniture, tapestries, even 5,000 church bells.

War damages have been estimated by successive Polish Government commissions from $750 to $1,000 billion (2017). The material damages to Warsaw alone were assessed by a special commission in 2005 at $54 billion. Warsaw was 85% destroyed and the loss of life was over 200,000, the damage to the health of the survivors is beyond valuation but the Poles began rebuilding their capital almost before the dust of the Wermarcht bombings had blown away.

It is very hard to understand why the West ignored the Soviet attack and occupation of Poland, the indifference politicians and journalists showed to the suffering of the Poles. Survivors were much affected by this painful indifference to the Soviet atrocities and it is a mainly untold story to this day. My family adapted to a new life in a new country but it was a largely unsympathetic one.

I am hugely conscious and proud of my roots, as a daughter of Kresy survivors, and I continue the story on the theme of the prequel, Midnight Train to Siberia with the homage it deserves. I feel it is important to show where a complete disregard of common rights can lead especially today when anti-Polonism is on the rise again.

Polish people surely deserve that their Holocaust merits the same as the Jewish Holocaust and that Germany in particular makes the proper restitution, as it is Israeli political and media activists are demanding restitution from Poland and actively spreading anti Polonism.

**All Polish people suffered hugely during WW2
and we must remember them all.**

'I eventually started writing my biography after the gentle encouragement of my daughter Tereska, who urged me to start writing my family history in 2003 but I just didn't know how to start, where to begin and then one day at the age of 79 it came to me. I started and I looked forward to writing every day.'

Alicja Góral – Sybiraczka

– my Mother, who embodies the spirit, passion and soul of the Polish people.

Introducing the family Radomski-Góral

My grandparents, Kazia and Adam my mother Alicja, Aunt Janina and Janusz my Uncle at the time of the invasions lived in Równe. Kazia's brother Walery and his wife Ziuta, sons Włodek and Zbigniew and daughter Marysia were living on their Osada Krechowiecka (named after Adam and Walery's regiment the 1st Lancers Krechowiecki) just outside Równe and near to the Ukrainian Russian border in the eastern borderlands of Poland. My Grandfather Adam and Great Uncle Walery had been awarded Osadas on the borderlands after the Bolshevik war of 1920 as reward for the success of Poland regaining territory lost in previous partitions.

On the 10th February 1940 on a bitterly cold day at 5am Stalin's Secret Police, the NKVD, burst into my grandparent's home waving guns and screaming at them. They were arrested as 'anti Soviet elements,' told they were to be exiled to Siberia, stripped of their land and home and given half an hour to pack some belongings. They were then taken to an assembly point outside Równe in a horse drawn sledge passing many of their neighbours awaiting the same fate. Stalin viewed these Military settlers as a danger to his plans to Sovietise parts of Europe as this was the most likely group of people to stand up to him and his plans.

There were 5 mass deportations of the military and civilian populations of eastern Poland in 1939-41 with a clear distinction made between the February 1940 deportation and the April one. The February military deportees were targeted as 'special settlers' and sent to zones selected in isolated areas and administered by a special branch of the NKVD. They were sent to 13 Oblasts, Arkhangelsk, Yekaterinburg, Irkulsk, Molotov, Vologda, Omsk, Novosibirsk, Chelysbinsk, Gorki, Czkalovsk, Kirov, Ivanovo and Yaroslavi. Other deportees were sent mainly to Kraij-Altai, and Krasnoyarsk, Komi, Mari, Yakut and Bashkiv.

From their home in Równe they were transported in cattle wagons towards the deep snows of Siberia and the Arctic regions, the train stopping at Gorki after 17 days then onto Sharya from where they had to walk many miles in very deep snow to the labour camp, Poldniewica, the first of 3 camps, later to Duraszewo and finally to Derewalka. Their only crime was being Polish and being 'an enemy of the people.'

They were expected to work for their communist masters, clearing forests to lay tracks for a railway line, from dawn to dusk on the most meagre rations. Many perished through malnutrition, disease and the cold. Used as slave labourers they were worked until they dropped. A deportee was a 'nonperson,' a slave of the Soviet penal system. Upon arrival at the prison, labour camp or penal colony they were told by the Commandant: 'Here you will live and here you will die, niechevo, hairs will grow on my palms before you are free.'

By the middle of 1941 most of those Polish citizens had been imprisoned in subhuman conditions throughout Russia, from the Caucasus to the White Sea, in Steppe, Tundra and Taiga, from the Urals, Kazakhstan and onto the mountains of Russian Asia. At the same time 222,000 Polish servicemen arrested in 1940, were imprisoned in Siberian Gulags.

Life was awful from the very beginning but their spirit and determination was so strong, it saw them through the hell of the labour camp, the towers, barbed wire fences, searchlights and the routine aggression towards them. Every day they prayed, 'do not despair, have faith the Bolsheviks will not break you.' They suffered incredible hardship and many starved. Survival was of the utmost importance and attitude was a crucial factor and I put their survival down to their faith and love for each other and their spirit, the spirit that Stalin wouldn't break.

They also had good luck on their side and the kindness of the friends they had made, including the generous acts from the Russians deported there after the Revolution in 1917 which added towards their survival. The Russian people gave shelter when needed and shared what little food they had. The conditions were brutal, lone women were forced to give up their children to Soviet orphanages or watch as they starved to death. It was heart breaking.

Upon Hitler's attack on the USSR in June 1941 Stalin, unable to withstand Hitler's forces on his own, had no choice but to enter into an alliance with the West and turned to Churchill and Roosevelt for help. Their condition was the release of his Polish prisoners and the formation of a Polish army. The Soviet Ambassador to the UK Ivan Maisky and General Sikorski on behalf of the Polish Government signed the first diplomatic agreement on 30th July 1941. Maisky then announced that the Soviet-German treaty of August 1939 relating to the territorial division of Poland along the Ribbentrop-Molotov line was no longer valid.

General Anders had been nominated as Commander of the new Polish Army by Genera Sikorski and it was his intention to get as many Poles out of Russia as he could and he did his utmost against a belligerent Stalin. Polish soldiers had been commissioned to travel to the various camps and Kolkhozes across the USSR to gather as many isolated families as they could. The area was vast and the terrain, mountains, forests the sub-arctic climate made it extremely difficult to reach those spread so widely.

Stalin agreed an 'amnesty' which assured the release of Polish POWs and civilian deportees which took considerable time to get through to the Poles across the vastness of the USSR. Many were never informed that they were free to leave, the 'amnesty' deliberately kept from them to retain their labour. However, by late 1941 25,000 Polish recruits had joined Anders' Army from the gulags (Buzuluk RU) with civilians joining them and they all headed towards Tehran.

Although Stalin officially complied he made things very difficult with inadequate rations, medical aid and equipment so General Anders demanded that his army be evacuated from the USSR to the Middle East to fight under British command. He also demanded that all Polish civilians leave with him. An invitation to the many Poles incarcerated in labour camps and gulags that they couldn't refuse despite their hatred for the Bolsheviks, they just wanted to fight the Germans.

In March/April 1942 33,069 Soldiers and 10,879 civilians including 3,100 children were evacuated from USSR and Anders' army operations moved to Tashkent in Uzbekistan. Civilian Poles from the labour camps also headed there and in August-September 1942 43,746 Soldiers from the Gulags and 25,501 civilians including 9,633 children were evacuated to Persia.

The Polish Embassy in Kubyshev in the meantime was struggling to help the many thousands of refugees moving south, fleeing their mistreatment and imprisonment, they were exhausted and suffering from malaria, dysentery, typhus and other ailments, especially the effects of starvation. Their physical condition not able to sustain them through about 4,000 km of Soviet terrain and they had to contend with the NKVD disrupting their journeys and intercepting them for their labour despite the safety to travel towards the Polish army assured them by the 'amnesty.'

Once discharge papers had been issued my family were faced with the arduous journey from Siberia to Uzbekistan. Like many Poles who made their escape from imprisonment in Russia, they were determined to join the Polish Army gathering in Tashkent. They had no other option and another struggle for survival began. With very little food to sustain them, often ill with dysentery and typhus, they weren't fit to fight and were separated at times but with great determination they journeyed on towards the Polish army. That was the only thing on their mind, to link up with the Polish army however long it took and they barely survived their ordeal.

The journeys from the labour camp took the family on the Trans Aral, Trans Siberian railways and into five time zones. Briefly, they travelled through the Ural Mountains, skirting the Kurgistan Steppes, through

Kazakstan and into Uzbekistan. From Bukhara they were taken to Vobkent and forced by the Soviets, determined to delay them reaching freedom, into hard labour for the Uzbeks. Their physical condition was desperate.

They were only able to leave Vobkent when reunited with Walery who had been searching for them. He had been posted to nearby Tashkent and advised Kazia to enlist my mother and aunt in the Polish cadets in Guzor. The girls set off to Guzor and my grandfather was posted to Iraq whilst Kazia stayed with my uncle Janusz in Vobkent. They were reunited with the girls in Pahlevi sometime later as Kazia had finally managed to enlist Janusz in the cadets. She was now desperately ill in hospital in Tehran.

Once in the safety of Pahlevi in Persia they were out of Stalin's reach and able to begin their recovery. By this stage they had other journeys to make, to Refugee camps from Pahlevi to Tehran and Isfahan then onto Ghazir and Beirut in Lebanon, where my mother married in 1946 an Englishman serving in the RAF. The family would eventually find a home in England, my Mother and her husband William and Aunt in 1946 and my grandparents and uncle in 1948.

On their arrival at Liverpool docks from Lebanon on 19.2.1948, Kazia Góral nee Radomska, born in Wróblewo on 23.2.1899 presented her Paszport 11445/43c issued in Beirut on 25.2.1943 and was presented with Alien Order A128294.

Adam Góral born Daleszewicze on 26.5.1894, presented his Paszport 11446/43c and was issued his Alien Order A128295.

'Permission to land at Liverpool was granted on condition that the holder registered at once with the Police'. They were not exempt from restrictions of the Alien Orders until 29.5.1961.

From Liverpool my grandparents and Uncle were assigned to Resettlement Camps in Pulborough, Horsham, Helstem and Ely over a period of time. They had clothing issued to them on 1.3.1948 as they had arrived in England with very little as had many refugees arriving in England after the war. Many of the refugees from Poland were initially subsidised by the Polish Government as they had been in the refugee camps in Persia and Lebanon.

My parents were there to meet them at Liverpool and it was a joyous and emotional day, I was 6 months old, the first born to a free family and it was my Mother's birthday. Very many tears were shed.

Some thoughts from my Mother, Alicja, regarding refugee families in England. – 'we made up small pockets of Poland, holding onto whatever fragments remained of our once normal lives. We spoke Polish, German, Russian, Hungarian, Czechoslovakian and Yiddish. We all felt out of place, we knew we were new to this country and that we belonged somewhere else... We were survivors and children of survivors and many of us had lost family members. Marriages were made in haste and some out of desperation, there was a deep need to have someone to hold and love. Most of us were still in shock and grieving for a lost Poland.'

Life in England as a refugee was difficult and my grandparents especially didn't tell many people of their past, they hid it and somehow dealt with their demons. Physically, the family gradually recovered, yet the mental scars were more difficult to heal. The family had lost absolutely everything, their home, livelihood and liberty and gone through a life threatening experience. There were times when something would trigger a memory and transport them back to the camp and they would feel the fear. I sometimes saw it in my Mother's eyes and manner and the way she would regularly walk up and down the long lounge struggling with her emotions, walking the memories away.

They would hoard food, treasure it, remembering the starvation in the camps. They always had to have enough food and my Mother's cupboards were crammed full of tins and packets and jars from the Deli. She and my grandparents never returned to Poland, they didn't take the opportunity to see their homeland again, the Kresy, it was now part of the Ukraine with the border changes made by Stalin.

I am but one voice, a grandaughter and daughter of an extremely brave family and I have gone through an emotional journey of my own to unravel their past, their suffering which was buried very deep, their stubborn resilience, belief and determination. The Radomski's were never far behind or ahead of the Góral's in any of the many routes covered from Poland to the USSR to Persia to Lebanon and finally to England where they were all reunited. They seemed to be connected by a very strong radar of their own, a very lucky family and their defiant spirit shines out still.

I dedicate this memoir specifically to my dahlink Mamusia Alicja, who at 97 still remembers the labour camp in Siberia despite suffering from Alzheimers and to the memory of my beloved grandparents, Kazia and Adam and the other members of the Góral and Radomski family's who have been my inspiration. My reason for looking into their history, which is my history, a big part of who I am.

There is an irony in the telling of this episode of WW2. Had my family not been deported to Siberia they would most likely have fallen victim to the massacre of Poles in Wołyn and Eastern Galicia, by the Ukrainian

Nationalists who razed their town Równe, to the ground and murdered those settlers who had escaped Stalin's deportations. Between 76,000 and 106,000 were victims of this barbarism, mostly women and children over the entire region, my Babcia's cousin Toscia and her two infant sons were burned alive. In 2016 the Parliament of Poland passed a resolution recognising the massacres as a Genocide and in the Ukraine to this day the UPA members are celebrated as heroes.

**A person is only forgotten if their name is forgotten,
the Góral/Radomski's are not forgotten,
their name is written into memory in this biography.**

Teresa Radomska 2021

A Happy Childhood

My Babcia Kazimiera Radomska was born on 23rd February 1899 in Wróblew a village in Sieradz County, Lodz, in Central Poland. Her father, Władyslaw Radomski was the son of nobleman Walerian, whose coat of arms in official papers of that time identified him as Bielawski. He had lost his estates after taking part in the Uprising against the Russian occupation in 1863.

The Uprising had begun on 22nd January 1863 as a spontaneous protest by young Poles against conscription into the Lithuanian Russian army and they were joined by Officers of the army and various politicians. The insurrection was unsuccessful, they were severely outnumbered and lacked any real support forced instead to resort to guerrilla tactics. Public executions and deportations to Siberia led many Poles to abandon the armed struggle and it resulted in even stricter Russian control over Poland.

Walerian Bielawski, my grand mother's grandfather, was one of many insurgents to be captured and imprisoned at Częstochowa in southern Poland for his part in the Uprising, he was charged and sentenced with expulsion to Siberia but escaped from the prison with the help of a relative Cardinal Bielawski and made his way with his wife and children to eastern Poland to a friend who owned the Rozienek estate where they would be safe. Dates are very difficult to pinpoint as the family has very little detail on Walerian, and I am assuming his son Władysław born in 1863 continued to live on the Rozienek estate later working as the manager. He met and married Sofia and had children Walery, Kazia, Bronia, Antoni and Eugenia and although I am short of detail on Walerian and Sofia there are photographs of the family included here.

My Dziadek Adam Góral was born on 26th May 1894 in Daleszewo, a village in Gmina Gryfino in the Gryfino county in north western Poland, quite close to the German border, where his Mother Konstancja worked on the estate of Count Erazma Rupniewski. She and the Count fell in love, had an affair and she became pregnant with Adam. The Count refused to acknowledge his son or to support Konstancja and she had to leave the estate to find work elsewhere. The stigma of illegitimacy was something to be greatly ashamed of in those days and Adam never forgave the Count for the way he had treated his Mother.

Konstancja later married Bolesław Góral who was working on the estate of Count Szczerbek. He accepted Adam and gave him a home in his cottage on the estate and brought him up with his half brother and

1

sisters. Adam worked on the estate until he was about 17 and in an effort to do something with his life he enlisted in the Krechowiecki Lancers, to train and fight for his beloved country to help free Poland from Russia's oppression. It was on one of his visits to his family back on the estate of Count Szczerbek that he met Kazia who was visiting friends. This was in 1914 on the eve of WW1 he was almost 20 and Kazia was 15.

They obviously got on very well and Adam fell in love with the 'beautiful Kazia' very quickly. After a customary courtship, in those days there were formalities to follow, Adam proposed to Kazia who accepted and he then left to join his regiment. He promised Kazia with the bravado of a young cavalryman, 'that the enemy bullets would not get him' and he would come back safely from war. However, following WW1 there was another war to fight, the Bolshevik War from 1919-1920 that both Walery, Kazia's brother and Adam fought in for Poland's independence until September 1920 when they returned victorious.

In the Spring of 1921 a group of Soldiers from a small village in eastern Poland, in the area of Gmina Łyse in Ostrołęka County set off towards Wołyn by train with their horses, sabres and saddles to take up residence on land of the eastern frontier recently reclaimed from the Bolsheviks. Adam and Walery had been granted the land on the eastern borderlands by the Polish Government as a reward for their war service.

Many military settlers had been given land and were to build their homes there. Having fought in the 1914-18 war and also in the Polish-Russian uprising in 1920 they had earned the right to the land which was in a terrible state and needed incredible planning and work to make it habitable and there were very few tools to do the job.

Progress was generally good and by 1921-22 the land had been mapped out into individual plots and Adam was busy building his own bungalow to be ready before he could marry Kazia. The military settlers lived in groups and worked together helping each other digging wells and building houses so they could start living on their own plots although to begin with they would live in dugouts.

Beginnings were very hard and there was unpleasantness from the neighbouring villages populated by indigenous Russians and Ukrainians who were hostile to the Military settlers but as time went on relations developed and cooperation and respect became mutual although at the outbreak of the Soviet invasion to come, the Ukrainians became extremely hostile.

By Autumn the settlement covered about 1500 hectares with 2 instruction farms of 45 hectares and 85 ordinary farms of 11-13 hectares with 2 hectares of meadows. The veterans had worked hard and Adam was almost ready to make arrangements with Kazia and their families for a wedding and they married in 1923 in the church on Count Rozienek's estate.

He and Kazia moved to Lipniki, a small village in the area of Gmina Łyse in Ostrołęka County shortly after their wedding and my Mother Alicja was born there on 19th February 1924. I haven't been able to find out why they moved there when Adam had his land on the Osada. The name Lipnicki is thought to come from the Lipa or Linden trees which grew in abundance in the village and surrounding areas. They then moved onto their newly built Osada and were happily settled there, almost carefree after the disruption and horrors of WW1 and the Bolshevik War. With the many other Polish soldiers and their families they worked the small plots of land to help re-establish Polish claims to the area previously lost in the partitions of Poland.

Wołyn, Powiat Rowne, Gmina Aleksandria
Osada Krechowiecka
– settled by the families Góral and Radomski

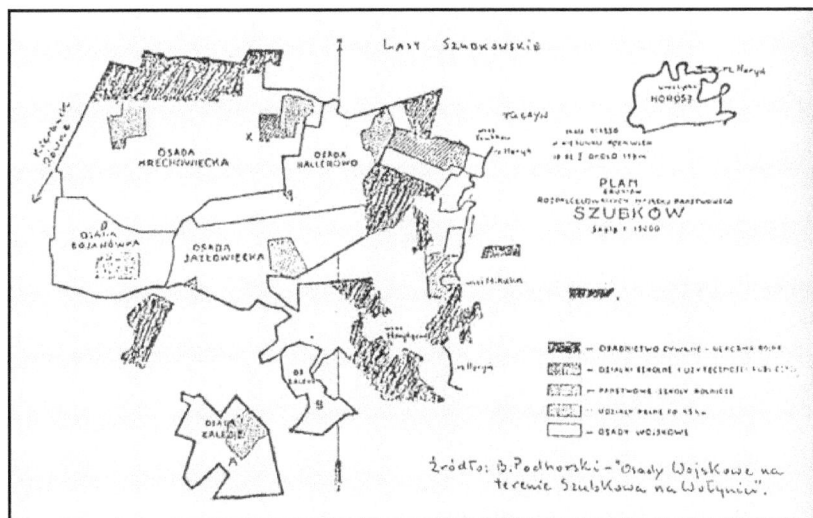

*The Osada Krechowiecka is now called Nova Ukrainka
and belongs to the Ukrainian republic. All towns and villages have been renamed
since the Yalta Convention in 1945.*

3

Although the family were happy with life on the Osada, Adam was not a natural man of the soil like his brother in law Walery and wasn't able to make the farm pay. He found work in the town and made arrangements to move the family into an apartment in Równe. By this time Jasia born in 1926 and Janusz born in 1930 had been added to the family. Adam rented his settlement on the Osada to a German family who were very grateful for the work and home and were better fitted to work the land. Adam only asked them as a favour to plant as many fruit trees as they could.

When Hitler recalled all Germans across Europe into his army, the German family visited Adam to thank him for his kindness and to say goodbye, they had brought baskets of fruit for him in gratitude. When the German family left Równe and before my family were loaded onto the trains to exile in Siberia the Ukrainians had taken over their Osada for 'safekeeping'.

Walery Radomski Kazia Góral Adam Góral Ziuta Radomski

Walery Radomski's house at Osada Krechowiecka 193?

Kazia made clothes, she was an excellent tailor and their finances began to improve. Life was better, the family lived by the river and the children went to a school named after the Polish Queen, Jadwiga. They were happy but there was always a worry about Kazia's health as she had a heart condition and suffered very frequent attacks which caused worry to the family, especially the children.

On summer vacations the family would visit Walery's Osada and they had wonderful happy, carefree times with their cousins, Włodek born in 1925, Zbigniew in 1927 and Marysia in 1930, they slept in the barn in the hay and enjoyed the beautiful fields, the forests and the river, picking mushrooms. It was an ordinary, simple life and the families were very close.

Kazia and Adam continued getting on with their lives day to day, as did most of the settlers and residents of Równe who were aware of some unrest but totally unprepared for the horrors soon to be unleashed upon them.

When that came on 1st September 1939 with the Germans invading their country and then on the 17th September the invasion by the Soviets it was still a huge shock to everyone and 'destroyed our life's work.' Then in February 1940 came the expulsions to forced relocation of all the military settlers to the forests of Northern European Siberia the Steppes of Kazakhstan, and as far as the frontier of Mongolia. 'We had no idea what lay in store for us and were extremely frightened'. Exile to remote regions of the Russian empire was not unknown to the Poles, after uprisings against the Russians in the 19th century many Poles had been exiled to Siberia. Those earlier exiles knew the reason for their expulsion, the new deportees of 1940-41 did not know where they were going or why. 'We would never see our beloved homes again, our lives had been ripped apart, changed for ever.'

'Without any warning in the early morning of 10th February 1940 armed Russian soldiers crashed through our door and ordered us to dress and pack. They would come back in half an hour and told us to be ready.'

This is the story of the deportation of my family by Stalin's secret Police, the NKVD, and the partitioning of Poland into the hands of the Soviet Union and Germany after the Molotov-Ribbentrop pact of 1939. Yet another example of German and Soviet plundering of Polish territories. The German terror in Europe from 1939 to 1945 was based on a primitive theory of race and the level of killing was without pity or mercy and unprecedented in the history of Poland and indeed the world. The Polish people were essentially in a state of slavery to both Hitler and Stalin.

Between five and six million Polish citizens fell victim to the Germans. Stalin's 'Eastern Plan', was based purely on class, of ridding the 'bourgeoise of the eastern borderlands' and spreading communism through the rest of Europe. It included a scheme to deport these 'enemies of the people' to Siberia and other remote Russian territories, and this was accomplished with the further loss of life to the Poles of over 2 ml.

I've included some personal testimonies from survivors with more detail expressing their own views on what happened to their country and people. Poland's history is a partly sad one, invaded by many of its neighbours, especially the Russians.

I'll begin with my dahlink Ciocia Jasia's remembrance of a reunion dinner at the White Eagle Club in Balham in 1991 and Danuta Mączka-Gradosielska's memories from home and a few others which basically tell a similar story in their own words. I've also included some notes from my Dziadek and Wujek Walery.

Janina Góral

'I am still under the spell of our reunion dinner on 23rd February 1991 in the White Eagle Club in Balham, London. For me my sister Ala and brother Janusz it was a deeply emotional reliving of the past. Before my eyes I could picture beautiful Wołyn, the Krechowiecka settlement and Równe. In a word, the land of my childhood, idealized through the prism of time. I remember Horyn, that dark and horrendous river, where we used to go swimming with Włodek and Zbyszek Radomski, when we used to come for vacation from Równe to stay at our Aunt and Uncle's at the settlement. I remember beautiful fields on the outskirts of Równe, covered in marigolds and the bewitching strong smell of 'sweet rush' and 'bird cherry' which I have never smelt or come across since in the rest of my days. I remember the forests surrounding the settlement, towards the Ukrainian village of Kozlin. I used to go to this village with my sister Ala and our Mamusia or sometimes our Babcia to pick mushrooms. It was also here in the woodland that the family Ławicki lived. They had four daughters and we befriended the girls. Their house was surrounded by fields of wild flowers. One field was white and the second purple. A tiny stream flowed through the forest, the water was crystal clear and the bottom was covered in golden sand and here lived tiny frogs. As children we sat on the bank of the stream catching the little frogs so we could touch them and examine them and later throw them back into the stream. I also remembered the road to Aleksandria which we used to walk with Ala and Babcia on Sundays to church. The views were beautiful from here leading through woodland. I relived these memories so strongly in my mind that it left me with a great desire to share them, because they underline the magic and the beauty of Osada Krechowiecka and the region of Wołyn.'

Selected excerpts by Danuta Mączka-Gradosielska – *family friend*

'Poland regained her independence in 1918 but our fathers had to fight with Soviet Russia for the eastern territories until September 1920. On

17th November 1920 an Act was adopted awarding land ownership to soldiers of the Polish army. The Riga Treaty was signed on 18th March 1921 and it was then that Poland's eastern borders were defined. The soldiers who qualified to receive land on the eastern frontiers of the Republic of Poland were soon demobilized.

In the spring of 1921 102 soldiers of the Krechowiecy Ułans Regiment were festively celebrating their last Easter in the home Regiment. A week later they set off from Hrubieszowto Wołyn, going by train, as military custom had it, each travelling in the same car as his horse, sabre, saddle and in uniform, by then quite badly worn.

The Regiment assigned them a few supply carts, two field kitchens, some equipment but no tools or farming utensils. For the first two months the veterans were provided with provisions for the people, and fodder for horses for 6 months from the garrison in Równe some 16 km away. The veterans travelled to Wołyn to start a new life on land of their own. They had hard pioneering work to do on land plots awarded them free 'for defending Homeland borders'.

The assigned terrain had no buildings, it was utterly desolated, so the veterans billeted themselves in the village of Horyngrod and immediately started by nominating a board of the 'work column' chief, warehouse manager, head of chancery and treasurer. The veterans eventually moved closer to villages Szubkow and Remel.

The veterans lived in groups and worked jointly, helping each other operating communal kitchens and building dug-outs and from September 1921 had to arrange everything for themselves. Some were helped by their families and those who were married were helped by their wives' dowries. Soon the land was mapped out into individual lots which took some time. By the autumn the settlement covered approximately 1500 hectares and consisted of 2 instruction farms of 45 hectares and 85 ordinary farms of 11-13 hectares plus 2 hectares of meadows. The Karlowszczyzna woods covered 200 hectares with a plot for a community house and a school of 4 hectares.

The settlement was shielded from the north by state owned forest over the entire length of 5 km. Through the middle ran a wide road from Równe to Tuczyn cut through with local lanes leading to neighbouring villages, Zytynia, Aleksandria, Remel, Azubkow, Kozlin and several others. These were large villages populated by indigenous Russian and Ukrainian people and in the early years there were unpleasant incidents. They were hostile and mistrustful of the Polish military settlers but as the years went by reciprocally correct neighbourly relations developed and in some cases there was even good cooperation and mutual respect.

Beginnings were very hard and many lived in dugouts. They started digging wells and building houses and they worked together so they could start living on their own plots as soon as possible. By 1923 almost all the settlers were married and the settlement flourished, much was achieved by joint efforts. A dairy operated in a rented house and in another house a school was set up. In 1929 a community hall was started and finished in the same year. Classes were being added, there were 7 and 240 children and the teaching staff also grew.

From 1930 the settlement was financially secure with a post office, a telephone operator and a cooperative shop. Scouts, guides and brownies and a farmer's association flourished and there was a bus route into Równe. There were orchards, plantations of sugar beets and tobacco the ponds were full of fish and there were herds of cattle, flocks of fowl and all the common effort of the settlers was bringing prosperity.

The local populations also benefitted from the settlers, they found work on the farms and there was access to better and improved breeds of cattle and fowl, better types of grains and seeds. The crowning glory was the building of the church in the Karowszczyzna Range in 1937.

The settlers worked as a group for their ideals and the common good and on a social level there were dances and social meetings, child raising courses and a health centre. A friendly atmosphere of solidarity prevailed where help was available for every need.

In 1931 the settlement celebrated its 10th anniversary with a community dinner for several hundred guests and cavalry veterans were present.'

Memories of Walery Radomski, brother of Kazia

'Adam and I and our fellow cavalry colleagues, were not only given the land as a reward by the new Polish state, it was also to increase the number of Poles in those territories where the Ukrainian and Byelorussian population prevailed. We were expected to take part in the economic and cultural life of these backward provinces and boost modern methods of farming.

The beginnings of the settlement were very difficult, there were a number of unpleasant incidents with the local populations in surrounding villages of Ruthernian and Ukrainian culture. There was an attitude of hostility and distrust on the part of the locals towards the military settlers although over time relations improved.

We settled the land and made a life for ourselves and the early years were extremely hard as the land was pitted with shell holes, trenches and other debris of war. We worked hard and made the land habitable and plentiful and our families lived a fairly happy and prosperous life. We managed to draw our Ukrainian and Byelorussian neighbours closer, removing the initial prejudice we had found as our neighbours had themselves hoped to acquire this land. Large parts of the land however were no man's land which had belonged previously to the Tsar's family, the Russian government and Russian landlords.

Our regiment the Krechowiecka Lancers, was allocated an area near Szubkow on the left bank of the river Horyn, in the county of Równe. The land Adam and I had chosen was part of a settlement peopled by couples very much like ourselves with a short short walking distance between the farms and quite close to the local village. Living in groups like this and working as teams we helped each other to build our homes together. The Osada was comprised of two training farms of 45 hectares each, 85 regular farms of 11 to 13 hectares each and two meadows of 2 hectares each. There were also plots for public use, the Karowszczyzna Wood of 200 hectares and 4 hectares for the settlement community centre and school.

The Osada was bisected by the wide well travelled road from Równe to Tuczyn with many country roads leading to various villages. Aleksandria, Remel, Szubkow amongst them, whose inhabitants were assimilated into the prevailing Ruthenian and Ukrainian culture and with the passing of years relations improved and cooperation and respect developed between us.

By 1923 most of us settlers were married, and the settlement was developing well. A dairy operated and a school was established. A great deal had been established by common effort and by the 1930's the settlement was in full bloom economically. Our families lived well and happily. As well as the school and dairy, there was a post office and telephone operator, a co-operative shop, a warehouse for grain and the offices of all executives of the farmers' association, the brownies, guides and scouts.

There were orchards, plantations of sugar beet, tobacco, the ponds were full of fish and the herds of cattle and flocks of fowl, cows and pigs, were evidence of the prosperity of all of us settlers. There was also rye, fruit trees, sunflowers in abundance, apples and cherries, grapes raspberries and gooseberries. Tobacco plantations, sugar beet and mollasses hops and the neighbouring villages benefitted from our hard work.

Selected excerpts from the memories of Franciszek Żurek.

On the morning of Sunday, September 17, 1939, a frightened Kazimierz Ferens, gave them the news that Soviet tanks and infantry carrying long bayonets on rifles had entered the streets of Krzemieniec. According to Antoni Żurek, on approach to Podzamcze, the Soviet officers told the local population that the forests and land now belonged to the Russian nation. In line with this approach, they began to divide the land and distribute it to the Ukrainian peasants. Only K. Ferens, fled his home in a panic and went into hiding at the home of his brother in law – forester H. Nowak. The rest of the settlers remained at their homes.

A month later, on Sunday 22 October, elections were held for a new Assembly of the People. The Poles who did not participate in the "elections", became the subject of persecution by the Soviet authorities who began a series of arrests. Franciszek Żurek, a 25-acre landholder was arrested (with his family) for trying to organise an election day protest on 23 October 1939. He was then deported to the depths of Soviet territory where he worked hard for two years, felling trees on the Shilka River.

He was finally sent to prison for keeping notes in a diary, and was released in Moscow on December 4, 1941. after the "amnesty" was granted. With great difficulty, he reached the army of General Anders. In his weakened and exhausted state, he fell ill with typhus, and after a few weeks, on 7 April 1942, died in Guzor on Soviet territory. There he was buried in a mass grave by his wife and a few of his closest colleagues, with whom he had shared the fate of deportation and exile.

Surviving Polish families were leaving Guzor in Uzbekistan for Persia. From there they travelled to Iraq, Palestine, Egypt, and by sea around Africa to England, Canada or Mexico. Franciszek Żurek's family left Guzar two weeks after his death, following this route, arriving in England in mid-September 1942. Four years after the war, in December 1949, Franciszek's wife, Stanisława and their daughters travelled to distant Australia. She lives in Niddrie Victoria.'

One of the reasons the military settlers survived the rigours of Siberia better than some was their experiences of forestry, gamekeeping, farming and generally hard physical work on the land. It may have prepared and helped them better for the job of felling trees and building shelters.

Gm. Czaruków – Osada Chrobrów

'The soldiers of the past, of the Polish army who took part in the battles for Poland's independence were given parcels of land taken from the division of larger estate holdings of the gentry.

There two of us children me 10 years and my brother Stanisław 15 years old lived. My Father was from Zyłomierza where at the beginning of WW1 he had finished his schooling at the Russian High School and was fluent in the Russian language. This is why he was able to take a job at the Town Hall in Charuków. We found out much later that he also worked as a civil engineer at the IKOP division and that this part of his work was secret.

Our parcel of land was 14 hectares which was quite large and we had newly constructed farm buildings. Father planted two big fruit orchards and sold the fruit as it became available. Our personal relations with the Ukrainians was fine as Father helped them with a variety of legal matters.

The town Łuck was about 25km from us and Father was often in Równe town and he was there when the Russians invaded Poland on 17th September 1939. The relations with the Ukrainians changed completely.

We lived at that time 'like rabbits hiding in the grass' but we continued living as normally as we could. We went to the Russian school and the Ukrainian children were nice to us although they were shortly to tell us 'soon you will go to the white bear's land.'

We repeated that to our parents and they knew very well what that meant. In secrecy Father prepared a hiding place, a dug out under the wall to the pantry and planned to hide there if the Russians came for him. Without warning in late evening from 9th to 10th February 1940 came 'bojcy' Russian soldiers with bayonets fixed to their rifles. They came with a few Ukrainian neighbours and told us to pack what we could and took us to the station. We could hear the desperate crying of people and the swearing of the soldiers. We were then packed into the train wagons.

We travelled for over two weeks towards the north of Arkangelsk 'oblast' and disembarked at the River Wyczegda. We lived in long single storey barracks in which each family had its own area. We worked cutting and sorting logs.'

These were just a few of the survivors of the deportations to Siberia. From an estimated 1.7ml deportees, it is thought only about 120,000 were able to reach the Polish army in Persia and very few survived even then, many suffering the effects of starvation, dysentery, typhus and malaria.

11

The Poles are a feisty, brave and strong people, which I can happily testify to, they got through incredible hardship to reach safety and from 9 members of my family having gone through Stalin's purges, 9 members lived to tell their story. One son of Walery and Ziuta, Zbigniew, regrettably did not.

Równe Market

CHAPTER 2

Invasion
The Germans

The Second World War was sparked by an attack on the Polish munitions depot on the Westerplatte in Gdansk, at dawn on September 1st 1939 by the German army.

However, Poland's future had been decided earlier, on August 23rd 1939, when the Hitler-Stalin pact was signed, it contained a secret protocol concerning the renewed partition of Poland along the Ribbentrop-Molotov line. The USSR and Germany spent the first 22 months of the war as allies and their pact was not a cold non-aggressive pact it was a most zealous partnership with the two dictatorships trading all necessary commodities of war. Grain, vital chemicals, arms and ships. Until of course Hitler invaded the USSR and Stalin then switched sides, completely taken aback by Hitler's Operation Barbarosa in 1941.

On 1st September 1939 without any declaration of war, Germany's invincible armies and air force launched a blistering attack on my mother Alicja's homeland, over a million and a half troops stormed into Poland, on three fronts, East Prussia from the north, Germany from the west and Slovakia from the south. This was the Blitzkreig, an attack by Hitler's enormous war machine, with 2,600 tanks and 2,000 aircraft against the Polish 180 and 420. The bombing of Poland was intense, Hitler was wreaking havoc and the Polish army began retreating and regrouping east near Lwów in eastern Galicia attempting to escape relentless German land and air offensives.

My family were living at their apartment in Równe at this time and Hitler's attack changed their lives dramatically, it was the trigger for the second World War in Europe. Germany wasn't the only power that invaded Poland that month, the Soviets were also on their way and were to invade 2 weeks later.

By early September German bombs were falling around their home causing massive explosions and Kazia, Adam and the children ran from the apartment into the courtyard amid the most incredible noise, it was terrifying and their two cats, poor things were running from room to room so frightened and confused looking for shelter. Adam's relatives in the west of Poland had warned him of the German invasion and told him to try and make an escape with his family as Hitler's troops would soon reach the eastern borderlands. Poland's fate was almost sealed.

The family ran out of the courtyard with the aim of getting to their Osada where they thought it would be safer. They were so frightened and Kazia and Adam dragged the children behind them and headed out of Równe. People were scattering, running for cover, screaming, there was confusion and chaos everywhere.

Huge billowing columns of smoke filled the sky, 'such massive clouds of smoke and flames, as red as poppy's'. They could see the German planes coming lower and lower and deliberately strafing the villagers with machine gun fire. Their town was burning and panic was everywhere. Huge craters lined the streets and they had to be very careful where they stepped.

They shouldn't have been out there in the thick of it, it wasn't safe anywhere but they were looking for a quick route out of Rowne and were also curious to see what was happening to their home town. Enormous mounds of rubble lay where buildings used to stand, bodies scattered everywhere, many having been crushed beneath the collapsed buildings. Most residential areas had been bombed and defenceless citizens were gunned down as they ran from burning buildings trying to find safety.

By the beginning of October 1939 'our country was shattered'. A month of fighting had almost destroyed Poland. A country of 34 ml people living on 150,000 square miles had almost ceased to exist. The last operational Polish unit surrendered on 6th October unable to counter the overwhelming German military attack.

The consequences of war were everywhere, every city, town and railway station showed the effects, with skeletons of buildings, ruined homes and depots.

My family had found shelter at the church and from behind its huge door they saw Kazia's brother Walery looking for them, arriving with his wagon and horses he had left his Osada as soon as he'd heard the bombs and had rushed to take them away from Równe into the comparative safety of the countryside. He could see they were in shock, Kazia was white and trembling and Adam was tightly holding onto Janusz, with Alicja and Jasia hiding behind him.

They were so very relieved to see Walery who quickly bundled them into the wagon. They covered the way back to the Osada through the country lanes very quickly, seeing many carts overturned with their dead livestock attached. They were very lucky to avoid any gun fire and they arrived safely. Luck was to play a most important part in the survival of the family. Alicja was in a daze and was wondering what had happened to their cats who they never saw again.

Hitler had authorised his commanders to kill 'without pity or mercy, all men, women and children of Polish descent or language, only this way can we obtain the lebensraum (living space) we need'. Himmler took him at his word, 'it is essential that the great German people should consider it as a major task to destroy all Poles.' Crimes against the Polish population were committed, the Luftwaffe indiscriminately bombing towns and cities, civilians killed by the security police and mayors and town officials hunted down and executed.

Map showing the partition of Poland according to the Soviet-German agreement, the Ribbentrop-Molotov pact.

The Poles were considered by the Germans to be sub human and were to be liquidated. By October 8th 1939 Jews and Poles were stripped of all rights and were made subject to special legislation. Rationing for the barest sustenance and medicine was imposed and young Polish men were forcibly drafted into the German army. The Polish language was forbidden, all schools and colleges were closed, the Polish press was abolished, libraries and bookshops were set ablaze. Polish art and culture across Poland was destroyed or looted, churches were burned and priests arrested and sent to German concentration camps.

Hitler's goal was to identify the Polish middle class and murder them. An estimated 40,000 Poles were killed in mass executions in Pomerania northern Poland alone before the end of 1939. In Poznań about 2,000 Polish intelligentsia were murdered and on 9th November 1939 Professors of the Jagiellonian University were summoned by the secret police, arrested and sent to concentration camps.

Community leaders, mayors, priests, teachers, judges and doctors were executed in public, much of the 'intelligentsia' was sent to German concentration camps spread across Poland. The first mass execution of WW2 took place in Wawer near Warsaw on 27th December 1939 when over a hundred Poles were taken from their homes and shot. There followed street roundups and other executions throughout the war. The goal was complete domination of the Poles, to terrorize them into submission and slavery. Western Poland was now decreed by the Germans as a new territory a 'General Government'.

In the spring of 1940 the Germans began the AB-Aktion (AuBerordentliche Befriedungsaktion) a concerted effort to eliminate what remained of the Polish intelligentsia. As many as 30,000 Polish Academics, intellectuals, teachers and writers were arrested and interrogated by the Gestapo. Most were sent to concentration camps, those considered especially dangerous were charged, a verdict proclaimed and the sentence declared. Those prisoners, around 6,000, were then taken to nearby woods and executed with a shot to the back of the head then buried in mass graves.. Prisoners from Pawiek prison were killed in Palmiry Forest, some near Częstochowa and others near Lublin

Jews were also being systematically murdered in the concentration camps located in German occupied Poland, where most of Europe's Jews were located after the pogroms in Russia during 1881-1884, having found a safer haven in Poland than in other European countries. The camps were Auschwitz, Birkenau, Treblinka, Sobitor, Belzec and Kulmhof. They would wear the Star of David as their sign and the Poles the letter P in a triangle as their sign. They were treated with equal brutality, deprived of all humanity and both Poles and Jews were condemned to death. They lived a little longer in the concentration camps but in the death camps, their murder was immediate, shortly after they stepped off the transports.

The Poles were also the target of extermination and as the population was larger than the Jewish population, the methods employed were different. They were removed from their homes, shot or immediately sent to Germany for labour and worked to death. The German war machine needed people for production and they could not murder the Poles all at once as they were doing with the Jews, Polish factory workers and farmers were needed.

Two days after the Wermacht slammed into Poland, both France and Britain, her closest allies declared war on Germany which was greeted by the Poles with great enthusiasm, people running into the streets waving flags believing their allies had come to their aid. Neither France nor Britain however, intervened nor did other nations of the world. PM Chamberlain dispatched instead the RAF to drop leaflets over German military positions commanding German troops to lay down their weapons and informed them that their declining economy would not withstand a protracted war. A futile and cowardly response.

It did not stop Hitler from carrying out his policy of Lebensraum with ruthless efficiency and establishing over 2,000 German concentration camps throughout Poland, some allotted to Polish Christians, some to Polish Jews as well as camps for women and children. The largest concentration camp was Auschwitz originally intended only for Poles who were its first prisoners in June 1940 in the first transport from Tarnow. There were 728 Poles mostly Catholic and 20 Polish Jews dubbed as Political prisoners and members of the Polish Resistance sent there by the SS. A group of German prisoners were also brought to the camp to act as Kapos.

From Free Radio Warsaw came the report of the bombing of Warsaw on 8th September 1939, 'Warsaw was burning, huge billowing columns of smoke filled the sky with thick clouds as red as blood, railway lines were so heavily bombed they became like twisted pretzels. Huge craters lined every street in Warsaw and other cities. There were enormous hills of rubble where buildings used to stand and protruding from the rubble were scattered bodies of people who had been crushed beneath the collapsed buildings. Military and residential areas were bombed and strafed. Defenceless citizens were gunned down as they ran for shelter from the burning buildings. Peasants were massacred as they worked in the fields and men, women and children were slaughtered. Churches, schools, hospitals, monuments, museums, all were targets for destruction. The Polish people, their culture and the very existence of the Polish nation were targeted by Hitler for annihilation.'

Warsaw, 'the Paris of the east was transformed into a wasteland, an open grave'. The devastation continued in 1941 by Soviet bombing, in 1943 by the Germans at the liquidation of the Warsaw Ghetto and in 1944 during the Warsaw Uprising. The city was 85% destroyed.

The Soviets

Whilst the German's were exterminating the Polish population on 15th September the Soviets began massing troops along the eastern Polish frontier. On 16th September Commissars went out among the men briefing them that 'this would not be an invasion but a liberation, freeing the workers from the unjust rule of the Polish landowners'. The plans for the 'liberation' contained a large propaganda element, fodder for the minorities of the Kresy, the Ukrainians and Byelorussians, Russia's 'blood brothers' who were 'trapped in territory that had been illegally annexed by Poland'. On the 17th September the Soviets invaded the eastern borderlands on the pretext of helping Poland against the Germans but the Polish population did not accept this, they knew the propaganda methods of their old enemy. Methods used to this day by Putin, glorifying the Soviets by regurgitatng that same old propaganda!

At five in the morning mechanised cavalry crossed the frontier followed by the rest of the army. The Poles were poorly prepared for the Soviet invasion and the eastern border was badly defended. The threat from the Germans had been clear for many months and most Polish forces had been focused in the west and the fighting had drawn many troops away.

As the massed forces of the Red Army advanced they swept all before them. Defensive positions were quickly overcome and Polish troops were captured or swept aside. During the first day the Soviets advanced up to 60 miles and it wasn't long before eastern Poland was theirs. Poland was now divided in half and the Kresy region was incorporated within the adjoining Russian border and Soviet citizenship was imposed on its Polish inhabitants. Tyranny would replace freedom so long fought for by the Polish people.

As the Soviet troops had broken through into Poland they unexpectedly ran into German troops who in less than two weeks had fought their way through to the east. The Germans fell back when confronted by the Soviets, handing over thousands of Polish prisoners of War to them who were immediately taken into captivity. Up to 250,000 Polish soldiers were taken prisoner, sent to the gulags or killed.

It was impossible for Poland to win against such powerful odds, trapped between two of the most powerful armies in the world. Although they were the first country to oppose the Germans, Poland may have had a different outcome had her allies, France and Britain come to her aid, but they had abandoned Poland to fend for herself but Poland did not surrender, she continued her struggle against both enemies until the end of WW2.

Approximately 20,000 Polish military forces who had escaped Poland, were fighting in France in 1940 and they and the Polish Government operating in exile, were evacuated to England. The Polish troops joined the British army, training in Scotland and its Airforce trained in Blackpool before joining the RAF to fight against the Luftwaffe in the Battle of Britain, where Polish airmen made their mark with the most 'kills' of Luftwaffe planes – a fact not mentioned during WW2 commemorations!

At the sound of the Soviet's 4,700 rumbling tanks, 3,300 aircraft and 620,000 heavy boots, families cautiously emerged from their homes to see what was happening. They had barely survived the German bombing and had lived day to day in a state of great fear. Adam, Kazia and the children had stayed at the Osada with Walery and Ziuta and their children, where they felt safer. When the bombing stopped Alicja rigged up the pony trap and she and Adam went back to their apartment for provisions and clean clothes and to look for food but the shops had very little, mostly taken by the Soviet troops.

What they saw when they came into Równe were Soviet soldiers dressed in shabby uniforms, the rear units trailed out along the roads and tanks, tractors and other vehicles that had run out of fuel, left by the roadsides. Soviet troops had expected to find impoverished peasants but instead had found a country wealthier than their own. The borderlands had been built up successfully by the military settlers after WW1 and also by the many Jews who had settled there and opened up their own businesses, living alongside their Polish, Ukrainian, Lithuanian neighbours.

The Russians began their rule of intimidation immediately, looting shops, occupying houses, flats and offices. They carried lists of names of people to be arrested for deportation, helpfully prepared by their Ukrainian spies, and they checked names off those lists whilst going about their business of harassing the Polish villagers. They had also hung from houses their red flags with portraits of Lenin and Stalin. 'They were a jumble of ragamuffins in their greasy coats and strange hats' one of Babcia's neighbours told her!

When Adam and Alicja arrived at the door to their apartment they found people there who had fled the troubles in Warsaw, who had made themselves at home after finding the apartment doors and windows open. The family had left in such a panic they hadn't had time to think of security, Adam decided to let them stay as they too were in shock and terrified with nowhere to go but they eventually moved out looking for safety elsewhere. Adam and Alicja got clothes and whatever else they could together and left for the Osada in the pony trap, carefully avoiding any Soviet troops on the way who were mostly busy looting and looking for food.

Despite the disruption and the aggression of the Russians, the bombs and the planes overhead, the craters and the horses lying dead in the road, Alicja looked around and tried to concentrate on the country side around her. 'September was glorious, nature just carried on around us, ignoring the turmoil' and she wished that she could ignore the turmoil around her as well but it was impossible.

On the way out of Równe she gazed almost in a trance at the beautiful fields covered in marigolds and wild flowers, the forests where they had picked mushrooms with their Babcia Sofia, the forests that Stalin and the UPA would later raze to the ground. They crossed the river and as they neared the Osada, the fields of white and purple flowers stood out against the clouds of black smoke in the sky. Alicja never forgot that scene, one of very many locked into her memory.

They continued without bumping into any Soviets although they did see a few of them ransacking the homes of villagers. Adam urged the pony on and they saw as they neared the orchards of Walery's Osada, the fruit ripening and acres of sunflowers, Adam's favourite flower which he was later to grow in England. The potato season was approaching and there was much work to be done in the fields but their lives were now on hold, their country was being destroyed and they couldn't do anything about it. Day by day Poland was dying around them and they couldn't see any help coming from their 'allies'. Alicja leant against her Father and cried quietly to herself, the reality was beginning to hit home.

The primary motivation for Stalin was class, he focused on those elements of society who might oppose communist rule and he targeted the people of the eastern borderlands. These lands had been settled by men like my dziadek Adam Góral and Wujek Walery Radomski and many of their military compatriots after the Bolshevik war of 1920. Stalin had not forgotten Russia's defeat and revenge was also his motivation.

One of Stalin's first moves was to deport to Siberia the military families, priests, lawyers, professors, all that he considered the 'elite'. These included the families of the eastern Borderlands where my grandparents Kazia and Adam had settled after marrying in 1923, to develop the land with other military families. Each deportation had a classification according to Soviet law, it defined the location, living conditions and in the end defined the chances of survival.

Like the Germans, the Soviets reigned in terror, a campaign of Sovietization was immediately started, taking over Polish businesses and factories, destroying churches. The Złoty (currency) was removed from circulation and banks were closed. Poland's educated classes were deliberately targeted because both the Germans and Soviets knew it would be easier to oversee the de-Polonization and control of the country if the 'elite' were annihilated.

The Russians then began their carefully planned deportation programme, sending Poles in huge numbers to Siberian labour camps in four phases up to 1941. On 10th February 1940 272,000, in April 320,000, in June 240,000 and in June 1941 between 200,000 and 300,000. Figures are taken from various sources, historians and scholars, the Polish Armed Forces and the NKVD and are open to further research which is continuing. My own research has focused on the Kresy history groups and other historical information which gave the numbers of approximately 1.7 ml.

The deportees of 10th February were designated as 'special settlers' (Spets-pereselentsky-osadniki), also labelled as 'enemies of the state' or 'anti-revolutionary agitators'. From specific Osada's between 100-150 families, the Radomski's and Góral's included, were exiled to the remotest regions of Northern European Russia and Siberia, Arkhangelsk district and the Komi ASSR, Sverdlovsk, Omsk, Tobolsk, Novosibirsk and Krasnoyarsk districts. They were under the direct supervision of the NKVD, the pre curser to the KGB.

Growing up with and experiencing my Babcia Kazia's loving character and sense of humour, which has prevailed amongst many members of the family, I can see how Stalin would have considered her and her compatriots the most 'dangerous of revolutionary agitators' and 'enemies of Russia' and his reason for such brutal action!

Within the 'special settlers' there were large numbers of farmers and forest workers from the Osada's, used to hard labour and together with the other less physically able, they could spread the load of the daunting work ahead of them and this group had a relatively higher rate of survival than many of the other deportees.

The Kresy Poles in particular, were damned in the eyes of the Soviets who hated them, thinking them all aristocrats and officers. They were however mostly enlisted, ex military men, Osadnicy and their families with other minority religious and ethnic communities, Jews and mainly Catholics of which most of Poland was made up of. In the same week that the AB-Aktion was ordered in Berlin in Spring 1940 Moscow gave the order to apply 'the supreme punishment, shooting of Poles' at random.

The April deportees, were POWs and mostly women and children, damned to exile for belonging to the families of men previously arrested by the NKVD, classified as (administrativno-vysslanye). They were deported to Kazakhstan, Aktyvbinsk, Petropavlovsk, Akmolinsk and Pavlodar. The survival rates were low and very few escaped the USSR following the 'amnesty'. The numbers of survivors for this group are unknown.

The June deportees were classified as (spetspereselentsky-bezhentsy) special settlers. Made up of Polish, Ukrainian and Belorussian and were mostly Jewish. They had fled German occupied Poland for the Soviet zone, others were refugees from eastern Poland who had escaped into Lithuania. They were regarded as 'politically suspect' and sent to Siberia, Sverdlovsk, Chkalov, Yakutsk and Arkhangelsk and lived in NKVD supervised settlements.

21

Very little is known of their fate as so few left after the amnesty, word hadn't got through to very many labour camps across the USSR and many thousands of Poles were left ignorant of what was happening, completely unaware that they could leave to join Ander's Army to fight against the Germans. The survival rate of those left in the wilderness of the USSR is likely to be low as they had little money, nothing to barter with and would have starved, there are no numbers of any survivors. There are quite likely relatives of deportees still living across the regions of the USSR.

These deportions were the final part of Stalin's ethnic cleansing programme and were almost on the eve of the German invasion of USSR, Operation Barbarrosa, with the last trains carrying the Polish deportees leaving eastern Poland as the German bombs were falling on the Soviets.

During the following weeks military POWs arrested by the Russians were shipped out of their camps and held by the NKVD whilst their identities were checked. They were then led away arms bound behind their backs and shot in the back of the head, their bodies disposed of in mass graves. This massacre at Katyn in western Russia was discovered in 1943 by the Germans and is synonymous with Soviet brutality. The dead totalled over 21,000 and included one prince, one admiral, 12 generals 81 colonels, 198 lieutenant colonels, 21 professors, 22 priests, 189 prison guards, 5,940 policemen and one woman Janina Lewandowska, an officer and Lieutenant pilot with the 3rd Military Aviation Regiment.

The culture shock faced by the Poles on arrival in the Soviet Union cannot be overstated. They had travelled in the depths of the coldest winter for some considerable time, through deep snow drifts and into deep forests. The only advantage was that they had accommodation in the labour camps built by earlier victims of Stalin's purges and ethnic cleansing of 1933, the Ukrainian Kulaks who had been left there to fend for themselves.

The deportees taken in the February and June 1940 deportations, sent to the north of Russia and Siberia were tasked by Resolution 2122-617ss of the Soviet People's Commissars of 29th December 1939, with 'clearing forests in regions belonging to the People's Commissariat of Forestry of the USSR'.

Work assignments were handed out to everyone aged 16 or over and it involved felling trees, sawing branches and hauling timber, even in winter when the temperature fell to -70.C and there was little daylight. 'If you didn't work you didn't eat' and the meagre rations were allocated only to those who worked, and who met the quotas. They were barely sufficient for the hard labour undertaken and the deportees began to starve and suffer dreadfully. My dziadek Adam and Mother Alicja were tasked with this back breaking physical labour in the most extreme of weather conditions.

Poland had to contend with the Germans and the Russians, their repressions and deportations to labour camps, hard labour within Germany and Russia and then the UPA who took advantage of the desolation of the country to wage their own massacres on the Poles. Murdering an estimated 100,000 mostly women, children and elderly.

The Ukrainians

The Poles of Wołyn and Eastern Galicia also faced the onslaught of the Ukrainian Insurgent Army which began ethnic cleansing of the area in March 1943. Their aim was to purge the Kresy of non Ukrainians from what was to be the future Ukrainian state and their savagery surpassed even that of the Germans and Russians.

When Soviet tanks had entered Nowy Dwór in Wołyn on 23rd September 1939, the infantry unit commanded by a captain riding a horse stolen from its Polish owner, gathered all the Ukrainians in the main square and said, 'on this day you have been freed by the Red Army from the yoke of Polish capitalism. This whole wealth accumulated by the bourgeoisie now belongs to you. You must exterminate the bourgeoisie! Your rulers will henceforth be peasants and factory workers. I will make arrangements for you to form police units composed of workers'. Soviet propaganda at its best!

With the Soviet invasion and the annexation of the area in 1939-1941 militant Ukrainian nationalist extremists saw an opportunity to cleanse Polish people from the territory they considered historically to be Ukrainian. They were distrustful of Polish territorial ambitions and were intent on exacting retribution for the Polonization which the Polish state had supposedly inflicted upon them. They wanted an independent and ethnically pure Ukraine modelled on Fascist principles, like Nazi Germany and Fascist Italy. They wanted to eliminate all Polish people from southern Kresy to prevent those lands from returning to Poland after WW2.

OUN and UPA nationalism was introduced by Ukrainian agitators in Ukrainian villages in Wołyn and also, in the spring of 1940 the Wołyn Jews showed their gratitude to the Poles by enthusiastically welcoming and supporting the occupying Soviet communists. They collaborated with them and it could be said they sowed the seeds of anti-semitism in Wołyn by their actions. The Poles hated communism with a vengeance and my Dziadek Adam was totally against Soviet state control and the brutality it engaged.

On 22nd June 1941 a terrible chapter began for the inhabitants of Wołyn with the German invasion of the USSR. The barbaric treatment towards the

Stepan Bandera

Polish people began almost immediately. The Germans had promised the Ukrainians a 'free Ukraine' and Stepan Bandera accepted this hollow promise little realising that he was simply a tool of the Germans, used for the mass extermination of the Polish population of Wołyn.

An order from 1942 states, 'liquidate all Polish traces, destroy all walls in the Catholic churches and other Polish prayer houses, destroy orchards and trees in the countryside so that there will be no trace that someone lived there. Pay attention to the fact that when something remains that is Polish then the Poles will have pretensions to our land'.

The Germans encouraged both sides against each other 'we have to do everything possible so a Pole when meeting a Ukrainian will be ready to kill him and conversely a Ukrainian will be ready to kill a Pole' – Erick Koch German Commander. The same as the Soviets with their encouragement to the UPA to 'exterminate the bourgeoisie' Poles.

Their methods were very similar to the German SS which the extreme Bandera faction of OUN-B admired. The group had a monopoly of power within Ukrainian society and had the support necessary for the massacres to take place and the opportunity. They also had the barbaric skills, honed when Ukrainian fighters had joined German SS and Police services where they learned the art of genocide against the Jews before approximately 5,000 deserted to join UPA in 1943 taking weapons and ammunition with them.

The terror campaign assumed a mass scale in the summer of 1943 with massacres in the Sarny, Kostopol, Równe the family home and Zdolbuny regions spread to Dubno and Łuck and eventually into Kowel, Włodzimierz, Wołynski and Horochow regions. On Sunday 11 July 1943 UPA detachments, supported by local Ukrainians surrounded and attacked 99 Polish villages in those counties, as well as in Łuck.

There was no warning for the attacks on defenceless Polish villages, Ukrainian neighbours came to the Poles with axes and murdered whole families. 'Villages were torched, Roman Catholic priests axed and crucified and churches burned with all parishioners inside. Isolated farms were attacked by gangs with pitchforks and knives, throats were cut and pregnant women bayoneted, children cut in two and the menfolk ambushed in the field and led away to be put through other atrocities'.

Ukrainian neighbours who had previously lived peacefully side by side with Poles now took over the empty homes and farms of the Poles they murdered. The initial hostility of the Ukrainians to the Military settlers in the borderlands had improved over the years with relationships becoming friendly with work for them on the Osadas and socially. However, they turned very quickly against them supported by the Germans and the Soviets who stoked resentment between them.

'The perpetrators could not determine the province's future, but at least they could determine that it would be a future without Poles.' – Norman Davies, Europe at War 1939-1945 No simple Victory

The Polish civilians of Lipnicki were ruthlessly slaughtered, their homes destroyed and the villages burned to the ground. Property and life-stock, farm machinery and equipment anything of value was looted and on that day alone it is estimated that there were 8,000 victims, mostly women and children and some elderly. The Ukrainian perpetrators used bullets, axes, knives and pitchforks. Those Poles who took refuge in the churches were not spared and suffered the same fate.

After the first murders the Polish underground began organising self defence units and the commander of the Wołyn District forbade any reprisals against Ukrainian villagers.

'I forbid the use of the methods utilized by the Ukrainian butchers. We will not burn Ukrainian homesteads nor kill Ukrainian women and children in retaliation. The self-defence network must protect itself from the aggressors or attack the aggressors but leave the peaceful population and their possessions alone.' – Col. Kazimierz Babinski, 'Lubon' Commander of the Armia Krajowa, Wolyn district – A most humanitarian attitude in view of the actions of the UPA.

My Babcia Kazia's cousin Tosia and her two young sons were murdered, burnt alive, the only detail we have of their murder. The Ukrainians were ruthless, savage beyond reason in their methods of killing, normally starting with young children. Poles abandoned their homes and fled to the cities seeking escape from their oppressors, the Germans, the Russians and now the Ukrainians!

UPA leaders who committed the genocide in Poland are today national heroes in Ukraine. Their victims number between 40,000 - 60,000 Polish deaths in Wołyn and 30,000 - 40,000 in Eastern Galicia, with the other regions bringing the total to 100,000.

This Genocide of the Polish people by the UPA was never formerly identified as such until 2008 when the massacres committed by the Ukrainian nationalists against ethnic Poles in Wołyn and Galicia were described by Poland's Institute of National Remembrance as bearing the distinct characteristics of a Genocide and on 22nd July 2016 the Parliament of Poland passed a resolution recognising the massacres as a Genocide.

Polish civilian victims of 26 March 1943 massacre committed by the UPA assisted by Ukrainian peasantry in Lipnicki, Kostopol, my Mother Alicja's birthplace

I've included some personal testimonies from survivors of the UPA atrocities and I cannot imagine how some of them actually lived through their ordeals. They recount how many of their relatives were horrifically tortured before being murdered. The UPA were Hitler's henchmen, supplied with arms by the Germans they also engaged in guerrilla warfare against the Polish underground.

Personal testimonies from survivors of the Volhynia (Wołyn) Genocide *– Polandpl/history*

'I saw my murdered friend ... his name was Pronczuk. When banderovtsky were killing his mother he ran to her rescue. The murderers chopped off his arms and legs and put him on a stool, he bled to death.' *– Wladyslaw Tolysz*

'In the first homestead we saw a horrifying picture, a boy aged not more than ten was impaled on a sharp pole at the gate ... Dead bodies of men and two women brutally massacred with an axe were lying at the doorstep.' *– Jerzy Krasowski*

'One of the Banderovtsky saw me and shot me at point blank but missed, he fired another shot but also missed and I managed to escape. My father and brother also fled from the house. My brother was shot, a

26

banderovtsky riding a horse caught up with my father and murdered him. My mother was standing in the entryway holding her baby in her arms, Banderites fired shots through the closed door, one bullet hit the baby in the chest and my mother in her arm. My mother jumped out of the window put the dead child on the ground and crawled into a rosebush near the house. The Banderites broke through the door, plundered the house and set fire to the buildings. The roof fell in, the charred remains of the house fell as far away as the rosebush so that my mother got painfully burned. This is how the tragedy of our family was sealed.' –

'In one of the villages near Detrazny after the pogrom a small child whose intestines had been ripped out was found in a hut. His intestines were splashed against the wall in an irregular shape and on one of the nails a piece of paper was hung which read, 'Poland from sea to sea.' – *Wincenty Romanowski*

'At daybreak I found my father's dead body in the farmyard, he was lying next to a tree trunk used for chopping wood and his throat was slit. I found my mother inside, she had marks on her head from being hit several times with a hammer and a stab wound from a bayonet in her throat. My sister Helena had a deep wound in the head from being hit by an axe so deep that her murderer had left his axe in her head. My youngest brother Edzio aged 2 was lying in a pool of blood with his small head smashed and a knife stuck in his chest. Lying next to him was my 16 year old brother Bronek. It was his voice begging for mercy that I heard for the longest time at night. When I took a closer look I saw something that looked like a lump of battered meat. His arms and legs were broken, it was him the murderer tortured the longest.' – *Michel Wojczyszyn*

'During the singing of 'Gloria' the first shots were fired at Father Bolesław Szawłowski and the congregation. I was in the church with my sister when I heard the murderers walking around the church and saying 'O toj jeszcze zywyj' ('Oh this one is still alive') I quickly grabbed a cap soaked in warm sticky blood and rubbed my and my sister's face with it and we pretended to be dead. People were choking from thick smoke so they tried to escape from the church, Ukrainians were shouting 'wychadi chto zywy' (come out if you are alive) and then they would kill people leaving the church at the door. They tried to blow up the church but we only felt a terrible tremor and then there was silence.' – *Jadwiga Krajewska*

'Three of my children, Stanisława, Janek and Leon were murdered by Ukrainians, I took my youngest son and ran out of the barn. I heard a loud noise and heard my son Jozio let out a horrific cry. I fell to the ground holding my baby in my arm, I felt pain in my left arm, blood was trickling

27

from the wound. The dumdum bullet went through the muscle and the bone of my left arm. I wasn't aware if my son Jozio was alive or not. I was very weak from the loss of blood.

I don't recall how long I lay there unconscious, I soon felt thirsty so I began to crawl. I was lucky because I saw my husband's brother Aleksander Soroka miraculously saved, appear. He brought me water so I could quench my thirst. I decided to crawl back to my house so I could die there. I lost everything I had in my life. Those I loved the most passed to eternal life. I wanted to join them there in the other world where God dwells.' – *Marianna Soroka*

Poland's suffering continued at an awful pace by three invading enemies and my family were at this time prisoners in a labour camp under the direction of the NKVD after a journey they barely survived and would never forget.

Had they been left behind in Równe they would almost certainly have fallen victim to the savagery of the UPA.

I had listened as a child to my grandparents chatting away, fascinated by the language being spoken which I was only just getting to grips with. Adam my Dziadek referred to the Soviets as Bolsheviks and wasn't very complimentary about them. I knew enough of the language to learn about their ordeal which later led me to write their story in the prequel to this. What most left an impression later on in life when I was more able to understand the circumstances was that despite the treatment meted out to them by the Soviets, my Dziadek and Walery and many thousands of other Poles who had escaped the USSR labour camps chose to fight with them against Germany!

The Polish people who survived the brutality of a tyrannical force, almost starved in the labour camps and in dire physical condition, journeyed over 3,500 km to join the Allies in their droves to fight against Germany and it is quite incredible that they willingly allied themselves to Stalin!

Their other option however was to remain as slaves of the Soviets in the labour camps and face the demanding physical work and continued starvation. The decision to leave the camp was made easily by Kazia and Adam, with many other hundreds from their camp they went into another desperate situation, a journey of over 3,500km to Persia to join Anders' Army.

The Allies

Two days after the Wermacht attacked Poland, both France and Britain, Poland's closest allies declared war on Germany. The news of this promised liberation was greeted with some enthusiasm by the Poles who flooded into the streets waving flags and singing. They were hoping their allies had come to their aid in their time of great need. However, neither ally intervened. Their response was cowardly, instead dispatching the RAF to drop leaflets commanding the German troops to lay down their arms! This military farce continued for several months, with British and French troops posted along the Maginot line and conducting pointless raids into No-Mans' land. A farce which was to become known as 'the phoney war.'

They also sat back when Poland was attacked by the Red Army on 17th September, which went on to take control of more than half of Poland. On September 27th, after a siege lasting almost three weeks, Warsaw surrendered to the Germans, and by October 5th all resistance by the Polish Army had ceased. They were totally outnumbered and outgunned, they stood no chance against such overwhelming odds and their Allies had still not responded. – The Poles waited in vain.

On the 29th September Poland was partitioned according to the Soviet-German pact and the two nations each specified their territorial claims, which divided Poland along the Ribbentrop-Molotov Line. The Allies were aware of this and still Poland waited.

Leo Amery MP, lambasted Chamberlain in the House of Commons for leaving the Poles trapped between two of the most powerful armies in the world, 'the Poles have been bombed and massacred and we are still considering within what time limit Hitler should be invited to tell us whether he felt like relinquishing his prey!'

My family meanwhile were in the middle of a wartime hell. Walery had heard from some relatives in western Poland, in Łodz, also under German occupation, that Adam's brother's in law had been arrested and killed when the prison they had been thrown into was set alight. Other relatives barely survived the war. On the Radomski side, Kazia's sister Gienia and her daughter Halina had been taken to the west of Poland by her brother Walery prior to the deportations, to join her husband and they had survived. We have no detail of Kazia's Mother Sofia, whether she survived and on the Góral side, Adam's sisters somehow saw it through to the end.

My mother Alicja's home, Równe was turned into a wasteland. The Germans had used twice the ammunition to bomb Poland than the combined artillery used against France and England, Warsaw was reduced to rubble. People were scattered everywhere, POWs were being sent to either Germany or the Soviet Union, soldiers and airmen who had escaped were making their way into Rumania and Hungary. The huge army of refugees created by the bombing who had abandoned their homes now had to find their way back or make their way to the Soviet zone, find new homes and work.

Their future was very uncertain and the war would go on until 1945 when they then had to contend with communist rule under Stalin and lose their freedoms which they had fought so hard to save. Whilst Germany and Russia were dictating the lives of the Polish people my immediate family were living through complete confusion and terror awaiting the next move of the Soviets. The Poles had been abandoned by the Allies and my family were in despair, their country occupied by two hostile enemies and a very uncertain and dangerous life lay ahead of them.

Churchill and Roosevelt

'In desperate times the enemy of your enemy becomes your friend.'

During WW2 the US Great Britain and the Soviet Union would never have been 3 way allies had they not shared a common enemy in Adolf Hitler. The only way to defeat Hitler was to put their personal and political differences aside in the name of global security. But, how much was each leader willing to sacrifice to make the uneasy alliance work? It seems that Roosevelt and Churchill sacrificed their common sense, appeased and bribed Stalin, almost grovelled, duped by their advisors Harry Dexter White, later unmasked as a Soviet spy, Sir Stafford Cripps a Marxist and Ambassador to the USSR and pro Soviet Harry Hopkins. Roosevelt and Churchill made a massive error in backing Stalin so fully and letting him get away with so much. They funnelled tons of much needed materials and equipment to the USSR, oil, thousands of planes, tanks and trucks without which Russia would have collapsed. What did they get in return? Stalin had purged his armed forces of many Officers and he was desperately trying to increase production of war materials. Roosevelt and Churchill should have used their aid to force Stalin to make concessions, over Poland for example, or to enter the war with Japan earlier. Instead, Stalin made no concessions and emerged the victor in 1945 with a new empire in Europe and territories in the far east that he turned into Communist states.

The further a society drifts from the truth the more it will hate those who speak it.
George Orwell

CHAPTER 3

Life as 'Enemies of the People'

'Poland needs to be destroyed as a country' – Hitler. Polish suffering at the hands of the Germans is widely known and has become an established account of WW2 history. Shortly after Hitler launched his invasion of Poland on 1st September 1939 Stalin did the same from the east on the 17th his invasion was in partnership with Hitler to defeat their common enemy, Poland. Which was then divided between them and the devastation of Poland, the horrors of the Holocaust, the persecutions, the executions and deportations, began in earnest. Stalin took about 200,000sq kms and 12 ml inhabitants annexing them directly to the USSR and Hitler took less territory and 20 ml inhabitants. It became the Fourth Partition of Poland.

The Soviet ideology was to completely change the entire framework of Polish life, they had invaded Poland to 'rescue' their fellow Ukrainians and 'help' the Polish people against the Germans but their aim was to impose a Communist revolution which meant the absolute destruction of all political, economic and social elements which would eventually bring Poland down to the level of Russian poverty. Stalin saw the opportunity to spread communism throughout Europe with Poland his main route.

Very quickly, after invasion on the 17th September, Stalin had the annexed lands transferred to the respective Russian republics of the Ukraine and Byelorussia and within a short period there were rumours circulating around the Osadas of deportation orders being levied on the settlers. This would be a huge blow for them but not totally unexpected, they had been waiting for Stalin's next move and somehow it felt a relief. Those lands inhabited by the military settlers, the provinces of Wolhynia, Polesie, Bialystok, Nowogrodek and Wilno were now completely under the control of the USSR. When the Red Army had crossed the Polish borders terror against the population began on an unprecedented scale and Ukrainian and Byelorussian gangs began to attack many of the settlements, looting and killing.

The Poles felt completely abandoned by their allies – 'where were they?' There was nothing they could do against their oldest enemy, the Bolsheviks, for whom they felt only hatred and 'a great despair settled in our hearts.' They and the country were powerless and they had never felt so fearful, vulnerable and alone. Their fears were intensified even further, when very soon the Russians had complete control of their home town of Równe. Poland was now under occupation by two enemies and a very different and dangerous life beckoned. Two dictators were using the family homeland for their own ends.

International reaction at the time was subdued as Britain was facing Germany alone and was hoping to recruit Russia as an ally against Hitler and wanted to avoid any public criticism of Stalin. The Russian deportations have long been ignored by the West and it is prohibited to mention the matter in the Soviet bloc where Stalin is held in the highest regard. The stories of the exiled Poles fully deserve to become part of the wider narrative and they are only now coming to light. from the telling of the story of my own family to the many accounts from children of other surviving Sybiraks and historians of integrity and honesty, rather than the revisionists.

Poland had the misfortune to be crushed between two brutal totalitarian states, both of them hostile towards Polish society. Germany on racial grounds and the Soviets on class. The measures employed against the racial enemy in the west of Poland were strikingly similar to those applied to the class enemy in the east of Poland and almost from the moment the Red Army entered Polish territory, the Osadnicy were singled out in an extensive propaganda campaign as enemies of the Soviet system. The NKVD manipulated the resentment Ukrainian and Byelorussian peasants felt towards the colonizers and the Soviet press in the occupied area labelled the Osadnicy as 'servants of the Polish Government' who 'brutally exploited the peasantry' and exaggerated their numbers greatly to 70,000 when the total did not exceed 8,000!

The NKVD then began to make arrests amongst various Polish groups, the main reason given was the military settlers' involvement in the Polish-Bolshevik war! They knew what their army dossiers revealed and there was also the conviction that all Poles of middle or upper class education living on the eastern borderlands were spies, men who would work powerfully against communism. They were a threat to the Soviets.

A reign of terror was unleashed against the Polish people of the Kresy region, the Soviets dropped leaflets urging the local Ukrainians and Byelorussians to rise up and rob and murder their Polish neighbours and whilst many were happy to be complicit there were those who helped their Polish neighbours in spite of a huge risk to them. Tensions had been inflamed towards the Poles by the NKVD and this resulted in bloody conflicts, criminals were released from prisons and encouraged to attack the Poles and the local militia were engaged to hunt down Polish officers, local government officials and the Osadnicy, the Polish military settlers that Stalin hated. Land and livestock seizures became common, intellectuals, rich people and priests were executed.

In the election of the supreme Ukrainian Assembly and in the Byelorussian Assembly there were many hostile accusations against the military settlers 'as faithful servants of Polish Fascism' and the determination to 'clear them from our land' was intense and they now had the backing of the NKVD to carry out their plans, there was 'no place for them in the Soviet order...' The Germans also stepped in with encouragement, money and training for the Ukrainian UPA. Life was becoming extremely dangerous for the settlers.

All citizens of Równe could see their 'liberators', using their power very quickly to arrest all policemen and Poles of any social standing. Towards the end of September the trains were full of Polish soldiers and officers sent by the Russians deep into the USSR. This was one of the first targets of the Red Army's attack in 1939, a premeditated act of revenge long in the planning and a retaliation for the Battle of the Bolsheviks in 1920 which had been won by Poland.

Large scale arrests were made of local leaders and reservists, government officials, police officers, political activists, landowners, businessmen, administrative elites and the clergy. With incredible speed they accomplished the absolute submission of eastern Poland, setting out new rules to Sovietize the lands The economy was devastated, with land and personal property confiscated and redistributed.

The military settlers and their families were to be banished from their homes and sent to labour camps as they were a particular irritant to Stalin, they were 'enemies of the people' even 'counter revolutionaries,' I had never looked upon my Dziadek as a counter revolutionary although he did tend to get a little heated when the Bolsheviks were spoken of! The military settlers were intelligent and hardworking men with minds of their own who would stand up to Stalin's doctrine, they despised communism and it's why Stalin wanted them removed. My Dziadek Adam was perhaps a little too outspoken about his own feelings towards the persecution and oppression that was communism but knew when to keep his counsel.

Stalin's priority then was the ousting of the military settlers from their properties, told they were safe under the protection of the Soviet authorities, the settlers' belongings such as livestock and farm machinery were already being divided up by the Ukrainian and Byelorussian villagers. the NKVD wasted no time, the Osadnicy were given just a short time to pack possessions they had amassed over 18 years.

My Mother Alicja has spoken of many villagers who did not participate in the campaign of oppression towards them and many good souls at great risk to themselves helped them. Some neighbours had refused outright to be moved and those who had been born in the region were allowed to stay, although they had to rescind ownership of their lands to the Russians and take in many Ukrainian and Russian families to lodge with them and 'help' them on their farms.

One evening the family were together at Walery's Osada, sitting at the supper table with only candles for light they were talking, angry that the Russians had come into their country like thieves, grabbing their land and its people on the pretext of helping them. 'They had come in the dark with their rifles at the ready, to shoot us if we came out of our homes. That's how they were helping us!'

Kazia, Adam and the children returned next morning from the Osada, to their now almost empty apartment, it had been looted as had many other dwellings in the village. Russian soldiers and tanks were everywhere, the schools were closed to the normal curriculum, only Russian teaching and Soviet propaganda were allowed. The days were of sheer terror, spent avoiding the NKVD militia as best they could and having to deal with the patrols checking bags at the edge of the village and the railway station.

There were long queues for everything which meant very long waits each day as the shelves were almost bare, no sugar, salt or soap or bread. Life had changed drastically and women stood in lines to try and get information about the whereabouts of their husbands who had been arrested. Terror and fear was in the atmosphere in eastern Poland. The family made a promise, to try and stay as close to each other as possible, no matter what.

Everyone was very nervous and on edge. It was impossible to cross the border into west Poland or Ukraine as the NKVD was paying well for information from the ethnic residents who were easily bought, old feelings resurfacing against the Poles. Anyone crossing the border would be dealt with harshly, an interrogation would take place with accusations of being a spy, then torture would begin. Wujek Walery was arrested coming back into Równe from west Poland and was sent to the Lubyanka prison and most likely underwent torture with many others.

Life was hard, very sad and gloomy, and the family felt helpless. Dziadek, in fear of being arrested by the NKVD hid in various safe places. He and the other military settlers who had been in the Cavalry during the First World War and in the Uprising against the Bolsheviks were considered as threats to Stalin's aim of spreading Communism throughout Europe

The family and many others had heard from their relatives in the west of Poland that people were being massacred by the Germans as they worked in the fields and men, women and children were routinely slaughtered just going about their daily routines. Hitler was targeting the Polish people, their culture and the very existence of the Polish nation for annihilation, Churches, Schools, hospitals and monuments were targets for destruction and Stalin was doing the same. There was no sleep in Równe, everyone waited, unable to do anything to change the situation and there were no allies to help them. "Where were the English and the French" questions asked by many of the Poles, who grew ever more afraid.

The settlements were gripped by fear and families were not sure what to do. Polish officials were being arrested every day and the Ukrainian Committee elected by the Russians, warned everyone that they would have to move out of their homes and that refusal would cost them their lives. Historical hatred was rife and the lawlessness was spreading ever wider. Walery and Adam's Osada's had not yet been chosen by the Committee but many other settlements had been, the larger ones with machinery and live stock for the Ukrainians who were going to 'look after everything for them.' By October 1939, the NKVD pestered the family each week, checking lists of family members and going over their possessions and the family also had to report to the militia office in Równe once a week.

Adam continued to hide with friends and life went on with much hardship and great fear and the NKVD troopers, mean spirited and aggressive searched their apartment looking for Adam, charging in with guns raised looking for any weapons they thought might be hidden, 'it was terrifying and It was only a matter of time before it was our turn,' and the family waited. Kazia did her best to ease the children's concerns, but it didn't really work. She had seen the effect their few neighbours acting as collaborators were having and their number was growing.

At the Osada Krechowiecka where Walery and his family lived, in Wolhynia, there were as yet no attacks nor was anyone yet arrested but everyone waited in fear. They were accused by the Russians, of being 'the most hostile group for whom there was no place in the Soviet order' and their numbers were hugely exaggerated to over 70,000! which led to further attacks upon the Osada's and started the eviction process in earnest.

The mass deportations that were to follow allowed the Soviets to annex the eastern provinces sanctioned by the secret protocol in the Molotov-Ribbentrop Pact signed with Hitler on 23rd August 1939 in which Stalin would take the Baltic states and Poland. The deportations were decided at the highest level, including Stalin, the head of the NKVD Lavrenti Beria and the People's Commissar of Foreign Affairs, Vyacheslav Molotov. It was personally supervised by Vsevolod Mierkovov, deputy head of the NKVD.

Deportation orders were issued in Moscow on 5th December 1939. The Council of People's Commissars of the USSR, had already undertaken resolution 2001-558 relevant to the deporting of settlers' families and those of the forestry service, from the territory of the western parts of the Ukraine and Byelorussia, which was confirmed by Stalin's instructions of the 19th and 25th December. Instructions for the field NKVD cells were prepared for 'cleaning up' the western parts of the Soviet republics of Ukraine and Belarus and deportations were carried out according to registered censuses compiled by NKVD officers in cooperation with local communists.

Also for exile were officials, forestry workers and employees of the railways, and peasants, those who were considered educated, middle class and those who were overtly religious. The Soviet authorities saw the deportations as a form of extermination of the Polish elite and of using thousands of Poles as cheap labour. The conditions in the Siberian Tiaga at many degrees minus of frost, famine and disease would kill many of the exiles. It was a very well planned crime against the Polish people.

Statistics on the numbers of Poles deported by Stalin are difficult to access. Historians differ in their interpretations and information hasn't been made available by Russia but it is known that the NKVD had information on every member of each family, that the deportation was to follow a routine of arrest, transport to the railway collecting point and then allocation to a particular transport and each transport was to consist of 55 trucks, one coach reserved for the escort and one for first aid.

In each truck to be bolted from the outside, 25 people were to be incarcerated, but the number usually exceeded 50. There was to be one hot meal a day and 800 grams of bread per person every 24 hours. This was not however the case and very many starved on that journey to Siberia. The NKVD regional heads sent progress reports to their superiors who in turn sent information to Lavrenti Beria. The journey of the military families lasted 3 weeks or more. 72% were sent to Arkhangelsk area, 9% to the Urals, 6% to the Vologda region, 6% east Siberia, 2% west Siberia, 2% Komi Republic and 3% to European Russia. They were to work in the forests, felling trees and transporting the timber.

Although a specific reason for the deportations was not given it is well known that the 'guilt' of the military settlers in particular was their military past and their loyalty to the 'bourgeoise' Polish Government. Another reason for the swift removal of the military settlers is that the NKVD were probably aware and apprehensive that these military settlers owned firearms and may have posed a threat to them. The overall supervision of the February deportation was undertaken by Bera's deputy, V.V. Chernyshev and the Osadnicy were given the status of 'special settlers' by the NKVD and they would live under their supervision.

Those deported on the 10th February 1940 were taken to Arkhangelsk, where most of the military families were sent, Krasnojar, Krai, Komi and also to Sverdlov and Irkutsk districts. The conditions on the day were terrible, with the temperature at -40. Sentenced to clearing of the forests and construction of railway lines, the exiles would fight hard each day for survival and apart from the extreme cold, there was hunger and appalling living conditions. Vermin and countless bugs infested the barracks and repression by the Soviet guards was a daily hazard to contend with.

Orders had been given to the settlers to quit their homes in the Osada's Krechowiecka, Hallerowo, Bajonowka, Jazłowiecka, Bolesławice and Woronów. Very little time was given to pack belongings that they had accumulated since arriving at the eastern borderlands. The military settlers, the primary targets, were to be taken during the first deportation on the night of 9th/10th February 1940. Although post war figures state that some 272,000 military settlers were taken in that first deportation the tag of military had been applied to many of the civilian population as well.

The family waited, Kazia knew and was fearful that they would very soon be arrested as Stalin was making his intentions well known. Outside the snow was thick, the winter had been severe and inside the house it was quiet, they were warm in bed and fast asleep. They came on 10th February 1940, a day that is still engraved in my Mother's memory, at 5 o'clock in the morning, with insistent hammering, it was so loud they all jumped up in their beds, terrified '…open the door in the name of the Soviet Union, immediately…' and when they had gained entry the family were subjected to an aggressive barrage of orders in Russian.

'There were 4 Soviets armed with rifles, 2 Ukrainian Police and 2 Jews who were also armed.' Told by the 'leader' waving his gun at them, that they were 'a threat to public order' he read out a decree of deportation… 'Do not run away, your house is surrounded by soldiers, you have an hour to pack…'

'They ransacked the rooms and ordered us to dress quickly, shouting all the time and jabbing their rifle buts at us. They pushed everything over and so many lovely things were broken, papers were torn and photographs were destroyed.' 'Pottery was thrown around and clothes strewn across the floor and the children were sobbing and numb with fright.' – *Unknown deportee.*

They were too scared to move, scared they'd be shot, as this was what had happened to others. The Soviets searched for Adam who was still in hiding with friends, then looked for guns and stole whatever they could. 'Be ready to leave in an hour' the leader said and left.

The remaining Soviets urged them to get dressed quickly, pack their belongings and get outside. The decree of deportation was read out to them again and they were ordered to 'get your possessions.' Any resistance was out of the question. They were terrified and weren't allowed to move freely. The leader asked again where Adam was and Kazia very quickly said he was away helping her brother Walery on his Osada.

'Regardless of the weather conditions or time of day or night the villagers to be deported would be surrounded and forcible entry made into their homes. At gunpoint the family would be given 10 minutes to 2 hours in which to pack their belongings and then driven or made to walk to the nearest railway station.'

'The NKVD fell like wolves with rifles and daggers to our house and began to destroy holy pictures, they broke furniture and challenged us, accusing us of being Polish bourgeoisie. They asked where Daddy was, where the weapon was that Daddy did not have. They tore up the floor boards, threw clothes out of the closets and broke the beds. After an hour of them trying to destroy the house we were ordered to gather together, allowed to take some clothes and only 5kg of flour. We were led onto a sledge and taken to the station, treated as a laughing stock.' – *A teenage boy's recollection, from Dubien in Wolhynia.*

The family did not know where they were to be taken and were afraid to ask. The militia were all heavily armed and were very intimidating and seemed to be enjoying their power. They would not allow the children to move around the house but there was one friendly one amongst the 8 militia who quietly said to Kazia, 'take as much food and clothing as you can' and she went to the larder with Alicja and Jasia and packed salt pork, flour, potatoes and as much else as they could into sacks. Kazia was chilled, she knew immediately where they were being taken, Siberia.

Although the children were almost paralysed with fear Kazia made sure they were busy collecting things to take, despite the guards wanting them in one spot they also wanted them to be quick. She hurried them from one end of the house to the other to focus their minds not to fall into a state of panic. They were young and so very scared but they quickly packed everything they could into a big basket, some pots, a kettle, as many warm clothes as they could wear and carry, it was well below freezing, -40C a dreadfully severe winter, the coldest for very many years. She managed to take money, watches and some jewellery she hoped they would be able to barter. She luckily wasn't seen by the guards who would have put these prime objects into their own pockets.

Kazia's grand father, Walerian Bielawski (1834-1883) who had a big estate in Złoczów on the Romanian and Hungarian border, had been threatened with exile to Siberia after taking part in the January uprising of 1863 and was caught by the Russians. It was yet another of a series of national revolutions against the Russian empire by the Poles. Its failure and the brutal suppression that followed led to the complete Russification of Poland for decades afterwards. He had been involved in the Uprising in Podolia, once under the Polish crown and then annexed into the Russian empire in 1793. He was wanted by Ochrana, the secret police force of the Russian Empire, was arrested and imprisoned at Częstochowa in southern Poland and condemned to death by hanging or exile to Siberia.

He escaped with the help of Cardinal Bielawski a relative, and was forced for safety reasons to change his name to Radomski and was never able to return to his home town, lost his lands and estate. He later worked on the estates of some of the rich gentry he had known in Rozienek. He was married (no detail of wife) and had a son Władyslaw (no record of other children). Now his granddaughter Kazia was to become a victim of the Russians.

Kazia glanced through the window and saw a large horse-drawn sledge waiting outside and she realised she could take more items putting all into a pillow case, they would be invaluable to them on their journey into exile. She took a crucifix and a picture of the Blessed lady of Częstochowa and despite the harrying of the NKVD troopers, had the presence of mind to take the family photograph albums. She must have known they would never see their home again.

Those photo albums travelled with the family for over 20,000 km. They were well guarded, it was the history of the family a treasure and they went everywhere and have given a most important record of the family Radomski/Góral. It's why there are so many photo's in this memoir and which I am forever grateful for such a wonderful gallery of our incredible forebears.

This poem describes the similar experience of another family who were sent to Siberia at the same time, February 10th 1940.

In February's snow-filled sleep our world collapsed, Its successor perilous – new-shaped existence. The night-clad Soviet fist directly lunged, Crushing our nest – the family home. Coercive hands – calculated, merciless – Hammer the door, wrench the handle. Understanding dawns... here's Nemesis... Nemesis. A fleeting prayer, 'Lord, by Thy Shielding...' Carted like cattle, in wagons clamped, Through merest window's slit beyond our view Slides our dearest Polish land: sanctum sanctorum, Europe's usual martyr shedding farewell tears. What follows – the grey dolour of Russian fields; Drained, strained comrades on station platforms ranged; Leaded skies – cloud sheeted; Listless eyes; life – lost hands; Vacant steppes, Siberia, the buran' Disembodied wail; Kirghiz' indifference. In gaping Saman shacks the first year groans Long as eternity – mine-shaft black – Amid Life's blood-drained emptiness ...But God stood with us! *– Maria Waridoda*

Kazia had realised that the Soviets had been planning this for some considerable time as in the course of a single day they had collected over 250,000 people. They were ordered out of their home and onto the waiting sledge, one of many in a convoy of sledges loaded with families who like them, had been arrested as 'enemies of the people.' Some neighbours stood outside their houses watching as the sledges went by and waved. Within a short time they were on their way out of the town with the many sledges and horse carts filled with people from the neighbouring villages and saw many others heading straight towards Lubomyrka station. It all seemed very well organised and was over powering. Kazia was in a daze, stunned and incredibly frightened, the children were trembling, they needed Adam desperately but didn't know where he was.

They were on their way to the assembly point in the main square of Równe where many people were already gathered and as they arrived at the Parish offices they were met with very loud crying of children. There were about 20 other military settler families all very scared of what was to happen to them, Kazia and the children waited with the others for further orders, it was incredibly cold, birds had frozen on the branches they slept on. They sat there on the sleigh watching small groups that had begun to gather outside with food for friends and relatives, some came just out of curiosity. The NKVD then began to separate the single men from the women and children.

They were checked off against the NKVD lists which had been meticulously put together and ordered into the Parish offices. A little later

40

a long string of large wagons collected them and moved off down the main road to the outskirts of Równe, towards Lubomyrka station. As they moved along the high street out of the town they noticed how very quiet it was, afraid of possible rescue attempts the Russians had ordered all inhabitants to stay inside. 'Anybody found on the street when transport starts will be shot without warning' the NKVD Kommandant announced through a loud hailer. Slowly the wagons moved forward and when they arrived at Lubomyrka they saw a very long train waiting for them.

There were many hundreds upon hundreds of people standing in heavy snow, wrapped up against the cold and there the train sat, big and imposing spewing out clouds of smoke. When Russia had invaded, Adam and many of his co military friends had gone into hiding fearing that because they had fought the Russians they would be arrested and imprisoned or exiled and they were right. How was Kazia to get word to him?

Some of those gathered were known to the family and aware of where they were going and amongst them were some people who hadn't been given any time to pack belongings and were taken to the station with very little. 'There was the family Mitoszewski from our apartment block in town, standing there with hardly anything but luckily, some of their relatives had heard of the deportations and rushed to the station with food and clothing for them.' The Russians wouldn't let them near so the family started screaming and crying and making such a fuss that in the end they let them through. A young woman with a baby and infant was told to bring only what she could carry, her husband had been arrested and she had come only with the child she carried and the infant holding her hand. The NKVD did not care, they were heartless and the poor woman and her children would probably not have survived.

Adam had escaped all the searches by the Russians and had found out that he would be able to travel with them as married military men were to be allowed to go with their families. Word of the deportations had got through to where he was hiding and he had rushed to the square but missed them. He had then run like the devil desperately trying to find them, checking the apartment and then the Osada and eventually reaching the station seeing them waiting by an enormously long train, he was incredibly lucky and the family were very relieved to see him. Luck would play a major role in the survival of the family on several occasions, luck and prayer.

Adam and Kazia had noticed that only the Polish army settlers and their families were taken away from their town that night and to them it didn't seem a coincidence. What they were to find out later was that Stalin had worked out the detailed deportation plan towards the end of 1939.

That same night all along the eastern borderlands many ex army settlers and their families were arrested and taken from their homes. The Russian dictator was settling old scores, he had been embarrassed at the loss of the Bolshevik War and his own part in it.

The hopes of the Russian leaders of pushing their revolution beyond the borders of Russia were dashed at Warsaw in 1920. Western observers were amazed but relieved at the reversal of fortunes as it seemed that Poland would be overrun by its larger Soviet neighbour, leaving eastern and central Europe vulnerable to Communist Russia and its armies.

The Red command had badly mishandled the final stages of the march on Warsaw and much of the controversy focused on the actions of Stalin. He was serving as a member of the revolutionary military council of the SW front, one of two prongs of the Red Army's invasion of Poland. In early August 1920 the SW Front was attacking Lwów, the Polish stronghold in Galicia, while the other prong of the Red Army's advance, the West Front under the command of Commander Mikhail Tukhachevsky, was aimed directly at Warsaw.

On 11th August Sergei Kamenev the Red Army's Commander in Chief ordered the SW front to send its main fighting force, the elite cavalry unit known as the Konarmia, northwards towards Warsaw to aid Tukhachevsky's weak southern front. Stalin refused to obey this order and the Konarmia continued to fight at Lwów allowing Polish leader Jósef Piłsudski to launch his counter attack into the gap between the West and South West Russian fronts, smashing Tukhachevsky's weak southern front. Stalin's subordination had cost the Red Army a strategic point and the war was won by Piłsudski and his Polish fighters.

It was just two of these Polish fighters Adam Góral and Walery Radomski, whom Marshall Piłsudski had rewarded by granting them parcels of land in the eastern borderlands to secure the border and to show his gratitude to them. This helped to protect the country from it's unfriendly neighbour and more than explained the family predicament. Stalin was out for revenge and those who defeated the Red Army in 1920 were to be 'dealt with.'

The family looked at the imposing train and saw that it stretched a great distance, Stalin had planned this well, in the course of 24 hours the NKVD and their Ukrainian militia arrested people for deportation from most of the eastern borderlands and had filled the train to capacity. 10 trains had already passed through the station filled mainly with professors, teachers, real estate owners and families of military servicemen like them.

They were ordered, at gunpoint, by the Ukrainian militia and NKVD, to move towards the wagon, one of the NKVD was a Jew, the local shopkeeper they knew so well but he wouldn't acknowledge them, so they didn't acknowledge him either just in case it caused any problems. Lists of those to be deported had been drawn up on information provided by collaborators from among the Jews, Ukrainians and local communists and trains had stood waiting for long periods at the railway stations in towns and villages across the region. Columns of trucks, wagons and sleighs requisitioned from the peasants had stood ready for days and Soviet army units, the NKVD and the local militia composed of Jews and Ukrainians, awaited orders.

The train consisted of freight box cars, more suitable for the transport of cattle and the Soviets must have worked hard and long to plan for so many people! Each box car contained primitive beds made of wood planks, like shelves and in the middle stood a metal barrel transformed into a stove. When the stove had fuel it would produce more smoke than heat but it would allow the deportees to cook the food they had brought with them.

At the urging of the militia they stepped into the wagon where the walls were covered in frost, it was incredibly cold. There were windows with small metal grilles set high in the walls which gave out very little light. Everyone would have to make do with a small space on the floor if there was no room on the bunks. In the corner of the boxcar a hole had been cut into the floor and separated by just a blanket which was to serve as a toilet. It isn't difficult to imagine the awful smell that arose from there, not to mention the concerns for social customs.

The friendly trooper who had arrested them was there to help them again. He made sure that the potatoes and pork and rest of the food and bundles of clothing stayed with them as the militia confiscated as much as they could, they were ruthless. Any opportunity to settle old wounds they took with sadistic pleasure. But this particular man felt sorry for them, he had a good heart. He had done his job, with compassion and had taken a risk because if his friendly behaviour had been noticed he would most likely have joined them in Siberia! The family wore as many layers of clothing as they could and it would probably save their lives.

That freezing February day was a day carved into Alicja's memory and is with her to this day at 97 years of age, she can never forget even through her dementia. Adam and Kazia looked back towards Równe with tears in their eyes, bidding farewell to their beloved home, where they had brought up 3 children and lived happily, their life and dreams now shattered. The wagon door was opened wider and more were pushed in to be almost on top of people already sitting on top of cases, bags and mattresses and they had to squeeze through a few people, managing to climb onto an upper bunk. The door was closed and locked and silence and darkness fell all around them. People talked quietly amongst themselves, "how long have you been here" asked Kazia of one of her neighbours, '2 days' they said but some in the other wagons had been locked in for up to 4 days, not allowed to use the toilets in the station. Throughout the night they heard many more horse drawn sledges and lorries arriving and people being thrown into the trains. At the sounds of people being loaded they called out to them hoping for any news but no one had any information.

It was incredibly cold, 'it got through to our bones and our breath froze in the air and no matter where you put your hands or how tightly you arranged your clothing, the cold got through.' It was dark and they waited for hours, the train shunting back and forth. The night of their seizure was one of incredible grief and pain, they were being treated like criminals, dangerous to society, now without a home and country.

As a child, from an early age I was aware of some loss as I listened to my family speak of their beloved homeland, the pain of leaving never left them and I heard those words of loss very many times. I saw sadness in my Babcia's eyes, my Dziadek's quiet, thoughtful manner and I saw my Mother often pacing up and down the lounge trying to clear her memory but I didn't make sense of it all until my teenage years.

Ziuta, Walery's wife, with her children Władek and Marysia, were in another wagon further down the track, but they didn't know this until much later. Her other son, Zbyszek, was with his father Walery, who was taking his sister Genia and her daughter Halina to join her husband Władislaw in western Poland. Zbyszek had been determined to join the Polish resistance and was anxious to do everything he could for Poland. He avoided the deprivations of the Russian labour camps, but what he actually went through must have been equally dreadful. There are very few details of his time during this period. All that is known is that he was killed in controversial circumstances shortly before being able to join his family in England.

Details of the journey into Siberia is credit to Danuta Gradosielska Mączka aged 15 at the time of the exile of the Kresy settlers, who kept a diary of the journey. I have been able to compare her detail with that of my Aunt Janina's and they complement each other extremely well.

They had been ripped away from all that they loved and put onto a journey into a terrifying unknown, a land that would prove to be very hostile to them. Kazia had closed the door of their home and on their life and she never saw her Mother again or her relatives in the west of Poland. Her sister, Eugenia, (who she was to see again), niece Halina and her husband Władislaw, survived the war living under the repressive communist state, where nothing was private and where one family member could be turned against another because only loyalty to the state mattered. What was spoken was spoken in secret because so called friends might report you to the Police.

Journey to prison camp – adapted from a sketch by an unknown artist

The train began to lurch backwards and forwards on the tracks and all of a sudden it made one last heave and slowly moved off. They were utterly bewildered, in shock and terrified and they sat there trembling, they had never known such fear. Neither children nor adults realised that something even worse was to come, they looked around, huddled up closer together and waited, it was another moment that Alicja never forgot. It was just after Midnight and they were on a Train to Siberia and imprisonment.

Their journey into exile was beginning. From Lubormyrka station on 12th February where they had spent two days in the wagon it took them through Zdolbunow and on February 13th they changed into Russian trains which were much larger and would suit the tracks, more people had been pushed into the wagon and it was very stuffy. The rhythmic clicking

45

of the train wheels on the tracks did nothing to calm their nerves. They were distraught, weeping and so terribly cold. By 15th February they stopped at Iwanko, and were given bread and water, it was very frosty but sunny and they were still locked into the wagon. Alicja looked through the grill at the top of the wagon hoping to see something, anything of Poland. The train travelled slowly, at a snail's pace, stopping frequently, but when it stopped at any station they weren't allowed out of the wagon.

Most of the prisoners had candles so they could see inside the wagon, but these would soon run out as did the fuel for the stove until the guards eventually brought some on one of the many stops and they were able to cook the provisions they and others had brought and share amongst them. After a couple of days they realised it was just best to accept the situation, they didn't know how long they were to be in the wagon and there was absolutely nothing they could do to change the situation.

'The journey was simply indescribable, during our sleep we froze to the walls, our hair, clothes and bedding. The train rocked so badly that people were falling onto the burning stove and onto the ground from the bunks. After 3 days we were given some water and when we could we caught snow through the window but when the guard noticed he beat the butt of his rifle onto the dish and broke it. At the end of March we came to Irkutsk region in Tajshta. In the barracks where we were placed we were told to forget about the rotten bourgeouise Poland forever as here we are to end our lives and work.'

– Resident of Grodno, wife of non-commissioned officer of Polish army recalls.

The journey would follow a pattern, it seemed the train would move as slowly as it could through sleeping towns at night to avoid notice and halt on a branch line out in the country during the day to refuel. Signal delays and long stretches of inhabited country meant over running the schedule until well into daylight the next day. On these occasions there was near panic from the Soviets and train staff. Alicja often wondered from her perch on the top bunk, what civilian Russians standing on station platforms made of the very slow, long lines of trains crawling past them.

Ethnic Poles, were a minority in eastern Poland but were the majority of those deported and no social group was spared, this included workers, artisans, peasants, foresters, soldiers, judges, the clergy, professors, scientists, attorneys, engineers and teachers. where many hundreds of thousands suffered awful misery and many perished in circumstances defying description. Anyone listed as an 'anti Soviet element' was deported and this was the most unfortunate ordeal that had befallen my family.

The land, as far as the eye could see was flat and there were a few dilapidated buildings a few scattered settlements and mud huts with thatched roofs and small windows, which looked dirty and run down. It was very gloomy and when the train stopped Alicja saw other deportees who seemed in worse condition than they were. Babies were hungry and were crying and mothers were in despair. Day after day, night after night they heard only the constant moan of the wheels on the tracks picking up speed, taking them further and further away from their country.

Passing daily through villages, fields and forests, all covered in snow. It was bitterly cold and the wagon walls were frozen and their skin froze on contact. In the mornings when they awoke they had to prise their clothes away from the walls. They were dejected, wondering what was going to happen to them. They talked amongst themselves, held each other and waited for the next move and prayed and sang patriotic songs and hymns. Their faith was all that was holding them together as they travelled into Soviet territory.

There were stops at intervals to fill up with water and coal and at these times they were given buckets of hot water and cabbage soup (łapsza) but they could only drink the water, as the cabbage leaves were inedible. They were sometimes given soup with fish heads floating in which despite their hunger they left and just drank the thin soup with the black, sour bread which was handed out at intervals of two or three days, it was hard and they dipped it into the putrid water, it's disgusting but it's all they have. A sense of powerlessness has settled on the wagon and they feel very vulnerable.

Passing into Soviet territory at Szepetowka on February 16th, it was much colder and everyone had noticed the big drop in temperature and put on any extra clothing they had. They were given coal and water and were able to cook a meal on the stove. They were hungry and tired but glad they had brought so much with them. They pass through Orzenin, Korosten and Owrucz, where they again are given coal, water and some potatoes but are still kept locked in the wagons. They see a bleak landscape, flat and endless snow covered fields, forests and towns, and villages through the open door before it was slammed shut.

The train passes over the river Prypet (scene of the Chernobyl disaster in 1986) on 17th February, and travels alongside fields and pastures that looked like ice rinks and they go through small villages and Alicja sees orchards and forests of pine, oak and birches planted in rows all along the railway tracks and there are rows of firs that protect against drifting snow. It's dark in the truck and the air is hot and reeks of human waste. Those sitting on the floor are shoulder to shoulder and rocking back and forth with the movement of the train.

She continued to look out of the small shutters hoping to still see Poland, just a small sign of her homeland but they are now in deepest Russia and she sees kolkhozes, (collective farms) and small houses. The train stops and they get a whole bucket of much needed water and some coal for the stove. At the next stop there is a small hut at the station with outside taps and running water and they are allowed out of the wagon and fill as many buckets as they can for the many thirsty people. Some villagers approach them carrying bread and bottles of water but are sent on their way by the guards.

On 18th Feb the train travels slowly over the Dneper bridge with yet more flooded fields, mostly frozen and forests of pine, oak and birches. There are again rows of firs along the tracks which would continue for most of the journey. Alicja sat on the bunk looking out of the small shutters, she was very cold and very sad. Janusz was by her side trying to keep warm and they cuddle up and together gaze through the shutters. They had stopped at Gomel an industrial town where two of the men in the wagon were allowed out to get some broth and returned with two buckets which were divided up amongst the starving occupants. When the train stopped to refuel and was ready to continue the journey, it didn't wait for those who had got off to find food or water or just to stretch their legs, it would move off regardless leaving those unfortunates to find their own way and many never saw their families again, they would freeze to death.

Adapted from a sketch by anunknown artist

On 19th February Alicja's 16th birthday, one which she would never forget, they pass through Bryansk and Orzel and on the 20th Feb they cross the river Don and the train starts to veer further north. Late at night they stop at Karaczew where they are given soup. They are allowed to leave the train and despite the awful cold several get out to stretch aching limbs to see where they are. Alicja and Jasia take the opportunity to look around and get away for a moment from the cries of the hungry babies and crying mothers who cannot feed them as they have no milk. The guards ignore their pleas for milk just sneering at them. Other mothers begged for water only to be ignored. Many of the deaths on the journey were of babies and children, thrown from the train into the snow by the guards. The mortality rate was high, the guards incredibly cruel and uncaring and would continue to be throughout the journey.

The condition of the human freight in the box cars defied description. There were now only about 30 as some had already died, squashed into the wagon some slept on the wooden bunks while others were on the floor. Beria's instructions had been for only 30 per wagon but the NKVD just packed them in regardless. In some wagons there were up to 80, which must have been unbearable and tiring with people only being able to stand. Deprived of food, warmth and the most basic sanitary requirements, thousands perished during the journey, which was of course Stalin's intention. Their bodies were left by the side of the track and it was heart breaking, no burial was to be given to the deceased who were mostly children and the elderly. Worst was seeing young mothers losing their babies or infants, unable to survive the cold and lack of milk, holding the lifeless child in their arms, silent with grief and if a guard noticed he would grab the child, throw it out of the train and would do the same to the dead mother only days later.

In the late afternoon of 21st Feb they reach Aleksandrowka and 22nd February sees them at Rybna station and they take on coal and water and carry on towards Holworsk and Woskriesensk where they notice many destroyed churches, Catholic and Orthodox. God doesn't exist for the Soviets, only Stalin. Next stop is Oriechowo where they collect snow in buckets and after it thaws, which seems to take for ever, they wash off the dust and grime. They are covered in lice and scratch constantly. Many are suffering, children and the elderly the most, children dying from hunger in the arms of their parents and being left in the snow, it was hard to witness.

The monotony of the landscape come to an end when Alicja saw a range of hills, and dry river banks, sandstone cliffs and bundles of peat piled up. She saw a large barn and a stable with sheep, stacks of straw and small huts. They are now all desperate to be free of the box car, packed in so tightly, under guard in locked wagons, sleeping in such crowded spaces. The slates on the roof are rattling adding to their frustration, they haven't eaten for two days and at 4pm they are given dumplings made of white flour and some cabbage soup. It's watery and sour but they eat it. The Soviets had only made meagre provision for their 'passengers' leaving them to suffer from hunger and thirst. At best they got one bucket of water for the whole wagon a day.

On 23rd February in the early morning the train heads towards Pokrowa passing through nice countryside and again they are surrounded by endless stretches of flat land covered by sand blown around by the wind. It is sometimes boring for Alicja watching from the grille but it is something to take her mind off the lice eating away at her, it is also bitterly cold. They pass through Pietruszki which is a big station, with many tracks and they are given soup with noodles but not any water, they can't wash and the conditions in the boxcar are awful. The lice spread from one person to another and everyone is infested. 'There is much unhappiness, a few days ago a woman gave birth and the child didn't survive, there was nothing for the new mother to feed her child and she was desperate and how she cried for her little one.' The guards did nothing at all to alleviate her agony.

The endless plains stretch before them, the train rumbles on and they stop at Untow and get off to talk to people they meet on the platform and hear of very many other Poles being deported. In the evening they arrive in Wlademir and rush to get out of the boxcar, to use a toilet and get water but there is no water and no toilets so they head to the bushes and trees. They are given thick barley and wheat soup which they eat very quickly, they ask for water but no one is listening. People faint, there is so little food and the effects are beginning to tell on very many. Alicja constantly looks out of the tiny shutters to see where they are, and mostly sees other steam locomotives loaded with people like them.

On 24th Feb they cross the frozen river Volga and the situation in the wagon is desperate. Alicja and Jasia are now taking it in turns to look out of the grill and see very many destroyed churches, Christianity was not compatible with Communism and the Soviets destroyed many. They are given coal, water and cabbage soup and the NKVD tell them if there are no delays they should reach their destination very soon which will be Gorki near the Volga river. Someone begins to sing, over and over Boze coś Polskie (God save Poland) and others join in, they are bitterly cold but haven't given up.

They arrive late afternoon and they leave the train and walk to an Orthodox church where they will stay the night. There is no fire and it is bitterly cold and they spend the night on the floor. Kazia and Adam look at each other and wonder how they and the children will survive the hardships to come.

On the morning of Sunday 25th Feb they leave the church with the Sieradzkis, the Zajdels and others from the Osada Krechowiecka for a smaller train and are told they will be going further north and given more coal and bread. They see on most days many planes flying over and anti aircraft guns and other military equipment as well as trains loaded with tanks. They notice that the main train they've left is going further north east, and they wave the others off hoping that they survive, their friends and neighbours the Mączka's from their Osada amongst them. Meanwhile they are heading towards Sharya and Kotlas.

Kotlas was a deportation facility, a transit prison location where deportees were held whilst awaiting transport to their ultimate destinations further north and east. The camp system was spread out along the railroad line, with camps, camp offices and camp stations every 5 to 10 km along the rails and there were also farm camps. No statistics exist but it is believed that a few ml people have passed through its portals, with the numbers peaking during WW2. It had operated from the late 1920's and very many others, Estonians, Lithuanians and Latvians passed through in 1939, also victims of Stalin's deportations. In 1940 very many of the Poles from the eastern borderlands were transferred through Kotlas to the forestry work camps in the Taiga where most perished in the forests. – *Irina Dubrovina – Sovest.*

They had travelled for over two weeks and many hundreds of km and they began to be gripped by fear and panic, not sure sometimes if they were shaking from fear or the cold. Their food supplies were very low and they didn't know how much longer they were to travel, there was little interaction between them and the guards. Many were sick from the cold and the lack of proper food, but worst of all was the lack of water. Some had scraped snow off the roof of the wagon as they had been so thirsty.

They had left many bodies at the side of the track having no time or strength to bury them. No one had any energy and all they saw around them was deep snow and very high snow drifts. Many babies and infants had died and some of the elderly and they were left in the deep snow most likely to be found by the wolves. The grief of their relatives was unrelenting and people were full of sadness.

They board the smaller train towards Sharya and the journey continues very slowly and at just after midnight on 27th February they stop at the end of the track and have reached Gorki where they have to wait until the following morning to disembark with several other families. Their next journey will be onto Sharya a journey of 690 km and from there the NKVD tell them they will head to the labour camp which is about 15 km away from Sharya and is called Poldniewica, The later camps they are moved to are Darowatka and then Duraszowa during the course of two years which are only a short distance from the main camp Poldniewica.

On 28th February 1940 they brace themselves for yet another journey after a gruelling one so far of over 2,000 km from Poland. They board another train, tired and frightened and the inhabitants of the wagon are exhausted, dirty with lice and starving. Some are trying to catch snow through the grille to quench their thirst and they are desperate. Kazia and Adam do their best to reassure the children who are wide eyed and very frightened. The next day on 29th February, after arriving at Sharya the door of their wagon is thrown open and the guards are pointing guns at them and shouting for them to get off the train, a wilderness of snow stretched before them. So much snow!

There were endless wastes of snow, forests and nothing else. It was almost blinding and they were exhausted and very hungry. They saw horse drawn sledges and more guards waiting and they're told to quickly collect their belongings as it started to snow, these are then put onto the sledges and they are instructed to follow the lead sledge. The snow is very deep and small children like Janusz who was only 10 struggle although his sisters Alicja and Jasia also have difficulty as it's up to their waists but the exercise keeps them warm and eases the load on the horses. They looked at each other for reassurance and slowly set off resigned to their fate. The elderly and those barely surviving, are at least able to travel in the sleighs including Kazia.

Sharya is in deepest Russia, a town in Kostroma Oblast on the left bank of the Vetluga river and dates back to the days of the Russian Empire of 1849. It gradually increased in size under the Soviet era and now has greater devolved power after the dissolution of the Soviet Union.

The bedraggled group were forced to march at gunpoint, although there was little point of the guns, there was nowhere to escape to! They walked through the very deep and heavy snow heading to the labour camp. The lead sledge headed off slowly towards the forests, deeper and deeper into the white cloud of snow and it was very quiet and still and after what seemed like hours, wet, very hungry and exhausted they reached the labour camp. The snow storm had by now became a blizzard and they were desperate for shelter. They were in the furthest labour camp, Posiolek Poldniewica. Szarynskij region, Gorkowskaja Oblast.

There had been considerable distress in the wagons, pregnant women had lost their babies and infants had died, not able to survive the inhumane and cramped spaces and having to relieve themselves in a bucket or through the floor had made the situation considerably worse, it was hellish. They went for days without food or water having to catch rain and scrape snow off the roof to quench their thirst.

The guards did little to help them ensuring a high mortality rate. There were suicides as powerlessness had overtaken many, they were completely under the control of the Soviets. Many men quietly raged at the Bolsheviks, my Dziadek amongst them. He struggled to keep his rage to himself even when Poland became an ally of the 'Bolsheviks'.

Less than half the people crammed into the boxcars, survived the long journey to Sharya. Many had starved and those who had left the train to look for food in the forests, would have frozen after becoming lost. Parents buried their children, digging graves with sticks into the deep frozen earth hoping that roaming wolves wouldn't unearth their bodies. Families were decimated, children orphaned and survivors were already suffering the effects of malnutrition.

At one of the stops on their journey they had seen other trains taking Russian 'dissidents' even further into Siberia and those who had died or fallen were just left piled up on the platforms or by the side of the tracks, their families unable even to cover them to give them some dignity. The thought of leaving loved ones behind in such circumstances must have been unbearable. They were pushed beyond anger and tears, beyond protest and grief, until without any energy some would just sink into acceptance, hoping somehow to survive. Only their faith, confidence and love for each other and their determination to survive, kept the family going.

That they had all been together on this journey was a stroke of luck as the assignment of people to boxcars had been random. They had been forcibly ripped away from all that they had known and worked for and put into the terrifying unknown, to a land that would be difficult to work and live in. The stove in the middle of the car had mostly spewed out more smoke than heat and they had been frozen for most of that unbearable journey but had physically kept close together. The train went very slowly, the Russians ignored them and when they stopped anywhere, few approached them to help, it was as if the Russians had been forbidden to speak to the 'capitalist bourgeoise' from Poland.

When they had first boarded the train they had made a point of getting to know their fellow passengers. They were all Poles, Catholics and Jews and like them had similar stories to tell. Some had been arrested for refusing Soviet citizenship, some for a made up crime they had no way of proving they didn't commit and so very many of them on this train alone perished on the journey towards Siberia.

'That freezing and gloomy day 10th February 1940 when we left our family home and with tears in our eyes, bade farewell to our beloved town, is engraved in my memory.' – *Maria Kielan*

Stalin thought the extreme conditions of the labour camps would ensure the liquidation of the 'enemies of the people' but he did not reckon on the resilience or the faith of the Polish people, especially those of the eastern Borderlands, those 'simple people', my family, the Polish Military class, representative of the multi-ethnic Polish State.

What the Bolsheviks had failed to do in 1920, they succeeded in part in 1939 through the signing of the Ribbentrop-Molotov pact. The Red Army took the eastern borderlands as the Bolsheviks had intended and then went on to deal with their slayers of 1920, the Osadnicy.

Whilst the Poles of the eastern borderlands were being deported to the USSR, those left behind fell victim to the Ukrainian Nationalists and the Ukrainian Galiizen Division who were planning the massacre of Polish citizens with the support of the Germans, ethnicly cleansing the Poles in eastern Poland, soon to be Ukraine under the USSR. The massacre of Poles in Wołyn and Eastern Galicia were carried out by the Urkainian Insurgent Army (UPA) North Command which included the cleansing of Równe, home to the family.

My family without any doubt would have fallen victim to the UPA's savage methods, having lived and worked amongst many Ukrainians who were very quickly turned against the Polish population. It is estimated that there were between 76,000 and 106,000 victims, mostly women and children at the hands of the UPA in the Wołyn area alone. Of the Jewish population at the hands of the Germans from this area, approximately 26.000 died which made up about half of the population of Równe. So very many deaths from just a small area of Poland.

Their lives were filled with loss, hardship and displacement, they would have a desperate life ahead of them and it would be their resolve, faith, spirit and sense of humour that sustained them through the deprivations of the Russian labour camps.

'To choose one's victims, to prepare one's plans minutely, to slake an implacable vengeance and then to go to bed..... there is nothing sweeter in the world'
– J.V. Stalin

CHAPTER 4

Surviving Siberia

The exile of Polish citizens by the Soviets between 1939 and 1941 is still not familiar to many people, what Stalin was doing to the Poles barely reached the West and when he became an ally of the two main WW2 powers, any discussion of this episode was discouraged.

The true story is only now emerging having begun very slowly in the post war years, over shadowed by the better known German occupation of Poland and the rest of Europe. Stalin's actions were no less brutal and yet despite the evidence of survivors and written testimonies, the West seems to think his crimes were not as evil!

Their walk at gunpoint from Sharya had taken many hours and they were exhausted. They arrived at a school in a small village where they were to spend the night in freezing conditions. The NKVD told them they would be marched to the labour camp, Posiolek Poldniewica, in the morning. They were all very frightened, the group looked at each other got their children together and made a circle in the middle of the floor. There was no food, water or heating and they resigned themselves for another long walk in the morning to the labour camp and a very undecided future.

Arkhangelsk is a region in north European Russia on the river Dvina near the White Sea. It was the seaport of medieval and early modern Russia until 1703. It has significant wood resources with forests mainly of pine, birch, aspen and fir which cover 86,000 square miles and it was to this area of north European Russia that many Polish military families were exiled by Stalin.

Forced labour was used extensively in the USSR as a means of controlling people, as manpower for government projects and reconstruction in a Police run system of colonies and special settlements, ultimately working people to death. Conditions were harsh and deadly and it was a way for the Soviets to imprison anyone for any reason.

It was deemed a necessary tool by the Bolsheviks to rid the country of internal enemies while using their labour to achieve stronger socialist unions and it was no different during wartime. In July 1937 with war imminent Stalin ordered the removal of Germans from Soviet soil on the grounds that they were working for the enemy. A month later the liquidation of Poles was also approved by the Politburo and in 1938 many others, Latvians, Estonians, Romanians, Greeks, Afghans and Persians were swept up in similar operations. They were arrested, shot or placed in the forced labour system.

In order to de Polonize all newly acquired territories, the Soviet secret

Police, the NKVD, rounded up and deported the Polish nationals to Arkhangelsk, the Urals, Kazakhstan and Siberia, in an atmosphere of absolute terror. There were four waves of deportations of entire families from 1940 to 1941.

There were several categories of labour camp:-

Corrective labour camps – the principal type of punitive institution in the Soviet Union, with 5 classes, exile colony, ordinary regime camp, intensified regime camp, strict regime camp and special regime camp.

The 3 main labour camp inmates were 'Kulaks,' 'Osadniks' (my family) 'Ukazniks', then the dedicated criminals, 'thieves in law,' and people sentenced for various political and religious reasons.

Exile colonies were for prisoners who were deemed to be 'solidly on the path to reform.'

Ordinary regime camps held prisoners serving sentences of less than 3 years for less serious crimes or, serving the initial portion of longer sentences for major offences.

Intensified regime camps were for men sentenced for more than 3 years for serious offences.

Strict regime camps housed those convicted of serious state crimes, political dissent, political crime and especially those considered 'especially dangerous recividists'.

The *special regime camps* were for those with commuted death sentences and 'especially dangerous recividists'.

Prison officials had the power to change a prisoner's category depending on their behaviour, moving them from a camp to a prison where conditions would be even harsher. Apart from the lack of freedom the semi starvation diet was the most punitive aspect of the labour camp. The quality of food was extremely poor, there were no fresh vegetables and the fish, which was the main protein was rotten. Food was often infested with maggots and cockroaches, the poor diet and the hard work resulted in illness and many deaths. Hunger was used as a weapon, it was a tool of war for the Soviets.

The labour was strenuous, fatiguing and quite often dangerous, with broken old tools and primitive machinery. Failure to meet the high production quotas was punished with lower rations and withdrawal of correspondence or parcels from home. Living quarters were not well heated or ventilated and clothing for the prisoners was wholly inadequate for outdoor work especially in temperatures that could fall to -30 in winter. There was over crowding, poor hygiene, toileting and washing facilities. Medical treatment if any was poor.

The size of the inmates' ration depended on the percentage of work quota they delivered and whilst this compelled many to work harder, depending on the size and needs of their family, it only accelerated their exhaustion sometimes causing death.

After the German attack on the Soviet Union in June 1941 the conditions in the camps worsened drastically.

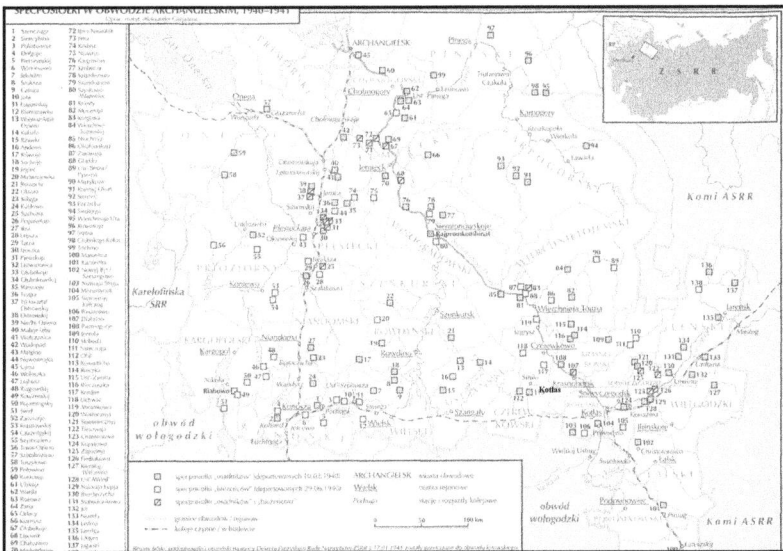

Map of Labour camps in the former USSR and Arkhangelsk

The camp routine was made up of a long list of orders given after the early wake up call, the instructions shouted out by the guards each morning to the inmates assembled in the dark, freezing cold outside their barracks. Then came the line up and marching in line into the forest to their forced labour. They had to gather all their strength to cope with the daily routine and then later in the day waiting in line for the meagre rations, a piece of black bread and maybe a bowl of watery vegetable soup, it was simply not enough for people working at incredibly hard labour.

Siberia is one of the most sparsely populated places on earth. During the winter average temperatures range from -23C to -45C, almost impossible for the body to function and if the intense cold didn't kill the arctic storms would do Stalin's work. They came with very little warning and would quickly cover the working parties in freezing white fog. It was to this vast wilderness that up to 1.7ml Poles were to be used as forced labour in lumber camps, excavating canals, laying railway lines, mining, working in factories and on collective farms.

Those transported to the isolated regions of north eastern Russia to the Siberian Steppe or the deserts of Kazakhstan had a low survival rate, succumbing to major ailments such as tuberculosis. Those deported to the western Siberian Russian-speaking communities often fared a little better. There might have been a medical student or a nurse in the community and some basic medicines available.

The deportees were housed in posiolki, settlements of wooden barracks or huts surrounded by high fences. Many ex military Osadnicy deported in February 1940, amongst them my family the Góral-Radomski's, ended up in isolated lumber camps in Arkhangelsk in north western Russia, where the accommodation was basic and over crowded. The barracks would be heated by wood burning stoves which kept the inhabitants from freezing but there was no running water. Some were housed in Russian villages and the freezing temperatures, hard labour and lack of food and medicines contributed to a very high death toll.

To the Soviets these families, 'enemies of the state,' were a resource to be exploited, a disposable workforce. Men would be separated from their families on the day of deportation and sent to other camps. Sometimes the men and boys lived in the family camp but were sent to work very deep into the forests for weeks or months on end. This would leave many women with children alone to support them with very little chance of survival.

Men and women over the age of 15, my Dziadek Adam and my Mother Alicja, carried out heavy and dangerous manual labour for 10 hours a day six days a week and they would receive a daily ration of a few hundred grams of bread and a bowl of watery soup, but only if the quota was fulfilled. 'If you do not work you do not eat', was the Soviet mantra and they were either paid in vouchers or cash. Many of the Polish families had brought items to barter and they were able to with their Russian neighbours. Some families received parcels from Poland including seeds and could grow vegetables in the short summers. Babcia Sofia, Kazia's Mother sent parcels for as long as she could. The Osadnicy with their farming backgrounds fared better than the townspeople and knew what to collect in the forests.

In some camps the children were sent to Russian schools to learn about communism and this fate fell to Janina, Marysia and Janusz.

Women and children were sent to collective farms in Kazakhstan and Uzbekistan, placed in local communities and usually treated with hostility. The living conditions were dire, filthy and infested with vermin. Life was tough and food sometimes non existent. The death rate was extremely high due to the extreme changes in temperature and exhaustion, malnutrition and disease. Mothers were in despair for their ill and starving children. The authorities were heartless and made no effort to help them, the basic conditions of the posiolek depended very much on the Kommandant.

The brutality of the gulag system is well known. Instigated by Lenin and perfected by Stalin, to remove counter revolutionaries and undesirables from society by placing them in camps in the most savage of environments and starving and working them to death. In 1942 alone, Soviet statistics tell that 352,560 people died in the gulags and in 1943, 267,826 died from illness, exposure and over work. Many were shot, the Soviets were ruthless.

Stalin had developed the system which was wound down in the late 1950's and finally abandoned in 1960 but they continued in all but name until the collapse of the Soviet Union in 1991, but I would be very surprised if there were not still some in the Russian wilderness. There were many hundreds of them and deportations continued up to the late 1950's. In 1956, the Supreme Soviet Presidium decided to rehabilitate the majority of the punished peoples authorising them to return to their region of origin. However, this did not include the Crimean Tatars, the Russian-Germans or the Meskhetian Turks. These three groups were neither rehabilitated nor allowed to return to their regions of origin but condemned to remain in exile deprived of all rights.

After leaving the train at Sharya, the group my family were with had finally reached some wooden barracks at a logging camp. They had walked for hours, had frostbite and were covered in lice after the long journey from Poland. Many had died on that gruelling journey. The barracks had previously been a prison camp for Latvians and it had a huge gate at the entrance which Alicja thought looked quite intimidating.

It was very quiet and still, no birdsong or sounds from any animals, it was so quiet. The camp was surrounded by a very tall wooden stockade with guard towers at the corners, and it looked exactly what it was, a prison. There was a wooden fence around the camp and there was nowhere to run to. The gates were locked only at night but the guards manned the towers 24 hours a day. The barracks were surrounded by forests which extended for hundreds of kilometres. There was nowhere to go to so any attempt to escape was futile and they were watched constantly, those who did escape froze or starved to death in those forests.

There were 18 barracks poorly made of rough wooden logs, and these would house about 2,500 prisoners, with 12 rooms in each barracks and a stove to be shared between two rooms. Each barrack would house 14 families and the barracks for the guards and the Kommandant were set further away in a clearing in the forest. The gaps between the logs were stuffed with moss and clay and were full of bugs of all sorts. There were clouds of bugs and insects that came out to feed on their blood at night, piercing their skin and also tiny flies and mosquitoes which bit and stung them incessantly. Multitudes of lice were also a huge irritant but as time went on they would gradually become used to them. The floor crawled with cockroaches and the fight to eliminate all these irritants would never be won.

Adapted from a drawing by Sobierajski

The family stood looking around their living quarters, and could see they would have many problems keeping warm as there were many large cracks in the walls through which the cold would creep, and at times the temperature would fall to minus -30 degrees, sometimes colder. They were all checked off yet another list by the NKVD, and some families were packed off into the unknown, being marshalled off out of the gates. Those left which included my family, were allocated a tiny space to live, one family on higher bunks, one on lower bunks. There was just enough room to lie down, and they would have to sleep tightly together, holding each other for warmth and comfort. They looked around them and resigned to their fate with the several other families they were billeted with helped each other to settle in and found themselves somewhere to store their belongings.

Chief of the NKVD, Beria had informed Stalin that 'in all the Posioleks the barracks are not prepared for the winter, there is a lack of stoves and unglazed windows, as yet normal conditions do not exist for the deportees, families live in cramped barracks, poorly supplied with food and medical care for them is sparse, which leads to epidemic illnesses.' Conditions would not improve.

The NKVD was all powerful in Siberia, were the overseers of the labour camps and they were always ready to punish any Poles for any offences which could be severe. One man was sentenced to 10 years hard labour for criticising Stalin and others were imprisoned for singing religious songs. The more frightening contact with the NKVD was at night when officers would come into the huts in the early hours, usually about 2am to question and check up on them.

The questions were usually aggressive, centred on any missing male member of the family. Ziuta, Walery's wife was constantly asked where her husband was and all she did know was that he had left to take his sister Gienia and her daughter Halina to the west of Poland to be with her husband. What she didn't know was that he had been arrested and charged as a spy on his way back to collect his family and imprisoned in the infamous prison in Moscow, the Lubyanka.

After arranging their belongings they were called together, made to stand outside the camp gates awaiting instructions when the Kommandant arrived with his dog and several guards. He looked quite imposing and had a huge bushy moustache, he began pacing up and down with his hands behind his back, in front of his 'audience' glaring at them with contempt. It was bitterly cold and they were stamping their feet to keep warm. He welcomed them by telling them to "Settle down and work because you'll never get out of here. Hairs will grow on my palms before you leave this place. Forget about Poland, it doesn't exist and never will.'

On hearing his views many were outraged. They looked around at each other and a voice from the back said, "That's what you think." It was Ziuta who stood up to him then and several other times. She was so small in stature, but she could be very assertive and she took outrage at this 'oppressor' who dared to doubt her passion for her homeland. This man, the highest authority in the camp, had insulted everyone and she couldn't hold back her feelings, the arduous journey had taken it out of them all! There did come a time when she was able to remind him of those words.

Life in the camp depended on the Kommandant, his powers were wide and the settlers could not question his decisions. All transgressions were liable to a fine or a few days in custody in the lock up. Being late for work was punishable by 3 months hard labour and a reduction in any payment they received. Settlers were arrested for simply having evening devotions and expressions of anti Soviet views had the same fate. Ziuta had been instinctive in her comments and it seemed the Kommandant had let it go, for now.

The very next morning they heard the heavy tread of boots outside the barracks, it was still dark and they hadn't slept well, they were cold to the bone and so frightened. A guard opened the door and 3 of them stepped in with their 'daily assignments.' They were to be sent to work in the forest to fell the trees and were issued with axes and saws. They were given half an hour to get dressed and eat but before breakfast each person was called into the Kommandant's office and given a form to complete which specified the reason for their 'resettlement.' The authorities would only accept one reason, 'enemies of the state' and there was no alternative but to sign. This condemned them to a sentence of 25 years hard labour in Siberia. They walked out of his office stunned, the thought of 25 years in this hell was too much for some of them, they hadn't committed any crime!

There were mornings at roll-call when the Kommandant would say to them all, shouting at them, 'you Polish Lords will die here, Poland never existed and never will. Here, he said, pointing at the forests, here you will die, Polish dogs.' Then turning on his heel he would leave the prisoners with angry looks on their faces as they went off to work in the forest.

They had only time for a breakfast of balanda, hot water mixed with flour, and a piece of very hard black bread. Not very nourishing, but it had to do. This would now be their daily diet, along with 400 grams of slightly less decayed bread. Compared with what they were to live through later, these conditions didn't seem impossible? They still had their strength and warm clothes from home, but it would be difficult to come to terms with their life as exiles! They already missed their home badly.

The Guards came back and ordered them out of the hut and they were all lined up, shivering in the cold. They had put as many clothes on as they could and they waited, there were about 50 of them with axes and saws, including my Dziadek Adam and Mum Alicja. They were urged on walking past the high wooden fence and towards the gate, the guards shouting 'come on come on, form lines' they were being continually checked by the guards, from the front and back. Two guards came out of the watch tower and the gates were swung wide open. There were 4 watch towers Alicja remembers, and she looked up to see sentries perched in the others, watching their every move.

They moved out of the camp and towards the forest keeping their heads down against the icy wind and intense chill, which cut them to the bone. The snow crunched under their boots and with the guards' urging they hurried on. Beyond the boundary of the camp the biting cold and the head wind stung their faces and their hands were already stiff with cold. Adam and Alicja rubbed them together and pulled their collars and scarves tightly and silently thanked Kazia for bringing their fur hats and scarves which they would have to guard carefully. They would later be given fufaika, a thigh length buttoned to the throat kapok-padded jacket and a pair of padded winter trousers and rubberised canvas boots which came to just above the ankles. On top of their own clothes, this did help towards keeping some of the extreme cold out.

'Attention, attention from the leading guard, keep to your lines, no talking, watch where you're going.' The column slowly moved forward, Adam looked at Alicja to try and reassure her and they walked on with as much confidence as they could muster. It hadn't snowed for a few days and the lane was quite worn from previous columns marching this way yesterday. Everyone hunched their shoulders, looked ahead of them and moved slowly onwards, they were all very despondent. The sun was rising over the forests and on any other day it would have been a beautiful sight.

They passed the wood processing building and moved out onto the plain right into the wind and the snow which stretched all around them and in the short distance were the forests where they would be working. By this time, they had marched for about half an hour and the frost had caught Alicja's scarf where she had breathed on it and formed an icy crust, her feet were almost numb as were her hands and all around her people were clapping their hands and stamping their feet trying desperately to get warm but being urged on by the guards.

They went to work in that Arctic weather with their saws and axes, trudging deep into the forest to fell trees in deep snow every day. Alicja's job was to strip the bark from the birch logs, load them onto a cart to be fed into the saw mill. Life from now on would be very difficult for them, they lived in complete isolation, there was no radio, no newspapers; they were not even able to talk freely. They did master some Russian in order to get by, it was very similar to Polish, and it helped them to trade what they had brought with them for food with the local Russians.

Meanwhile back at the barracks Kazia and other women who had been excused hard labour due to health problems and age, were faced with the most dreadful sight. They had been very cold during the night despite all cuddling up together under the blankets and rugs she had packed. She had noticed thick ice on the window panes and white cobwebs of ice all along where the wall met the roof, conditions were simply awful. The bunk beds and mattresses were infiltrated with bed bugs so she and a few of the other women organised themselves to clean bedding, they removed it and beat it with branches to rid it of as many of the different kinds of bugs there were. In the summer the bunks would be dragged outside and boiling water poured over them to kill the bugs.

It barely made a difference and exacted a toll on everyone. The bugs attacked them at night and sucked their blood out of their under nourished bodies. In the mornings they would see the creatures scurrying away full of blood and they could easily be squashed but there would be an army waiting to replace them. On top of this there were the lice that crawled into their scalps and clothes and played havoc with their skin. It had all very quickly become a part of their existence and Kazia wore herself out trying to give the family a clean bed at night.

The one range stove in the barrack used for heating and cooking burned continuously, there being a plentiful supply of wood from the forests. They also used the stove for drying their clothes, which were always wet from walking through snow up to their waists and they were still damp in the morning, there was never enough time to dry them thoroughly.

The stove was also a magnet for cockroaches crawling up the chimney and other bugs, which absolutely covered it. 'It is amazing what you learn to live with, what you accept as normal when you get up in the morning in this strange place.' Nothing was done to get rid of these vermin and a typhus epidemic broke out with many deaths in the camp. The Kommandant ignored pleas to help with this situation and the lack of hygiene due to overcrowding, lack of soap and very primitive toilets (outhouses or slop buckets) was far worse in the summer months. Contaminated water later caused a typhoid epidemic and many died without any strength to fight.

After cleaning the bedding Kazia, Jasia and Janusz would walk to one of the different villages they had found on their wanderings and exchange some of the belongings Kazia had packed, many small items to barter for food, sugar or potatoes. The winter was severe and had brought incredible hardship and people would collect as many stores as they could, any food that came into the camp was very quickly snapped up.

We Poles, said Słowacki (a Polish Poet 1831) "must learn to breath underwater," and this stubborn mentality helped them through every wretchedness the Russians threw at them.

Those under age which included Jasia, Janusz and Marysia, had to attend school to be indoctrinated into the Soviet ways which didn't quite penetrate their stubborn Polish minds and when they could they would escape the classroom and walk along the railway tracks to look for any of the settlements and people who might have some food. They were aware that there might be wolves or bears in the forest but luckily never saw any, their hunger overcame any fears they might have had.

The courage of the women in particular stood out, those faced without husbands, fathers or brothers had the impossible task of feeding and protecting their children and the physical skills needed to carry out the work, they somehow managed to survive and then were able to take on the arduous journeys ahead of them. Like my family, their faith and strength got them through each day. Mothers with babies found it hard, they would lose milk due to malnutrition and had to improvise with watered down honey and flour but it wasn't enough to save their children.

Everyone scratched, day and night, the lice were everywhere and many suffered from malaria, shivering so hard. Alicja remembers one of Kazia's new friends, Genia, with unbelievably swollen legs who was shaking with a very high temperature, whatever she ate she couldn't keep down and she became terribly thin. She began to lose her strength and her family cried as there was no medical help and within a few days she died. Those who died had to be buried twice as the ground was too hard in the winter to dig through so they were preserved in deep snow until the spring which must have been doubly heart breaking.

Relations with the guards were varied. The highest authority was the Kommandant and at times he was hard and at other times forgiving. Some guards pushed them mercilessly to work, but there were those amongst them who were considerate. Some of them suggested ways of preserving their strength, discreetly and the family were quietly grateful for their kindness although it was noticed that these few guards did not stay long at the camp!

One of them had initially frightened Alicja, he had looked very scary and was quite brusque but when she got to know him better he turned out to be a good natured guard who didn't put many into lock up or haul them off to the Kommandant on the flimsiest of excuses. He was very kind compared to the many who weren't.

Guards would come to their hut in the night and question Adam, asking him what political news he was receiving in their letters from Poland, despite them being heavily censored. They would threaten him saying that 'political activity' could be punished and he would be sent to another gulag many km away. Adam explained that he was not receiving anything political, he wasn't interested in politics. The troopers did not have any hard proof and stopped questioning him.

They would then call out Kazia and shouted at her to frighten her, asking her the same questions to which she answered in the same way as Adam had. They told her she was lying, would never see her children again if she didn't tell the truth. Kazia then became angry and shouted back at them that she was working hard, wasn't lying and they eventually backed off. The guards took sadistic pleasure in taunting their prisoners for any minor reason. Adam and Kazia were so very lucky as they could have been arrested. They stood up to the NKVD and how proud am I of my Babcia and Dziadek, and my Polish heritage.

In Siberia winter came early in September, and spring came late, in May. Work in the forests was in teams and Adam and Alicja became a very close team. Everybody above 15, or those considered big enough and strong enough – this included Włodek, had to work in order to eat. Here in Russia this was the rule – if you didn't work you didn't eat. The under-16s, including Jasia, Janusz and Marysia, went to the camp school to learn Russian.

Those who couldn't bear the incredibly harsh conditions, mostly the elderly, numb with cold, arms and legs swollen and hungry and ridden with lice so close to death, very soon gave way despite trying their hardest not to. So many of them, forced to trek daily across frozen wastes, so weakened they collapsed were left in the forest, stripped of their clothes and left to die, becoming food for the wolvers. Loss of life meant nothing to the Soviets, to them the imprisoned were just work horses and there would always be others to replace them.

Day after day at six o'clock in the morning Alicja and Adam and all the other workers had to get up in the dark, roused by the guards and hurried along to get ready. Marched off in columns out of the camp through the plains then into the forests, guards front and behind them constantly being checked. They would have to wade into deep snow up to their knees and in some places their waists, to fell the trees. The men would cut the trees down while the younger people removed the branches and stacked them into big piles ready for the horses to drag them away on wagons to the processing depot.

There was a sawmill with electrical saws and generators and the men worked in groups cutting railway sleepers or props and pit stops. The younger men and women cut wood into slices with electric saws and fed them into a machine which cut them into cubes, which were then used for fuel in the substation. There were many accidents as it was difficult to use those tools with frozen hands and there wasn't medical or nursing help at the camp and people died from infections to their wounds.

Alicja and Adam took the wood they cut to the drying house and as it dried the wood sent out a gas that was highly noxious, it would sometimes send heads spinning and made Alicja dizzy but she couldn't refuse to work and continued through the dizziness and nausea, no work meant no bread ration and no pay which hurt all the family. If she had refused she would have been sent to the 'coop' or detention cell, a small freezing cold shed in the woods.

Circumstances suddenly changed, they were not paid for many weeks and the rations barely sustained them. Finally, the Russians began to pay them for their toil but the wages were very low, just a few roubles, but it helped them to buy some goods from the nearby villagers. They were forbidden to have any contact with the local people, but hunger forced them to break the rules. The Kommandant mostly overlooked this in the beginning, as he realised he needed them to be strong enough to work and meet the deadlines imposed on him from headquarters.

Their work was back breaking, some worked in the collective farms or mines, while others slaved in the quarries. Most worked in the forests felling trees regardless of their fitness and health, braving the most inhumane climatic conditions so that the Russians could continue the railway track that had ended at Sharya, where they had left the train. The Soviets intended to build deeper into Siberia to give easier access to other labour camps and the 'special camps' and gulags. How my Mother at only 16 survived the physical toil I will never know.

Some of the more able and experienced men were given the responsibility of building new barracks. They worked very hard for slightly better wages and larger rations of bread. These projects were usually completed in good time as accommodation was needed for newer intakes of prisoners as there were many more 'undesirables' coming into the camp.

Although the prisoners did not present any danger the NKVD spied on them constantly. They had their informers and it was necessary for everyone to be constantly on their guard. They had to watch what they said because 'the walls had ears'. If someone was suspected of 'political activity,' a 'denunciation' would be made against them by a person who would then be rewarded by the authorities for their help, by assigning them lighter work, or extra rations of bread. To a hungry person, as they all were, but who was of a weaker character, the acquisition of an extra piece of bread was possibly life saving!

Arrival at camp – adapted from a drawing by an unknown artist

All transgressions were punished, sometimes a fine, sometimes a few days in custody. The powers of the Kommandant were absolute, with the settlers having no possibility of questioning his decisions, which made some of his future actions regarding my Dziadek very interesting. One could be arrested for devotions to the Blessed Virgin but the Osadniks did not capitulate.

Despite the dreadful conditions imposed on the Polish deportees, they maintained as best as they could their cultural and religious activities and made every effort to keep their identity. There are drawings and illustrations of camp life, illustrated in (Stalin's Ethnic Cleansing) and some wrote on scraps of paper keeping diaries, one was a friend of the family 15 year old Danuta Mączka from the same Osada as my family who kept a most incredible diary. The families conducted prayer meetings despite pressure from the guards telling them there is no God, only Stalin!

The days were long and if they were lucky Kazia, Jasia and Janusz were able to give the workers hot water with maybe raspberry twigs that they'd foraged for during the day on top of the daily sour, black bread which didn't have much taste, but took the edge off the hunger pangs. Kazia also sometimes managed to find mushrooms. There was very little else to eat. They had received some seeds from Babcia Sofia but these were not yet ready for planting. Everyone was desperately hungry and sad, they were aware of having to be careful and the stress was beginning to tell. Of all the memories that my Mother remembered, the one in sharpest detail concerned food, it would come back to her clearly and unbidden. There was never enough of it and the thought of it always nagged them. 'Some would have given a handful of diamonds for an extra piece of bread in those circumstances, because only food had value, it was beyond price'.

Sometime that month a northern snow storm hit the camp, it blew in without warning and it covered the workers with a white fog. For 3 days the cold was so intense and the winds so icy cold that not even the well fed and clothed guards ventured out and the workers resorted to using ropes to find their way around the camp. They had even less food over those 3 days and on the 4th day work was resumed regardless of the weather. On this day Adam saw a horse frozen, the poor over worked thing abandoned by the guard. He and a few men tried to cut some meat off with their axes but they just bounced off they were too blunt, but they did get some meat off and took it back to the cabin cooked and shared it. It didn't last very long and Adam went back the next day after sharpening his axe only to find that there was very little left of the horse. Others had got there before him.

One day Janusz had seen the Uzbek guards brutally beating a man to death, he had allegedly killed their dog cooked it and shared it with his family. Janusz saw his hands up in prayer, begging for his life, screaming that his family was starving and Janusz ran, afraid at such brutality, it didn't happen very often but left a mark on those who witnessed it.

There was a small village about three kilometres from the camp and the villagers, mostly Russian 'dissidents', were very kind to them. They held markets on occasion and the prisoners were able to buy or barter for much-needed food. At the last moment before boarding the sledge to leave Równe, Kazia had grabbed as many scarves, and other small items and trinkets as she could and filled her pockets and sacks knowing they would probably exchange well. People from the collective farms around the camp would sometimes come to the fence to exchange food for clothing with the prisoners which would later be a life safer for them.

The Russian villagers on the collective farms and villages, had been exiled from their homeland after the Russian revolution of 1917 and like them had been given little notice. They had been arrested and physically removed from their homes, loaded onto transport and brought to this wasteland to work on collective farms. They had not been able to take many possessions with them and had arrived with little but the clothes they stood up in. They were then expected to build their own homes and work for their Russian masters, sending a great proportion of their farm goods to the major towns, probably via Kotlas, surviving on very little themselves. 'Yet they were able to help us, they were so kind especially the older ones who could empathise with what we newer prisoners were experiencing, we were so very grateful to them.'

There were many good Russians, but the Soviets soon filtered these out and sent them either to the Gulags or collective farms across the vast wilderness of Russia. These older Russians couldn't even be open with their own children, who would without hesitation report them to the authorities for any outspoken comments. Their children had been indoctrinated from early school age into the ideals of communism so they knew no other way. A similar country today would be North Korea, the inhabitants under constant surveillance and control.

One old Russian, Constantin, had become friendly with Adam and they chatted to each other whenever it was safe. They were both very much against communism and spoke out about it but as the NKVD jumped on the slightest anti communist remark as being almost treasonable, they were extremely careful. The village markets soon stopped, because prisoners and villagers were getting too friendly, which was not tolerated by the Russians. Everyone had to be careful of what they said and did from then on. Maybe they had been careless and had been overheard saying something completely innocuous but considered anti-communist and were now punished for it!

There were two occasions in the labour camps when the family experienced absolute terror. The first took place in Duraszewo camp, where they lived with three families, two Polish families and a family from the Ukraine, who weren't very fond of the Poles and more often than not worked with the Russians to gain special favours. The atmosphere at times was tense and Adam wondered if they had been put amongst the family to spy on them. Extreme hunger affects the mind in a very negative way as do old adversities.

During their incarceration they tried very hard to keep their spirits up. Sometimes singing and dancing, and they were singing one evening when all of a sudden the door opened and the Kommandant stood there with his rifle and dog and told Adam to go with him. It wasn't the usual evening head count, when guards would come with their dogs. The family froze, knowing that so many men had been taken by the Kommandant for interrogation and were never seen again. They didn't know why he was there and were terrified thinking about what might happen. All of a sudden the Kommandant seemed to change his mind, he spun on his heel and walked out without saying a word leaving them confused.

The Kommadant never mentioned the incident again and they later learned that the father of the Ukrainian family had sent his son to the Kommandant to tell him that Adam had been making fun of the Russians, which was completely untrue and malicious. From then on they were even more alert and the Ukrainian father was even more hostile, as his spiteful effort to gain any indulgence from the guards had failed.

The family were still receiving packages from home, which were thoroughly examined at the regional office before they were able to collect them. Sofia, Kazia's mother, had been able to send parcels and they had exchanged letters with her for a little while, heavily censored of course, it was such a comfort to keep in touch, and to know that she had so far survived, as she was now quite elderly.

The regional Post Office was a long walk from the camp and they had to collect the mail and packages, walking through muddy country roads and fields and in winter very deep snow, which made it very difficult. It took most of a day there and back and Jasia and Janusz used to go together, with Marysia tagging along sometimes. They often didn't get back to camp until after dark, absolutely exhausted but so happy with their post, although sometimes they were empty-handed and despondent.

These letters and packages seemed to cause the authorities great discomfort and they began to show a lot of interest in them. The prisoners shared all their news from home with each other and this raised their spirits hugely. Some of the letters contained news that the NKVD regarded as 'political' and it was easy for them to eavesdrop in the barracks, by just standing in the corridor by a door listening in to what the prisoners were sharing.

Senior NKVD officers would arrive at the camp unexpectantly to investigate, questioning people about their political views, 'where did all the news come from, who was writing these letters' and then they would threaten them saying that this 'political activity' would be punished in a gulag. Had they had irrefutable proof of any 'political activity' they would have most certainly arrested and imprisoned anyone and the unfortunates would never be heard of again! All gatherings were then banned and very suddenly, there were no letters, no contact from home and no parcels of desperately needed food and seeds. They had been confiscated by the NKVD, which wasn't a surprise.

One evening after work Adam in desperation made the decision to take Kazia's wedding ring, (his had already been bartered) and despite his emaciated state, go to one of the villages to look for food and he set off for one of the nearest which was about 2km away. His family was slowly starving, it was a struggle to maintain the work commitments, and "if you don't work you don't eat" was the Russian principle. The situation could not go on much longer, the family had to survive, they needed food desperately.

Kazia, Jasia and Janusz had been able to collect sorrel and chives from the meadows on warmer days and had also spent time fishing not far from the collective farms and as well as the mushrooms and cabbages it had kept them going although the situation was now desperate. They had seen bodies being collected by the Uzbeks and loaded onto arbas, skeletal corpses, Poles from various collective farms and prison camps, dumped into ditches that would become their graves. It was becoming an everyday occurrence.

It had not snowed heavily and was still light as he left the barracks and he looked around for any guards, the searchlights hadn't yet come on and it seemed clear, he was very nervous but he set off in determined mood running towards the path to the village and after a short time safely reached it. He knocked on the door of his friend Constantin who helped him to exchange the ring for potatoes and flour from some of the other villagers. He was exhausted as the trek to the village had taken a lot out of him, the snow was deep and he was feeling the effects of malnutrition, but he had to get back. He had a hot cup of tea with Constantin and his family before he set out on the return journey.

He had only been going for a short time when it started to snow quite heavily, the storm had come down very quickly and he lost his way completely. The cold hit him hard and his face was numb, it was way below zero, everything looked the same and all he could see was a wall of white swirling snow, the big white flakes falling on him, he was very cold and he noticed the light was slipping away as he struggled through the drifts. The sky had become darker and he hoped he wouldn't have to survive the night in this wilderness.

He was desperate, this time the Kommandant wouldn't be so lenient he thought. He couldn't go any further, he couldn't see a thing, no path, nothing but a blanket of snow. He stopped, gathered his thoughts and collected some kindling from under the trees and bushes which was still fairly dry and he was able to light a fire, with his battered old army lighter, although it took some time as his fingers were almost frozen.

He then squatted down by the flames in total despair, clinging onto his sack of food, wondering if he'd see his family again or if the wolves would get him. Which way should he go? He had no idea. He was so tired, so cold and so hungry, and he was becoming disorientated. He thought it was hopeless. How would he get back? What should he do? Oh how he needed Kazia, his rock. He cried until he shook, he just wanted to sleep and felt at a complete loss, how had he got into this nightmare? And how could he get out of it? He was distraught, it had all come to a head and he was in a complete panic, all his army training was to no avail.

With the snow falling heavily around him still not seeing any landmarks, let alone a path, he prayed as he'd never prayed for a miracle, a way back to his family. The Poles were deeply attached to their religion and praying was a means of helping them through many problems. Praying had given Adam what he needed, an incentive. All of a sudden, with what little strength he had left, he got up, his mind absolutely set, he had decided on a direction. He put aside his hunger and weariness and started walking, his life and that of his family depended on action, one foot in front of the other, that's all he had to do. His body was beyond exhaustion. He was soaked by the snow which had got through to his bones and he was achingly cold. His hands could barely keep hold of his precious goods, but he was determined about one thing – to get back to the camp. His family was waiting for him. It was a major effort and every muscle cried out for rest.

The snow flakes seemed to be easing, a light wind was starting to gather pace and the night sky was clearing, he could see the moon and the stars so very bright and around him a frozen, white emptiness, he was even able to notice how beautiful it was. His nose and cheeks were frozen numb and his eyes were watering as he pulled his jacket up around him trying to shield his face, his lips were cracked and so cold. He recognised a clearing ahead of him and realised he wasn't very far from the camp. He stepped on huge sheets of ice cracking and crunching under his weight and the wind suddenly stronger pulled him along, sliding along those sheets of ice. It helped him a little as he was exhausted with very little energy left and he couldn't feel his body.

After what seemed like hours, he arrived at the outskirts of the camp and at the gates stood two figures, one tall, the Kommandant with his rifle and the other his dog, by a large fire. The fire was like a magnet, drawing Adam ever closer to someone he really didn't want to face. Should he go round the other side of the camp? Try getting in another way? But it was surrounded by wide open spaces and the forests were so far away. So many escapees had never made it, they just disappeared. And he was so tired. He felt resigned to his fate. His legs shook and were about to give way as he made his way to the gates, but his fear suddenly left him he was ready to face the Kommandant.

"Góral, where have you been?" said the Kommandant, and Adam answered, so close to anger, the adrenalin taking over, "I had to go for food for my family, they are starving, I had no choice, you left me no choice," he screamed. The Kommandant was taken aback, not expecting this from one of his prisoners. "We'll talk about it in the morning" was his response and he went through the gates back into the camp, leaving Adam just standing there, exhausted almost to the point of collapse, confused and not sure what to do next.

Kazia had been watching out for his return and ran up to him, grabbed him and pulled him back through the gates and into their barracks. The children were still awake, curled up on the bunk together waiting for his return. They couldn't sleep, how could anyone sleep? They'd kept as quiet as they could so as not to alarm the guards, and after keeping their feelings in for so long they just burst into tears. They were so relieved to see him. Every day was torture for them, wondering whether they would survive it, avoid the guards and their aggressive behaviour, have any food to eat? It was beginning to tell on all of them.

Adam still held the potatoes and flour, he had never let go of the sack and Kazia had to prize it away from his frozen hands before throwing a blanket over him and dragging him to the burning range, his ears burned and his nose and chin felt like pins and needles, he would have to thaw out slowly and it would be painful. The dread the family had felt that night was never forgotten. There were many occasions over the first few years of her new life in England when Alicja would very suddenly be reminded of these times. 'They just crept into my thoughts without warning and would leave me in such a state of panic for some time. I still think of them occasionally, but without some of the awful panic,' over the many years since then those thoughts haven't left her, she remembers Siberia when her father went into the forest to get them food and how frightened they had been although these thoughts are fading over time and dementia.

Adam had risked his life to keep the family alive, he had seen their physical state, they had lost a great deal of weight, and were wasting away in front of him. Their muscles ached so much it was painful to move. Alicja and Jasia couldn't lift the heavy saws to cut the trees and were anaemic, lethargic, dehydrated. Their skin was becoming cracked, they were so fatigued, how could they work? It was far worse for Kazia, this was having a dire effect on her heart and she was struggling to get through each day despite her determination.

In spite of everything, the Kommandant seemed to have a conscience. He had been kind to the family on two occasions. After the signing of the Amnesty in 1941, he simply vanished into the night with his wife and dog. Where could they have gone to find safety? Or had he been sent to fight the Germans?

I remember my grand parents telling that story so many times when we all got together. Each time something would spark the memory and they would all chip in with their thoughts and each time they found a reason to laugh, to look back with humour and then it would go quiet but not for long and chatter would continue around what prompted the memory.

Ciocia Ziuta also risked her life, although in a different way. She was quite outspoken, the words she aimed at the Russians and Ukranian guards could have had enormous impact but she seemed to escape any significant punishment. She was a very small woman with a massive heart and personality. How could an NKVD guard possibly take delight in responding harshly to the insults of such a little person, a 'non-person' at that? What bravado could he have gained in the barracks in front of his fellow guards? The sheer strength of human spirit and unbreakable bond between the family got them through unimaginable privations.

The prisoners were finding the winter months extremely severe, temperatures falling to -40, and the snow and frost were intense. All prisoners had been given padded trousers and anoraks filled with wool and wore shoes made from wicker, and around their legs they wrapped strips of woollen pieces from their shoes to their knees. They were very light and warm if wrapped around properly and with some added clothing they had brought with them Alicja and Adam were able to cope a little better out in the forests.

Life was very sad and very hard, and could be demoralising, but the youngsters amused themselves after work even on an empty stomach by singing hopeful songs and praying when they could. Praying in groups wasn't allowed but day after day they hoped and prayed that some time soon, somebody would rescue them from this inhuman land. Children and the elderly were dying in their hundreds and there had been many burials in the hard icy snow. Some of the deportees could afford to have relatives buried in the cemetery at Monastyrek in Kotlas but many of the dead were buried in the ice ground of Siberia.

The year progressed and after the snow melted they had to dig deep into the ground cutting trees whilst others worked to lay the railway tracks. Standing in deep snow digging all day and coming back to the barracks cold and wet and tired for something to eat, and of course there was very little and they usually went to bed hungry. They had by then finished the food Adam had risked his life for sharing it out as carefully as they could. They lay close together for warmth and comfort, holding tight. At times there was no bread because no food was delivered. When they received a parcel from Babcia Sofia it cheered them up and they smiled.

People were dying every day of dysentery and typhus, malaria and starvation, the privations of life in the camp were hitting hard, the family were living on roots and the herbs that grew on the bank of the river, the very barest necessities of life! There was grain in the fields around the forests and wild fruits which some of the smaller children gathered when the guards were distracted, they filled their pockets and returned the next day to do the same. The guards knew what was going on but turned a blind eye, some of them seemed sympathetic to them.

There had been many deaths in the workforce, younger girls and boys as young as 13 were now being sent deep into the forests and forced to do very heavy labour. Hardly able to carry the heavy axes they were marched into the forest in the same columns, with the axes on their shoulders and worked tirelessly cutting down trees and trimming the branches. Alicja was lucky as she worked with Adam who insisted on being with her despite threats from the guards. Other fathers started to follow his lead to work alongside their children to protect them. Once the Kommandant saw the benefits of families working together he raised little objection and now Jasia was also working in the forests.

The Kommandant's orders had been to keep his prisoners going for as long as possible as their labour was important to the cause! One of the awful aspects of this ordeal was the contempt and hostility of the guards towards them and if people didn't die from the cruelty, the frost, the deep snow and extreme temperatures would see them off. In this climate their lips would chap and ears would freeze and it was very difficult at times to breath.

The day was from dawn to dusk and at the end on leaving the forest they would be gripped by the fear of the wolves out on the open plains watching their every move. They would wait and watch them, it wasn't a very long walk but a fearful one before they eventually reached the safety of the camp seeing the clear strip with the guards and barbed wire of the camp they would relax knowing they would soon be with Kazia.

They still had some clothing and trinkets to exchange for food, and would have gone to the Kolkhozy to get some potatoes or flour so that Kazia could cook something for the family but the Kommandant had put a stop to the visits. They had very little to eat now during the day, usually just a piece of bread and a drink of tea made of raspberry twigs. They had no coffee, so they experimented with a brew made of acorns and called it coffee which wasn't very tasty. In June some were lucky enough to get seeds from relatives and grew potatoes, cucumbers, beans and onions and it was warm enough to bathe in the river and get clean. In the summer months they picked mushrooms and cranberries in the forests and they could sustain themselves as they were plentiful, Kazia and Janusz spent most of their time searching for anything to eat.

Did anybody know they were there? Perhaps no one knew they had been forcibly deported? Exiled from their homeland. They felt they had been deserted, forgotten. What was happening back home in Poland, how was Sofia coping, life was very difficult to bear and the guards were very cruel which put a great strain on them all.

The guards would come around each night for roll call with their dogs, at a different time each night to try and catch them out and to keep everyone constantly on alert. Some were very rough with them and abused everyone verbally. If a girl happened to be pretty she would be singled out for attention, but mothers and fathers kept a keen eye on their daughters.

The youngsters had accepted the situation more easily than their parents who were very depressed, only waiting for the day when they would be free again. To think of escape was impossible as there were always guards and dogs around. The camp was surrounded by wide open spaces and then the forests which very few escapees made it to or through. Accidents, starvation and sickness took its toll on the prisoners, but the most distressing cause of death was psychological. Anyone who lost faith in their survival did not last more than a few days. It was quite unnerving.

Kazia and Adam, although quite subdued, never, ever gave up hope, somehow they knew they would be free, that they would survive. They never doubted it, their resolve served them well.

After a few months in the camp at Poldniewica, the family were moved to a smaller camp, Duraszewo, in August 1940 which was about four kilometres away. They were sent with four other families in carts with their few belongings and hoped they would be housed in better conditions. The routine was the same, they had to work as hard as they had done before, on even poorer rations and conditions. At the new camp they met the Krawiec Family, Bruno and Maryan, their sisters Krysia and Irena and their parents which was to lead to a very close friendship over many years.

Bruno and his brother Maryan fought at Monte Cassino once they had escaped the camp. He later met and married Halina who had lost both her parents in the Russian labour camps where they had succumbed to the privations. As orphans, she and her two sisters were eventually sent to India after reaching safety in Persia from the USSR. Of all the groups of Polish orphans escaping the USSR into Persia in 1942 the largest group was sent to Africa. The Commonwealth countries were very hospitable to the many refugees fleeing the labour camps and accepted many of them willingly unlike the US and UK.

Wigilia 1941 had been and gone and with it the memories of their homeland that had been brought to their minds. Christmas decorations and barszcz, uszka, śledzie, fruit and cakes and everything else that came with the memory of Wigilia. The snow kept falling and it was dark and Kazia prayed that they would return from the forest safely for the potatoes and soup and dark Russian bread that she had prepared. They were together which was the most important thing and another day had gone by safely as she saw them appear at the edge of the forest.

Winter was well established when they were told they were going to be moved again, they were being sent to a smaller camp, Deralwelka with 6 other families. Moved by sledge, on another very bitterly cold day, it was February 1941, very frosty and the snow very deep and food was becoming even scarcer. It was a year since they had been taken from their homeland, hundreds had died through starvation, exposure to the climate and injury. Kazia had some spare clothing and trinkets left and exchanged some of them for potatoes which was all they could get from the market. The Kommandant had relented and allowed several families to visit the villages again for food, but by then they also had very little to barter for, the villagers were stockpiling for another hard winter and couldn't let them have very much. The new camp was a slightly better one and they had a family area to themselves, it was surrounded by forests and the narrow gauge railway came by the camp which made them feel less isolated.

The guards took them through the usual routines of how much they were expected to do each day, when they were to get up, when to assemble outside the barracks and their days followed a routine, the physically demanding work continued with great difficulty, felling trees and building the railway line further into Siberia, their health was suffering and was becoming a matter for great concern to Adam and Kazia. Signs of acute hunger were beginning to show in the children with gnawing pains in their stomachs, hunger pangs and Alicja was slowing down with very little energy and low moods, it was a constant battle not to give up.

One of Jasia's jobs was to collect water from the well at the outskirts of the barracks. It was a long walk and it was her dreaded chore as the snow was always very deep and it made it difficult to walk. A thick layer of ice covered the opening of the well and she found it difficult to get the bucket into the opening. She always carried an axe in this weather and she carefully made the hole bigger and got the bucket down. The walk back was exhausting with the heavy bucket and Adam usually met her half way if he wasn't in the forest. She was also beginning to show signs of exhaustion, finding each day getting more difficult to get through.

The snow was heavy and was to cause many problems. The temperature was low and the wind freezing, many did not have proper boots or clothing, what they had been issued with had worn out. There were several accidents with people slipping on scaffolding carrying heavy boards, people went down with colds and pneumonia and every morning they put on the same wet and cold clothes they hadn't been able to dry on the range. Everyone went back to the hut each day frozen, soaked, sometimes trees would fall injuring people and they would be brought into the barracks in great pain. The equipment was primitive and caused accidents and they didn't have any medical help and so few of the injured would recover.

There was one young girl of about 14, Ewa, who was exhausted beyond endurance working for her siblings having lost her parents. She left the hut at dawn each day and returned in the evening and then had to prepare a meal, clean the hut and wash and repair clothes with some help from her younger brother, her younger sisters were too young to help. She was exhausted and had to face the most strenuous demands to cope with the extreme cold and hard labour with a malnourished body. She had the responsibility for her younger siblings and they did what they could to help her. If she had asked the Soviets for help they would separate them and she would never see them again. It isn't known if she and her young siblings survived the camp or were shipped out to a Russian Orphanage.

Spring was late in 1941 and they were recovering from another extreme winter. They were still receiving letters from home which were very heavily censored so they didn't really know what was happening outside the camp. There was no news of the War but the Soviets were still so full of their alliance with the Germans. People in desperation tried to escape and two young men did but were recaptured, badly beaten and imprisoned. No one tried to escape after that.

The Poles took great comfort from praying, it gave them strength to get through each day although the Soviets were determined to stamp this out, telling them there is no God, there is only Father Stalin! It was relentless. If a parent tried to stop his child from attending the school he would be punished with prison or heavier work. Despite the threats they prayed when they could, it was their faith that got them through this terrible ordeal. Adam and most of the prisoners hated communism, seeing it as oppressive and would not bow to Stalin's indoctrination methods. Communism had genuinely transformed society but in a very destructive way. The regimes' policies caused famines that killed millions and never before had any government terrorised so many of its own people.

One day whilst Alicja was cutting branches off a tree and putting them onto a bonfire she noticed a young man sitting on a fallen tree with the foreman, watching her. When she finished work and she and Adam were walking to the barracks, the young man walked along with them. They talked, and when Alicja got to the barracks he told her he was a member of a young communist party (Comsomolts) and that he would come and see her again. Adam very watchful, called her into the barrack then, as it could have been a very difficult situation.

They didn't want to antagonise the guards but also didn't want to encourage any friendships either, especially those of a romantic nature, as this might have led to an even worse situation. The young man did come again several times to their barracks and each time he brought a balalaika and played for her, and 'I didn't even remember his name', said Alicja. Adam wasn't happy that he was seeing her and did his best to quietly discourage him. The last time he came he very solemnly told Alicja he loved her but that he had to go to war. She never saw him again. This young Russian was the very first man who expressed romantic love for her and she didn't remember his name! Soon after that the guards began leaving them to their own devices. There was hardly any bread and anything else was rotten, completely inedible.

By late Spring 1941 they had been forbidden to visit the kolkhoz to barter for food but rules had been broken because they were starving and people would break out of the camp at night despite the search lights and try to get back in without being noticed although the guards watched them constantly. Those who were caught were imprisoned in the cellar in the admin block where there wasn't any heating and they froze.

There were times when the villagers from the Kolkhoz, knowing the dire conditions in the camp would hide in the bushes on the verge of the forest bringing them some food to barter. The Camp stores sometimes had food and clothes but of very poor quality and line ups would start very early and they often went away empty handed. There might be salt, cookies and shoes and people would crowd in but there was never enough for them all. Those kolkhozniks hiding in the bushes would catch their attention and Adam would take a risk and go up to them to see if they had anything. They were very kind people and shared their spare rations whenever they could.

Everything, especially food was now being sent to the front for the Russian soldiers who were now fighting the Germans on Russian soil. The guards seemed restless and the prisoners sensed something was happening. One day, June 22nd 1941, they found that the guards with their dogs had left the camps. They had just disappeared overnight, then news filtered through from some of the villagers who had been watching from the outskirts of the camp that Germany had declared war on Russia. Maybe Russia would become an ally of America and Britain? Everyone began to hope that things might change.

The absurdity of the situation was that the prisoners were saved by Poland's first aggressor, Hitler, with his attack on Russia. Churchill had persuaded Stalin to release all Polish prisoners on Soviet soil to allow them to fight against the Germans, becoming allies with the USSR who now had German troops deep in her territories and Stalin desperately needed allies and re-established diplomatic relations with the Polish Government in exile in London. He agreed to grant an 'amnesty' to all Polish citizens who had been forcibly deprived of their freedom and exiled to Russia in 1940-41 and when this news came through to the camp, everyone cheered, they were elated.

Amnesty, a period during which a law is suspended to allow offenders to admit their crime without fear of prosecution, a general pardon especially for offences against a government. The Poles had been arrested without having committed any crimes!

The amnesty referred only to a one time immunity in the USSR, for those deprived of their freedom following the Soviet invasion of Poland in September 1939. The signing of the amnesty by the Presidium of the

Supreme Soviet on 12th August 1941 resulted in the temporary stop of persecutions of Polish citizens under Soviet occupation. General Sikorsky, on behalf of the Polish Government, signed the first diplomatic agreement on 30th July 1941.

The agreement also included a special statement concerning Polish prisoners of war and Polish civilian deportees in the USSR. Stalin promised to release Polish prisoners of war and the huge number of the deportees who had been exiled to Siberia. The Soviet Ambassador to Britain, Maisky, then announced that the Soviet-German treaty of August 1939 relating to the territorial division of Poland along the Ribbentrop-Molotov Line 'was no longer valid.'

Picture of one of the many burials endured by parents of a child who could not survive the utter deprivation of life in Siberia

Stalin had put the Poles in those camps to work them to death, and if it hadn't been for the 'amnesty', he would have succeeded. Poland's history shows Russia's greed for her land, to expand the Russian Empire even further and seek revenge for past uprisings. It was also Stalin's intention to spread Communism throughout Europe via Poland. The Russians' hostile feelings towards the Poles were returned in full.

Although emaciated by disease and exhausted from the harshness of the life they had led, the survivors were ready to make their way in their hundreds of thousands from the most remote corners of Russia, out of the camps and towards freedom and their Army. They were to leave behind so many of their number, buried in crude graves and those too exhausted, aged and worn down by starvation to be able to make a journey of any distance, even if it meant freedom.

Very many of these poor people were skeletal, wearing only rags, their feet covered in paper. They were so very thin, as the family and everyone else was but these people looked old and wrinkled. They were bloated and their skin was yellow, their eyes sunken. They were so weak some of them couldn't stand up, mentally they hadn't given up but physically they were incapable. There were not enough of the prisoners who were strong enough to help them and they had to be left behind. It was heart-breaking for Alicja and the family to watch and it would be another image of very many that stayed with her, she would never forget those they left behind.

Many of the prisoners had not been told about the formation of the Polish military units on Soviet soil, the news was kept from them, they were not told about their rights and obligations to join those Polish units until a young Polish soldier had walked into the camp shortly after the' amnesty' and surprised them all. He confirmed to them what had happened and said it would be best for them to head towards Persia, a journey of over 3,500 km where the Polish army was forming under British command.

The NKVD did everything in their power to limit the number of Poles leaving as they needed their slave labour. After the German attack on Russia the conditions in the camp worsened drastically, quotas were increased and rations cut which led to a sharp rise in mortality which made the prisoners more determined to take action during the short period they had to leave. They had to make haste as the window would not be open for long and after listening to the young soldier they were now even more determined to join the Polish army. They did not trust Stalin with very good reason, they had to leave as soon as they could.

General Anders, their Polish military leader, had been freed from the Lubyanka prison in Moscow and news then reached the camp confirming that the Polish army was reforming under his command in the Middle East, with some units being formed within the Soviet Union. Everyone was excited and wanted to join the Polish army. They knew what they had to do, but not how to do it. Leaving was not as simple as it might seem, 'amnesty' documents and transport had to be arranged, and there was much to do and think about. Only in flight from Russia could safety and freedom lie and they had to move fast, the journey to Kotlas would be their first aim.

Not many weeks after the amnesty had been declared, Uncle Walery had walked into the camp, he was unrecognisable, he was very badly bruised, very thin and gaunt, with long hair and dirty clothes and a beard down to his chest. Despite his malnourished condition he had found the strength to look for them. Walery had been coming back to collect his own family when he had been caught by the NKVD had been arrested accused of being a spy and transported to the Lubyanka prison. He had avoided the deportations but was then sent to a prison at Swierdlowsk then onto a camp in the salt mines of the Urals, many hundreds of km from their camp. He had been lucky as there was a lot of movement along the Soviet lands with many people leaving camps heading towards the Polish army.

There were transports and centres set up for the deportees to register at and he had managed to get onto some of those transports but had also walked many km to reach them. He also met with other Poles who were wandering the plains looking for their relatives.

Ziuta had earlier found out where he was and written to him to make sure he knew where they were and contact had been maintained between them. Despite such isolation, no papers, no radio, contact was always somehow made. Word was always able to get through, although it did take some time.

It was so very difficult for them at this time and they longed for freedom, anxious to leave but there was now a typhoid epidemic throughout the camp and the death toll was unbelievable leaving very many orphans to fend for themselves wiping out whole families. It lasted for 2 months and the population of the camp halved. They had lost so very many friends and had to learn to keep their emotions on hold, it was the only way to function. The camp authorities let them trade with the villagers again and they had food to build their strength for the arduous journey they were soon to face. They still had to work in the forests and were driven very hard and mentally found it extremely difficult.

They felt downtrodden and it brought many to despair but to lose courage now, to let the Soviets destroy their spirit would be disastrous. The days seemed endless, life was monotonous and they were very sad. They were physically and emotionally exhausted and always hungry but they prayed and kept their faith. So many more tragic deaths through accident, death through illness of friends was difficult to cope with. Climatic conditions and cruel treatment by the guards and near starvation was taking its toll by the day.

Alicja had another friend in the camp, Elzunia, who was 14 orphaned with a sister of 7 and a brother of 12, she was the head of the family and worked in the forests as a lumberjack with grown men. If she didn't work her family would starve as there would be no rations. The Soviets made sure she worked as hard as the men did and produce as much as them. They were heartless, 'the more of you that die the happier we will feel'. There were 10,000 orphans from the labour camps who arrived in Persia after the amnesty, they had somehow managed to travel from the USSR towards the Polish army in the most malnourished of conditions.

In August 1941 an NKVD officer had arrived at the camp to confirm to people that General Sikorski, Commander in Chief of the Polish army and Premier of the Polish Government in exile in London, had signed a pact with Stalin. The family and those around them were overjoyed. They were told they would receive documents quite soon stating that they were free to leave.

The first discharge papers were issued on 5th September 1941 for some of the surrounding camps and very soon groups departed to travel towards the Polish army, so very eager to fight. By October other groups were getting their discharge papers and travel documents. The family hadn't yet received theirs but waited with patience. It was getting much colder and the wait for papers was getting longer and it looked like they would be caught in the beginning of the harsh Siberian winter, a very difficult time to travel the distances ahead of them.

The Kommandant explained that there were very many people waiting at the station in Kotlas and not enough wagons for them all. He asked them to be patient but they were keen to get out of this prison. Without the travel documents though they couldn't leave as they wouldn't qualify for food stamps for soup and bread at the station canteens. Some of the older boys so very keen to fight ignored him and left.

In November 1941 Antoni Maj, the camps' representative and the Kommandant were notified that it was time to transport some of those who wanted to leave and horse drawn sledges were sent from the collective farms in the area. Over 700 Poles left the camp and were taken to the nearest railway line in the middle of a forest. There was no station and they had to wait for 3 days and nights in the open in deep snow for the train.

There was plenty of wood available and camp fires burned continually to keep them from freezing. When word reached them that the train was on the way they gathered as much wood to load onto the train as they could for the long and cold journey to Kotlas which was over 450km away. A few hundred Poles from camp Dorovatka near the railway line joined them making a very large grouping and they hoped there would be room for them all.

The train arrived and they loaded on and when it left there were many tears and high emotion, people were excited but afraid. The journey ahead was again unknown to them, it was over 3,500 km to their destination, meanwhile, Adam and Kazia and several others still waited for their official papers to leave.

It was now a war situation, the captive Poles left in the camp awaiting their papers had now become Soviet allies and it was a very strange feeling for them! They weren't getting paid and were still expected to work but at least they were getting 800 grams of bread and watery soup a day. Their main concern was their documentation and there were just a few of them left in the camp in this situation. Soviet soldiers needed shelter and the prisoners were moved to a very small hut. Adam was angry thinking that the Kommandant had other motives in keeping them there and was ready to 'escape'. Kazia was more measured and argued that they settle down and wait.

From the Russian wastelands there were almost 200,000 POWs who were released from the gulags to form the Polish army on Russia soil. Stalin would cut off their supplies however and the NKVD would sabotage them at many stages of their journey so General Anders in 1942 ensured they were evacuated to the Middle East making their way by whatever means they could to Persia, Iraq, Syria and Palestine under the main command of the British army, but under his command whilst ensuring them safe passage out of Russia. This exodus included many thousands of women and children and very many orphans.

At about this same time relations between Stalin and the Polish Government deteriorated over disagreements over the borderlands between the eastern provinces of Poland, Stalin insisting they should be absorbed into the Soviet Union after the war. Vyacheslav Molotov, Soviet Foreign Secretary, was in London to press the case for the territories of Poland and the Baltic states, formerly carved up by Hitler and Stalin.

Stalin was keen to have the Allies endorse this same deal. The British Government thought this utterly immoral and Churchill refused, only granting a general treaty of alliance and no promise of any territory but this was overturned at the Tehran meeting and later at Yalta with Roosevelt's support. Stalin would have his territories and the Iron Curtain would later close down on Eastern Europe.

Although Germany was beaten and the Allies had won the war, The Poles were the real losers. Over half a million fighting men and women and six million civilians died. About 50% of these were Polish Christian and 50% Polish Jews. Approximately 5,384,000 of the Polish war losses were the victims of prisons, death camps, executions, annihilation in ghettos, epidemics, starvation, excessive work and ill treatment. So many

Poles were sent to concentration and labour camps that virtually every family had someone close to it who had been tortured, interred or murdered there.

There were one million war orphans and over half a million invalids. The country lost 38% of its national assets (Britain lost 0.8%, France 1.5%) and the country was swallowed up by the Soviet Union, including the two great cultural centres of Lwów and Wilno. So many had died in the camps, of disease, bad water, mosquitoes, ill treatment and starvation. They had been worked to death and told they would never leave.

Families' buried their dead in the mud, under little mounds of earth, singing their patriotic songs, some of the coffins lay on the high water table unable to be buried. Yet so many did survive, mostly by simply believing they would, with their determination and resilience and their faith, it saw them through. They had indeed 'learned to breathe under water.'

Deportation had been a way of eliminating economically strong and intellectually enterprising elements of Polish society, a plot designed to weaken the Polish population of the newly Russian occupied eastern borderlands, it also strengthened the Russian speaking population.

Those frail and starving people had incredible, psychological strength and refused to abandon their beliefs. They had shown a heroism and resourcefulness in sustaining their physical lives under terrible conditions and also their humanity and friendships and their concern for others which helped them to survive. They worked together as best they could for each other and would need every resource to survive their journeys towards Tashkent.

Kazia, Adam, their children and her brother Walery and his family had no alternative than to wait for the documents that would guarantee them food and water at the various stations along the route to Tashkent. Without them they would starve as so very many did in their impatience to leave the camps to fight.

They were still one strong unit and had survived this far because of that, the strengths I had seen growing up in such a close and loving family almost devastated by war.

Two of the labour camps in the Gorkowski Oblast where the Polish military families from the Kresy were exiled to in 1940

'If you are afraid of wolves, keep out of the woods' – J.V. Stalin 1936

CHAPTER 5

Liberated – Kotlas to Bukhara

In Operation Barbarossa in June 1941, the Germans invaded the Soviet republics, Ukraine, Byelorussia and Russia. Stalin now needed allies and as a condition of joining forces with the USA and GB against the Germans, he grudgingly agreed to the repatriation of all Poles on Soviet soil. This was the price he paid for the Soviet-Polish pact of 31st July 1941 which re-established already tenuous diplomatic ties with the Polish Government and began the creation of a Polish Army to be assembled on Russian land.

Although Stalin ordered the release of Polish POWs from the gulags and labour camps, he allowed only a small proportion of them to leave, about 114,000, over 1ml were still detained and the NKVD were to obstruct the passage of those fleeing refugees towards reaching any checkpoints. Due also to the endless sabotages from the Soviets the Polish Army was quickly evacuated to Iraq, Persia, Syria and Palestine coming under British command with General Anders ensuring as many as possible left the USSR safely.

At the camp, local men and the guards were quickly mobilised into the Soviet army, food, coal and kerosene were diverted to meet the army's needs and all others left in the camp were faced with starvation but they at least had an escape to plan and freedom to look forward to. Their remote settlement had been shocked by the news on the camp's radio of these events, which always followed a familiar pattern, announcements with a build-up about Soviet bravery and large German casualties and then admission about a Russian retreat, Soviet casualties were concealed while German forces were in full retreat on all fronts!

Leaving the camp was not as easy as it seemed and preparations had to be made for a long and arduous journey of over 3,500km. The food situation in the camp was dire, the prisoners were at the end of their strength and most had exhausted any items they had to barter. The Kommandant tried to stall their departure but unable to block them from leaving he made no effort whatsoever to help them.

In general the Soviet authorities made it almost impossible for the Poles to leave the gulags and camps as had been provided for in the agreement with the Polish Government. The re-classification of the prisoners as 'free citizens' guaranteed nothing, as the Soviets did not recognise their right to join the Polish free army nor their right to leave the USSR. The prisoners had to achieve this on their own, and it was hardest on the single women with children who had lost their husbands.

A few days after the radio announcement a telegram arrived at the camp from the Polish Embassy in Kuybishev. It stated 'that all officers, the soldiers of the military settlers and those who were able to serve were to report to the nearest HQ of the Soviet Army, from where they would be directed to the new Polish Army. All Soviet authorities had this information and those who reported to them would receive the necessary travel documents and food stamps.' Many of the Soviet 'authorities' ignored this information and diverted the Polish transports leaving the USSR towards collective farms along their route out of the USSR.

Camps Poldniewica, Derawalka and Duraszewo, elected a representative who would go to the army posts set up by the Polish Embassy scattered throughout the region, who would have information about what the deportees would need to do with their newly gained freedom and how to move on to the next stage of their journey from the USSR. They would need to know how to progress now that they were able to travel freely regardless of the cynical tactics of the NKVD.

Antoni Maj was the representative of the remaining prisoners. He was from a village in eastern Poland, Jadwipol and one of four children of Ludwik and Stanisłowa Maj. His father had a small farm and was a forest ranger working for Prince Janusz Radziwil. Antoni had just returned for a short visit to his parents in the Kresy with his new wife and happened to be on the deportation list held by the NKVD. Many years later when he visited his Aunt in Poland she told him that shortly after the family had been driven away by the NKVD, their Ukrainian neighbours descended on their property like vultures!

Antoni would need to visit the Polish embassy in Kuybyshev, (named after the Bolshevik leader Valerian Kuybyshev who took the city in the October revolution of 1917) which was the administrative centre of Samara and about 800km away. He had to argue very strongly to get transport to the railway station in Sharya about 90km away, which the Kommandant very reluctantly agreed to. The journey was long and the deportees would have to get used to the vast distances to be travelled across the USSR in their journey towards Persia.

Kuybyshev is a major river port situated at the junction of the Volga and Samara rivers in close view of the Zhiguli mountains and in 1941 the prospect of Moscow falling to the invading Germans seemed so likely that it was chosen to be the new capital of Russia. The Communist party and governmental organisations, diplomats and leading cultural establishments were evacuated there. After the Russians defeated the Germans most of the area's 1.5 ml German inhabitants were dispersed into exile or into hard labour camps. In 1991 the city was given back its historical name of Samara.

Antoni returned a week later with the necessary paperwork which gave him authority to act, a certificate from the Embassy officially nominating him as a spokesman for the refugees. Alicja remembers when Antoni got back and told them they were free and able to go where they wanted, there was such joy and tears of relief!

The Polish Ambassador to the USSR, Stanisław Kot, and his small team had the enormous task of organising relief for the hundreds of thousands of Poles dispersed throughout the vastness of the Soviet Union. The first task was to find them, as they were spread over such a huge area. The aim of his delegates was to set up orphanages, feeding centres, hospitals and schools throughout Russia for all who had been released from the labour camps and to somehow get them all to where the Polish Army was being formed. Embassy delegates were sent all over Russia to arrange this massive programme of relief.

It took time to organise the necessary individual papers (the amnesty document which would serve as the family identification and passport and as a one-way travel permit to the destination of choice) and transport from Kotlas, and Antoni, with several able assistants, was working hard to organise everything, he had a huge job on his hands. Transport was to be arranged for the entire community to go south east, as the Polish army was being formed in Buzuluk, in the southern Ural Mountains. General Władislaw Anders, commander of the Polish Army, had set up his headquarters there. Without the amnesty papers everyone would be faced with hunger, as the papers entitled them to soup and bread at various station canteens. It also helped prevent any arrest by the Soviets.

However, Adam's papers were withheld and the family couldn't leave and were in absolute despair. There were several other families denied permission to leave who were also considered 'social undesirables' for their part in the Uprising of 1920, the Russian-Polish war, when all around were busily getting ready to leave, the 'social undesirables' were being held back. The records of the men in question, their military history and political views were known to the authorities, it was why they had been arrested in February 1940 and the NKVD had made objections to them leaving because of their military history! 'I cannot describe our feelings of hopelessness. We were absolutely desperate and how we wept.'

The Soviets went out of their way to postpone as many departures as they could, determined to keep their slave labourers as long as possible and they refused to allocate places on a train for them. However, a few days later Antoni successfully acquired the necessary amnesty papers for all the camp residents remaining including the 'social undesirables' and tickets would be allocated for them despite the Kommandant's efforts to prevent them leaving.

Those in the most remote labour camps of the Kotlas region didn't hear of the amnesty for months and as soon as they could they moved south desperately seeking recruitment into the army or at least their protection. Many from this remote region would need to make rafts to drift down the rivers to reach the nearest railway station and at Yarensk every family who wanted to leave had to build rafts, which then meant cutting down trees, gathering vines and boiling them to bind them to the logs before setting sail. It was long and tiring work. Those who decided to travel in later winter had to make sledges and cope with the snow up to their armpits in places which made their escape very difficult. They trudged this way for over a week covering incredible distances of up to 60km a day they were so determined.

From the moment they heard of the 'amnesty' tens of thousands of Poles travelled south from their labour camps towards General Anders and his army. Some hitched rides on carts, some walked, some sailed part of the journey on basic boats, some boarded cargo trains again, keeping alive by eating raw potatoes or weeds and grass. Many thousands died of mainly typhus en route, Uzkek villagers would open train doors and skeletal bodies would fall out.

The family were at last free to go leaving the labour camps behind them and Antoni had got them all together before leaving and told them to guard these identity papers very carefully as without them they would be arrested and sent back to the camp or worse and they wouldn't ever see freedom.

Although they were free to go there was considerable hardship to endure before they were truly free of the restrictions of the Soviets. Some of the families in the camp stayed behind by choice, they were mostly White Russians or Ukrainians with communist sympathies and they didn't see any reason to travel into more conflict and danger. Although how they would survive in that inhospitable land, in one of the most extreme geographical and climatic regions in the country? They would have to survive a harsh and sometimes deadly climate, hard labour and meagre food rations!

On 28th December 1941, after a very unhappy Wigilia, with little to eat or celebrate, with their papers in their grasp they started to pack everything together, they had a horse and sledge borrowed from Constantin, Adam's

Russian friend, to take them to Kotlas. They were frightened that it would all go wrong, but also excited, it was desperately cold and there was a lot of very deep snow and they had heard from the Soviets that the German forces had now reached Moscow and Leningrad. How would this affect their journey? The camp was now almost empty but for the graves of over 270 of their fellow countrymen, women and children, driven to their deaths by the extreme cold, overwork and starvation. Only about 10% of prisoners in some camps survived to escape.

Kazia, Adam and the children looked back on almost two years of abject misery and hardship and took a very deep breath realising they were on the way to freedom although with a mountain to climb. They had their few scraps together including their most precious photo albums, hugged each other, and with 3 other families, looked ahead to the journey towards Kotlas 450km away, with lighter hearts and great determination. They travelled many miles on foot, with Kazia on the sledge and were able to stay overnight with local Russians they had met previously at one of the markets. They had probably saved their lives as it was bitterly cold.

They started early the next morning on the long journey to Kotlas which would take a few days but they were focused, they thanked their Russian hosts and set off. Everyone was happy because they were moving away from the dreaded labour camps, going south towards the Polish army in Bukhara and away from Stalin's grip. Their hearts were lighter and their shoulders already dropping. As they were about to leave army trucks appeared at the farm with Russian soldiers on their way to the railway line in Kotlas and asked them if they wanted a lift. They couldn't believe their luck, Russian soldiers – and so friendly! They left the horse and sledge for their Russian friends and got into the trucks.

There was a lot of movement of Russian soldiers at that time across the plains of Russia after Hitler's attack and the soldiers were very helpful. The trucks passed over the river Dwina, which was frozen, it was -20 degrees and extremely cold, the wind was very strong and they shivered from cold and excitement. There were three other families with them on the truck and they would support each other throughout the harsh demands of what would be an arduous journey.

They reached Kotlas late afternoon on 30th December and saw a very crowded station, people were begging for food, so thin, eyes so dark and they couldn't ignore them as they made their way to the station forecourt. It was full of Polish families, all hungry huddling in rags because of the cold and like them eager to board any train out of Russia. They waited in line for 400 grams of bread and a bowl of soup and this was marked on their permit of travel. They had paid for their place on the train as Kazia had saved what she could and bartered for the rest, it cost her 80 roubles per person. There were about 7 families from their camp and they waited at the station for 3 days, waiting as train after train packed with Poles passed through the station without stopping. They had been reassured that there were Polish officers there to help them along the journey but they didn't see any.

Kotlas was the first town they had seen as newly freed people and they noticed when coming in that most buildings were of wood, the only brick building was the NKVD headquarters and a smaller building for the district communist party. There were wooden walkways each side of the streets and the roads were just dirt. Most of the inhabitants were ex Zeks (Prisoners) who had been allocated to live in Kotlas after their release from the labour camps. Some had worked on the Kotlas-Vorkuta railway and many others in the mines in Vorkuta district, the canals and dams.

Kotlas is a city at the tip of the Arkhangelsk Region and lies at the junction of two wide rivers, the Northern Dvina and the Vychegda. It has a river port, a shipyard and rail junction as well as a timber processing combine. It was probably inhabited from ancient times and was only granted official town status by Russia in 1917. During the 1930's Kotlas became the place to where Kulaks were deported and made to work as slave labour in the forests, they were affluent and independent farmers in the Russian empire who emerged from peasantry and became wealthy by their own hard efforts and had resisted Stalin's collectivising of the peasantry and refused to hand over their grain to detachments from Moscow.

During 1929 and 1933 peasants with a couple of cows or 5 or 6 acres more than their neighbours were labelled as 'kulaks' and 'class enemies' of the poorer peasants! Lenin described the kulaks as 'bloodsuckers, vampires, plunderers of the people and profiteers, who fatten on famine' and according to his political theory and his Marxist revolution, he intended to liberate the poor peasants and labourers. In practice however, government officials seized, with violent force, kulak farms killing resisters and deporting others to labour camps, which existed in the area until 1953. It was Stalin however, through one of his 5 year plans who caused the worst famine in history, the Holodomor, which killed millions.

2nd Jan and the train arrives late. It's made up of lots of boxcars and they join the long line, lucky to get on as so many were fighting for a space. They have tickets and were allocated seats amongst the Poles from the gulags and POW camps. The family were to witness a sight that would be a constant at each stop on the journey to Persia, the burying of people who had died on their long trek to freedom. They had already seen lightly covered mounds on the outskirts of the station which were the graves of Poles from the earlier arrivals.

The sliding door of the train is left open and the only sign of guards were the uniformed men driving the train, no NKVD guards to shout orders at them. At every station these men had to negotiate hard with the NKVD to have the train moved onto the next station and they also arranged food for the Poles at the communal feeding places. They didn't bother them and the family began to feel a little freer. There were however still the many watch towers manned by guards near every settlement on route.

There were men designated at the stations to bring them food, soup, bread and boiled water and being classified as military transport enabled the newly freed Poles to receive small rations for which they had to show their identification papers. At other stations and city's there were Polish Consular officials to help them on their way.

The train moved towards Kirow and they began to relax a little. After arriving at Kirow station, a journey of 520km they were faced with many hundreds more people waiting on the platform. Some were able to board, but others were left to wait for the next transport. People sometimes waited many days for a train, vulnerable to the weather and thieves. They were very often shunted onto a side rail to wait, as other transports carrying military equipment were given priority and they sometimes heard Russian soldiers singing. They also had to be very careful if they got off the train as they would set off without any warning.

The journey from Kirow to their main destination Bukhara, was over 3,000km, and they braced themselves for a very long and gruelling journey. Everyone sat huddled together and chased hunger away with the little food left, ground oats and potato pancakes. As they moved on from Kirov through forested countryside with small villages at intervals the watch towers were less frequent as they moved onwards on the Trans-Siberian route. They were able to get out and stretch their legs, very aware that the train could leave the station without any warning. Many people were caught out by this and were separated from their families, never to see them again, as had happened on their way from Poland to Russia.

They were heading towards the Ural Mountains and had to change trains several times, there were hundreds upon hundreds of weary travellers heading towards the Polish army and the trains were very crowded and also very unreliable as everyone was to find out. Some of the routes were guarded by a network of spies and the NKVD who only worsened the evacuation process by relocating thousands of Soviet citizens at the same time. This was a deliberate ploy to cause as much difficulty as possible and an attempt by the NKVD to resettle as many deportees in the poorest part of Turkestan as they could. They thrived on creating problems for others but in this they failed as so many determined Poles got through to other south eastern republics of Russia. The Polish spirit was unbreakable, they would not let the Soviets get the better of them, they still had the spirit that had won them the Bolshevik War.

The Ural Mountains extend for about 2,500km and run from north to south through western Russia from the Arctic Ocean to the Ural River and north western Kazakhstan. It is probably the richest range of mountains with salt, silver and gold mined there since the 1500's. Famous for its gems and semi precious stones, it forms the boundary between Europe and Asia and during the German invasion of Russia the mountains became a key element in German planning for the territories they expected to conquer. Faced with this threat the Soviets evacuated a large part of these territories especially the industrial units and three giant tank factories were established in Sverdlovsk and Chelyabinsk out of the reach of the German bombers and troops.

Everyone was tired and hungry as they pass through Zuyovka but their spirits are good and the children chat to their companions and stay very close to their parents. They spend their time watching the countryside go by and sometimes see elk and the odd brown bear which excites them and they see many wolves. They pass stations the names of which they couldn't remember. If the train stopped for any length of time it was for the disposal of the dead, both young and old died but most frequently death hit the former gulag prisoners, so badly malnourished.

The bodies were not buried, as no one had the strength to dig graves, emaciated children died in their mother's arms and it was heart wrenching to look at the mothers abandoning the bodies of their children to be devoured by wolves in the forests or the jackals in the deserts. Sometimes the train wouldn't stop for many hours and the decomposing bodies would have to be thrown from the moving train. How many thousands of Poles were left by the railroad tracks in Russia during that trip to freedom will never be known.

They stop at Molotov for 2 days to allow Russian troops to go through ahead of them, troops heading to fight the Germans who have invaded their country. Would the fleeing Poles have any contact with the Germans? It was a thought that crossed Adam's mind constantly. They shared their thoughts with others, but sometimes were just lost in their own, thinking of home and wondering if they would ever see it again. At times they just huddled together to give each other warmth and the reassurance to go on, Kazia always had a word of comfort or humour to keep them going. She truly was the glue that held the family together, they had always been a close and happy family but were even closer and reliant on each other now.

'We journey on and it's been many days of exhausting travel. We never know when there will be a hold up and we make the best of the delays to hunt for food'. The journey continues over the river Kama, to Shalya, Kuzma, and Hropik going through a more industrialised countryside. 'We get off at Hropik and stretch our legs and as usual we look for food. We find the queue for the bakery which is so very long, many people as dusty as we are in threadbare clothing and so very thin and we probably looked the same. When the bakery started selling bread the queue moved slowly forward but after about ½ an hour it stopped as a convoy of NKVD lorries had arrived and they took the whole batch of bread, we were very hungry and very angry.'

They travelled through the most beautiful landscapes of forests, valleys, rivers and mountain ridges, and arrived at Swierdlowsk on 19th Jan a major station in the Ural Mountains. This time they were able to get out and speak to friends from other wagons and see the happy faces of people who didn't seem to have a care in the world for the first time in two years. Alicja and Adam go out to look for food, they had their papers and were able to get soup and bread. Their train was classified as a military transport but it didn't make any difference to the speed at which they travelled, it was very slow as they were shunted onto side rails to let the troop transports through which sometimes left them waiting for hours at a time.

Swierdlowsk was formally known as Yekaterinburg, founded in 1723 and named after Peter the Great's wife, Yekaterina. It was the mining capital of the Russian Empire and a strategic connection between Europe and Asia. She gave the city the status of a district town in Perm province and built the main road of the Empire, the Siberian route through the city when it became a key city to Siberia. It is on the eastern side of the Ural Mountains and is surrounded by wooded hills, several lakes and rivers being located on a natural watershed.

Yekaterinburg was also the place of imprisonment and execution of Tsar Nicholas II, his wife and 5 children together with their loyal servants who had chosen to accompany them. They were shot, bayoneted and clubbed to death on 16-17th July 1918. Killed by Bolshevik troops led by Yakov Yurovsky under the orders of Lenin and the Ural Regional Soviet, Yakov Sverdlov and Felix Dzerzhinsky. Their bodies were then taken to the Koptyaki forest where they were stripped and mutilated. Initially thrown down a mine shaft called Ganina Yama, the bodies were later disposed of in unmarked graves in a field, Porosenkov Log. Russian President Boris Yeltsin described the killings as one of the most shameful pages in Russian history.

The Soviet leadership claimed in September 1919 that the family was murdered by left wing revolutionaries and then denied outright in April 1922 that they were dead. The Soviet cover up of the murders continued until 1926 when they acknowledged them after a publication of an investigation by a White émigré. The burial site was discovered in 1979 by an amateur sleuth but the existence of the remains was not made public until 1989 during the Glasnost period. The remains were confirmed by DNA and forensic investigation and they were reburied in the Peter and Paul Cathedral in Saint Petersburg in 1998, 80 years after they were killed. Key members of the Russian Orthodox Church did not attend the funeral disputing the authenticity of the remains.

They had been travelling for many long and very uncomfortable days, always hungry and it was very hot and dusty and there would be much hardship to follow. At some stations they saw huge piles of salt and wheat, the salt being sold on the black market by the matchbox at a very high price. At other stops there were quite unpleasant scenes with men driving horse-drawn carts collecting the corpses of those who had died, eventually giving in to illness and starvation.

Jasia, Janusz and Alicja took the opportunity to explore Swierdlowsk, as they had been assured that the train had to refuel and take on provisions and would not be leaving until the next morning. There were many buildings and beautiful monuments along the streets, one of Catherine the Great, but in the end they were too malnourished and weary to really look at the sights so headed back to the station.

As they approached the sidings they saw a very long train filled with people who were probably being transported to the camps the Poles had come from. Their cries for food and water were desperate, there were many such transports of human misery heading into Russia, many Germans from Kuybyshev which had a large German population. As Hitler had invaded Russia the Soviets were rounding up all Germans from across the regions and sending them to prison and labour camps in Siberia, Uzbekistan and other Russian areas. The children quickly ran for their wagon and climbed on. This had frightened them as it immediately brought back memories of their own journey into Russia from their homeland. Adam had been told by one of the 'officials' at the station that the Polish recruiting office had moved to Kuybishov which he shared with his companions.

From Swierdlowsk on 21st Jan they continue through the Ural mountains towards Chelybinsk 250km away. They disembark to search for rations which are now becoming very scarce and they manage to get some hot soup. The next stop is Orenburg where Polish Officers are there to help them on their journey. There were Polish army units camped along the route from Siberia to Tehran. The train then heads to Kartal and Aktyubinsk after taking on more fuel and some time for rest, it's an even longer journey of 1,670km and the train stopped in a siding by open fields. The landscape is very different here with houses of brick or mud.

They had passed a village a short way back and they were very hungry, they always were and Jasia and Janusz decided to try their luck and search for food but they had only gone a short distance when a loud whistle was blown announcing the train's departure and they raced back. They wouldn't eat that day. Trains had been changed there for Oktiabirsk a shorter journey of only 102km and they get out again to look around for food and there are many people waiting who tell them they've been there for days and that there isn't any food.

These had been very long, arduous journeys, so far over 3,000 kilometres, it was hot and everyone was filthy and exhausted and had lost track of time. The shortage of food and the unwashed bodies and clothes were irritants, but they were together and safe, that was important.

The train rumbled on to Shalkar and the Aral Sea, now on the Trans-Aral railway, and finally, after a journey of about six weeks and a total of over 3,500km, they arrived in Tashkent, the capital of Uzbekistan. It was a drab and very old station, still marked with the Turkish moon and star. Everyone was exhausted, hungry and filthy, they disembarked and sat on the platform, talked to friends, looked for food and waited. This had been a most fatiguing journey and very many didn't make it despite their determination. Worn down by starvation, typhus, dysentery and malaria with no energy left to go on, they just dropped. The girls would be chatting to their friends one day and the next morning their friends didn't wake up.

The surrounding fields and platforms were filled with Polish escapees from the Russian work camps. Representatives of the Polish authorities milled around doing as much as they could to provide food and basic shelter. More trains of Polish refugees were arriving every hour which made matters even worse. The assistants from the Polish Consulate started to explain to them how to reach the local Polish Army unit. 'Once you join up' he said, 'you'll be safe, the Russians won't be able to touch you, you must get into a uniform.'

After several hours they board another train which stops first at Samarkand, a journey of 300km. They get off and will have to wait on the platforms for 2 nights, some of the passengers were to wait for barges to take them to Nukus on the Aral Sea and Russian military trains were let through. They were exhausted, they hadn't slept well on the platform and were very hungry, they board another train and after 200km they reached Bukhara, where some of them were told to leave the train. They said their goodbyes to their friends, including the Krawiec family, Bruno, Maryjan and their sisters Krysia and Irena and their parents, as the family and others were going further east. They had become very close to the Krawiec family and would meet them again.

Many years later my Mother Alicja became friendly with Halina a Polish woman, while taking my younger brother Chris to junior school in Birmingham in 1962 and she was taking her daughter Elizabeth. She invited her to her home once and "I noticed her wedding photograph and I said I recognise that woman" and Halina said but how can you, she's my mother-in-law? 'Just then a tall dark man walked into the lounge and we recognised each other immediately. He was Bruno from the Krawiec family to whom we had said goodbye in 1942 in Bukhara.' There were many hugs and tears, 'how can you hold back tears when such vivid memories suddenly overwhelm you' Alicja remains friends with Halina to this day, Bruno died some years go.

During the journey south they had suffered many hardships, typhoid, red and common dysentry raged, food had been scarce and the death rate had risen higher than ever but everyone had held on to the hope that the Polish army would be there to protect them at the end.

They were now in Uzbekistan, the site of one of the world's oldest civilised regions. An ancient Persian province, it was conquered by Alexander the Great and the Nomads, Arabs and Turks over the centuries. From the 4th century BC to the 16th century AD Bukhara and Tashkent, situated as they were on the major trade routes to China, India, Persia and Europe, were centres of prosperity, culture and wonderful luxury. The Uzbeks invaded in the 16th century and extended the domain over parts of Persia and Chinese Turkistan. The empire then began to break up into separate principalities, one being Bukhara. Sorely weakened by warfare, these regions were conquered by Russian forces who took Tashkent in 1865 and Bukhara in 1868. These areas then became vassal states of Russia and after prosperity, peace and luxury came communism, domination and poverty.

It seemed the end of the line and there were very many hundreds of people gathered, cold and dirty, hungry and waiting for someone to tell them where to go, some were on the platform and some had stayed in the boxcar. The train would go no further, it had made a very short stop, and no one moved, they didn't want to get off as they thought they would never leave the USSR. They had a very unsettled and fearful night in a field across from the station.

Next morning the Polish civilian authorities came and assured them that they would remain there only temporarily and that the boxcars were needed for military purposes. They were persuaded that resistance was useless and reluctantly they left the train.

Bukhara was very busy with Uzbeks with very colourful straps around their caps and midriffs and Turkmen in black khalats, long robes with huge caracul hats lined with long haired fur band around the outside. The roads were full of people riding camels and donkeys loaded with bundles of dry twigs and bales of cotton. Lists were being drawn up by the 'authorities' dividing the occupants of the train into smaller groups and the thought of further forced labour crossed the minds of the waiting Poles.

They waited for another night in the field and were terrified of their prospects. Morning came and they were given their instructions by the Uzbek authorities, they were being sent to a Kolkhozy. Their fears about working in forced labour are realised! They had wondered what their fate was going to be, knowing that the Soviets were keen to retain their labour and prevent them from leaving, they were not surprised at this turn of events. They were still slave workers for the Russian collectives! Adam, Władek and Walery had left for the recruiting office in Bukhara which had re-opened and said they would be back as soon as they could thinking it was safe to leave them.

They had been assured by the Polish authorities that this was only temporary, until the problems of feeding and accommodating the large numbers of Polish Army volunteers had been overcome. Kazia and other mothers were most anxious, the Russians had been taken by surprise at the numbers volunteering for the Polish Army and had made attempts to limit the terms of the amnesty made with the Polish Government.

The numbers attempting to reach Buzuluk and Kuybyshev where the Polish Army was being formed in camps at Totskaya and Tatishchev, were an embarrassment to the very inefficient Russian rail system already under strain from the wartime demands of Soviet soldiers. To this end, without consulting the Polish authorities transports were secretly ordered to bypass Buzuluk and travel towards Kazakhstan and the fleeing Poles were affected hugely by this, left fending for themselves in desert and collective farms almost cut off from civilisation.

The many numbers of Poles involved had completely over run the Uzbek, Tadzhik and Turkmen Republics. They were now at the vast Steppes of Northern Uzbekistan and access to the collective farm was possible only along a dusty clay road. In the long severe Siberian winters, this route was snowed over and in spring, when the snow melted the road vanished under a raging torrent of ice cold water.

Some hours later, several arbas, with mules driven by quite wild-looking men wearing black fur hats got off their carts and through gestures told the weaker ones to get on board the arbas. Kazia was allowed to ride and those like her who were too weak or ill to walk. This time their walk to enslavement just outside Vobkent was about 30km or so and the stronger ones set off walking. Alicja, Jasia and Janusz follow the arbas confused and frightened. They were captives again, were in shock and very frightened. Kazia was almost in despair but she knew that Walery or Adam once in uniform would find them.

By lunchtime they still hadn't eaten and had just reached the Kolkhozy, which was in very barren countryside, with clouds of dust everywhere. It filled eyes, mouths and noses and made everyone cough and almost choke. The Uzbek took them to a big clay hut with an open fire in the middle full of smoke with a group of people with strange faces looking curiously at them. 'We had never seen an Uzbek before, and the Uzbeks had never seen a European before.'

They were strong sturdy people, with broad yellow faces, flat noses, very prominent cheek bones and cool dark eyes. 'We just watched each other, it was a strange meeting, but despite the differences, especially in appearance, they were friendly towards us.' They would need these new recruits to work for them! Early evening came and they were so hungry, they were given some uruk, dried fruit to eat, for which they were very grateful. The diet from then was frozen turnips and linseed cakes and cattle feed, which was tasteless and indigestible. After eating each family was allocated a kibitka, where they were to sleep.

They had no lights, no beds or furnishings. The huts were fashioned from home-made clay and bricks mixed with straw, and the roofs were either thatched or tiled with a hole in the middle. The village foreman managed to get some boards and straw, so they had something to make beds with although they didn't have any bedding.

A kibitka of the nomad Uzbek tribes,
also known as a yurta

They were free to mingle with the local population of many mixed ethnic origins, the native Uzbeks of Mongolian race and European Russians who like the Poles had been deported there. There was no escape from this isolated and inaccessible settlement. The land around was flat and had a small tree covered area where the Kommissar lived. On the northern side of the Kolkhoz was a forest plantation and a small lake with a supply of fresh water, there was a store and a post office and the offices of the NKVD headquarters.

The NKVD told the Poles that anyone wishing to travel beyond Tashkent needed to obtain special permission from them and that the Polish deportees especially were not allowed this privilege, 'they had been misinformed that they could travel freely.' However the family knew that if they had a relative in the Polish army they were allowed to leave Uzbekistan, which is why Adam, Walery and Władek had left to reach the army HQ to get into uniform but the Soviets did not share this information wishing to keep them on Soviet soil.

Their first priority was a long soak in the lake after weeks in the trains it felt so good to be able to wash their hair and clothes. They were filthy, covered in lice and scratching.

Work was organised by the village master, who came to their kibitka in the morning with a horse drawn wooden cart and asked them to follow him into the fields, where he explained what had to be done. They were made to clear the cotton fields of the stems of the previous seasons' plants and various other dried weeds which the Uzbeks used for fuel. They later had harder work assigned to them, which involved digging irrigation canals and carrying soil from one place to another to level the ground for the cotton fields. It was work far beyond their strength, but if they didn't work they wouldn't receive the dhzugara, similar to wheat, – their 'payment.'

The Mothers left to fend for themselves looked around them and shrugged, they had no choice. Kazia would not be able to handle the strenuous work with her heart condition and would look to the children to help out, even Janusz.

The younger people picked cotton in the fields and the norm was for everyone to produce three large bags of cotton a day, which was very difficult for the Poles being malnourished and in such poor health. The Uzbek women did manage to achieve the norm but with difficulty, they bent into the work stooping, using both hands with very few breaks throughout the day. Even infants were taken by their mothers to earn their 'payment'. Some of the men working at harvesting the crops, shoe making and repairing wagons had come from the Osada's in Poland and were skilled in farm work and proved to be very useful despite their poor condition.

Other groups were sent to weed the planted wheat and barley crops which stretched for many kilometres across the Steppes. They laboured for seven days a week from dawn to dusk with meagre nourishment, perhaps a little water, cold tea and bread. The work was very hard, women were bent double moving along the rows of wheat in heat of 50C pulling out the rough wormwood and everyone returned to their kibitka's exhausted. The sun was extremely hot and the wind which often brought with it sandstorms, burnt them and dehydrated them quite badly.

As well as terrible hunger people succumbed to typhoid, fevers and dysentery, they were all terribly ill. They ate anything they could find, hog weed, nettles and sometimes when they were brave enough, stole melons and apricots. They even hunted for hedgehogs, lizards and crows. People were haggard and swollen with hunger and they died and those with enough energy dragged their bodies to ditches and covered them with branches. No one had energy to dig graves, they had to drag

104

themselves through each day.

The Kolkhoz administrator told them what was to come later in the year, that at harvest time the whole of the Kolkhoz would move onto the steppe to gather and cut the hay working into the night and how important it was that the harvest was good for the survival of the population as the state would take a fixed amount of wheat and if more than this was not grown the population would starve in the winter months. They listened with other ideas on their minds as they had between them been planning an escape. They would not survive more strenuous labour, they were almost physically spent.

All the children gathered what they could, mushrooms and wild berries in the forest plantation and everyone queued up daily for their food provisions from the store. They gathered firewood for cooking an evening meal and Kazia tried to have something ready for her exhausted workers, Jasia and Alicja. Their standard fare was a soup called zutyerka, salted boiling water with pieces of dough and potato.

On a good day Kazia added an onion and cabbage and if they were very lucky Janusz caught a fish from the lake. Kazia was the source of their survival, her sacrifices and heroism, and all-embracing devotion got her family through this most awful ordeal. The family owe her everything, especially her resourcefulness after Adam had left, her superhuman efforts and for offering them the last spoonful of soup from nettles, a crumb of bread or a potato, leaving herself with very little.

In September the potato harvest would also begin and this again involved back breaking work, and by this time the weather would be colder and it would be the rainy season. The Administrator showed them how the potatoes had to be collected and put into large casks made from wood with large heavy iron handles and that the best of the potatoes of course would go to the state. He was planning for what he thought would be their future, his to decide.

The deportees however, had no intention of seeing the potato harvest, already making plans to leave. They were all suffering from various illnesses and wanted to use their remaining energy for the trek towards Tehran which was another lengthy journey of many km. They took in the detail on their rounds with the Administrator giving nothing away to him of their plans.

There were also dairy farms at the Kolkhoz and in the summer the workers would be sent far out into the steppe to guard and milk the cattle. There was no accommodation and they would have to build their own shelters. Again the women had to meet a quota of cheese and butter and would be fined if they produced less than expected. They were given very little milk for themselves or their babies or any other dairy products as generally the entire produce of the farm was sent to the authorities. This was Stalin's collectivisation.

There was no meat or fruit or vegetables and their bodies were badly undernourished, they were always hungry and were growing thinner and weaker. It was relentless, and it was now critical they made their escape as soon as they could. Most of the workers, were women and children who were extremely weak and malnourished.

After the amnesty, when they had received their evacuation papers, on 27th December 1941, with most of the men heading to join the Polish army most women had been left to cope on their own and were not expecting further forced labour, which was not the intention of the Russian-Polish pact of 31st July 1941. Also, unless the women were related to one of these men who had joined the army, they wouldn't be able to leave the kolkhozy and the fate of many of these women and children, left under Soviet control, is unknown.

The Soviet methods of working surprised the women, despite Stalin's movement for industrialisation and collectivisation in agriculture the tools the women were expected to use were ineffective and quite primitive and the work was not organised well and it looked like the appearance of work was more important rather than the actual output as the overseers never seemed to be there overseeing which was an advantage for these emaciated workers!

This land, had once been known for its riches, but through communism and collective farming it had suffered poverty and severe hunger. Before the October Revolution of 1917 it had been regarded as a paradise.

There wasn't much help from the Polish authorities at that time as they were so far stretched organising the evacuation of so very many thousands of fleeing Poles from such a vast area. They did at times meet some delegates from the Polish Embassy on the roads, recruiting personnel from amongst the deportees to help with the organisation. The Russians went out of their way to disrupt everything they possibly could. They were determined not to let their labour go free. Stalin's grip was tight.

The solidarity of their Polish group remained strong in spite of being scattered over such a large area and daily contact was continued whilst at work in the fields with their Polish friends and many new ones amongst the locals. Although they hadn't been able to see Ziuta as often as they had liked, they were too exhausted for the walk to the other Kolkhozy.

106

The trains, trucks and food were now being diverted to serve the needs of the Russian army while all the exiled Poles were left to their own ends for their daily bread again. The amount of food they received was dependent on the weight of cotton they picked or the number of heaps of soil they had moved, 70 being the required quota. They were given maize flour and sometimes dried fruit, again only so much per working person. It wasn't much and they didn't always get it. Everyone was hungry and at times there wasn't any flour, so Kazia picked some weeds and boiled them so that there was something to make a meal from. Survival was the order of the day, Jasia and Alicja were the workers and Kazia and Janusz searched for herbs, sorrel, anything edible.

Things were getting desperate, would they ever eat a proper meal, would their hunger pains ever go away? Janusz was still gathering what he could from the plantation, but had to be careful not to be poisoned as had almost happened when he mistook something that looked like a beetroot. The most prized item would be a dog or cat but this was almost impossible, there were some creatures like frogs and lizards but for the moment he left those alone.

By this time they had heard a Polish army unit was in Kermine about 400km from their kolkhozy. Word had reached them confirming that families who had a member in the army had a better chance of getting out of these inhumane conditions and children could join the cadets and this would allow them to go to the Middle East, where the main Polish army HQ was.

Their 'amnesty' papers had by now become useless, deliberately invalidated by the Soviets! Thinking their families would have been safe, Adam, Wujek Walery, Włodek and other men had left to go and enlist in Kermine Adam was immediately posted to Iraq and others were sent to the Middle East and the remaining families were forgotten, left to their own devices.

They weren't aware but at the time Wujek Walery had been left behind in Bukhara in an Army camp and he was able to come back for them, another stroke of luck for the family and the main reason that they were to survive. He was able to get them out of incredible difficulty. Food was so scarce, everyone was very thin and working so hard and were so very miserable, and Kazia was desperate to feed her family. Their love for each other and faith had got them through incredible hardship but they knew they also had a great deal of luck on their side.

Sometimes children would catch a dog but they weren't brave or strong enough to kill it quickly with a hard blow to the head so instead they pushed it into a sack and suffocated it, so desperate had they become. This land had once been so abundant with pheasant, quail, wild goats and game, all now extinct, victims to Stalin's collectivisation programme.

The Uzbeks were generally quite friendly, they spoke in their own language but addressed them in Russian and as Kazia spoke Russian and most of the deportees had picked it up in the labour camps, they were able to get along quite well. Soon after this Kazia was taken ill with typhus and had to go to the medical station and Alicja helped her there as Jasia was having to work, 'one of us had to work'. The foreman had obtained an arba for them, pulled by mules, and they got Kazia to the hospital in Vobkent. Alicja had to leave her there and walk the five kilometres back to the collective farm.

The children were now alone and they prayed that Kazia would soon recover and be back with them. A couple of days later they were lucky enough to get some maize flour from one of the Uzbek women in exchange for an embroidered handerchief so Jasia and Alicja baked some buns. The next time they visited Kazia in the medical centre they took her some of those buns. They were only able to see her from the window as she was on an isolation ward, but though she was still very ill she recognised them. The children walked back to camp with lighter hearts, knowing she was still alive.

They met one of their neighbours on the way back, Ivan, a Russian, and former sailor in the Tsarist navy and for his service he had been deported to Siberia. He had been very kind to them. His wife and daughter had remained in Russia, free citizens and once a year they travelled the long distance by train to see him. The family came across many older Russians, some devout members of the Russian Orthodox church, who after the Communist revolution had been exiled to Siberian gulags. Believers had to be secretive about their faith to avoid persecution by the NKVD who were especially vigilant in all USSR communities. Children were taught to spy on their parents and religion was never discussed.

So many people were ill, they bartered and begged for food for their survival and many hadn't the strength to get up, many had blackouts from the hunger. They were exhausted and desperate but never ever defeated, they were determined to join the army but hopes of getting out of the USSR alive were fading. There was no more flour, no food to share and the situation was desperate. There was a great shortage of drugs for treatment of anything, certainly no antibiotics, children were going down with measles and diphtheria, pneumonia and pleurisy and many did not survive.

Traditional herbal remedies were relied upon which sadly did not work.

The next time Alicja went to the hospital to visit her Mother the Sister on the ward told her she would soon be discharged and Alicja was so happy when she left the hospital she ran across that bridge with such relief. They all three went to visit Kazia together a few days later with a donkey to collect her from the hospital. She was still very weak and wobbled on the donkey but somehow managed to stay on and they got her safely back to the kibitka. The children were so happy to have her back, although she would need nursing and some nourishing food, and as usual there wasn't any food to be had. The fact that she was with them somehow gave them all the strength they needed to carry on.

Soon after Uncle Walery arrived at the collective farm from Bukhara in uniform, he had come to take his family further south so that they could be closer to the Polish army and have a better chance of surviving and then hopefully he could follow Adam to the army in Iraq. Ziuta and Marysia were in a collective farm further away, which was a very long walk, and they hadn't been able to see each other very often but had managed to keep in touch and to be together sometimes despite objections from the overseer of the kolkhozy.

Only uncle Walery's immediate family could be registered and allowed the necessary papers for food and travel and because Adam was already posted to Iraq, Kazia and her children were left with nothing, no food or money and no papers had arrived for them to travel. She was still recovering from her illness and was far too ill to work and the children were in despair. With only Alicja and Jasia working how could they all be fed?

Kazia had made a decision, despite being forbidden to approach them by the Soviets she and Walery contacted one of the liaison officers at the Polish Consulate Trustee and 'encouraged' him to let her enrol Jasia and Alicja into the young cadets school in Guzar so that they would be looked after. Janusz was too young, so Kazia and Janusz would stay behind at the Kolkhozy for now waiting for their papers from Adam.

Włodek, Walery's son, had already left to enlist and Uncle Walery then persuaded Kazia to go closer to where he was stationed so that she and Janusz would have a better chance of survival and it would be easier to get him into the cadets. Unless you had a family member in the army or were in the cadets, basically in a uniform, you wouldn't be allowed to leave the collective farm. So many of the deportees were left at the collective farms and their survival is unknown.

The Kolkhoz authorities would not allow them to move but with intense opposition from Walery and Kazia, she and Janusz did move to Bukhara nearer to Walery. Kazia would later persevere despite further opposition from the Soviets and the overseer of the Kolkhozy, to get Janusz into the cadets and then permission to later travel south. It would take time and argument but in the meantime Alicja and Jasia would shortly be on their way to Guzar to join the cadets and to receive medical attention, food and at last, freedom.

Many thousands died travelling on foot from the labour camps through the Russian Steppes, they had no food or water and their clothing wasn't fit for the sub-zero temperatures. Even when they reached safety, already sick and emaciated, Stalin would not allow them food and the NKVD made it very difficult for the American Red Cross to provide the refugees with food, medicine or clothing. Stalin's plan was to kill as many as he could either from starvation or on the battlefield. His intention was to send the fledging Polish Army straight into battle against the Germans. General Anders the Polish Commander of the 2nd Army Corps refused, his aim was to get as many of his countrymen out of Russian imprisonment and fit to fight.

Later in March 1942 he negotiated with the allies for an immediate evacuation, which was one of the largest in modern history but his attempts to get the release of the remaining Polish prisoners and deportees in the USSR failed. Stalin refused to give them up insisting they were now Russian citizens and part of his labour force, he had reneged on his pact with the Polish Government, the man was evil.

Alicja and Jasia left Kazia and Janusz in Vobkent, to join the cadets leaving Wujek Walery and the rest of the family in Bukhara, knowing that their uncle would help Kazia and Janusz, they were in safe hands. They were quietly confident that they would all meet up soon. For now Adam and Włodek were in Iraq with the Polish army and the sisters set off for their journey via the station in Bukhara, to Guzar the Polish enlistment centre and Cadet School in Uzbekistan.

The Polish and British governments were now aware of the deportations from Poland but were completely unaware of the conditions of those exiled Poles. Everything had changed on 22nd June 1941 when Germany invaded the Soviet Union in Operation Barbarossa. This proved to be the salvation of the Polish exiles from regions of the USSR and saved many lives in the 'amnesty' of 1941 granted to the deportees in the Polish-Russian pact.

A world at war had forgotten the many hundreds of thousands of starving Poles in captivity in Stalin's forced labour camps. After being told by the camp Kommandant that 'hair would grow on my palms before you leave here' the Soviets now needed these Poles but still disrespected and enslaved them! Stalin suddenly found his country was in danger from the Germans and the destiny of my family was changed that day in June 1941 when Hitler had attacked Russia.

Stalin had agreed to Churchill's plea to release all the Poles held in captivity, he was in need of allies to fight the Germans and he had agreed to the creation of the Polish army from these released prisoners from the gulags and prison and labour camps. This army was comanded by General Władislaw Anders who rather than mobilise the new army against the Germans as quickly as Stalin had wanted, held back to allow the Poles to recover their health after 2 years of captivity and to also allow as many as possible to flee the camps.

This did not please Stalin who then put a stop on any further release of Poles in August 1942 leaving many hundreds of thousands on Soviet soil, they were now citizens of the USSR and their future was cast. He withheld food from women and children travelling with the men, who mostly starved and his NKVD did all in their power to disrupt the travel of those heading towards the Polish Army, yet these people were travelling to fight with the Russians against the Germans!

I've included a series of notes on recollections of some Sybiraks fleeing the labour camps in Siberia,

'From Kharitonovo where people worked as foresters and loggers, we left 14th October 1941 on a small steamer over the river Vychega to Kotlas. The place was awash with Polish families, all hungry and huddling in rags because of the cold and like us anxious to board any goods train travelling south. Reached Tashkent and the collective farm end of October. Christmas 1941 was a cruelly cold winter, very little fuel in the collective farm, Engels, in Kagan. Searched the fields for frozen carrots, turnips and potatoes. Typhoid epidemic and many died. Conditions were terrible in the half ruinous Uzbek huts in which we were housed.

By Easter, April 1942 news filtered through of the Polish army being formed in Vrevskoye and Cadets, girls and boys being enlisted into the cadets. Many left for Tashkent and then by train to Vrevskoye. Many girl cadets were sent onto Guzar. We left Guzar on 11th August and by then many cadets had died from dysentery and hepatitis and on 14th August arrived in Krasnovodsk and on 16th August aboard ships for the 2 day journey to Pahlevi in Persia. It was like a fairy tale, the shops were full of goods and we spent our time sunbathing and swimming and we had plentiful food and fruit. This lasted until October 1942 when we left for Tehran.

The journey on army trucks took us through the most beautiful scenery, sparkling with flowers, greenery, vineyards and rice fields and the tree covered slopes of the mountain of Elburs on the horizon. After an hour or two the scenery changed as we wound our way through high mountains and deep ravines and a wilderness of bare rock to an almost uninhabited sandy plateau through Kazvin to Tehran. Underwent quarantine. Left cadet school end October and joined family in Camp 3. Left Tehran in August 1943 for transit camp in India. Left India in November 1947 for England.'

'Xmas 1941, people receive certificates, documents of release, representing freedom, where to go, people knew that in Kotlas there was an agency dealing with Poles so when we were supplied with sledges in early Jan 1942 we ignored the hard frost and headed there. There were very many of our compatriots from many different Posioleks, like us intent on moving south. They were all haggard, wrapped in rags, but full of hope and determination. A herd of human bodies clambered onto the train and fell onto the bunk beds. We passed through forests, mountains and steppes. The train would stop whenever and wherever and we passed through Kirov, Svierdlovsk, Czelyabinsk and Tashkent. Every station looked the same, drab and miserable and covered with multitudes of people. At these stations the dead were taken off the wagons and taken for mass burial.

Went onto Turknenia where Polish units were encamped March 1942. Were worked on collective farms. Many fell victim to typhoid and dysentry. In Hospital recovering. Lived in a mud hut surrounded by an apricot grove. End of March 1942 heading to Krasnovodsk to join cadets. Soviets on the station preventing the sick from going on board the ships. In Pahlevi Persian men selling pancakes and hard-boiled eggs and cigarettes. Underwent quarantine. End of August next stage towards Africa and sit out the war. In 1948 join family in England.'

'August 1941 Liberated Poles left their places of exile, posiolek Lednya on the river Vychegda. Working in forests and housed in little villages built by previous deportees. They headed south towards Kermine, clad in rags and tatters and not all of them reached Kermine. A lack of water and unbearable sun caused outbreaks of typhoid and dysentery from which thousands died. On arrival in Kermine we saw an Uzbek leading his arba loaded high with corpses and skeletons. They were Poles from the collective farms and he stopped by a ditch and offloaded them and this became their grave. This was an everyday occurrence. We stowed away

112

on trains as there was no official transport for us to leave Siberia. End up in England at end of war after India.'

'Nov 1941 from Posiolek Komartikha on news for the formation of the Polish army, deportees were heading for Kotlas and on arrival we camped in Kotlas railway station in fearful conditions with vermin infesting the concrete floor. The cold was intense and we had to endure this for two weeks before once again finding ourselves in cattle wagons but the atmosphere was entirely different. We had no planned route but knew we were heading south to the Middle East. There were very many stops as the green lights worked in favour of the Russian army transports.

At each stop the corpses of dead children were taken off. The entire route was strewn with the bodies of children. By Jan 1942 the transport came to a halt at an oasis in Uzbekistan. Not far from Sari-Assiya there was an assembly point for Poles. All healthy men joined the army and all those too ill were taken by ambulance to the hospital in Denau. Many had chronic inflamation of the lungs, dysentry and anaemia. Hundreds spend several months in hospital recovering then onto collective farms housed in Kibitki, June 1942.'

'September 1941 Many men left the camps, Yeluga, as soon as news of the amnesty had been announced. Telling their families that they would let them know when and where to join them. Unfortunately in many cases no news ever came and the families were left to sort themselves out with relevant documents'. 'November 1941 rest of the family set off for Kotlas on foot walking several km a day and at night stop at ancient villages, luckily finding places that took us in and often gave us food. Reaching Kotlas in Dec there were thousands of people arriving from all points of the compass, all waiting for trains to take them south.

There was a Polish Mission there but it could offer no help at all only advising us to make our own arrangements. Friends we met there warned us to be very careful of our belongings. There were Russian escapees from the gulags and some Poles who had been there for some time with nothing. We got a train, throughout the journey the carriages would be uncoupled and attached to other trains. Supplies ran out, there was very little food available. People were getting lice, it was filthy. The route was difficult to judge, but we did go through Kotlas, Kirov, Perm, Sverdlovsk, Chelyabinsk, Karaganda and Tashkent. Onto collective farms, cotton growing.'

'When we reached Kotlas the sight that met us made our hearts drop, we were faced with thousands of ill looking starved people camping under open skies whose number stretched down both sides of the railway tracks

113

and well into the forest clearing. Many at the end of their strength died from hunger, whenever the train stopped the corpses were taken and placed on the platforms. Trains stood at sidings for hours as army transports took priority. Typhoid, dysentry and other infections decimated many people'.

Of the Polish prisoners deported by Stalin 415,800 died and were buried in registered graves, 434,300 were either lost or disappeared and 681,400 were never allowed to leave the USSR. My family made it out of the Arkhangelsk region, and were on their way towards Uzbekistan and safety but they experienced sabotage by the NKVD throughout the journey to Tashkent.

From the 20,000 Poles sent to the Kolyma mines only 170 made it to the Army camp on the Volga. Prisoners released from the Navaya Zemlya gulag walked more than 3,000 km to reach the camp and the only survivor died on the day he arrived. The 3,000 sent to work in the lead mines of North Kamchatka all died of lead poisoning.

After Germany attacked Russia on 22nd June 1941, General Anders had been freed from prison and he then sought to form an army from the men imprisoned in Russia. He was initially told a blatant lie by Stalin that only 20,000 men had been captured by the Russians but he ignored this lie and began the formation of an army corps and had within weeks established a HQ's southeast of the Ural mountains. Troops and deportees started to gather in the area of Buzuluk after fleeing their respective labour camps and gulags. The first parade of the army corps from the words of General Anders were as follows:-

'There for the first time I saw 17,000 soldiers paraded for my arrival. I shall not forget the sight as long as I live, not the mingled pity and pride with which I reviewed them. Most were in tattered relics of Polish uniforms. There was not a man who was not an emaciated skeleton and most were covered with ulcers from semi-starvation. To the great amazement of the Russians including General Zhukov, who accompanied me, they showed a fine soldiery bearing. Old soldiers cried like children during Mass, the first they had attended for many months. For the first time I took the salute of a march past of soldiers without boots. They had insisted upon it. They wanted to show the Bolsheviks that even in their bare feet they could bear themselves like soldiers and march towards Poland.'

This parade of skeletons was on the 14th September 1941 and was the beginning of an army that was only allowed to begin to leave Russia a full year later and it would be over a year later before the soldiers were

114

ready and fit enough to be transported to Italy to be trucked up towards a shell-pocked mountain that was the strategic key to the Valley of the Liri River and Monte Cassino. The 12th Podolski Lancers would win the battle to raise their Polish flag at the top of that hill and these were the men who had marched past General Anders in their bare feet such a short time ago, proving their point to the Bolsheviks.

To someone who does not know the Russians as intimately as my family did, it would seem that all of Russia's cruel hostility against Poland would cease when she became Poland's ally against Germany, especially when, with the treaty of July 1941, the Polish army was formed to increase forces against a common enemy, Germany. Stalin had no intention of giving up the eastern territories seized at the beginning of the war. His aim was to dominate all of Poland and turn her into a communist state, and it was clear from the later Yalta conference that the Allies would not oppose Stalin's plans, that Roosevelt would again give in to 'Uncle Joe'. Without Polish representation or that of any other occupied country, the existing annexation of the eastern half of Poland had been decided. The Poles, their ally, had been betrayed and abandoned.

The forming of the Anders Army in Buzuluk

General Anders had the deepest loyalty to these men.

The Yalta agreement had consigned Poland to the "Soviet sphere of influence" and for many Poles to return to their homeland meant death or another deportation to a Gulag in Siberia. Many settled in the UK, US, Canada, France, South America and several other countries. Unless you were a communist, there was no future in Poland. Adam and Kazia, Walery and Ziuta and their families did not return to their homeland to live and the younger members only visited on holiday. Marek Skocyzlas son of Marysia and grandson of Walery and Ziuta, moved to Poland after College and still lives there with his family.

The sisters were looking forward to joining the cadets although were reluctant to leave Kazia and Janusz but hoped that it wouldn't be too long before they were able to be together. They were heading towards Guzar which was a reception depot and health inspectors at that time were rounding up the very sick for isolation in hospital. During their stay here many civilians and soldiers would die like flies from typhus, malaria and dysentery, suffering from the deprivations of the labour camps and gulags.

The trek to freedom was being made at huge physical cost to the Osadniks and there would be many stops along the route for anyone who needed medical treatment. The journeys had been exhausting on top of their treatment in the labour camps and most of them were almost spent of energy, physically and mentally but they resolved to carry on towards the Cadet School.

Flight to Freedom

The relocation of the Polish army took place in January and February 1942 and was spread over a massive area with the journeys between the camps taking many days through Kazakhstan, Kirghizstan and Uzbekistan. The HQ moved to Yabgiyul, south west of Tashkent, the 5th Infantry Division was in Dzhalyal Abad almost on the Chinese border, the 6th Infantry Division was in Shachrizyabs near Samarkand in south Uzbekistan, the 7th Infantry Division was in Kermine in central Uzbekistan and the 8th Infantry Division in Czok-Pak in Kirghizstan. The set up had taken time and further organisation would prove to be very difficult.

The 9th Infantry Division was near to Ferghana in Uzbekistan, the 10th Infantry Division in Lugivoy in south Kazakhstan, the Artillery at Karasu in Tadzhikistan, the Engineers in Vrevskoye in east Uzbekistan, the Armoured forces in Otar in west Kirghizstan and the army depot in Guzar in south Uzbekistan not far from where the family were in the Kolkozy. Communications were poor as the telephone only worked for an hour a day and the camps were primitive, thousands of tents pitched on a wide and muddy plain. It was a massive undertaking.

From 7th August 1941 an Embassy of the Polish republic existed in the USSR and opened 19 delegation centres and provided a network of social workers for the protection of Polish citizens, 10 such centres being in Kazakhstan and Soviet southern Asia. At the time of the breakdown of Polish-Russian relations in April 1943, 271,325 Polish citizens came under the remit of the Embassy and the Embassy's welfare activities faced constant hindrance from the Soviet authorities including the arrest of its social workers. Russia was treating its ally with utter contempt.

Bukhara to Guzar

Jasia and Alicja were looking forward to joining the young cadets in Guzar, in preparation for joining the Polish forces. With many other girls from the collective farm in Vobkent they travelled by arbas to the station in Bukhara. Alicja wasn't well and would struggle to cope with another long journey but there was no alternative. Kazia had made sure that the girls were getting closer to the Polish army by enlisting them in the cadets, she stayed behind with Janusz who was too young to join and she was also nearer to where her brother Walery was stationed.

The sisters witnessed complete mayhem when they arrived at Bukhara station, so many starving people lying on and around the platforms barely able to move waiting for a train to freedom. Many had been stranded and hunger and sickness had taken a huge toll. People were lying in the streets and on the railway concourse begging for food, 'many were skeletal covered in rags, their feet wrapped in newspaper or dirty cloths and held together with string, many were barefoot, very thin and almost yellow in colour, they were bloated, shapeless with sunken eyes and looked very old and shrivelled.'

They would have to sleep in the open air whilst waiting for the train and there wasn't any food. 'Those who haven't experienced starvation will never understand the desperation to put food in your stomach, to stop the gnawing pains, the contractions and the awful tiredness'. So many had eaten tree bark to prevent the agonising pangs of hunger. The girls found it frightening as they noticed, especially during the night, people wandering around stealing what they could, any piece of clothing, anything to exchange for food, they were so very desperate. Most of the deportees had by now bartered away everything they had for a piece of bread and had no choice left but to steal. The girls tucked their few belongings closer to them and settled down to wait.

The train eventually arrived and they scrambled on and sat on luggage in the corridor and after many uncomfortable hours they arrived at their next stop at Kogon, were given water and food and then continued through Karaulbazar travelling all night through the desert to Qarshi and arrived in Guzar in central Uzbekistan after 3 days travel. It was a relatively short journey, about 200km and the 7th Division of the Polish army was there looking very smart in their British uniforms but very tired and haggard, handing out food and water.

They were almost as haggard as the girls and all the sisters wanted after seeing them was to join the army. By now Alicja was becoming quite ill and was struggling with the exertions of travel and lack of food, Jasia, although a little stronger was also feeling the effects of malnutrition, the hard labour and the extreme climate.

The Soviets noisily ordered them off the train but Polish personnel stepped in to help and it was reassuring to see them, they were from the detachment of the Polish army unit and the Polish military hospital camped nearby, with a transport company and an army field kitchen. They advised them to stay where they were and to refuse to go to any village or collective farm, to ignore any instructions from the Russians and they would get them on their way as soon as possible.

People had come from all over Russia to join the army of General Anders and were always debriefed on arrival at their particular centre. The place and date of their deportation and the destination in the USSR were noted for the records and this information was sent to every Polish unit in Southern Russia where Polish people were assembling. Details were also taken of people they had met on their way and travelled with to gain as much information for their records.

Those who arrived at Guzar who were thought to have infectious diseases were quarantined at a medical unit and would later be sent to a camp hospital. They had their clothes collected and burned and were showered, deloused and some had their heads shaved. They were given sheets, blankets and fresh clothes which had been provided by the Red Cross and then shown to their living quarters at the Cadet School.

The name Guzar means 'valley of death' and from what Alicja remembers it looked and felt like a valley of death. Here nature conspired against life. It was a sandy desert, and from May the temperature could reach 103°F. The steppe would turn into a desert with dust so thick you couldn't see through it. The water would dry up and the local Uzbeks would leave the valley in the summer for the shade of the nearby hills. Many Poles died here on the threshold of freedom, from dysentery, typhus, malaria and other tropical diseases, it was too much for their grossly malnourished bodies, they were skeletal and exhausted.

This was one of the places where General Ander's army was formed in 1942. It was the Organizational centre of the Army and the Auxiliary Centre for Women's Service, a field hospital and the main camp for typhoid quarantine.

At the Cadet School the sisters were given food and medical attention and were able to rest, they were so relieved at not having to work in the fields for the Uzbeks. Soon after the sisters arrived Alicja contracted typhus. The living conditions in the labour camp and the Kolkhozy had been dire. Rats and other vermin were endemic in the huts and lice and fleas were something the families had to get used to. They continually scratched and were never able to sleep properly due to the parasites. They now had to contend with other creatures, plagued by huge black hairy spiders and scorpions they had to check their clothes and footwear each time they dressed. A bite could be fatal and Alicja did have one lucky escape.

Neither of the sisters gave up and somehow, like Kazia who had struggled with her heart condition, they found the strength to live through each day. They must have inherited some instinct for survival which saw them through everything. As a family they had promised themselves that they would never give up, if they did they would never be free, they would starve, be killed by their captors or risk being separated and never see each other again. They were finding it very difficult to live up to their promise.

Alicja remembered one day when her fever had passed she was allowed to leave her bed to go to the window to see Jasia, and when Jasia saw her big sister she burst into tears, Alicja didn't realise that she had lost most of her hair and looked like a skeleton having lost so much weight. The sisters were so upset because they couldn't even hug each other and they missed Kazia's support dreadfully. Jasia was so afraid her sister would die she looked so awful and she left wondering if she would have to make the rest of the journey alone.

The family were all separated at that time, Adam was in Iraq, Jasia and Alicja in Guzar and Kazia and Janusz in the Kolkhozy in Vobkent. At that point they didn't think they would ever see each other again and this caused great heartache but they persevered, they would find the courage. Eventually Alicja did recover well enough to be discharged from the medical station and went back to the Cadet camp and soon both sisters regained some of their strength.

Days at the Cadet school were filled with many activities, an early start at 6am in the morning and after breakfast exercises and then beds to be made, marching to be practiced and shoes to be polished. The girls took to the routine with energy and there was always laughter and at night time the sisters giggled and chatted with the other girls. The cadets would see on a daily basis lines of horses pulling carts stacked high with bodies on the way to the makeshift cemetery, it was an upsetting sight they would get used to, some of those on the wagons had been their friends.

They were being well looked after and had clean clothes and shoes on their feet. They had arrived at the collective farm in threadbare, filthy rags their padded clothing finally wearing thin and with sore, bare feet.

The cadets were excited to learn that General Anders was to visit their camp and they all gathered to hear him address them. He told them that very soon there would be a better life and they must be patient. Seeing him gave them the hope and courage they needed. General Anders was responsible for this exhausted tribe fleeing from Russia via the Urals and the Steppes, south and eastwards, through central Asia to the Caspian Sea. There were many, many thousands of them. This army of his was unique, not only was it formed in exile but it travelled with all its dependants, husbands, wives and thousands of children, many of them orphaned.

He must have been overwhelmed at the huge demands of the Polish

Exodus but he was determined to lead this group of his countrymen out of the USSR, onto the oil barges and decrepit ships to the safety of Persia. The sisters continued to work hard with the cadets but missed their family badly. They would quite soon be moved nearer to Port Krasnovodsk on the Caspian Sea and their thoughts were with Kazia and Janusz hoping they had been able to make their move from Vobkent. The sisters were moving further and further away from them.

The Polish authorities would be sending the cadets on to Krasnovodsk by military train and trucks, towards the Polish army post in Kitab, one of many scattered over southern Russia. Always moving the escapees closer to the main point of assembly, the Polish army in Pahlevi, westwards towards Persia and the cadets were made ready to move again, only waiting on the General's orders.

Neither Jasia nor Alicja were yet very strong physically, Alicja couldn't eat the food provided as it was very fatty and she now had yellow jaundice on top of the typhus. Corned beef and fatty soup and lamb given by the British soldiers caused havoc with their digestions which had only been accustomed to dry bread, no one could tolerate the rich food. Jasia would take her ration back and exchange it for fruit as her sister needed nutritious food but Alicja was too ill to be interested in food of any sort. Jasia later told her that she was in such a state she only wanted to die. Then she went down with dysentery and they both urgently needed a hospital bed and were moved to the Medical Station.

Their shrivelled stomachs would have to become slowly accustomed to richer food, any food. Their care at the medical station slowly revived them although the effects of starvation and disease would stay with both for some considerable time. It wasn't until 1955 after the birth of her third child that Alicja began to put on a little weight and start to regain her physical fitness. Her mental fitness never fully recovered and it would be the same for the rest of the family.

Many of the cadets had been ill from their enforced labour but were now ready to be moved towards Tehran. Care and proper diet at the Cadet School had given them strength, they would be getting closer to freedom at Port Krasnovodsk which would then take them to Pahlevi and even further away from the brutality of the NKVD. So many people died from typhus, dysentery and malaria on this route alone. Those who survived looked like living ghosts and remembering this brought huge sadness and tears to my Mother over the years, it was very difficult to see so many deaths when they were so near to freedom.

The sisters were happier now they were getting fitter and they had each other for comfort and confidence although Alicja was struggling to regain her full strength. To have your sister to rely on and to share the tribulations of the journey was a blessing. They missed their parents badly especially after having been so ill and they wouldn't have survived if they had been left to cope with this arduous journey on their own, many others had made this journey alone, their family members having died in the camps or on this journey and it was a huge test of character for them.

Guzar became one of the largest Polish cemeteries in the Soviet Union, the station at Kermine, a recruiting station 'was one huge refugee camp.' 'The local cinema was turned into a hospital for infectious disease and here without any medicine, surgical measures no food other than the occasional piece of black bread, hundreds of men lay on the ground suffering pain. In these conditions thousands died, their shrivelled remains put into boxes to be taken by strong men to communal graves dug at the town's peripheries. Once the ditches were full, the bodies were covered with quick lime and topped with soil.'

Guzar to Krasnovodsk via Bukhara – March 1942

The orders from General Anders came soon after his visit to their camp and they were on the move again. They were fed and prepared for the journey but Alicja was still very weak and could barely stand let alone walk and couldn't carry anything, even the very little they had, so Jasia carried their few belongings tied around her back and she too struggled to get to the station but the cadets helped each other working as a team.

They were to leave by military train towards Krasnovodsk then transfer to wagons. When they arrived back at Bukhara station from Guzar, travel details were changing by the day, they were greeted with a long passenger train, not a cattle wagon as they had travelled in previously. At this time they hadn't heard anything from Kazia and Janusz and they were very worried as it must have been desperate for them left in Vobkent and they were moving further away from them. However, whilst the sisters were on the train crawling through the mountainous part of Uzbekistan heading towards Port Krasnovodsk, Kazia and Janusz were also heading in the same direction, but at that time none was aware of this.

Janusz would have had to join the cadets for him and Kazia to get out of Uzbekistan but he was too young and too short and hadn't so far been accepted but Kazia had other ideas and wouldn't be beaten. She put paper in his shoes to make him appear taller and at the next attempt of joining he was accepted. She had managed to get Janusz into the cadets by sheer perseverance and they could then make the journey towards the Polish Army and the sisters.

In order for the Poles to be able to leave Russian soil, General Anders had conscripted everyone, male, female, and even children into the Polish army, he had put as many as he could into a uniform to ensure they got out of the USSR. When the amnesty had been signed on 30th July 1941 he had been a prisoner in the Lubyanka prison in Moscow and was very quickly released on 4th August to officially take up his command of the Polish Forces on 8th August.

The cadets travelled by train from Bukhara and then army wagons through Guzar, Ashgabat, Turkmenistan, through mountains on the right side that divided the USSR from Persia and the sandy desert on the left, on the Trans Caspian rail route following the old Silk Road. Through Qarshi and Kasan, finally arriving at Port Krasnovodsk, about three days and 1,500km later. The train had moved so slowly and for some reason would often stop in the middle of the desert. They realised later that it was to take off bodies. Dysentery was raging and the toilet spilled into the carriage, conditions were awful for everyone and disease spread very quickly.

Port Krasnovodsk to Pahlevi – March 1942

After almost falling off the train at Port Krasnovodsk, through sheer exhaustion, they suddenly found it very hard to breath, the heat was intense and many found it very difficult to stand, dizzy from hunger and exhaustion, they had no energy. Polish personnel met them with food and water and then showed them the tents on the nearby beach where they were to spend the night. They were tired and hungry but spent the night in a relaxed atmosphere and with the thought that freedom was so close they slept soundly.

The next day in a sandstorm so thick they could barely see, they made their way with the other cadets to the harbour, but not before cleaning the sand from themselves with greasy water, which didn't help at all, it just smeared the sand even further over them. They looked awful and laughed at their futile efforts! The sisters were so full of hope they didn't mind waiting a little time to board one of the boats that would take them to Pahlevi, with so many thousands of people it would take some time. They chatted and made new friends amongst the other cadets.

Some of those small boats that ferried the Poles across the Caspian Sea on the last leg of their journey to freedom were vessels of hope but were in a dreadful condition, some were made of only planks of wood and propelled by paddles and others were just empty oil tankers. They were badly overloaded without drinking water or sanitation but they would serve their purpose.

Alicja & Jasia in Pahlevi c1942

Whilst they waited the sisters noticed the people around them, the look in their tired eyes, staring and drained of any sparkle. I have photographs of my family taken in Persia and the striking feature is their eyes, I can only describe as empty of emotion.

Some people were so traumatised they couldn't raise themselves off the ground to board the boats although they so desperately wanted to, while others refused to give up the fight and kept going. The distances they had covered were exhausting for even the fittest of them, the weakest had a psychological mountain to climb and the ship would become a graveyard for very many.

Jasia and Alicja with the cadets, boarded one already quite full, so very many people already on board and so little space, but they managed to squeeze into a corner on deck as Alicja so desperately needed to lay her head somewhere. At this point she still felt so ill she didn't 'care if the ship sank'. She wasn't coping at all and it was lucky that the sea was calm. Jasia looked round at the sights that met her, sights she would never forget.

Most of the people on the boat were ill and there were many deaths over the course of the voyage, mainly caused by dysentery and typhoid. They were packed so tightly it was very difficult to lie let alone sit. People were only skin and bone, filthy in rags and crawling with lice, some almost naked, with the very weak trying to hold each other up. They were so very determined to see it through and get to Pahlevi and away from the Soviets.

What children there were amongst them were in an even worse state, naked and with lice under the skin. Tuberculosis was in children under 5 years of age, their stomachs blown up with their limbs and faces shrivelled up. They were so ill and weak and unable to even cry, they were mostly orphans with no adults to care for them. Alicja remembers a young girl badly emaciated waiting to board, holding her tiny sister very tightly, her sister so very thin, when she was approached she whispered 'I could only save my sister.' There were many similar heart rending stories but there were also tales of happier accounts, of parents finding their children, although very few.

The Polish representatives witnessed terrible sights, 'collections of skeletons covered in rags, feet wrapped in newspaper or dirty cloth tied with string, although many were barefoot. There was not a normal face to be seen, they were either very thin the colour and texture of yellow parchment, or bloated and shapeless like the face of a drowned man. Their eyes sunken and completely lifeless or glowing feverishly. They looked old and shrivelled although some of them must have been young'. And these were some of the fittest to leave their prison camps.

The sisters witnessed dead amongst the dying, with typhus, dysentery, malaria and frostbite and they were simply thrown overboard, their bodies pulled along by the ship's wake towards Pahlevi. There was only a handful of the thousands on board who could be called healthy. It was a distressing sight that stayed with the sisters for many years and they moved closer together, Alicja was struggling and Jasia was aware of the battle she was having and held her close.

The boats and small ships that ferried the deportees across the Caspian Sea on this stage of their journey were their last hope. Every available space was filled, terribly overloaded and a lack of clean drinking water and basic sanitation added to the huge death toll from dysentery and typhoid. The sisters remained on deck with the other cadets and many others, all so determined and the sea air revived them a little.

After 3 days they could see Pahlevi in the distance with a very long beach and the ship crossed the Russian-Persian border and anchored at the Port. The sisters disembarked and stumbled onto a beach covered in hot pebbles roasted by the sun. Some walked across barefoot before finding shelter from the sun under empty fish crates. They were exhausted by what they had endured in Siberia and the long journeys since had taken a huge toll.

From the heat, hunger and physical exhaustion Alicja was too weak to stand, she fell to her knees with the many hundreds of others and kissed the land of Persia, they were free and safe from the Bolsheviks. She sat and didn't move for some time and then cried, heart wrenching sobs which shook her exhausted body. Jasia looked on, tearful and quite lost and gently put her arms around her big sister and held her tightly, sitting together both sobbing quietly. They desperately missed their Mother and it hurt but they realised they were free, safe at last.

Other cadets had moved towards them and formed a circle around them, all hugely emotional, they sat together and wept. When they looked around them they couldn't believe their eyes at the beautiful sight that met them, a blue ocean so very calm and on the beach were palm trees. At last they felt really and truly free and were almost calm. The nightmare of Soviet Russia and their precarious journey was over for now and they saw in the distance tents stretching over a huge area.

They had made it, they were in Pahlevi in Persia, on the southern coast of the Caspian Sea, and as they made their way from the boats they saw before them a city of countless white tents. It was an oasis, with large walnut trees, vineyards and streams, the river banks covered with flowers and shrubs. The air was cooler from the mountains, but there would be danger from malaria as they were to find out.

It was here after their exodus from Russia, that they had found their first real shelter, courtesy of the Shah of Persia. Alicja was very weak but with enough strength to be happy. How had they found the energy to make the journey? From Kotlas in Russia to Port Krasnovodsk in Uzbekistan to Pahlevi in Persia, including the journeys in between was over 6,500km. A journey of escape few people make in a lifetime.

Their countrymen who had already arrived ahead of them shook their hands, hugged them and patted their backs and life was feeling a little bit better. A photographer nearby was recording events, a photographer by the name of Lt. Col Henry Szymanski, a US Army Liaison Officer. He was to take photographs of the true state of the malnourished refugees, which were classified until 1952.

Roosevelt and his propaganda team of communist sympathisers and journalists through the Office of War Information (OWI) and the Voice of America, (VOA) issued photographs of healthy looking refugee children, dressed in clean clothes and well nourished holding loaves of bread in baskets. His reason? To hide the truth of Stalin's crimes against the Polish nation from the world.

Many more would arrive, 'exhausted and in rags, impoverished, covered with sores, louse infected, without hair, resembling strange creatures more than human beings. They made their way with the last of their strength to the medical stations or the Recruitment Commissions where they would die from exhaustion, having wasted away on the very threshold of a new life'.

'Evacuation staff made up of Poles, British, Persian and Indian officers arrived in Pahlevi to find several boats ready to offload their cargo. They were grim faced as they surveyed the human wreckage being unloaded, their faces expressed pity and disgust that once healthy people had been brought to such a state of misery. Spontaneously the Polish officers knelt on the sands with the 'cargo' and silently thanked God for their safe journey and freedom. Emotion was strong and very many of them wept from sheer joy.'

They then watched the small boats continue their shuttles to the main boat to collect the corpses of those who hadn't survived the journey. Bodies were laid out on the beach and covered with sheets and those who had lost relatives walked down the rows hoping to discover their own parent or child, or sibling, it was heart rending.

When the British and Persian officials had watched the Soviet oil tankers, small boats and coal ships list into harbour at Pahlevi on 25th March 1942 they had little idea how many people to expect or what physical state they would be in. They had watched the ships arriving, over loaded and struggled to put a plan together to save a nation. Only a few days earlier they had heard that civilians, women and children were to be included among the evacuees and this was something they were not prepared for, they had no idea what to expect, it was mayhem, yet the organisation was slowly catching up.

Persia at this time was occupied by the Russian and British forces and relations were strained, the country was badly affected by political instability and famine and the Soviets and the British sent all the resources from Persia to the frontline of Europe despite Persia declaring its neutrality. This makes the compassion and hospitality of the Persians even more exceptional considering the conditions the country found itself in.

With the Polish refugees there was an immediate affinity from the moment they had arrived into this land. My Mother often spoke of the generosity of the Persians and how they made them so very welcome. The debt and gratitude felt by the exiles towards their host country is written of in most memoirs and the kindness of the Persian people is spoken of everywhere.

A makeshift city of over 2,000 tents had been erected along the shoreline of Pahlevi to house the refugees, it stretched for several miles on either side of the lagoon, a huge complex of bath houses, latrines, laundries, bakeries, sleeping quarters, disinfection booths and a hospital, provided by the Persian army. Unoccupied houses in the city had been requisitioned and even this was to prove not enough to provide for the many thousands of refugees coming through to the army bases.

Alicja and Jasia were so happy to be met by British troops, Polish soldiers in British uniforms and Polish liaison officers who reassured everyone. They had to walk through disinfection spray, which wasn't very pleasant, were showered, given food then issued with new uniforms of army cadets after their old uniforms were burnt. Whoever was healthier helped the weaker and the sick, many of whom had crawled on all fours to get away from Stalin's slavery.

They had been infested with lice, in terrible shape, hungry, broken and in rags, 50 died from exhaustion alone every day, 3,000 died within 2 months of arriving and the many orphans that arrived were moved into children's homes in Persia, mainly in Isfahan. Those with any infectious disease were quarantined in medical stations for a few days and Alicja who was still suffering from typhus would shortly be sent to the camp hospital.

Like in Guzar they were allocated their living quarters in tents, where they could lie down and rest, given sheets, blankets and fresh clothes if needed by the Red Cross. The sisters were beginning to relax although both still quite unwell and were missing their family so much.

No sooner had the cadets got ready for the night than came torrential rain and the tents pitched on the beach for their first night just couldn't keep the water out or hold up against the wind. They were absolutely soaked, but managed to get the tents back up with some help from the Polish officials and then fell back into them and slept like logs.

In the morning the sun was shining and everything dried out and all was well. Jasia and Alicja didn't yet know but Janusz was looking for them.

He had already arrived in Pahlevi a week before them and was quite established, wandering around the tents each day looking out for his sisters as each of the loaded transports came in. Kazia must have used every ounce of her charm and persuasion on the liaison officers to get him accepted into the cadets so quickly, unless he'd grown six inches!

When Jasia and Alicja bumped into him a few days later they couldn't believe their eyes, the three of them together again was wonderful. They embraced each other and wept, they couldn't speak, it was too much, too emotional. They sobbed and held tightly onto each other, but Alicja's legs gave way and she dropped to the ground overwhelmed by the sheer emotion of their reunion. It took some time to get their breath back, they hadn't known if they would ever see each other again. Kazia had separated them to get at least two of her children to safety with the cadets and had stayed in Vobkent to ensure she could do the same for her youngest child. My Babcia was my inspiration to write this story, as she must have been to her children, to encourage them to fight their way to survival.

Of course the first question from the sisters was 'where is Mammy?' Janusz said she was in Teheran in hospital, over 600 km away, sent there with the families of the cadets. He had come with the cadets to Pahlevi and started his search for them almost immediately. He had food, boiled eggs and some Polish wódka, the sisters had never felt so much joy, you can't imagine it. And how had he got the wódka? he'd bartered for it and also for the eggs from the Persians. The Persian people were very welcoming and offered them dates and nuts and raisins, pomegranates and boiled eggs. Some were able to eat these offerings but to many they were too rich for their malnourished stomachs.

Alicja forgot about her illness and rejoiced that they were out of that desolate land, really and truly out of Russia. They were in a Paradise, almost all together and heading towards a better life, just to be together would make it a better life. 'Stalin had tried to take away my family, the joy of my life.' It had been over two years since the Russians had stolen into their country and deported them to Siberia packed into cattle wagons, 'but my God it had felt like a lifetime, and the aching, mind numbing fear, no one truly understands how it feels to be free again.' – *My Mother's words.*

'There were no guards with rifles and dogs in Pahlevi, we could open and close doors ourselves, there were no locks, no feeling of fear, no having to look over our shoulders or watching what we said in case it might be interpreted as anti-communist! After two years of imprisonment and persecution in those gulags, in a land that was desolate and uninhabitable, digging into the ground and felling trees, working in snow up to our waists.

We had dug through permafrost and had mostly existed on weeds, black stale bread and water, working to the point of starvation and exhaustion, and the Russians came to Poland to help us! To save us from the Germans.'

'The utter joy and happiness, to smell and breathe freedom, light and air, gifts beyond imagining, it overwhelms you.' 'Oh God, those who didn't live through it can't possibly imagine, it felt like being reborn.'

In Pahlevi they were treated with kindness and understanding by the Polish, Persian and British officials. The Russians who were also in Persia were avoided at all costs.

The only aim in fleeing the USSR, was to enlist in the Polish Army, and head towards bases at Tashkent, Kermine, Samarkand and Ashkhabad for which the Soviets had allocated very little food and provisions for them. For the many hundreds of hungry women and children who were camped on the military bases there was nothing. Stalin had cut their provisions, his cruelty knowing no bounds, these people, mostly starved in his labour camps and gulags, were heading out of Russia towards the Polish army, to fight with the Russians! The Polish army in response to Stalin's petulance enlisted as many of the civilians as they could into its ranks, even children regardless of their age, to save the people from starvation but it was too late for many.

In Pahlevi, the sisters' training as cadets continued, they had been issued with identity cards and were now fitter after their rest and medical treatment and wanted to join the army instead of the cadets but when the sisters went to the Women's Volunteer camp they were told they were far too young. They had all been inoculated against various diseases, given more rigorous disinfecting procedures, fed good food and the liaison officers instilled them with hope. Their dream of joining the army would have to wait a little longer.

They sang songs of joy, part of their training, to let out the anguish and terror they still felt and instil confidence and morale. They knew, here and now, that Jasia, Alicja and Janusz and Kazia were safe. Adam was safe in Iraq, and they just prayed that the five of them would remain that way and although they were not yet all together, they very soon would be. Kazia was in Teheran and all the cadets were going to move there quite soon and the children were anxious to see their Mother, their rock.

Walery and Ziuta and their family were also safely in Teheran. the grapevine that had developed was amazing you only had to ask one person if they knew Walery Radomski and if they'd heard from him or knew where he was? If they hadn't they most likely knew someone who probably had. The power of the spoken word travelled well over such a vast land it was amazing, slow but effective.

Pahlevi to Teheran – April 1942

Within a couple of weeks they were to be transferred in army transport wagons to bigger more permanent camps in Teheran, Mashmad and Ahvaz. There was a constant line of trucks waiting to transport the exiles by a very twisting and treacherous road from Pahlevi, over 600km across the Elburz mountain range. It was to be a hair raising journey and the road was open to traffic for only 5 months of the year as snow drifts, avalanches and floods made it impassable for the rest. On one side of the road there were deep ravines, which was really frightening with the drivers negotiating the hazardous bends at speed, and there had been an instance of a wagon toppling over the mountain.

They boarded the wagon and Alicja sat on the floor so she wouldn't be able to see anything of the route, she was terrified at the thought of going over the edge. Everyone seemed nervous but Jasia didn't seem too bothered, she had recovered better than Alicja and chatted to the other cadets and admired the beauty of the mountains and the villages in the valleys. Janusz had gone on an earlier transport with the younger men. The route via Qazvin was beautiful with scenes below them of olive groves and fruit trees.

Alicja remembers little of the journey only that they stopped during the night at Qazvin and stayed in an empty school, it was such a relief to stretch a little and have a drink and the drivers could have a rest. They made an early start next morning as it was still a long way to Teheran, but the road was better and Alicja didn't have to sit on the floor this time. The journey took them through the most beautiful scenery, past vineyards, flowers and rice fields, the tree-covered slopes of the mountains of Elburz.

The scenery changed as they wound their way between high mountains and over deep ravines with less and less vegetation and then just bare rocks. At last they came down to Tabriz, arriving later in the afternoon into Teheran itself and driving into Camp 1 which was run by the Red Cross. The Persian people had provided buildings and many other amenities for the sole use of the refugees.

Camp 1 consisted of two brick buildings within a brick wall enclosure on the outskirts of Tehran. In the larger of the buildings beds were arranged on platforms and families would hang blankets for privacy around their very cramped living quarters. As more refugees arrived 500 tents were erected around the main buildings with washrooms and showers and a field kitchen which provided 3 meals a day. At one time the camp held 7,000 refugees and the tents were replaced by mud-brick barracks which housed as many as 80 people.

Tehran also had 5 transit camps, administered, financed and set up by the Polish delegation of the Ministry of Labour and Social Welfare. One for the army and the others for the civilians in various parts of the city. Camp 2 was a collection of tents outside the city and this was the largest. Camp 4 was a deserted munitions factory, Camp 3 was situated in the vast garden of the Shah and was surrounded by water and trees, Camp 5 was in Shemiran.

There was also a Polish hospital in the city, an orphanage run by the Sisters of Nazareth and a convalescent home for sick children and a hostel for the elderly. The Queen Alexandra Royal Army Nursing Corps was also there to help the refugees. The Cadet School was financed by the Polish Government in exile as was most of the care for the Polish refugees.

People who were already in the camp came out of their tents, searching desperately for their relatives. And who should be there to meet them but Janusz with Marysia who had travelled on an earlier transport with Ziuta from Tashkent. But again no Kazia, where was she? Ciocia Ziuta told them that Kazia was still in Tehran Hospital, seriously ill. They were in this beautiful city of Teheran, happy at being reunited with Janusz and the others with the worst behind them, and they were greeted with this terrible news about Kazia.

Starvation had left a terrible mark on them all, but on top of Kazia's heart condition it had almost taken her life. She had ensured that the workers in the labour camp, Adam and Alicja and then Jasia had eaten, if only weeds and water and hard stale black bread, she had often gone without. They were now in a completely different land and the contrast was worlds away from Siberia but they were faced with losing their Mother.

Many refugees were taken to hospitals before being sent on to civilian camps to recover and the staff at the hospital in Tehran had a huge Polish contingent newly arrived from the USSR. It was run by Persians with help from Polish doctors and nurses and the Polish Red Cross who listed names of the evacuees and Pahlevi's processing centre then sent them on to other army or refugee camps to help other refugees link up with family members. It was well organised.

'Teheran was beautiful, the hospital was large and we were very well looked after, the roads and trees and cars, the limousines and the people beautifully dressed. I'd never seen such beautifully dressed women, lovely looking and the men quite handsome, after the rough and ready NKVD it was a delight'.

The Poles were welcomed by a people who were extremely kind and respectful of their situation who were also very generous towards them, especially with their time. They met them with smiles and gifts of food and clothes making buildings and facilities available for them. It was noticed by the Persian army that the Polish soldiers saluted them in the street, the British or Russians didn't show them this courtesy.

It was a city of hustle and bustle, shops were full of goods, the Persians carried baskets on their heads and sold all manner of goods, dried fruits, cigarettes, boiled eggs and much more. The Persians couldn't do enough for them and they were all very indebted to them but at this stage the family had next to nothing, having bartered away most of their possessions some time ago. Two years of living with the deprivation imposed by the Russians had not prepared anyone for the overwhelming sight of shops full of goods and the cleanliness of the town.

They were able to bathe and enjoy the fresh sea air and eventually enjoy the good food. To the wearied Poles, nothing more than skin and bone, a plentiful supply of fresh fruits helped with their physical recovery, however the climate, with its baking heat was giving rise to dysentery, typhus and scarlet fever. It's thought that between 115,000 and 300,000 had made it to Teheran from the USSR but were in such bad shape that as many as 50 a day died.

By the end of 1943 the Ministry of Religion and Public Education of the Polish Government in Exile established 6 kindergartens, 8 primary schools and several secondary schools and lyceums. Within a short time the Polish community had set up their own theatres and opened art galleries, formed study circles, ran their own radio stations and published Polish newspapers, gathering their people together to strengthen and maintain their Polish roots.

Life was getting better for them but a setback to the community was the death of General Sikorski in a plane crash on 4th July 1943. He had just visited the troops in the Middle East and the circumstances of his death left the Poles feeling the tragedy keenly. There were many questions about the security of the plane he was travelling in and suspicions towards the Soviets were high.

To many thousands of Poles liberty was almost within reach, or so they thought. Most able bodied men and women of military age had enlisted, as had those who had recovered and were later assigned to military camps. Thousands had travelled south to join the Polish army to fight with the Allies but their stay in Tehran would be short as the army quickly evacuated to Lebanon and this included the Polish forces being reformed there.

Stalin had by now put a complete stop on any others leaving the USSR, he now considered them to be 'Soviet citizens' and the last Polish deportees escaping out of the USSR arrived in Pahlevi on 31st August 1942. Most like those arrivals before them, joined the allied armies in the Middle East and the rest, mostly women and children remained in Iran for up to 3 years.

There were 25,000 Polish civilians living in Persia in 1942 and by 1945 about 4,500 remained in Isfahan and Tehran. In 1946 there were approximately 6,000 Poles in Lebanon, some including orphans were sent to Commonwealth countries, Canada, Africa, India and New Zealand as well as to Mexico, diverted there by Roosevelt.

In Teheran's Dulab cemetery there are graves of thousands of Polish men, women and children, it is the largest of several, row upon row of gravestones have the same date, 1942, the only footprint of this sad and forgotten journey. 'In Isfahan in the Roman Catholic church candles are the only flickers of remembrance of almost 3,000 Polish men, women and children who died on the point of freedom.' Teheran had been a beacon to almost half a million Polish citizens escaping the labour camps and gulags of Siberia and so few lived even after reaching safety.

In later years relatives would send letters to the caretakers of these unmarked graveyards asking that a candle be lit on one of the many hundreds of headstones. Letters would arrive to the Polish Embassy in Teheran inquiring about a parent or relative buried in one of the graveyards. Almost 3,000 Polish souls lie here, so very far from home, victims of a tyrant. I wonder if any candles flicker to this day in remembrance of those Polish men, women and children?

Statistics are few, but it is estimated that approximately half of the 1.7 ml people deported to Siberia were still alive at the time of the 'amnesty' but news had been deliberately kept from them and very many thousands had died not knowing. In general, the news of the amnesty had spread very slowly and many of the camp Kommandants either did not believe it or chose not to believe it. After so many lies over the years from the Soviets some Poles also found it hard to believe. To suddenly find that the Soviets were their friends and would be fighting on the same side was hard to take.

However, it seemed that the attitude of a minority of Soviets had changed and they allowed some prisoners to take their possessions and make their way to stations where transport would be waiting for them.

The Soviets and the NKVD did all they could to obstruct the refugees on their exodus out of Russia, Stalin's cruelty would sometimes specifically target Mothers and their children on their escape from Russia. There had been a convoy of 23-25 wagons of Polish Civilians travelling to Persia in the winter of 1941 which had been diverted to the sidings by the NKVD, ignoring the Polish soldiers who were waiting for Polish transports from the USSR camps. The station was Czkalow now called Orenburg, close to Totskoye. They were kept in the sidings for 3 days with the doors locked without food, water or fuel.

When the NKVD allowed the Polish soldiers to eventually approach and open the doors, the occupants, women and children were frozen solid. The group of Polish soldiers had a doctor with them, Dr Maria Chmurzyna, also a soldier who reported that the occupants, mostly Mothers and babies were dead in every wagon. A consequence of Soviet brutality and a wholly shameful and unnecessary act and to those Polish soldiers opening the wagons it must have been almost impossible to withhold their hatred and hostility towards the Bolsheviks with whom they were now allies! No Russian has ever been held accountable at the Nuremburg trials, for the crimes they committed against Polish citizens!

Shortly after they had arrived in Teheran in 1942, the evacuees had been asked by the Polish officials to write about their experiences under the Soviet regime in Siberia. This was mainly to collect information that would be used to help nullify any annexation of eastern Poland after the war. The exiles also formed the first large group of people in about 20 years who were exposed to life in the Soviet Union and allowed to leave. 'Testimonies may constitute a precious source of evidence enabling us to reveal to world opinion the truth about Russia' one official noted. Of the tens of thousands of handwritten reports collected about 20,000 ended up in the Hoover Institution, including many written by women, approximately 2,000. Children too young to write drew pictures.

However, many of the Poles so very grateful to have been safely delivered from their labour camps and gulags, were advised to keep silent by the Soviets and Americans and many complied, although had they known of the propaganda perpetrated by the Voice of America (VOA), staffed by communist sympathisers they may have declined.

Many others who followed in the last wave of liberation in August 1942 also kept silent about their treatment even when the Soviet Union was exposed as a murderous tyranny. Their history however is not completely lost, like the exiles who escaped from the grip of Stalin, their children especially have not been silenced and they continue to highlight the story of Stalin's exile of their families from the Kresy, in the eastern borderlands.

Very few of the evacuees who passed through Teheran during 1942-1945 would ever see their homeland again. This included my grandparents Kazia and Adam and her brother Walery and sister in law Ziuta, as their fate was sealed in this land of freedom in 1943. Stalin, Churchill and Roosevelt met in the capital of Persia, Teheran, to decide the fate of post war Europe. Their secret discussions assigned Poland officially to the zone of influence of the Soviet Union after the war.

Poland would lose its independence and territorial integrity and the eastern borderlands would be absorbed wholesale into the Soviet Union. The Polish Government was not consulted or informed of this decision until some time later. Polish soldiers, 48,000 of them, would lose their lives fighting for the freedom of the nations whose governments had secretly betrayed them in Teheran. The decision was made known to the world in Yalta, Crimea in 1945.

My family took away from Persia a lasting memory of freedom, friendliness and sympathy and their time there is shown in the many photographs taken in that generous and beautiful land, included in this memoir. My family never forgot the hospitality and friendship of the Persians and the Shah of Persia and the debt they owed to them. The country had stood as a beacon of hope and freedom to them on their journey of escape.

CHAPTER 7

Sanctuary and Recovery

QUEEN ALEXANDRA ROYAL ARMY NURSING CORPS – QARANC

Russian and Polish Prisoners of War and Refugees WW2 34th British Commonwealth General Hospital

An eyewitness account from the journal of Principal Matron Lieutenant Colonel Annie Hughes 1942 of Queen Alexandra's Royal Army Nursing Corps.

The history of the modern day QARANC can be traced back to the Crimea War. Florence Nightingale took 38 women to work as nurses and nursing attendants at Scutari Hospital from 1854 to 1856. She was recruited by the Secretary of State for War Sidney Herbert to lead the women in tending the wounds of the injured soldiers. He had identified the need for a nursing service because soldiers had little medical care and treatment and were dying from neglect as well as their horrific wounds.

Camel convoys were the chief means of transport in the mountains which were still covered with snow and with narrow, deep ravines on either side making the road difficult and dangerous, but the Royal Army Medical Corps units got through to Pahlevi and started to unpack in readiness. Before the day was out. Someone looking vaguely through the blizzard spotted three ships approaching – if you could call them ships, they were not fit for the use of human beings or cattle – across the Caspian Sea. The vessels anchored and rapidly disgorged their contents of humanity on the beaches. What a shock for everyone – this sight would never be forgotten! The smell was too awful to describe. There were thousands of both sexes of all ages, packed like sardines and they could not lie down or even sit. They were emaciated, being skin and bone only, filthy and lousy, the dead and the dying all mixed up together, sent over without food or drink, no sanitary arrangements and with the weak trying to hold each other up. They were dressed in bits of old, dirty rags, some almost naked, with no shoes and crawling with bugs. Practically every disease in medical history was evident there, typhus of the worst type, dysentery, malaria, tuberculosis, frostbite, some with limbs almost dropping off with disease. There were just a handful of the fairly healthy mixed up with the typhus cases. They had received no medical attention, the kiddies' bodies naked but covered with embedded lice under the skin. Tuberculosis was at its worst among children under four years of age, their little tummies all blown up, limbs and faces all shrivelled up and outlining only the bone formation and they were too ill and weak to cry.

My Mother Alicja was in tears telling me of the sights she had seen in Pahlevi, she couldn't have described it more vividly. My family had received medical attention along the route to Pahlevi and although in dire physical conditional they were not in as bad a state.

The bath unit and disinfector could not be used for all the cases, many being too ill and the numbers too great to be dealt with. Our chief anxiety was to get them to the hospital at Dosham Tapu for immediate treatment so we sorted out those able to make the journey. The language question was a drawback at first, having an all Indian staff and the patients Polish and a few Russians but this was soon overcome, being only a minor detail. Over one thousand were admitted to the hospital on the first day. We had only five hundred beds so the remainder as a temporary measure had to lie on folded blankets on the ground. The fatigue party put up more tents where the patients lay. With only four of us to cope with the nursing side we tried to get some of the not so ill to help with the washing and feeding. At first they refused, for after seeing so many of their compatriots die, they were terrified of catching typhus. This went on for four days and in the end they had to be compelled to help. We had to work day and night with practically no rest, taking only a hurried meal and when that was over getting back to find hundreds more lying on the ground waiting for attention. An improvised operating theatre was set up under canvas, with two pieces of board on trestles forming the table, instruments were few, field ambulances' equipment only and these were boiled in old tins on charcoal first to deal with the cases of gangrene and frostbite. This work was done at night as the numbers arriving during the day was so great and it took time to get them settled.

The hospital now had 1,500 patients desperately ill and dying. More refugees began to come over the frontier, so a camp had to be organised nearby to accommodate them. Often they had to look after themselves. This camp eventually held 25,000, a daily visit being paid by the medical officer to attend to those reporting sick.

This Indian hospital was called the 34th British Commonwealth General Hospital, I was told there was a 500 bedded hospital in the stores at Teheran Station waiting for a British hospital to come up the line if it was necessary but when headquarters in Baghdad heard what was happening they released this hospital to us. HQ then sent several officials over by plane, these including Sir Edward Quinan and Sir Henry Maitland Wilson the C in C. At nine o'clock the following evening Principal Matron in Persia arrived, also a matron from one of the large hospitals in Shaiba. We did not expect them and no preparations had been made for them. I could not stop to welcome or speak to them as there was so much work to do. These ladies immediately donned gowns, masks and gloves and worked alongside us throughout the night. The matron of the hospital had not been seen and did not know of the arrivals until we went to our Mess for a break and well earned cup of tea at 6am. It was during this break I was able to give details of what had been going on but we were almost too tired to talk. They remained with us and helped for a week. The Principal Matron sent a signal for immediate reinforcements and twelve QA Sisters arrived within 48 hours. The authorities were afraid of sending too many along at this time as it was too dangerous, the Germans were shelling Stalingrad and were expected over the Caspian Sea. The few Sisters sent gave us time for a short break and reorganisation of the hospital routine. The mountains surrounding the valley were from 5,000 feet to 180,000 feet high and by now it was beginning to get very warm. The brass hats visiting us were amazed at the amount of work being done.

Before the Principal Matron returned to Baghdad she informed me I had to take charge of the Teheran area and camps. This was a terrific undertaking and responsibility which rather took my breath away. I was now acting Principal Matron with the rank of Lieutenant Colonel and I got down to the duties. The previous Matron was posted to the Middle East.

Amongst the refugees we found Polish medical officers and some nursing staff from Polish hospitals and after feeding them up and giving them clothes they were put on duty in the hospital. Clothes had been collected from various people and even the Americans sent hampers over to clothe the women. This was a great beginning and we felt the work was progressing, they being able to speak the same language and looking after their own people. They turned out to be very good workers, several students working as nursing orderlies and grateful for being given the chance to help. A few weeks later more patients began to arrive, more beds had to be made, women and children from the camp helping to make mattresses with straw collected from packing cases. The hospital now had 2,000 patients.'

I found a few well educated women amongst the campers. They also came along to help in the hospital kitchens but before they were able to help, clothes had to be found as they only had dirty rags on. Some of these refugees were fully trained matrons and sisters from Polish hospitals who had been taken as prisoners. Their bodies were covered with weals, scars and cuts and they had sore feet from tramping many miles. The American Embassy in Teheran gave us wonderful assistance in getting things, as did the Indian Red Cross. As prisoners, it appeared the higher the class the worse the treatment given. These ladies had been made to clean lavatories, sweep roads and help the men to cut down trees.

One day I approached some of their medical officers and General Anders, asking them to give Red Cross lectures and this was done, with over 200 students. I had some of my RAMC lectures with me and these were interpreted into their own language. On examination they passed out with good marks and eventually they were dressed in khaki and given the same grading and pay as the soldiers. They soon picked up in health after receiving good food and treatment. As the men got discharged from hospital they reorganised a unit and started training again. How they dreaded this time. It was pathetic to see them go because the training was for active service.

I found a matron, a very experienced woman, amongst a batch of refugees. She had been in charge of a large medical training school in Kraków and had remained behind until her hospital had been evacuated. She had also been very badly treated. I took her under my wing as an assistant matron and trained her how to organise and run a field hospital. When the patients started to get their discharges in fairly large numbers, the Polish Government started to open up hospitals of their own in the Middle East. The Polish Matron was appointed their matron in chief and the nurses trained at 34th CGH also went.

The removal of the dead was a problem. The Nursing Sepoys (Indian) would not touch them, it was in their religion and considered unclean. The lower caste Indians called Sweepers had this duty to perform. There were hundreds of dead amongst the new batches arriving and due to the climate and diseases their bodies had to be buried within a few hours. Wild animals prowling around would often carry the bodies away. A large tent was erected to receive the bodies and this was guarded day and night. In the shadow of an 18,000 ft mountain the Polish refugees dug a large common grave, quite a number having to be buried as unknown.

More QA's and Indian assistant nurses arrived making the number up to 30. The Indian Government had sent sisters and nurses over to help. I was fortunate in having the loyalty of all my staff which included British, Indian and Polish, 170 in all and through good team work there was no illness amongst the staff. I think that working and sleeping in open tents kept everyone fit. The staff having been increased we were able to take proper off duty time with a clear conscience. This time was spent going into the city for shopping and sight seeing. In the early days the city was out of bounds to British sisters as we had been threatened with death, the Persians accusing us of bringing diseases to Teheran but as nothing happened they began to realise we would do them no harm and they would benefit from our shopping. The shops were full of wonderful things but much too expensive for us to buy though by this time our garments sadly needed replenishing. Stockings could not be bought for less than £5 a pair in Persian money, shoes being £6 to £20. After appealing to HG in Baghdad an Officers' shop was opened in the town to where British male and female uniforms were sent by plane. Even our shoes were past repairing.

German paratroopers had been seen coming down, some having been captured in the Caucasus so in July 1942 British and American troops began to arrive in the north to meet what they thought was going to be a grave situation. The enemy was advancing and was expected to cross the Caspian Sea or come over the mountains. Guns and bombing could be heard in the distance. The authorities thought the work as far as the Poles were concerned, had finished. So the 34th CG Hospital began to pack up. British and American hospital units began to come up the line. They were lucky in taking over a half finished modern German hospital that had every luxury. They were horrified to find that a large Indian Hospital was under canvas on the plain and remaining through heavy snows and heat but I would not change my life for the comfort of bricks. My British staff were redrafted to their units but the Indian nurses remained with me.

Refugees were still coming through at the rate of 5,000 a day, by 6th April 19,000 Poles had been moved and when the number reached 44,000 we thought the movement had finished. News came through that it was possible a second evacuation would take place later though by now only a skeleton staff remained.

Some of the new arrivals had walked across the country from Siberia, many high ranking officers amongst them. They were given no food but just turned adrift and told to make their own way. They had been Russian prisoners and the Russians were too busy defending their own lines. Only a few survived the ordeal, hundreds dying before they reached the frontier, all ranks helping each other along. It was hard to believe they were human beings. A few Polish women joined them on the walk, these women showing their marks of ill treatment. Most of the females were able to go straight to the camp. I found several pregnant and arrangements were made for their own women to deal with them.

The winter season was coming on with snow on the plains many feet thick, being crisp and hard to walk on and the air was like champagne. A fatigue party had to be detailed to go around periodically to knock the snow off the tents to prevent the weight from collapsing them. The winds in the Persian hills were bitterly cold. The hospital was now very busy. German troops continued to advance and Stalingrad was invaded. They were pushing down towards the Caucasus, hoping to penetrate to the river Araxes in the North of Persia.

Settled in once more my patients improved sufficiently for quite half their number to be transferred to the camp to be looked after by Polish nurses who had been trained in the hospital. At this stage it was feeding up that they wanted and their own cooks gave them the kind of food they were used to. Doing the rounds of inspection in the kitchens I was amazed at the queer concoctions though they smelt good. And how these poor creatures could eat, even those in the hospital.

General Sikorski and General Anders gave a banquet at their new Persian HQ to meet all the high rankers of their own army. The Colonel and myself were invited as honoured guests. It was a wonderful dinner all Polish and what intrigued me most was that they started their courses where we leave off, they ended with soup. This was the first time for me to taste Vodka but was not impressed. After this a letter in Polish was sent from HQ Evacuation Base, Polish Army in the East.

The Polish army had been greatly reformed having been put into khaki uniform given by the British Government. Even boys of 14 had to join up as they were needed for further fighting, their one aim being revenge. They certainly appeared very bitter. I met many of their great generals and leaders who were very appreciative of all that had been done for them and I received many letters from the men and women of Poland.

The unit was awaiting orders for the next move and one morning when I too was wondering where our next place would be, I met our Indian Colonel waving his hands over his head and in a terrific flap, they do get very excited when in a fix. The reason was that a ship had been sighted crossing the Caspian Sea. At first it was thought to be an invasion because no one expected any more refugees to come that way as it was too late to escape Russia, unless they tramped over the hills of Turkestan or the wharf at Krasnovodsk. Already 6 Germans had landed by parachute about 70 miles south of Teheran, 3 more dropped near Mosul and 3 landed in SW Persia so the military authorities blocked all frontiers leading into Persia and Iraq with troops. I think about 8 frontiers.

When the ship had anchored we saw it was a very small vessel of the type we call a cattle boat. It was very old and one wondered how it made the crossing as it was certainly unseaworthy. It just made it though actually, it was not meant to arrive. The sight of its cargo was again too awful to describe. It was supposed to have on board 1,000 babies from 3 months to 10 years old. There was difficulty getting to know their ages. The older children could not help us because they were strangers to each other and much too ill and weak to talk. With more than 200 dead and many more dying the stench was awful. They were naked and caked with filth, emaciated to skeletons and looked more like very old people. Their eyes could barely be seen having sunk so far into their sockets. They had blown up tummies, suffering from abdominal tuberculosis, typhus and dysentery. There was no one looking after them on the journey, no food and no one to say when they last had a feed. They had been in homes and orphanages, belonging to no one, some having been picked up on the streets in Russia where probably their parents had been killed. The older children look at us with fear and terror and it took some time to convince them that we wanted to help them. The OC and his staff were concerned because they were babies and felt it was impossible to do anything for them but when told they were in my responsibility they sighed with relief.

I recruited some kind motherly women from the camp and a few Polish nurses. There was also a Polish children's hospital matron amongst them. I felt the children would feel more at home with their own people. A large building in the grounds was turned into a suitable place, with mattresses on the floor. They were taken there after they had been cleaned up and given nourishing fluids. Old sheets were collected and torn up to cover their wizened little bodies. I did not think they would survive but given treatment and good attention from the very kind foster mothers it was amazing how they picked up and only a few died.

Then when the time came to get them up and teach them to walk the question of clothes was again a problem. Our Red Cross could not help us and I appealed to the American Red Cross. Through the kind and helpful wife of a British Consul within a few days large hampers arrived with lovely woollies, dresses and shoes, also little baby sets, all hand knitted, having been flown over from America. All had a good rigout and I don't think the little mites had ever seen or been clothed in such lovely things. Coats, shawls and bonnets also arrived and it was a pleasure to see their faces. All the Polish women and nurses had a good cry over such kindness.

The day arrived when we had to part with 500 of them. They were sent to India to finish their convalescence and to be safe. The very poor women, to show how grateful they were, made a rag doll dressed in Polish national costume and presented it to me. I loved this little doll, the gift spoke more than words, it was the thought. I had the children for roughly 6 weeks and here is a copy of the letter they sent to me after they had left.

The matron of the Polish Civil Hospital sends her deepest gratitude to the Matron of the 18th Indian Gen. Hospital for her kindness to the Polish children during their stay at the 18th IGH.

In spite of the lack of knowledge of the Polish language the Matron was always attempting to understand and assist the Polish children for which we are ever so grateful.

The Polish people shall never forget the acts of kindness displayed at the 18th Indian Gen Hospital. *– Signed H. Wydecka Teheran, Persia.*

The Poles recruited into the army, were assimilated into battle formations of the armies of the western powers while the civilians and children were placed in temporary camps in Iran, India, British East Africa the Middle East and even Mexico.

In all of these places were many of the families of the military settlers from the eastern borderlands of Poland, the homeland of my family.

From the middle of 1942 Soviet repression of the Polish representative units increased. On 5th January 1943 the Council of People's Commissars, without notifying the Embassy of the Polish Republic, issued a decree whereby they placed all the Polish centres under Soviet control. On the 25th April 1943 Polish-Russian relations came to an end. The Soviets began forcing Poles left on USSR territory, to accept Soviet citizenship, those who refused were imprisoned, many died, among them military settlers from the eastern borderlands, the Kresy.

I've included Matron Hughes' account in her own words, it describes perfectly the atrocious physical condition of the Polish refugees on their arrival in Tehran and is in complete contradiction to the reports and photographs submitted by the Americans. The refugees had suffered dreadful mistreatment at the hands of the Russians throughout their imprisonment in the labour camps and the OWI staffed by communists, with Roosevelts support, did their utmost with propaganda to present a very different story.

Sanctuary on the Caspian Sea

It was now early summer of 1942 and the family were settling into Camp 1 in Teheran after receiving such a warm welcome from the Persians. They still hadn't had any news about Adam, and so desperately needed him, he and Walery had reported to the Polish army unit in Kermine, the nearest army HQ to Bukhara and he had been posted to Iraq. They only found this out later through Antoni, who had worked so hard to organise their journey from Siberia. Walery had been searching for them through the Red Cross and Antoni reassured them that they would soon meet up.

The day after their arrival in Teheran, Jasia and Alicja went to the hospital to see Kazia. She was very ill, but so happy to see them, her face lit up and she was so relieved to know they were safe. It was a hugely emotional reunion.

Hospitals had opened in Pahlevi and Isfahan with the assistance of the Red Cross and the Polish-American Relief Organisation. Included also were the Queen Alexandra Royal Army Nursing Corps. Acting Principal Matron Lieutenant Colonel Hughes, has documented in her diaries first hand detail of her care and that of her nurses, of the Polish refugees from Russia at the 34th British Commonwealth General Hospital in Teheran.

Five refugee camps had opened in Meshed and Achwaz, as well as hostels for the elderly and an orphanage and community centre. Yes they were all safe, but Kazia and Alicja were very ill. Exhaustion and the sudden change in living conditions caused diseases to break out, primarily dysentery and typhoid, and many people died so close to freedom. Grief touched thousands of people, those they knew and had grown close to on their long journeys, were dying around them. 'One day they seemed to be recovering and the next they had died. It was heart breaking, very hard to accept, people were groaning in pain, others had staring eyes were gasping for breath and others would never breath again.'

Perhaps the sudden calm after so intense a mental pressure and physical hardship had been too much to bear and the body so weak had given out. It was so very sad and it affected everyone hugely. Many hundreds of bodies were to lie in the Dulab cemetery in south Teheran having almost touched freedom. Soon the family had to choose what to do, where to go as the refugees were being moved constantly to make room for others.

Jasia reasoned that because Alicja was so weak after having typhus and yellow jaundice, and Kazia was still in hospital, they should both remain in Teheran and wait with Janusz until they knew more about Adam's movements. They all thought this was perhaps the best idea allowing them time to recover. The rest of the cadets were being sent to Palestine, as were the more able-bodied men and women of military age to prepare for active service with the British forces in Palestine.

So with Jasia on her way to Palestine, Kazia, Janusz and Alicja stayed in Camp 1 in Teheran waiting for news of Adam. Ziuta and Marysia also stayed with them, both recovering from typhus and dysentery, before Marysia too could also join Jasia and the cadets in Palestine. Walery and Włodek had by now joined the forces in Iraq having travelled there from Kermine.

After much liaison with the Red Cross Adam had found out where the family was and reassured that they were safe and recovering from their trauma felt sheer relief. For the time being, recovery from illness was the priority for them all and it wouldn't be until a few weeks later that he would be able to travel to see them on leave from Iraq. For now he relaxed knowing they were safe and being cared for.

The family slowly recovered and regained their strength and looked forward to their reunion with Adam, life was becoming more relaxed and being together helped their recovery. When Adam arrived from Iraq it was a very emotional reunion. He stayed for two weeks and it was wonderful to be together and the family began to breath a little easier. The relief they felt at being free was overwhelming, sometimes they forgot and the tension hit them and they would gasp for air. They were all having difficulty getting used to these new circumstances. There were no guards with barking dogs intimidating them but everyone was still edgy, expecting aggressive orders from Soviet guards. It would take some considerable time for them to adjust, they knew they were free, but it was difficult to believe that freedom was really theirs, the restrictions of the labour camps had left a huge mark on them.

In January 1943, the Soviet Government sent a communique to the Polish Government based in London informing them that all Poles remaining in Russia who had originated from the provinces now under Russian occupation, including the eastern Borderlands my family's homeland, would be considered Soviet subjects. Stalin was determined to hang onto his Polish labour and dominate Poland with communism.

The Russian authorities had offered no assistance whatsoever to the Poles left in the labour camps. Many through age, exhaustion, infirmity or lack of dependents, had been unable to leave, not fit enough to make that most arduous journey to join the Polish army. They were condemned to endless captivity. In Kazakhstan alone 120,000 people can trace their Polish origins and there many survivors remained, often in abject poverty.

Day by day Kazia was slowly recovering and the day of her discharge from hospital arrived. Alicja remembers the day she went to collect her as a very happy one, just being together gave them all confidence, being apart had greatly unsettled them. Kazia, Janusz and Alicja, were in Camp 1, in Teheran for now, but for how long no one knew as the authorities were moving people all the time to make room for those Poles still arriving from Siberia. Many thousands were still making their escape from Siberia towards the Polish Army very many walking the 3,500+ km and very many dying on this perilous trek.

There wasn't enough space for them all in the Teheran camps so after receiving medical attention many refugees were sent to the British colonies, some to India and some to Africa. Many of the orphaned children were sent to Isfahan, further south in Persia where schools were being organised for them. These young children were in such a state of shock, having lost their parents, some their entire families, they were almost comatose. Some had siblings to help them bear the awful situation but many were totally alone in the world. How would they cope with this trauma at such a young age?

Wherever the Poles were sent, schools were immediately organised so that children wouldn't miss too much schooling and they hadn't had any schooling to speak of whilst in the Russian labour camps for the past two years, except for having to learn Russian and being schooled in the communistic ways of their Russian masters. Parents did their best to make sure this didn't happen, reinforcing the Polish ways and identity in the barracks. They were determined their children should remain Polish, and they mostly succeeded.

Kazia and Alicja were recovering well getting quite fit after their illness and Alicja had even put on a little weight and was beginning to feel happier. She had got a job in the camp sewing with Ciocia Ziuta, which was wonderful because she was earning some money and she and Kazia would go to the shops and buy some material to make clothes. They had arrived in Guzar and Pahlevi in rags, without shoes and had been given clothes by the Red Cross but they needed to make their own and to be able to rely on themselves. Working and earning some money would help their confidence greatly.

They heard from Adam, who had been very ill with typhus in Iraq, he sent them a letter and photograph of himself with Jasia, she and the rest of the cadets had stopped there on the way to Palestine and completely by chance, they had found each other whilst wandering around the camps. The family always seemed to be able to find each other when many others only faced disappointment!

Strange and wonderful things did happen whilst the Poles were escaping the Russian labour camps. On one of the trains from Swierdlowsk near the Ural mountains, they had noticed a young girl approach one of the men waiting to get into the wagon. She said "Daddy, is it you?" The man didn't pay any attention, lost in thought, but the girl persisted, and the man then looked and recognised her and burst into tears. They hugged so tightly and she told him that her mother and sisters were further down the line in another wagon. They had been separated many months ago and never thought they would see each other again. Very few families survived as a unit, and this was one very lucky family, as were my own family.

It was now 1943, they had all been found, although not yet all together but they knew where each other was and it seemed like a miracle. They were on the move again as the authorities were more actively sending people to Africa, India and other Commonwealth places for safety until the war was over. Kazia didn't want to go to Africa, she didn't want to go to any of the places they were offered, so she instead chose Isfahan further south in Persia. If they stayed there, they may be able to go back to Poland, she thought?

All their meagre belongings were collected and they made ready for another journey, waiting with many other families at the gates of the camp. They boarded buses which were quite comfortable after the trucks they'd travelled in from Pahlevi to Teheran and the roads were in better condition along the edge of the Great Salt Desert. It was very dry, they didn't see any vegetation, trees or people for very many miles and the villages were very few. It was just desert for most of the 448 kilometres journey and enduring the very high temperature was very difficult.

The journey lasted many hours and they were desperate for food and water. They had stopped along the route at various shelters, hamlets and shacks and had found shelter to rest for a while, but there was no food and very little water. Only occasionally did they see an oasis and took on as much water as they could. The route took them through Varamin, Kashan and Qom and was a very slow journey.

When the buses eventually rolled into Isfahan they were completely taken aback at the beautiful surroundings. Trees and flowers bursting with such vivid colours. Homes were surrounded by very large gardens and they were to spend the night in the courtyard of a large building which they learned later was the palace of the Armenian Bishop.

Next day they were all allocated their living quarters and happily settled in. Many buildings had been made available for the refugees and after a week or two of rest and finding their bearings, Ciocia Ziuta got a job in one of the schools as a carer and Alicja got a job in a hospital, in charge of the stores. She wasn't in this post for long because the manager heard that she had been in the Girl Guides in Poland so he offered her a job as a secretary of all the Scouts and Girl Guides in Isfahan, she had the necessary experience and it was a job she would enjoy.

Of course it was a much better job and as well as a secretary she was also made a Cub leader. She thoroughly enjoyed the job, her Cubs were called Krechowiecy, after Adam and Walery's cavalry regiment. Life was very pleasant in Isfahan, the old capital of Persia, as it was known then. It had once been a major empire with settlements dating back to 4,000 BC, a monarchy ruled by a Shah from 1501 until the 1979 Iranian revolution when Iran became an Islamic Republic.

Time had marched on, it was now 1944 and Kazia, Alicja and Ziuta were all busy and enjoying their jobs and making friends. Janusz was happy at cadet school but Kazia was not very well, the climate was making it very difficult for her, Isfahan was very hot, it was 35 degrees and it didn't agree with her heart condition and the ailments she had succumbed to along the many arduous journeys. She had difficulties breathing and the stress on her heart was beginning to tell, maybe because of the height above sea level.

Adam was soon to be discharged from the army, he had developed a stomach ulcer and hadn't fully recovered from the debilitating typhus and wasn't now considered fit enough for military duty. In the end he was to be discharged as being unfit for service and he was hugely disappointed at his inability to be with the troops to see active service and fight against the Germans, he would at least be able to serve at the military unit.

Like his fellow deportees, he had been able to control his feelings towards his new ally, Russia, although with some difficulty. He had somehow contained the hatred he felt towards the Bolsheviks for invading his country, transporting many hundreds of thousands of his countrymen to Siberia and trying to crush the Polish spirit. In this last case, Stalin had been unsuccessful! Instead, taking the lead from General Anders, all the Poles recruited into the Polish army from the labour camps and gulags, had sworn loyalty to their former captors and like him only wanted to fight the Germans.

In Isfahan there was an Anglo-Polish club where many Poles and British airmen who were stationed there would meet. The Poles had been well fed and clothed by the British Army and were beginning to relax and were ready to enjoy some socialising, especially the younger ones. Film shows were held there with concerts and meetings and one evening at a film show a young airman asked to be introduced to Alicja.

His name was Taffy and he started talking to her about where he lived in Britain although Alicja didn't understand much of what he said, her English wasn't yet that good. He walked her home that evening and she really wasn't very impressed by him. One afternoon Alicja and her friend Irena were in the club with two other airmen and Irena introduced Alicja to them, one was called Harry and the other Bill.

After that initial encounter they met occasionally when Harry and Bill were off duty and they would have a game of cards. The airmen were wireless operators and their job was to send weather reports to the Forces. They also helped Alicja and Irena to learn English and Alicja and Irena

149

continued to socialise with them and the other Poles and Airmen.

Soon it was Christmas 1944 and the family had a very quiet, and reflective one. Their thoughts were of home and Wigilia, which the Poles celebrate on Christmas eve. It is the most important culinary event of the year. At one time dinner consisted of 12 courses, representing the 12 Apostles, but today it is far more modest. Even to think about those 12 courses was too much for their recovering appetites, but mouths watered thinking about the Uszka (little ears) with the barszcz (beetroot soup), fried carp with mushrooms and sauerkraut, gołąbki (cabbage parcels) pierogi, soused herrings and of course the poppy seed roll and cheese cake. It was something else to focus their minds on and look forward to in the future but what wonderful memories. Janusz did manage to barter for a bottle of Zubrówka and they quietly celebrated their freedom.

There was an English mission in Isfahan run by a lady called Mrs Mentle, and she had organised a party for the English airmen with their guests for Twelfth Night. Alicja and friends met at Irena's flat and Taffy had assumed quite wrongly, that Alicja was his girlfriend and that he was taking her to the party, which was a huge surprise to Alicja, but she reluctantly went along with it as the party had been prearranged.

The group arrived at Mrs Mentle's and it was quite a large place with plenty of room for dancing. There was a gramophone and lovely records were playing and couples were dancing, mostly to Glen Miller tunes. Alicja loved dancing and Taffy just sat there, hardly speaking to her and didn't even ask her to dance. She later learned that he couldn't dance and Bill had taken him to another room to teach him a few steps of tango. He was useless, so in the end Bill asked her to dance and they danced together for the rest of the evening. Alicja was never sure where a Lancashire mill lad had learned to tango! But she was pleased as they had a lot of fun and she was beginning to relax. Bill was also more talkative and easier to get on with.

Once the dancing was over, they all started the walk home. Taffy tagged along with them still thinking Alicja was his girlfriend, yet making no effort to talk to her! She was now confused and obviously out of step with the mind of a Welshman! Bill was walking behind them and she thought, 'I'm not walking with this dummy', so she called to ask Bill if he was going the same way and stepped back in line with him and they walked together the rest of the way. The night was so beautiful, a full moon was shining and it was starting to snow lightly, and she'd shaken Taffy off. Bill walked her home and then went on to his station.

She and Bill became quite friendly and met several times at Mrs Mentle's but soon after that he was posted to Teheran. In the meantime Adam was notified that he had to go back to Teheran to join his army unit, and Janusz and Kazia were to go there with him, to Camp 3, which was much better equipped to deal with the many people needing medical assistance. It was a place with many green trees and bushes and a little stream, and this would better suit Kazia's health and she would be nearer to medical aid.

Alicja was still at her post as a secretary in Isfahan when she heard that there was going to be a nursing course in Teheran so she decided to go with the family as Ciocia Ziuta thought they ought to enrol. The course was to be held at the Polish Red Cross HQ and Alicja hoped that Bill would find her. She liked him, he was good company and very loving and attentive.

There was another journey to pack and prepare for and within a few days they were waiting for the transport at the edge of the camp to take them to the station. They travelled by bus through Qom, Kashan and Varamin arriving back in Tehran at Camp 3. It was 1944-45 and the time had gone very quickly for them. They often thought of Poland and their home in Równe but at this stage could not see any way they could ever go back.

Alicja and Ziuta's nursing lessons started shortly afterwards and they were quite enjoying school again. They were informed that when they passed the exams they would be posted to the Middle East, Egypt, Palestine or even Italy. When Kazia found out she wasn't happy with this and she wouldn't hear of it as they had been separated many times already and she couldn't bear another parting, so she persuaded Alicja to take a job as a typist in the camp where they were living. She had already spoken to the Camp Overseer about Alicja and hoped he would be helpful. Jasia was with the cadets and settled and Janusz was at school and Kazia wanted and needed Alicja near to her.

As she had passed a typing course previously when they were in Camp 1 in Tehran she was confident. She went to the Camp Overseer and introduced herself and all she had to do was type a letter of application and she was offered the job. She was quite happy to be a typist in Camp 3 if it meant staying close to Kazia, and not put any unnecessary burden on her, her Mother needed her support and she reluctantly gave up the nursing course.

While she had been on the nurse's course Bill had been looking for her in Isfahan, as she hadn't let him know where she had moved to and he had to look for her over a huge area that was Persia but in the end quite easily found out where the family had moved to from the Red Cross.

Adam, who had just re-joined his army unit in Teheran, was informed that he now had to go to Egypt to be formally discharged. All this would take time and they knew they would all be leaving Teheran fairly soon for a journey to Lebanon and another refugee camp. 'We were being moved all the time but we never knew when or where to.' It was quite unsettling but they were at least being looked after well for which they were so grateful.

The authorities had a massive job on their hands with all the refugees still coming through to Pahlevi from the USSR labour camps. Room had to be made for all those who were arriving in such great numbers and the medical stations were almost overwhelmed. Those people would need the care and medical help that the family had been given to recover from the horrendous situation they had been forced into.

The Polish representatives had witnessed terrible sights alighting the boats in Pahlevi, 'skeletons covered in rags, feet wrapped in newspaper or dirty cloth tied with string and many were barefoot. Their eyes sunken and completely lifeless or glowing feverishly. People had been almost dying on their feet, they were so emaciated, only skin and bone filthy and crawling with lice, trying to hold each other up' and so very determined to see it through to Pahlevi away from the Soviets. There were many deaths, mainly from dysentery and typhoid.

In the meantime everyone in the family was occupied, Kazia now recovered had a little job sewing, Alicja was typing and Janusz went to his school lessons and Ziuta was working in one of the hospitals. They had acquired a dog they called Ass and were living in tents and they knew they would soon be on the move again. Events always moved fairly quickly, there was never enough time given, not much warning, just time to pack and wait for the next transport to the next camp, which they heard would be in Beirut in Lebanon.

Alicja & Kazia – Isfahan c1943   *Jasia & Adam – Palestine c1943*

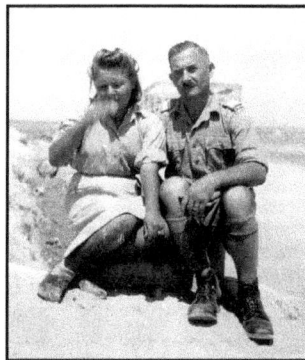

CHAPTER 8

A New Life

It's 1945 and the family had learned of their next destination and from Teheran where they had been since early 1943 they had to pack quickly and immediately move all the way to Beirut in Lebanon, a journey of around 1,800 km. Firstly by train from Teheran to Arak, staying overnight, then by army lorries to a camp in Baghdad where they stayed only for a few days as the intention was to move them on to the next destination without too much delay. Before they were moved from Teheran, Bill had to leave for Iraq but before he left he had asked Alicja to marry him. He must already have asked her half a dozen times and each time she had said no. At that time she had seven 'boyfriends,' just friends really that she had met in the different camps on their travels, all of them in the forces in Palestine, Egypt and Iraq. Each one of them was writing letters to her and they were all Polish.

You can imagine her predicament. She was seeing Bill, an Englishman, so very loving, declaring his love for her and refusing to take no for an answer. She continually said no because she couldn't bear to leave Kazia. After so many separations and such hardships she would find it extremely difficult. She was only 21 and trying very hard to adapt to a new and very different life and also trying to absorb all that had happened to them.

The next time Bill asked her to marry him they were having a day out in the mountains at Demavent, where the Shah of Persia had his summer residence. It was Bill's last day in Teheran and it was a beautiful day. They had their favourite place to sit, a tree stump by a little stream and it was a very calm place and so peaceful, they sat listening to the sounds of the stream which was slowly running by and watched the sun and the shadows shimmer on the water. It was very romantic and Alicja felt it was an ideal place for a proposal. As they sat there, Bill was telling of his love for her, asking her to marry him again because he knew he would have to leave Teheran with the RAF very soon. He didn't know when or where he would be posted to and he was anxious for an answer, the right one!

Alicja had slowly stopped writing to her other 'boyfriends' and had continued seeing Bill, and on this his last day of leave in Teheran, she finally said yes, she would marry him, he loved her so much. But was she doing the right thing? She had wanted to say yes, but there was so much else to think of, her family and their future was still so unsettled, they had been reunited for such a short time and she would have to leave for England and they would have to stay behind.

Bill left Teheran a much happier man as he headed off with all the other airmen for Habbaniyah in Iraq. Alicja missed him after he left, but he wrote every day and as soon as he got to his camp in Habbaniyah, he wasted no time in applying to the RAF authorities for permission to marry her. The Lancashire lad who could tango had claimed his girl and wanted to make her officially his without delay!

It was going to take a long time for the formalities to be arranged and agreed and in the meantime they were getting on with life and preparing for more travels. They were used to packing up by now and were ready for the transport for the next stage. It was a long journey but they were by now fairly well recovered. The Red Cross had to make room for the other refugees coming into the country from Siberia and were moving many of those who had recovered and able to journey onto other areas. They were taken to the main station in Persia for the first leg to Arak and then by large army lorries to Baghdad. From Baghdad the journey continued on by train moving towards Lebanon and crossing the Turkey-Syria border to reach Aleppo in Syria. It wasn't very safe for them to be transported at that time because there was much unrest in those countries. British and French troops were in Syria in May 1945 at the time of the Levant crisis where there were nationalist protests against French occupation which was opposed by Churchill. He sent in British troops and a ceasefire was enforced, the French withdrew and Syria gained full independence. The family eventually got through the borders after some delay in sorting out the papers and permission to cross.

Aleppo was the second city of Syria, today the scene of civil unrest between President Assad and rebel forces, a civil war raging. There have been many previous conflicts with the Syrians, against the Persians, Greeks and Romans until Arab Islamic conquest in 636 AD. Since the 3rd millennium BC Aleppo was a flourishing city, a meeting point of many commercial routes in the north. A centre of trade with France, Turkey, England and Holland, it now lies mostly in ruins, bombarded by heavy weaponry, the ancient mosque and minaret devastated by artillery.

When they reached Aleppo British soldiers were waiting with hot drinks, for which they were extremely grateful as they hadn't had anything to drink for 24 hours. There were also Polish soldiers in British uniforms looking happy and confident, it was so reassuring to see them. They had waited for them despite the delays until the middle of the night. In Aleppo they had to transfer from the passenger train to the goods train for some reason, and this was to be the last part of their journey. They spent a nervous night in Aleppo, very much aware of the unrest but knowing there were British soldiers on hand to protect them they were reassured.

From Aleppo all the Poles were allocated different places which meant separations from newly made friends. Alicja, Kazia and Janusz were to go to a house in a village on the top of a mountain, it was beautiful, right by the Mediterranean in a village called Ghazir, just outside Beirut. It was lovely, but Kazia wouldn't be able to make the walk up and down the mountain, her health was still so precarious but they would have to manage for the time being.

It was nearly Christmas 1945 and Adam was now officially demobbed and was coming to join them. Jasia was coming from Palestine and Bill had got leave and he still had to officially ask Adam for Alicja's hand in marriage. When Bill and Alicja were apart waiting for official permission to be married he wrote her countless letters, sometimes two a day, and she still has them. It was going to be a very memorable Christmas, as it was their first together as a family for three years. It was to be a quiet Christmas though, as they were still unsettled and unsure of the future. After Christmas Bill would have to go back to Iraq and Jasia to Palestine, where she was at teacher training college and was also still a cadet, but for the moment it was a happy time and they were able to celebrate.

Lebanon was a beautiful country. The name means white, a reference to the snow-capped Mount Lebanon, its beauty took everyone's breath away. The youngsters would walk along the Serpentine to the sea coming back up the steep incline with the cedars in the background, it was rather exhausting but they were young and enjoyed it, they had physically recovered well.

Bill had got permission from Adam to marry Alicja, although her parents did have their doubts, it was now a matter of waiting for permission from the RAF and also from the Archbishop of the Catholic Church to be married in a Catholic church. This was necessary because Bill wasn't a Catholic at that time, so they had to wait for the necessary authorisations.

It wasn't until many years later that Alicja realised the historical importance of the countries they had journeyed through, there were many other things to think about and her concentration then was purely on getting through one day at a time! Whilst she had appreciated the beauty and the wonder she had not been aware of the significance. They had set foot on some of the oldest continuously-inhabited cities in the world, dating back to earlier than 5,000 BC. A once in a lifetime holiday in better times.

Bill was still writing her two or even three letters every day, keeping her up to date, she though wasn't a very good letter writer, so didn't write to him as often. How he found the time to write so many during such times!

Soon after Christmas Adam had asked permission from the authorities to move them from the house on the mountain to nearer the Serpentine because Kazia was having terrible difficulty walking to the shops and church. In the meantime Alicja was the main shopper, the 'little donkey' bringing the shopping home and caring for her mother Kazia.

Within a short time they were offered a place with an Arab family and Kazia was much happier because walking to the shops was much easier and she didn't feel so isolated. Her heart condition was so bad she had difficulty breathing, and walking any distance especially uphill wasn't helping her. That Kazia had survived so far was a wonder, she had incredible strength of mind and tremendous will. My Babcia Kazia has been my inspiration, my muse, she has left an amazing impression on me and I had to record her and the family's story. I also inherited her sense of humour which had served her so well during a horrendous time.

It was now 1946 and they were looking forward to planning the wedding. As Bill's parents were in England they were not able to come; it would have been impossible for them to travel. Bill eventually got permission from the RAF to be married and they also had approval from the Archbishop to be married in a Catholic church. This all took about six months, but the time flew by.

Now it was time to arrange the date and the Polish priest who was to marry them arranged the ceremony for the 9th July. Kazia and Alicja went to Beirut to get some material for her wedding dress. It was very lovely heavy crepe, which the tailor would make into a most beautiful gown designed by Kazia, who had trained in Warsaw as a tailor in her teens after WW1.

Bill's parents had made their intentions clear to him, they were not happy he was marrying a 'foreigner' and a Catholic and would not give their blessing to the marriage. Kazia and Adam, although liking Bill, weren't sure about him either feeling they hadn't known him long enough. They also weren't happy about it being a 'mixed' marriage, but especially concerned that Alicja would move to England. The family had not long been reunited, their futures so uncertain, they had no idea where they were to be sent next? Back to Poland under Communism and possible arrest? It was a huge concern to them.

The Poles in the Middle East would eventually be given the choice by the authorities of settling in England, America or Africa or going back to Poland. Like many thousands of other families mine had lost absolutely everything in their homeland, there was nothing to go back to. My Dziadek Adam and Wujek Walery feared that they would be arrested again by the Soviets having fought in the 1920 Polish-Russian war against them, the

Russians never forget, their record keeping and memory being meticulous and a score to settle top of the list.

Not many years later it became known to the family that former military deportees, especially from the eastern borderlands and servicemen who had returned to Poland were treated extremely harshly by the Soviet dictatorship in post-war Poland. Without trial, many were imprisoned either on trumped-up charges as spies or 'enemies of the people' and sent to gulags, some just disappeared and others were executed, as in the case of Witold Pilecki, a Polish war hero who was an embarrassment to the Soviets.

Alicja's parents, although uncertain about the marriage gave their blessing to the wedding and Alicja was busy learning English as communication was still a little difficult. Despite all reservations the wedding was set for the 9th July at 6pm and Alicja seemed in a state of bewilderment. She was seeing everything through a very thick fog and it just didn't seem real, so much had happened over such a short time for her to absorb.

Jasia and their cousin Marysia, also a cadet, were coming from Palestine and preparations were going well but as the date approached the priest informed them that the wedding would have to be on July 10th instead. The wedding rings had been engraved for the 9th, so they had to stay like that although that wasn't important.

Two days before the wedding Bill and his best man Eric arrived from Habbaniya and Jasia and Marysia arrived the same day from Palestine. Two of Alicja's best friends were present, Nusia and Irena. Walery and Włodek were in Iraq with the British forces and weren't able to get leave to be with them for the day of the ceremony and Ziuta was with them and couldn't attend either.

The day of the wedding came, lovely, hot and sunny. Whilst waiting to go to the church, the family and their guests sat under the lemon trees and grapevines on the terrace at the house they had rented. They were excited but also a bit nervous, Alicja's parents hadn't envisaged their daughter marrying in the Middle East but in a small church in Poland! It wasn't a big wedding as it might have been back home, a fairly big event with lots of family but it would be one to remember in a most beautiful country.

All the Polish refugees were being supported by money from the Polish authorities to cover their living needs and had income from jobs they had. They didn't have much, having lost everything, the Osada in the country and the apartment in Równe, the Russians and Ukrainians having taken all their possessions. 'Friends' and families of the NKVD had not wasted time moving in. But they were free, and it was such a lovely day although they sometimes couldn't help but think of what they had lost.

There were about 20 of them in the party. Alicja's friend Irena, was her maid of honour and dressed her to be ready at the church for 6pm. When Bill came to the house to meet them he was quite nervous, it was so different for him coming into a foreign family and their customs, although he liked the family very much, he felt a bit lost but he did look very smart in his RAF uniform.

It was only a short walk to the church, and it was a beautiful evening in Ghazir when Bill and Alicja walked slowly up the hill towards the church. She was carrying flowers and holding onto that calmness, she was only 22 and Bill, who was 26, was stricken with nerves. They chatted, and then entered the church. Alicja thought there would only be her friends there, she hadn't wanted a big wedding but she was quite popular within the Polish community and was also in the church choir, so word had got round and everyone seemed to know about her wedding.

The church was full, mostly with Poles from all the different refugee camps they had been in, friends from Persia, army personnel. There were also Arabs from the village who had heard that a Polish girl was getting married and were curious about a European wedding. It was a wonderful surprise, and she was so happy. Bill was still very nervous, yet surprisingly Alicja now seemed quite calm as they stood together with Adam for their wedding vows.

They were married in a French church, by a Polish priest, in an Arab village, Ghazir, not far from Beirut. When they came out of the church Janusz took photographs, some of them showing her parents looking quite serious. It was early evening and warm and they walked the short distance home meeting Kazia and Adam on the doorstep welcoming the newly-married couple home with bread and salt, as is the Polish custom. The guests arrived soon afterwards and they had a drink, probably a very generous shot of wódka if Janusz was pouring and some wine. It wasn't a lavish wedding, but supper was delicious. In later years at each special occasion or get together, they always called Janusz's shots of wódka, a 'Polish measure.' Janusz had a very good arm! And this talent seems to run right through the family.

With the help of Jasia I've been able to put together a few details of the wedding supper. Alicja also recalled that Kazia cooked everything on two primus stoves, very primitive, but there was nothing else. They had very little to their name, but were in a very safe haven, and of course they had each other and they held on tightly to that.

How Kazia was able to prepare such a wonderful feast was a lovely surprise but she had always been so resourceful. There was barszcz (beetroot soup), mushroom pierogi, (meat parcels), herrings with apples, beetroot salad, fried chicken, meat loaf with stuffed eggs and rice, meat balls and rice, mizeria (cucumber salad & soured cream) gherkins, olives, pitta bread, pancakes and oranges, dates and grapes. Most of which the family enjoy to this day.

She must have sold her soul, what a banquet! And what a wonderful recovered memory. It had taken a few phone calls with Ciocia Jasia but we had got the wedding menu in the end. They would have had something very similar back home in Poland.

Although it was a happy occasion the wedding photographs show everyone in a very serious mood, under the surface they were still feeling the effects of their experience in Russia, and would suffer flashbacks for many years to come. The family was to be separated yet again as Alicja was going to England with Bill, and this was heavy on her parents' minds. It was very difficult to hide their worries.

Later in the evening when most of the guests had left, Bill and Alicja danced on the terrace under the vines and stars, to some lovely music, mostly tango. It was a reflective, quiet moment, but there was a slight problem – they had no bed for the night. The Arab landlord had double-booked their room and there was only one other room for the whole family. They didn't find out about the double booking until later in the evening so it was impossible to make other arrangements. That night Bill slept on the roof garden with Adam, Eric and Janusz and Alicja slept downstairs with her sister, Marysia and Kazia. So their wedding night was a little different, but still memorable!

They were happy and it didn't really matter as it was such a minor thing in the circumstances. After that they made other arrangements and it was only for a few nights after all. Bill was then taken ill with papadach a tropical disease with a very high fever and was due to go back to Habbaniyah. So only a week after the wedding they were to be separated. With Bill and Eric his best man, back on duty Alicja was left without her husband, she was however with Kazia, Adam and Janusz, her sister Jasia and cousin Marysia had gone back to Palestine to the cadets.

Soon after the family moved house again, nearer the centre of Ghazir, closer still for Kazia to get to the shops and church. The family lived quietly, shopped and saw friends and waited for their future to be decided. Bill continued writing wonderful letters that kept Alicja going. He had to wait for all RAF formalities to be completed for taking her to England as his wife, and they had to cover quite a lot of officialdom before that happened. Alicja was feeling very guilty, sad and apprehensive about leaving her family and also very anxious about what to expect in England, meeting Bill's family, it was almost too much for her.

At last in October, Bill came to collect her, all formalities now concluded. He stayed overnight and the following day they would leave for Cairo. She packed her suitcase and had to say goodbye to her family. It was very, very hard because she didn't know if she would ever see them again. They all cried, it was heart breaking and her parents were distraught. It was an incredibly sad goodbye. She never knew how she managed to leave them. She and Bill reassured them that they would do all they could to help them to get to England but it didn't stop the tears, they were desolate.

Bill and Alicja travelled from Ghazir by taxi to Beirut and from there took another taxi to Haifa where they stayed overnight at the YMCA. Next day they took a taxi and then a train to Jerusalem, where they stayed for two days and were able to see something of the city. They didn't see very much or stay very long because of the rebellion, with terrible unrest at the time and they couldn't move around freely and Bill had to report to camp. They left Jerusalem heading for Cairo by train, which was a very long journey and although they were very newly-wed their start to married life wasn't very romantic. The journeys they had to take were long and uncomfortable, over 250 km so far and it was all very tiring, with trouble spots along the way. Alicja was also so sad missing her parents, knowing they were inconsolable after losing her so soon after their reunion following the trauma and hardship of Russia.

After a journey to Cairo of 280 km they took a taxi to the hotel, the Hermitage House, and at last they could rest on a comfortable bed. After their rest they took a shower and went down to the dining room to have something to eat. It was lovely food, and it was the first time they had eaten fresh dates from the tree. They spent six lovely weeks in Cairo at the expense of the RAF, waiting for a boat to take them to England as Alicja wouldn't fly, she was still in such an anxious state.

It was very hot during the day, so they went out in the evenings to open-air cinemas or to the Gropis café in Cairo, where they danced among the palm trees in the gardens, getting back to the hotel in the early hours of the morning. They had to be cautious because of the tensions in the Middle East at that time, it was quite frightening as troops were on the streets in large numbers, on high alert, and they could feel the anxiety in the ordinary people. Tensions had escalated after the bombing in July of the King David

Hotel, which was the administrative HQ for the British forces in Palestine. The Irgun, a militant Zionist movement were apparently responsible.

This had been in response to a raid on the Jewish Agency by the British authorities on Black Sabbath. The British had confiscated incriminating information about the Jewish Agency's involvement with violent acts and this information had been taken to the King David Hotel. The Irgun were determined to destroy this information and planted explosives in milk churns in the basement. To avoid suspicion they had dressed mostly as Arabs and the guards were easily overcome. The explosion caused the collapse of the southern wing of the hotel, causing many deaths and injuries to those who were in the road outside. Despite this state of unrest Alicja and Bill made the most of their extended honeymoon.

Thoughts of a survivor

Jan Wojcik, a well known journalist and the 'Voice of Solidarność,' during his last broadcast on Radio, said: "I was forced to leave half a century ago and it is where I left that most essential part of my being, "my heart. Poland is inside me". After 50 years of wandering he went back to his birthplace, Volhynia.

"There had been a delightfully developed Osada in which had stood my home, surrounded by a garden and fertile fields" he wrote. "Nothing, but nothing, remained of any of this. Everything had been razed to the ground. Even trees and forests had been put to the torch so that no one could ever recognise his roots, and wouldn't dare put a claim to it."

They craved the very roots,
Desired the furrows groove swallow the top soil deep
So that nothing, no surface remained,
No linking with the past –
No past – no history of her and of this nation
Whose prediluvian line was nurtured here
Through countless generations.
They sought to smooth over the marks, The tiniest traces of dust.
Disfigured, drove, dispelled,
Divided the heart from the head. But one granule they quite overlooked, The grit of the Land itself
– *Feliks Konarsk*

My cousin Marek Skocyzlas, son of Alicja's cousin Marysia, made a claim in his Grandfather Walery's name for the return of the lands of his Osada, but was unsuccessful.

Married life began with a mixture of conflicting memories and yet more unrest, but Alicja and Bill knew it would only get easier from here on and were looking forward to married life. Tensions would however be fraught in the early days in England.

Sunny Beirut to foggy Blackpool

At the beginning of November 1946 Alicja and Bill were to journey to Port Said to board the ship Durban Castle which was bound for England, it was a passenger ship converted into an army carrier. They left Cairo by train for a journey of over 200 km travelling alongside the Suez Canal. When they arrived in Port Said in the early evening of 1st November, Alicja saw in the distance a very big ship anchored some way from the shore, and while they were waiting for their papers to be checked, she wondered how they were going to reach it and get on board. It was such a long way out and she was beginning to feel very nervous. It was already dark when the time came to board the ship and they were told by the sailors that they would have to walk on pontoons all the way up to it. The military and their wives were lined up in their hundreds, the women very wary and mostly young brides of the English servicemen.

The group started to walk towards the pontoons and stepped on, putting one foot in front of the other very carefully, not daring to look between the gaps. When they got to the end of the pontoons which seemed to take for ever and was very difficult to stay on as it wobbled so much, they had to climb up ladders on the side of the ship and seeing the waves lapping between the ladders and the pontoon was very frightening. All this was happening in the dark and although the ship was lit up to give them some light to see where they were putting their feet, it was moving all the time, even while they were boarding the steps and they were all very relieved to eventually reach the deck.

There were hundreds of people on board, many of the newly married included women from Greece, Egypt and Poland and other Europeans and their military husbands. Everyone was allocated cabins, and Alicja was to share one with two other military wives. Their husbands were in separate cabins and had to sleep in hammocks. Alicja saw Bill only on deck during the day as they couldn't even have meals together. All the Servicemen were down below deck and were only allowed to see their wives during the day on the decks. The journey was terrible, it lasted nine days, and throughout all that time Alicja was seasick and couldn't eat anything. Every time she walked into the dining room and saw the waves through the portholes she immediately had to go back to the cabin, she just couldn't face any food and Bill fed her on dry cream crackers when they met on deck. It was a horrible voyage, very miserable, nothing but the high seas all around them. Alicja wished she'd never come, and there was no way of getting off. It seemed a very stormy crossing to her, although Bill thought it was calm! Perhaps if they had been together it would have been easier to bear.

Six years after that day in February 1940 when her life had changed forever, she was going into the unknown without her parents travelling to yet another country not knowing what to expect. She would be meeting Bill's parents and wondered what they would be like, it was all very difficult to deal with on her own. She was still only 22 and desperately missing the family. On the last day of the voyage she felt the ship stopping and she looked through the porthole to see land, green grass and trees. 'You can't imagine my joy to know that I would be able to put my feet on firm ground again'. Alicja thinks she had breakfast that morning, but doesn't really remember, she was too happy realising she was to be on land again.

They left the ship that morning, November 9th 1946, and Bill was with her when they disembarked at Southampton. After they had collected their luggage they went to a little café and for the first time in her life (but not the last) she had English fish and chips, which were delicious after all that time at sea. It was her first big meal since Cairo not having had very much to eat on board the ship and it was so tasty. Mum would always enjoy fish and chips.

They now had to take the train to Blackpool in the North of England, via London and travelled almost all night arriving at Blackpool North Station at 5am in the dark, in a very thick, cold fog. Alicja had never seen anything like it. It was so depressing, unwelcoming, grey and damp and she thought to herself that she would have gone back if she could and what a contrast to the beautiful countries she had just left. They took a taxi to Bill's parents' house, and arrived in the dark. A tall, white-haired woman, his mother Alice, opened the door and Alicja thought, 'she looks nice, I think I'll be happy here.' She embraced Bill, the son she hadn't seen for five years, and Alicja was just standing there in the hall waiting whilst they hugged before Bill introduced her. Alice just said hello and that was all, there was no welcome for their son's wife, no embrace, no friendliness, no warmth on her part. Alicja was away from her own parents, missing love and warmth in a strange country, just a young woman but there was very little welcome for her and she'd had such hopes. It was decided fairly amicably and after the children were born, that it would be better for William to find them a separate dwelling and Alicja was to stay in London whilst he looked.

Alicja was with her sister in London for several weeks before Bill found a house for them, he had worked very hard to find somewhere as he wanted his family back as soon as possible. She came back from London with the children and they moved into their new home in Lytham St Annes and they couldn't have been happier. It was heaven being on their own with their two babies, they didn't have much furniture but they were happy. There was a cooker and Alicja could cook some nice meals, they had somewhere to sleep, there was a garden, she had a very loving husband and knew that together, they would get on with life and work towards their future.

All was not milk and honey in this new land, there were many difficulties to deal with and it was hard to adapt to a very different life, mixing with people when shopping for essentials for example, trying to converse in English, which Alicja still wasn't very good at. People weren't openly hostile towards her but nor were they very welcoming, just accepting of the situation. The Government had written to all the Polish servicemen (1946) in Britain advising them to go home to Poland, seemingly not knowing of the reception and the reprisals their allies would face from the Soviet dictatorship! The Unions were also hostile, making it extremely difficult for Poles to get any work despite the country being in a state of devastation and in need of labour to help with rebuilding!

The English also had to adjust to a different life. After a devastating war they had to learn to deal with people of many nationalities now living amongst them. It was a learning experience for them all. Many refugees would find it extremely difficult after arriving in England, alone, still in a state of shock and perhaps bereft of hope, they would search crowds for any sign of the family they'd lost in their exodus from Russia, scrutinising faces in churches, shops, on the bus and the street for any recognition of family or friends, hoping to be reunited with just one familiar face. They would search for many years.

As the years have gone by I have realised from growing up with my amazing Polish family just how very badly they have been treated, by both Stalin and the Western allies. It has made me quite angry, especially since their treatment has been ignored from 1940 to this day. I've used my displeasure proactively to try and bring my family story to light and hope that they and the many hundreds of thousands of other Poles deported by Stalin to Siberia, get their deserved recognition one day.

CHAPTER 9

Family Reunited

Stalin had achieved his aim, he had taken Poland and tens of thousands of veteran Polish troops lost their homes in the Kresy and other regions of Poland to the Soviet Union. This would have an effect on many of the service men, their relatives, wives and children, spread across the landscape of the war and those left at the mercy of the NKVD in Poland.

Churchill explained his actions at Yalta in a 3 day Parliamentary debate beginning on 27th February 1945 which ended with a vote of confidence. He was openly criticised and MPs strongly voiced loyalty to Britain's Polish allies, with 25 MPs drafting an amendment protesting against Britain's tacit acceptance of Poland's domination by the Soviet Union. The amendment failed and one MP resigned his seat in protest at the British treatment of Poland.

Churchill did however say that '…His Majesty's Government will never forget the debt they owe to the Polish troops and I earnestly hope it will be possible for them to have citizenship and freedom of the British Empire if they so desire. We should think it an honour to have such faithful and valiant warriors dwelling amongst us as if they were men from our own blood' (Sword, Davies and Ciechanowski 1989) This became known as Churchill's pledge, it caused concern in the Foreign Office and came across to the Polish allies as empty words, which they turned out to be!

In July 1945 Churchill and the Conservatives unexpectedly lost office to the Labour Party led by Attlee, the British people choosing the path of Socialism. The editor of the Daily Worker couldn't help himself by crowing that the Communist Party had eight 'cryptos' (informants) among the huge influx of new labour MPs. The balance of opinion within the Labour Party and the Left towards Poles and the Polish question was now very different. Although Attlee did eventually expel some of these 'lost sheep' from the Party, it was more pro Soviet than the anti Bolshevik Churchill and was much less favourable towards the exiled and displaced Poles.

Nothing better represents this attitude than the shameful exclusion of the Polish Forces from the Victory Europe Parade in May 1946. In fact there were strong feelings within the Labour Party and their Trade Union paymasters that as few Poles as possible should remain in Britain and that everything should be done to ensure their removal, including negotiation with the Commonwealth countries. Attlee had tried to re-interpret Churchill's pledge as having been merely an aspiration!

The Polish Government in exile had moved from Paris to London in 1940 and the British Government, press and the community had been largely sympathetic to the plight of the Polish people. However, in 1941 when Germany invaded the USSR and Stalin was forced to switch his allegiance to the Western Allies British-Polish relations were badly affected.

The British Labour Government wanted to maintain cordial relations with Stalin and ignored the Poles' outstanding war effort, their loss of land and belongings, population and family and tried to persuade the Poles in the UK to return to their homeland. Most Poles quite rightly felt betrayed and refused to return to Poland for a number of reasons, Soviet repression of their citizens in particular.

My Dziadek Adam and Wujek Walery could not return to their homes in the Kresy. It wasn't safe to do so, they had fought and won against the Bolsheviks in 1920 and for this reason alone they would have been sent back to Siberia, or worse. It was Stalin's reason for deporting the peoples of the Kresy in the first place! To return to Poland as ex military men meant practically committing suicide, they would be special targets for the NKVD, as 'potential nationalistic organisers/agitators', accused of spying and jailed. They would be prosecuted in phoney trials and even murdered, as many returnees were. Word had began to trickle to the Poles in England from their relatives, of the fate of those who had taken the risk to return home.

The London Poles began to get a bad press inspired by the barely suppressed pro-Stalinism of many Left liberal intellectuals and Trade Union activists. The Daily Worker, the British Communist Party's newspaper (later the Morning Star) called the Poles 'Fascist Reactionaries', 'landlords' and 'Jew baiters'. Words such as 'unrealistic', 'intransigent' and 'unrepresentative' began to be used by the Left. Pro-Soviet propaganda was increasingly written by sections of the press and accusations of right wing fanaticism against the Poles began, including organised marches against them by the Left. A hostile attitude the Poles were to endure for some considerable time!

The Unions were very open to Soviet ideology and an easier target for the KGB than the Labour Left Wing were, as they had the real power within the Labour Party being their paymasters. Jack Jones, leader of the TGWU the most powerful Trade Unionist and a hero of his day, was a paid up 'useful idiot' of the KGB who would rope in anyone who would be of potential help to their cause and the lure of post Soviet ideology is still strong within the Labour party front bench to this day, Corbyn, MacDonald, Abbott and others.

The Polish contribution to the war effort had been outstanding, they had formed the fourth largest Allied force in Europe and were the largest non British group in the Battle of Britain, yet despite being on the winning side the Poles saw themselves being as severely treated as defeated Germany. The loss of the eastern borderlands, the Kresy, was a huge blow to many Poles mostly from those 'lost territories' of the east.

They had been forcibly exiled and it wasn't safe to return, as a consequence the total number of Poles including soldiers and their dependants who arrived in the U.K. through the process of forced migration is estimated at 200,000. My grandparents Kazia and Adam like those other 'displaced' Poles, considered the Communist regime too dangerous to return to and we grandchildren were very lucky to be able to grow up alongside them embraced in their love and Polish traditions.

The Polish troops became an unwanted post war expense for a British Government feeling the financial strain of the post war economy. It became a regular subject in the House of Commons during 1946 and on 20th March the Sec of State for Foreign Affairs Ernest Bevan acknowledged the Polish achievements, 'as a major ally in the field, Monte Cassino and the Battle of Britain, Squadron 303 with the most kills and instrumental in cracking the enigma code ………'

And said further, 'I feel sure that the House would wish me to pay tribute to the magnificent services which these forces as one of our first allies in the late war, have rendered to the common cause throughout the whole long struggle. His Majesty's Government and I am sure the whole House are conscious of their debt to these men and are determined to deal justly by them.'

He also said, 'While we will not use force to compel these men to return to Poland, I have never disguised our firm conviction that in our view they ought to go back in order to play their part in the reconstruction of their stricken country.' How very noble, 48,000 Polish military died for the allies and freedom!

And that the British Government considered it was the '…duty of all members of those Polish forces to decide how to return to their own country.' Words spoken by another of Stalin's idiots!   This was in complete disregard to the complexities of any returning Polish citizen to Stalin's terror and revenge which the British Government was aware of, but they were in thrall to Stalin and his ideology and musn't upset him!

Bevan, later in reply to Anthony Eden regarding the future of Poles in Britain, said 'We are extremely anxious that the Polish troops should return to their own country, subject to that we cannot relieve ourselves of responsibility for those who feel in their conscience that they cannot go back.'

Those Poles who had been exiled to Siberia, berween 1940-1942 were in danger if they were sent back, many of them had already been assigned as 'enemies of the people' by Stalin for their fight against the Bolsheviks in 1920, there was no free Poland to return to. The Commonwealth countries were far more obliging to the Polish troops and Polish refugees than the country the Poles had fought on behalf of. One of the last directives from Bevan in relation to the Polish troops was 'speaking on behalf of the British Government I declare that this is in the best interests of Poland that you should return to her now...' what gratitude.

There were Polish troops still in Italy, having taken Monte Cassino and in Northern Europe, the military cadets were in the middle east and the majority of these Polish troops were not convinced. Having been deported by Stalin in 1940, fighting with Stalin and the Allies from 1941 they were now in the hands of ungrateful allies, communist MPs and Unions.

The problem of registration, supervision and settlement of the Poles imposed a great burden on the Aliens Branch of the Home Office and Police Forces throughout the U.K. In the end the Government passed the Polish Resettlement Act of 1947 which provided 'certain Polish Forces' with an Assistant Board to meet their needs.

My Grandparents Kazia and Adam and the family of Wujek Walery were housed in Resettlement camps, Pulborough in Sussex being just one of several. Most of the accommodation was in military units in 170 camps all over Britain, many in airfields vacated by British and American troops.

Polish Pharmacists and Doctors were given temporary registration to practice in Britain. These measures identified the Poles as a special case which caused ill feeling not only in the Government but in the wider public domain. Large numbers of Poles, after occupying resettlement camps of the Polish Resettlement Corps, later settled in London and industrial areas of the north. Many were recruited as European Volunteer workers others settled in the British Empire, forming large Polish communities in Canada, Africa and Australia. Some also settled in Mexico and the US

I didn't understand why my family had little respect for Churchill and Attlee and the post war Labour government. My Ciocia Jasia filled me in when I was about 16, telling me about the secret deal in Teheran, then Yalta, the V.E. day celebrations and the efforts to send the Poles back to a Communist state. The underhand ways of the Unions to block Poles working here and I also did some research and I realised why they felt this way.

I understood completely why most Poles had little respect for the post war politicians and government, I understood the huge injustice felt by them. The Polish had been betrayed not once or twice, but several times and I can only describe that as shameful. The fact that the deportations in particular are still ignored and many Polish achievements glossed over, condemns the British establishment. They betrayed their Polish allies and ignored their many sacrifices for this country.

The vast majority of Poles in the U.K. and across Europe post war had rejected their homeland under the Soviet puppet state and Communism. They chose to remain in the West where they could continue the political struggle for an independent Poland whilst maintaining their language, culture and traditions. My Grandparents missed their homeland dreadfully and thought they might return one day but their family was now in England and they made their lives here.

The Polish Re-settlement Act of 1947 was the first ever mass immigration legislation offering British citizenship to over 200,000 displaced Polish troops, it also supplied a labour force to meet the demands of a war-torn Britain as there was a lack of manpower for mines and agriculture. However, the Trade Unions agitated for Government legislation to forbid employers from taking on Polish workers. 'Foreign labour can only be employed when no British labour is available and willing to work' so jobs remained vacant and a ready workforce unused!

Jack Jones was a full time District Secretary in the Coventry TGWU branch overseeing union organisation during WW2 and according to KGB files he was 'first cultivated by the Soviet Union as an agent in the aftermath of the Spanish Civil War'. Given the code name Drim (Dream) the 'agent' enjoyed Soviet contributions towards his 'holiday expenses' and he was regarded by the KGB as a 'very disciplined and useful agent'.

His influence and that of the other communist Trade Union leaders would have a large impact on the jobs market post WW2. Labour had sold out the Poles just as Churchill and Roosevelt had. They had been determined not to let the 'Polish problem' get in the way of their partnership with Stalin. The 'Polish problem' so reminiscent of Stalin's NKVD Order 00485 back in 1937, on the 'Polish Operation 'signed off by Nikolai Yezhov in the period of the Great Purge.

Members of the public wrote to their MPs complaining about the Poles. 'It is time they were back in Poland, I am sure you will act sensibly and order them to return.' What a contrast to Churchill's rhetoric in the House of Commons, his pledge to the Polish people that 'his Majesties Government will never forget the debt.'

The Polish refugees would have an enormous job on their hands to find work and generally fit into a post war England. They had the Unions and the Civil Service to contend with from the beginning. Numerous organisations and Politicians, local and national, were keen to repatriate the Poles as soon as possible and forced repatriation was used in some cases despite knowing what was happening in Poland under the harsh Soviet regime. No-one returning did so without consequences.

Many Poles did go back only to be branded as traitors and their fate would be death or imprisonment, back to the gulag or labour camp. Those for whom homesickness was a huge motivator to go back were never heard from, there were no letters or calls although censorship would have prevented this. The British Government knew exactly what was going on in Poland but the truth was kept secret for political expediency. Why break a rule the U.K. and the US Governments had used throughout the war! Stalin, or as Roosevelt referred to him, Uncle Joe, was looked upon and promoted as the saviour of the eastern bloc, not it's oppressor.

These men and women had helped to win a war which they had fought from the beginning to the last and yet lost their freedom and country. Normal people living their lives had lost absolutely everything, except their names and spirit. Their treatment by the British Government and public was beyond contempt. It must have been so disheartening to those Polish refugees.

Despite the almost unsurmountable odds they would face over 200,000 of those Poles had chosen to remain in England and Scotland to where some had been demobbed. They would soon be joined by their dependents from wherever they had been left. The largest number of Poles were those who had escaped from Siberia, Arkhangelsk, Kazahkstan and other USSR zones with the Polish Army in 1941-42. Many were in displaced camps in Africa and India and some were in Mexico, spread across huge areas of the world.

My Mother Alicja had married an RAF serviceman in Ghazir and had arrived in England in 1946, she was living in Blackpool with her in-laws who were making her life unbearable. They were very unhappy that their son, had married a 'foreigner' and they treated her quite badly. My Ciocia Jasia had arrived before her and lived in London at college with friends. My Grandparents and Wujek Janusz were still in Ghazir, in Lebanon just waiting to join them with Kazia's brother Walery and his family. Permission to settle in England with my Mum, who had British citizenship would take some time and travel documents would also be needed.

Alicja eventually got news of her parent's move to England in January

1948 and was 'as excited as a child,' she hadn't seen them for almost 16 months and had desperately missed them, they were due to arrive in February and would soon be followed by the other family members, Walery, Ziuta, Włodek and Marysia.

As Adam and Walery and their families had been considered 'class enemies' by the Soviets it was an easy decision to make to come to England and not return to a Communist Poland. From 1945 up to 1953 Polish underground leaders that were still in Poland post war, had been sentenced to death and then executed for 'sabotage', and some 20,000 others were murdered. Former deportees and other 'undesirables' were also treated most harshly. England would be a safe haven, there was 'no future in Poland unless you were a Communist' my Dziadek used to say.

The family arrived in Liverpool from their temporary home in Ghazir, Lebanon, where they had been since 1945 after a very long journey from Port Said in February 1948. Alicja and Bill had waited at the docks for hours, looking out for them. The seas were very rough, too severe for the boat to dock for a day or two, so they had to come back, which was very frustrating. They did spy her parents and Janusz waving his scarf like mad and the excitement Alicja felt she would never forget. They were so close to reunion, it seemed so long since she had left them in Ghazir. When they were eventually able to disembark there was the formal process of registration and passport checks to go through.

Bill and Alicja waited in a reception area for a long time as there were many hundreds of refugees to be processed, so they tried to be patient until the family suddenly appeared, and she could not describe her emotions. It was so very intense that they could barely talk. They held onto each other so very tightly, oh how she had missed her family, her mother especially. It was so good to see them and to introduce them to their 6 month old grand daughter, Teresa. There was much to be joyful for.

The reunion, however, was very short lived. Adam, Kazia and Janusz had been allocated places at a camp in Five Oaks, near Brighton, and were to travel there by train. The family spent the short time together catching up on news and holding onto each other before they were called to be taken to the station with the many hundreds of others, for travel to the various Resettlement camps.

They stayed at Five Oaks camp for a few days to get over their journey and were then placed in Pulborough, registered with the West Sussex Constabulary on 19th February 1948.

They were interviewed and issued with Certificate of Registration (Aliens Order 1920) documents and recorded as Adam Góral born 26/5/1894 born in Daleszewicje, Poland, ENA9012204 (A12295), Polish Armed Forces 1941-1944

Kazimiera Góral born 23/2/1899 in Wróblewo, Poland ENA9012203, and (A128294), Janusz Góral born 6/1930 in Równe, Poland ENA 9012205. Then issued with clothing and food coupons on 4th March 1948. Clothing was issued by the Assistance Board, West Chiltington Camp 1/3/1948 and 4/3/1948.

They were to stay there for several months and were then moved to other camps, usually unused army barracks, in Horsham, Ely, which was surrounded by beautiful forests and reminded them of their Osada in Poland, and then they were moved onto Kelstern in Lincs. They would be moved again over the next 18 months eventually being registered at Monkmead Camp, Billingham, Sussex.

Alicja, Bill and Jasia visited the resettlement camps and the whole family were able to gather to see them in Lytham and London. Their registration cards record visits to and from Lytham St Anne's from those camps up to December 1950 and visits to and from Victoria and Brixton in London up to 1958. Each visit to and from was stamped by the Metropolitan Police or Lancashire Constabulary. They were finally exempt from registering their movements in 1961.

The only way to accommodate the large numbers of refugees was to place them in camps that had been recently vacated by the American and Canadian troops. There were many camps in the UK, most had been built in the early 1940's in rural areas, often in the grounds of large country estates, as well as military Hospitals, Army bases and Airfields. A Polish Resettlement Corps was raised in 1946 as a Corps of the British Army into which Poles were enlisted for the period of their demobilization up to 1948. The camps were given up by the MOD for housing Polish families and they were administered by a number of organisations and local authorities.

On arrival at the camp, travelling in army trucks, the Poles were very aware of the barbed wire that surrounded the camp and the tall watch towers which reminded them of the Labour camps they had been imprisoned in. Soon after arrival however the barbed wire fences and watch towers were taken down. They were registered and given I.D. cards and assigned to their Nissen hut. Everything had to be provided as the displaced Poles had very little, only what they stood up in and very few belongings. My Babcia still had the photo albums taken with her from Poland safely packed in her bags.

Their worldly goods amounted to very little.

The hut was furnished with beds, bedding, chest of drawers, chairs, and a table with some cutlery and plates. The sleeping area was sectioned off with a curtain so there was some privacy. In the centre of the camp was a cookhouse and communal mess room which catered for everyone to begin with but in time as more facilities became available, pots and pans and ranges, people cooked for themselves and were given their ration books.

Most of the buildings were Nissen huts made into hostels for single working men and a handful were Polish boarding schools run by the Committee for the Education of Poles. There were also a number of Polish hospitals. As people were finding their feet many moved out of the camps in search of work and accommodation. A large number emigrated to the USA, Australia, New Zealand, Canada and Argentina. Families were moved from camp to camp and by the 1950's the 200 plus camps had dwindled down to about 50. Northwick camp closed in 1970.

People in the camp came from many corners of Poland and from every walk of life. Factory workers, foresters, farmers, lawyers, doctors, nurses and teachers. There was a purpose built sick bay staffed by Polish nurses and doctors and those with serious illnesses were sent to the Polish Hospital in North Wales. In the early days language difficulties made finding work difficult but men and women found work in the canning and other factories.

Most of the Nissen huts didn't have internal plumbing and water had to be fetched from cold water taps and toilet and washing facilities were in separate blocks and there was a huge coke filled boiler house at the far end of the camp. For those who could not look after themselves communal meals continued until 1969 but many of the residents were self sufficient although they were some distance from any shops and this was a problem. One enterprising Polish man acquired a van and sold Polish sausage, sauerkraut, gherkins and lots of other Polish foods. Another sold bedding and clothing and the residents were soon able to become self reliant. Local buses were laid on once weekly and people were able to travel further afield. They all pulled together, helping each other through any difficulties.

By 1949 there were 16 Nursery Schools and 34 Primary Schools with over 2,000 children spread over the camps and hostels throughout the UK. The Committee for the Education of Poles in Great Britain administered the education of Polish Children. As in Tehran and Lebanon, schools always sprang up to educate the children whose education had been interrupted by the war and very many had missed out. To the Poles it was very important for the children to continue their education wherever they were and whatever the circumstances.

The Committee also concerned itself with the education of the adults and teaching them English to enable them to get by and find work. The children found it much easier to learn a new language than the adults although they persisted. Some children went to local English schools but most attended the camp schools. Some went onto secondary and some to grammar schools where it was strictly forbidden to speak Polish amongst themselves which was quite unfairly punished as some children still found it difficult to fully communicate in English. Kazia and Adam were only ever able to learn the very basics but managed to get by. Most of their time would be spent with their countrymen and family.

There was a Polish boarding school for the many orphans of the war and for those whose parents were too ill to look after them. Many Poles were still suffering the effects of starvation, typhus, dysentery and malaria they had caught in the labour camps as well as from psychological effects. There were two fee paying boarding schools and the Poles in Great Britain were successful in establishing 4 faculties at British Universities, Medicine at Edinburgh in 1941, Architecture at Liverpool in 1942, Veterinary studies at Edinburgh in 1943 and Balliol College in 1944.

Over the next few years more families arrived at the camps, many having travelled half way across the world, fleeing their imprisonment in Siberia through the Ural Mountains, Kazakhstan, Uzbekistan, Persia, the Middle East to Africa and India, arriving in England in the late 40's and early 50's. By the 60's people were leaving the camps as they became more prosperous and found homes and work further away. Many settled in the Midlands and London, were allocated Council houses and some of the buildings on the camps were later made into residential homes for elderly Poles.

Alicja's parents came to live with them in 1951 when they were able to leave the resettlement camps and Alicja and Bill started decorating the house in preparation, putting lino on the floor and varnishing the floorboards. With rugs on the floors it was looking much nicer. They were so excited and were ready to welcome them. I was 4 by then and my Babcia and Dziadek lived with us until I was nearly 8.

My grand parents found it quite lonely in Lytham as they didn't speak English very well and consequently found it very difficult to mix. Most displaced people coming to England after the war had headed to the capital, and small Polish and Jewish communities were springing up. St

Anne's was only a small town and there wasn't a Polish community for them to become involved with. They were still young enough to be more active and needed something constructive to do.

My brother Tony and I were at convent by then and although Adam and Kazia enjoyed taking us to and from school and teaching us Polish, it wasn't keeping them busy enough. Adam had his garden and Kazia busied herself in the home whilst Bill and Alicja were at work but it wasn't really enough, they needed people of their own age. They needed to be in a Polish community, and it wasn't long before they left to go to London, where the Polish community was growing. Alicja understood their needs and with sad hearts she and Bill saw them off to London.

My grandparents first lived with Ciocia Jasia and her husband Bolcio in Victoria from 1953-54 and then later in Brixton, helping to raise my favourite cousin Alec whilst they both worked.

My Ciocia Jasia had been in England before the rest of the family, in September 1946, and she had lived and worked in Everleigh, Wiltshire, as a teacher in the Polish Refugee camp. She then moved to Guildford after finishing her further education course. She had met her future husband Bolcio (Bolesław) in Guildford. He was a university graduate and physical training instructor who had taken part in the 1936 Olympics in Berlin, a footballer in Poland and a veteran of the Battle of Monte Cassino.

They married on 23rd July 1949 and settled in Victoria, London, their son Alec was born in 1950. In 1954 they moved to Brixton and later on to Streatham in 1962. In 1963, without any indication of ill health, Bolcio died of a coronary at the age of only 49.

My Wujek Janusz also shared the house in Brixton, putting down roots in a new country was expensive, so sharing costs, especially the purchase or renting of a house, was quite common. He later moved to Forest Hill, sharing the lower part of a large house with Kazia and Adam. He had by then married Pamela and had two young daughters, Anita and Krysia.

Adam was a devout Catholic and dedicated his life to charity, helping to raise money for the poor and starving in Africa. He was also active for the local Polish community and helped to raise funds for the purchase of their own church in Balham which to this day is a thriving Parish and has a meeting place for the Osadników Kresowych. This society is made up of the surviving relatives of the families of the eastern borderlands, survivors of Stalin's deportations. The president of this society is Ryszard Grzybowski, a friend of Jasia's, who is a leading member of this society; I met him at her funeral in December 2011 and have met him several times since at various Osadnicy events with other children of the Sybiraks.

When Bolcio died Kazia and Adam moved back to Streatham to support Jasia and Alec always on hand for whoever needed their help. In their later years they moved to a Polish home in Corby and later to Antokol in Sidcup.

Jasia remarried in 1966, to Bruno Misik, an artist, who spent a lot of his retirement renovating the Stations of the Cross at Balham Polish church. He died in 1990 and Jasia then devoted more of her time to the Polish community. She was a most colourful personality, some acquaintances likening her to Zsa Zsa Gabor the actress, having a very strong Polish accent and always being so beautifully dressed. She became a stalwart figure in the Balham Polish community, running social clubs for the elderly and lonely and a charity for Polish orphans in Warsaw (Pruszków Charity) for which she collected generous amounts of money by advertising in the Polish Press.

Jasia moved to Balham in 2000, where she cared for her then partner Stanisław Raymond, another veteran of Monte Cassino who had suffered serious head wounds and in later years developed dementia. This all took a huge toll on Jasia's health, and after Stan's death in 2009 her own health deteriorated dramatically and she battled hard over the next two years. In December 2010 she was diagnosed with secondary lung cancer and struggled with the considerable pain it caused her.

My Mother Alicja stayed with her several times 2010/11 and was there in November 2011 when she died whilst a carer was tending to her needs. The family knew it was inevitable but it was still an awful shock, as Alicja's little sister was such a vibrant person. I took it badly, as we had been very close and she was also my godmother. Alicja and Jasia had cared and fought for each other throughout their travels to and from the USSR. Kazia and Adam, Walery and Ziuta, Włodek, Janusz, Marysia and now Jasia, were all gone. Alicja was now the only one of the family left who had survived the wartime hell created by Stalin. She suddenly felt quite alone and is today at 97 imprisoned by Alzheimers.

The children of Sybiraks have organised several Facebook sites to exchange information of our parents' experiences of Siberia 1940-1942 and other USSR states. It is our endeavour to keep the memory of what happened alive by exchanging detail and supplying historical data to those who are trying to trace family members. Very many grandparents and parents had been unable to speak of their ordeal and for their children who only know a very basic amount of detail these sites are invaluable.

I have two friends with a Polish father and they know very little about their history from WW2 as their Fathers were unable to talk about it. My friends don't know their real names or where in Poland they came from and their fathers both died without sharing any information. Do they have family in Poland? Without a name or place of birth or area where they grew up or came from, which labour camp they were in, where they fought? They cannot trace their origins. A very large part of their heritage is missing. One of them is actively researching through the Polish history Facebook sites as there is more information available now than ever before.

There are also commemorative events that are organised by the site organisers and my cousin Alec and I have met members of families that were in the same Osada back in the eastern borderlands and the same prison camp as our family. It is hugely emotional to meet these people who shared so much with our family. I belong to Kresy Family and Kresy Siberia and several other of these history sites and I'll list them all at the end of the chapter for information.

After his arrival in England my uncle Janusz had gone to Glasgow to continue his education with a group of the cadets before moving in with Jasia and Bolcio in Victoria around 1951. He studied restorative dentistry but gave this up to move into the better paid hospitality trade in the hotels of London, the Berkeley, the Bedford and then the Savoy where he worked until retirement at 65. He met many famous faces here, the most memorable being the Queen Mother.

Marysia had come to England in 1946 with Jasia as cadets and later settled in West London with her parents Walery and Ziuta and her brother Włodek. They had arrived in 1948. She married Wiesiek in 1950 and later with their three children, Marek, Ania and Ewa, they moved to Brockley. Marek has lived and worked in Warsaw for many years and has three children, Adam, Marcin and Izabella. He is a grandfather to four baby girls. Stella, Augustyna, Janka and Jadwiga. The twins Ania and Ewa live and work in Kent.

It wasn't until some time after their arrival in England that Wujek Walery and Ciocia Ziuta had devastating news about their younger son Zbyszek, who had joined the Polish underground in western Poland at the outbreak of war. He had been shot by his 'best friend' in a terrible drunken, accident on returning to barracks after seeing Ciocia Genia in Lublin,. His friend had demanded to see Zbyszek's pass on entry to the camp and Zbyszek's reply was "but you know me, I've just shown you my pass," but his friend fired at point-blank range and killed him.

He was only 23 and he had survived the desperation of war only to be shot by his best friend! The exact details are unclear, and why his friend was drunk and on duty will never be known, the family was shattered. It isn't known what action if any was taken by Wujek Walery and Ciocia Ziuta, or what happened to the young man who fired the gun.

Those who stayed behind in Poland, Kazia's sister Gienia and her daughter Halina had survived the war with Genia's husband Władislaw in Lublin. Halina married Wiesek Morawiec, and both worked as doctors in Stalowa Wola. Wiesek died at quite an early age and Halina who was a specialist in rheumatology suffered from dementia in later life, and died recently, 2020. She lived in Stalowa Wola. They had a son, Maciej, who practises law in Warsaw and regular contact is maintained between him and myself and my cousin Alec via Facebook.

After Gienia died, Halina found a letter from Sofia her Babcia, whilst sorting out her belongings, The details are quite vague but it describes Sofia's experiences and survival during the Russian occupation and later behind the Iron Curtain. I don't yet have access to this information from Maciej so it isn't known what happened to Sofia or how she had managed to survive on her own during such harsh times, as she had been elderly during this period. Gienia had related some of these details to Jasia in the phone calls they shared over the years, but these details are vague as she had to be so careful in her contact with family in England. She was lucky to be able to get permission to visit her sister Kazia and the family on two occasions.

Conversations had to be short and they were not able to discuss personal details freely as there was constant surveillance in Communist Poland. Whatever was spoken was spoken in secret and quietly because there were situations when so called friends would report you to the Police, and even if you didn't say what this 'friend' had reported, you were still arrested.

Thrown into a padded cell where a suspect could find themselves banged up for months in solitary confinement on the whim of a reckless neighbour, then put into the interrogation chair where a suspect could be grilled to the point of insanity. The fake delivery vans patrolling the streets would snatch a suspected dissident off the streets. Spy cameras would be hidden in belts, ties and buttons and instruction manuals on how to destroy people's reputations were eagerly read by the Secret Police. This was happening when deluded English Lefties would take their holidays across the 'paradise' of eastern Europe. Only the Stasi in east Germany would outdo the NKVD?

Under Communism everything had to be shared, one family member could easily be turned against another, as loyalty to the proletarian class, the state, was all that mattered. In eastern Germany a third of the population were informants to the Stasi. I'm not sure of the corresponding figures for Poland's secret Police but I don't think they compare. The older Poles were open of their contempt for Communism and shared this with their children despite the penalties.

Specific relationships family, religion, culture and art were considered by the Soviets to be the 'base' of society, and were to be broken by the Communists as they associated with the old 'capitalist order'. Individualism, loyalty and truth would all be ruthlessly stamped out. It was a brutal practice. Tens of millions of people were murdered by many Communist regimes in many countries by Lenin, Stalin, Mao Zedong, Pol Pot, the Kims and the Castros.

The influence of the USSR post war spread to their satellite states of Poland, Hungary, Czechoslovakia, Romania, Bulgaria, Albania, E. Germany, Iran, Azerbaijan, Austria, Korea and Afghanistan, who all 'benefitted' from military, economic and political aid from the USSR. It is still interfering in European democracies, in the U.S , Montenegro, Ukraine and Syria to name but a few.

I didn't intend to go into an expose of Communism but my Dziadek's words from many years ago suddenly reverberated in my head. He always told me how the theory of Communism was brutal in practice because it was brutal in theory. It touched more than a billion people and killed millions. Stalin, my Dziadek said, 'was a brutal dictator, no different from Hitler or Lenin.'

Stalin continued his violent dictatorship, to abolish the so called bourgeoisie of the eastern borderlands, eliminating those people who would not easily relinquish their property, culture and beliefs, family and God. By fighting for their livelihoods and their country and believing in their God, my family were considered 'class enemies of the proletariat' and had to be eliminated. Stalin was fighting against a 'class' not individuals and was intent on discarding those individuals from Poland en masse, for the sake of the collective, or was it revenge for the Bolshevik war!

My grandparents loved their country but were never able to go back, it was too dangerous. They had heard what had happened to those who did return, especially those like them who had been exiled in 1940 and who had fought with the Allies.

They are my reason for writing this memoir, it is in their honour. I cannot ever imagine what they experienced during their time in the Arkhangelsk labour camps, or the precarious, long and exhausting journeys to reach freedom but I remember their courage, love and humour.

The many historical sites I've referred to relating specifically to Polish heritage are:-

• Sons and Daughters of Displaced Poles
• Silent Heroes of the Forgotten Holocaust
• Polish Culture
• I Love my Polish Heritage
• Shallow Graves in Siberia
• Unravelling Your Roots
• Poland's Long War
• Sybiracy
• Polish Media Studies
• Encountering anti Polonism

They are full of information and views and data is exchanged tracking down family members long thought lost.

CHAPTER 10

Journeys in Detail

One of the aspects of my Mother's journeys that gave me the biggest headache was researching the routes she took from her home in Poland, to Russia and onwards, as I've detailed below. It took some considerable time as I was determined to see how far the family had travelled, especially their many journeys from the Labour camp in 1942 through to their journey's end in England. The fact that they were in a dreadful physical condition needing to stop at various points along the route to Uzbekistan for medical aid, didn't take away their determination to get to the military points the Polish army were assembling at in the Middle East.

My Mother remembered the final stop in Russia and the names of camps they were in which helped me to track down the areas and train stations and with some encouragement she began to remember a little more. That it had all happened so very long ago was difficult for her and at 97 with Alzheimers she remembered very little although she hadn't forgotten the hardship and trauma of the camps, 'I remember but it doesn't hurt my head so much.'

It has taken time but I now have the completed journeys illustrated as accurately as I can, checked with my Ciocia Jasia, against the routes of a friend from their Osada, Danuta Gradosielska who had kept a diary of her deportation and some research from Mum's notes. They travelled through 5 time zones, on the Trans-Siberian, Trans Mongolian and Trans Manchurian railways.

I marvel at the spirit and determination of my family to have survived not only the deprivation of the Labour camps but the arduous journeys taken over so very many km to reach safety and freedom and to begin their recovery.

February 1940 – The Kresy, Poland

10th February 1940, their last night at home, arrested by the NKVD at 5am with a decree of deportation read out to them, they're told they were 'a threat to public order' and the family were then taken to the outskirts of Równe for the first stage of their deportation to the USSR. Transport had been ready and waiting for some considerable time.

Journey 1 – Równe to Gorki, Moscow Oblast – 2300kms

From Równe, the train heads out through Lubormika, Zdolbunow, Iwanko, Szepetowka, Orzenin, Korosten, Owrucz, River Prypet (scene of the Chernobyl explosion) Gomel, Brynansk, Orzel, over River Don, Karaczew, Alexandrowka, Rybna, Holworsk, Woskriesensk, Oriechovo, Pokrowa, Pietruszki, Untow, Wladimir and Gorki, a journey of 17 days in temperatures of minus 30 degrees.

USSR – Journey 2 – Gorki, Moscow Oblast, to Sharya, Kostroma Oblast – 690kms

They left the train at Gorki to travel onto Sharya, another 2 day's towards the labour camp. They stayed overnight in an empty and very cold Orthodox church and early next morning set out for the train to Sharya. On arrival at Sharya, they had to walk towards the labour camp, Poldniewica, Gorkowski Oblast, in very deep snow. It was about 20 km away and they were very tired as they had very little sleep. The other labour camps they are moved to whilst in the Archkangelsk region are Duraszewo only a short distance away, approximately 10 km and Darowatka, in the Gorkowski Oblast about 20 km away. I've been able to find two of the labour camps on map Specposiolki w Obwodzie Wologodzkim 1940-41. Duraszewo I'm assuming is not very far away and in the same Oblast but have not yet been able to locate it.

Poldniewica, USSR – December 1941

In mid 1941, after the news of the 'amnesty' was known to the prisoners many just left from their camp, Derawelka, eager to get to the Polish army, whilst many others gathered at camp Poldniewica about 20 km away to plan their escapes. They would have to wait for their official 'amnesty' papers, without which they would not be able to claim food at stations along the journey, the papers would also 'guarantee' their safety up to Uzbekistan.

They left Poldniewica camp in late December 1941 almost two years after arriving there, on hand made sledges staying with local Russians, they would have frozen without their help, it was bitterly cold. There was a railway line between Poldniewica/Poludnevitza and Darowatka which would make the journey out of the camps easier for all those heading towards Kotlas.

Journey 3 – Labour camp to Kotlas, Arkhangelsk Oblast – 457kms

Early next day they had a lift in trucks from a group of Russian soldiers they had come across purely by chance. There was much movement of troops across Russia at that time after Hitler's attack on Russia and the troops helped the group of 15 to Kotlas station. It had saved them many days walk in very deep snow.

The journey from Kotlas, took them through Kirov, Zuyvka, Molotov, Kama, Shalya, Kuzma, Hropik, Swierdowsk, Czelyabinsk, Kartal, Aktybinsk, Shalkar, Oktiabinsk, Aral Sea, Samarkand and then onto Tashkent, a journey through the Ural Mountains, the Kurgistan Steppes, Kazakhstan and Uzbekistan. It took about 6 weeks with many stops for aid at the medical stations set up along the route by the Polish army.

Uzbekistan - January-February 1942

They left the train at Tashkent, a group of about 30 people, and were diverted to a field to wait for over 2 days and nights without food or water. They were terrified as there were no Polish officials there to help them as there had been at points on the journey so far. The Uzbeks told them they would soon be moved. This was just another diversion by the NKVD together with the Uzbeks who had stopped them here to send them onto Bukhara, to a collective farm to work for them.

Journey 5 – Tashkent to Bukhara – 570kms

From Tashkent they boarded a train for the journey to Bukhara. They had been met by Polish officials who told them they would very soon be moved towards the army and to go with the Uzbeks for now as there was little alternative. There were so very many Poles fleeing the USSR and the Polish officials were almost overcome with the numbers.

Journey 6 – Bukhara to Vobkent – 35kms

From Bukhara they travelled to Vobkent in yak drawn wagons by Uzbeks to a collective farm. It had been an exhausting journey of hunger and of a hell unimagined with the Soviets generally disrupting the evacuation. Refusing to allow access to trains to help their exodus and diverting many of the transports towards collective farms, Kolkhozy, for the labour they still required. Stalin's grip was tight and would continue to be throughout their journey to Persia. Adam and Walery had heard via the grapeline that if a family member was in the army, in a uniform, it would help the other members of the family to leave and join them and the Polish army in the Middle East. They both left with this in mind, Adam was then posted to Iraq and Walery to Uzbeksitan, the families were now on their own. The stay at the Kolkhoz was thankfully short, circumstances moved very quickly and the sisters Jasia and Alicja would soon leave the kolkhoz to join the Polish cadets in Guzor. Walery had found the family as he had been assigned to an army base in Uzbekistan and had been searching for them. He told his sister Kazia to get the children into the cadet school and into uniforms urgently, as the borders would soon be closed. He knew how Stalin worked and he was right, Stalin would close the borders to the Poles in August 1942, keeping them in the USSR.

Journey 7 – Vobkent to Bukhara – 35kms

The sisters leave Vobkent and head back to the station at Bukhara in arbas to board a train to Guzor.

Journey 8 – Bukhara to Guzor – 217kms

They travelled from Bukhara to Guzor arriving at the Cadet school after a day, they were deloused given basic medical attention and issued with cadet uniforms. The 7th Division is here and despite their haggard faces the Polish soldiers look very smart in their English uniforms. The girls are happy and eager to join the cadets.

Journey 9 – Guzor to Bukhara – 217kms

The cadets then had to travel from Guzar back to the station at Bukhara as plans were changing all the time which was quite confusing. The new Polish army was constantly on the move. Stalin was cutting off supplies and the NKVD continually intervened to hamper the journeys. Alicja had typhus and Jasia had dysentery, both were very ill and Alicja would need hospital treatment.

Journey 10 – Bukhara to Kitab – 275kms

Next journey after Alicja had partly recovered, was by train from Bukhara onto Kitab where some of the army units were assembling. General Anders was ensuring that all the Poles leaving the USSR were being moved to be safe and closer to the Polish army, away from Stalin's clutches. General Anders visited their camp in Kitab and instilled much needed confidence in the cadets.

Journey 11 – Kitab to Port Krasnovodsk – 1,595kms

From Kitab another train journey through the mountains of Uzbekistan to Port Krasnovodosk (now Turkmenbashi) a gruelling journey and both girls were quite ill Jasia with dysentery and Alicja had typhus and yellow jaundice. It took several days with stops at medical stations for treatment and to recover. March 1942 – Mum's notes say she thought 'it was August' but I haven't been able to match this up.

Journey 12 – Port Krasnovodsk to Pahlevi across the Caspian Sea – 200kms

At Port Krasnovodosk they waited for two days and nights in a sand storm, amongst many people in terrible condition to cross the Caspian Sea, a 2 day sail. Some of the boats were just fishing boats and not in good condition but the sisters were able to get onto a larger more stable one which was very over crowded.

Persia (Iran)

In Pahlevi after a crowded but calm journey they were de loused again, their physical condition was awful, they were scratching and desperate to be clean. Given new uniforms and medical assistance from the Red Cross and the Queen Alexandra Nursing Corps they were sent to tents on the beach before being moved to a Camp in Pahlevi.

Journey 13 – Pahlevi to Tehran – 680kms

Janusz was looking for them in Pahlevi, he and Kazia had arrived a week earlier and she had been sent on to a hospital in Tehran. After a week they were moved to a larger refugee Camp 1 on army transport passing thru Tabriz, the Elbrus Mts, Qazvin and finally into Teheran. Whilst here they heard that 'permission' to leave the USSR had been withdrawn and many thousands of Poles were left in the Siberian wilderness. They had not been able to leave as the Kommandants of many camps had kept the 'amnesty' from them in order to retain their labour. They were in Teheran for about 1 year recovering and working before being moved to make room for other refugees coming through from Pahlevi's refugee camps. Alicja had yellow jaundice and was too ill to move to Palestine with Jasia in Autumn 1942 and she stayed in Tehran with Kazia and Janusz. Adam visited on leave. Alicja, Kazia and Janusz leave Tehran in Autumn 1943.

Journey 14 – Tehran to Isfahan – 448kms

Autumn 1943, from Teheran they were moved onto Isfahan through Qom and Kashan to another refugee camp and were there for possibly 1 year when Adam was recalled to his army unit in Tehran.

Journey 15 – Isfahan to Tehran – 448kms

Alicja meets William in Autumn 1944 in Isfahan, she and Ziuta enrol in a nursing course at the Red Cross HQ in Tehran. William is posted to Tehran and Adam has been recalled to his unit so the family all move back there through Kashan and Qom. They were also moved to make room for other incoming Polish refugees from the USSR.

Journey 16 – Tehran to Ghazir, Lebanon – 1840kms

Another move came for Adam to be formally discharged from the army in Egypt in 1945, due to ill health. From Tehran they travel in army lorries through Arak, Ahwez staying there over night, to a camp in Baghdad for 2 nights. They cross the Turkey-Syria border into Alleppo, transferring from a passenger train to a goods train. They were allocated a house in Ghazir and William proposes to Alicja before he is posted to Iraq. Alicja and William are married in July 1946 in Ghazir.

Journey 17 – Ghazir to Beiruit – 26kms 1946 –

In 1946 the family is allocated other accommodation and will shortly move from Ghazir to Beirut.   William collects Alicja on 1st October for their journey to England. They take a taxi to Beiruit after a very tearful goodbye to Alicja's family, they didn't know if they would ever see each other again.

Journey 19 – Beirut to Jerusalem via Haifi – 433kms

2nd October – From Beirut a taxi to Haifi staying over night then train to Jerusalem the following day. They stay a couple of days in Jerusalem at the YMCA.

Journey 20 – Jerusalem to Cairo – 740kms

3rd October – From Jerusalem a long train journey ahead through Palestine and into Cairo where they spend 6 weeks

Journey 21 – Cairo to Port Said – 203kms

5th October – A honeymoon in Cairo and a wait for a boat to take them to England from Port Said.

Journey 22 – Port Said to Southampton – 5,762kms

1st November - Leave Cairo and journey along the side of the Suez canal reaching Port Said early evening. They board the Durban Castle and arrive in England on 9th November and then travel by train to Blackpool, Lancashire – 423kms

I've worked out distances at approximately 23,000km over a period of 6 years. There will be some journeys not accounted for and I've checked dates and places against family photo's, my Mother's notes and information from Ciocia Jasia and others.
It's as accurate as I'll ever get.

Personal Recollections

Adapted from notes made of conversations with my Dziadek, Adam and Babcia Kazia, in their attempts to dispel the myths surrounding their beloved Poland and to educate me about my heritage.

Many look upon Poland as a backward nation that was defeated in a matter of days by overwhelming and efficient German troops, that Poland's army and air force were destroyed and that Poland capitulated within a very few days. The truth is very different.

Polish forces did not collapse, they fought for 35 days, the last battle of the campaign was on 5th October five weeks after the German attack, they were overwhelmed by a far greater force. Poland's losses were 67,000 killed and 134,000 wounded. The Germans expected to have a quick and easy victory but the Polish authorities had immediately begun organising Armia Krajowa to continue the fight, it was the first and the largest Resistance army in Europe. Poland's fight then continued on the 17th September when they had to contend with Stalin's invasion from the east on his excuse of 'coming to save Poland from the Germans.'

Poland did not surrender. It's Government continued to operate in exile throughout the War, first in France until it fell to the Germans and then in London until its dissolution in 1990. It also had an excellent intelligence service, Armia Krajowa. Before the war the Poles delivered models of Germany's top secret Enigma encryption machines they called 'bombas' to British and French intelligence, enabling the Allies to read key German communications throughout most of the war. It was not Turing who cracked the Enigma code as is commonly believed, it was Polish mathematicians, although he was able to build on the Poles' initial expertise and mathematical genius.

Poland held out in 1939 against the Germans, alone, almost as long as France, Holland and Belgium held out against the Germans with major British help in 1940. If not for the Soviet invasion on 17th September the Poles would have held out longer if they'd had the promised help from France or Britain, which did not come until much later.

I speak with pride about Poland's contributions to the Allied victory in WW2, their incredible efforts have been overlooked by the Allies since the end of the war, their exclusion from the celebrations on V.E. Day an insult, to which there has never been an official apology, although I believe former PM Tony Blair did acknowledge the exclusion. My family lost everything, almost their lives and I include many thoughts from Sybiraks who survived, especially from Sybiraczka Alicja, my Mother, and my grandparents in the main part of this memoir.

Alicja Góral, is 97 the only remaining member of a family who survived the deprivations of Siberia whilst very many didn't. Their graves are scattered along the routes to Siberia, the Russian plains, the Siberian wilderness and along the paths to freedom from Kotlas to Tashkent. There are also graves in the cotton fields of Bukhara where they were again forced into labour by the NKVD for the Uzbeks, the NKVD who trailed the escaping Polish exiles, sabotaging their escape efforts.

I spoke with my Mum very many times over the years before she was lost to Alzheimers, we had many nazdrowje's and she opened up a little each time. She didn't talk about this period of her life very much as it 'hurts my mind' and she gets emotional because she can't remember what she wants to say and I cannot anticipate it. She desperately wants to remember something specific and can't. 'What's the matter with me' she asks? I'm too upset to say, seeing her struggle with her memory, my Mother who was so strong throughout my childhood is now so reliant and vulnerable, sometimes impatient for memories of her homeland.

She remembers something, she is 'in a new place' maybe 1946 England? A young woman in a new country away from her family for the first time since their exile. She says she 'felt foreign and didn't belong'. 'I didn't feel at home at all, I didn't feel like my children were truly mine, it's very difficult to explain.' Maybe she means bringing up children who speak a different language which was perhaps a little alienating, especially to begin with. Although my brother and I were learning Polish from both Mum and our grandparents and were fluent pre school but she said she 'felt alien.'

I asked if Babcia and Dziudziu felt the same and she said yes they did 'they didn't feel as though they belonged here,' they were viewed with suspicion for many years.

Mum couldn't ever explain why she had never felt at home, she has been here since 1946 and was perhaps reluctant to mention the hostility. As children we knew of the hostility and were bullied at school because of our 'foreign Mother.' I wish I'd had this particular conversation many years before but at least I'd had the foresight to ask her to write her memories down 20 years ago after my Father had died. I thought it would fill her days and that it might have been a release for her. I was wrong, as she remembers Siberia and it still causes her stress. Sadly she can't remember her home in Poland, except for 'the bridge over the river.'

After WW2 many Poles in England as registered refugees, were given a hard time by the Labour Govt and the Communist supporting Unions, despite having been a major ally of the British and USA. Manual labour was needed to rebuild the country and the Unions put up many barriers to foreign refugees. Many Polish servicemen had been asked to leave the country by PM Attlee, although the Polish Resettlement Act of 1947 gave them reason to stay in England and make their homes here but many left for what proved to be more hospitable countries in the Commonwealth.

I've included personal recollections from individual Polish refugees in England, in their own words with some amendments for grammar.

Michał was born on 12th August 1927 in Boldury in the Tarnopol region (now deep in the Ukraine). He was the eldest of 6 children and in 1935 his family moved to another farm between Tarnopol and Wołyn where his father built a house. They were there in 1939 when war broke out.

The beginning of the war brought great tragedy, his Mother died on 1st September in the evening of the outbreak. His grandmother stayed with the family but his grandfather had to go away, it was the last time they saw him, murdered by Ukrainian bandits. Michał remembers that it was a beautiful autumn that year. In the 2nd week after the outbreak on the road between Beresteczko and Racichów many people were fleeing east from the Germans. In the evening the German planes started shooting into the crowds with machine guns and there was nowhere to hide, only open fields on each side. This happened every day until 14th September.

'Then the Russians arrived from the east and the refugees turned round and started heading back west. It was a terrible winter in 1939-40 and on the 10th February in the middle of the night we heard tremendous banging on the door. My father opened it to an NKVD Soviet agent who entered with a gun and several other Red Army people. They scattered about the house and two surrounded my Father and put their guns against him. We started crying uncontrollably it was so frightening, I'll never forget it, the picture of my father surrounded by those ready-to-kill soldiers will stay with me forever. We were told to take as much as we could as there's nothing where you are going.'

The family were taken by sledge to the station 24kms away, as they were leaving 'our big dog howled terribly and one of the Soviets shot him dead.'

They were put into cattle wagons and their long journey to Siberia began, they travelled for 22 days and the journey finished where the track ran out at Kotlas in Siberia. 'We endured 18 months at the labour camp before the 'amnesty' of July 1941 when we made our way south towards the Polish Army in Tehran'.

The family were separated by the end of the war and in 1947 Michał came to England spending his first few months in a re-settlement camp near Winchester. Finding work was difficult due to the Unions being dominated by communists who wished to please Stalin's whims, making the employment of Poles difficult but many firms sought to employ them.

The family were active members of the Polish community and lived productive lives in England.'

My mother Alicja, had a break down in her late 30's and my Ciocia Jasia and Wujek Janusz suffered mental health problems. There would also be flashbacks for them over the years, impossible for them to ignore. My grandparents Kazia and Adam suffered quietly although Kazia especially could laugh when remembering the Bolsheviks, she somehow coped. Adam involved himself in the Church and raising money for overseas children.

I know from speaking to family members of survivors and friends, that some knew next to nothing about their parents or grandparents, who had never spoken of what had happened to them. They're not aware of any living relatives they may have in Poland and children of Sybiraks who are researching their family history have little to go on. These days there are many research points as the history of Poland's WW2 is recorded in many areas.

Stanisław was born in 1936 near Wilno in north east Poland, his father was in the Polish army when Germany invaded Poland, the Russians invaded shortly after and very soon occupied the local area. On 10th February 1940 all 8 members of his family were deported by rail in cattle trucks through the depths of Russian winter to frozen Siberia. The privations of the journey led to the death of his youngest brother shortly after their arrival in Siberia.

There his parents had to work outdoors cutting trees, the older children attended the Russian school and the younger ones stayed in the camp.

The 'amnesty' of June 1941 enabled the family to leave the camp in late 1941. He remembers the arduous journey south after their release. 'my father was very good with his hands and built 3 sledges, my mother pulled one, my father pulled one and my eldest brother who was 12 pulled one. My sister who was 10 walked as there were 3 younger siblings.'

They managed to get to the station and then travelled by train to Uzbekistan which took several weeks, a journey of over 3,000 km, to meet up with the Polish army. His father joined the army and the family were supposed to remain and work in the cotton fields for the Uzbeks in return for subsistence. After 3 weeks his mother decided conditions were so bad that they should leave and follow the army. Obstructed by NKVD agents at train stations, Stalin needed their labour, they were luckily rescued by some Polish troops who grabbed them on board the train. This was extremely fortuitous given the terrible conditions other fleeing Poles experienced in Uzbekistan having got stuck there.

'There were some transports organised and we left Uzbekistan in 1942 for Persia, that's when we met my brother (must have been separated) and from then on we moved to one of the British colonies called Tanganyika in East Africa'.

Six years later the family sailed for England and were reunited with their father. Life was in Nissen camps in the Cotswolds and he finished his education in Northamptonshire. He met his wife at the Lifford Park school.

The family settled in England, some of the children going to University, one to Cambridge and some siblings eventually moving to Canada. Stanisław and his wife entered into the English and Polish communities and helped those Poles who came into England post 2004 needing help with the English language.

Like many refugee Poles he has sent parcels of food and clothing to various cities during post war Poland and even up to the 60's through various crises which occurred under communist rule in his homeland. He has not yet visited the area of his former home which is now in Belarus.'

Very many survivors were unable to speak of their ordeal, it was very firmly buried. My Mother only gave me a very basic outline to work on, it was far too painful to recall much detail but what she gave me was the backbone of the story.

Many young Polish people came to Britain after 2004 when Poland became a member of the E.U. and settled in Birmingham and increased the number of Polish Delicatessens popular with English customers as well as the Poles.

These new arrivals are unaware of the earlier wave of Polish refugees post war [they were not informed in their schooling under Communism] predominantly servicemen and their families, who had spent some years in Soviet labour camps and post war in resettlement camps within the British Empire recovering from their ordeal. There were also very many thousands of orphans.

Together with other groups of Polish people in London and Leicester, Birmingham etc, these people established thriving communities and only those who arrived as children or young adults survive to this day.

Those that I know of, include my Mother Alicja, family friends Danuta and Ryszard from the same Osada and labour camp and Halina a very dear friend of Alicja's.

Many of these refugees fought in the regular Polish units or resistance units against Germany in WW2 or were from families where their father fought with the Allies in the war. Some were from families who were exiled to deepest Russia or Siberia on the orders of Stalin, for their fathers' participation in the Bolshevik War, or simply viewed as 'enemies of the state' as my family were.

Others were from families whose members were forced into labour by the Germans in factories or on farms in Poland, Germany or occupied France.

Their lives had been greatly impacted by WW2, many arriving in England by troop ship, as my Mother Alicja did with her husband who served in the RAF or on large merchant ships after 1945. Some arrived during the war by small boat or aeroplane to join the Allied cause, many fighting in the Battle of Britain.

These Polish refugees have spent a large part of their lives in England, some were born in the re-settlement camps. They all found employment and became productive and law abiding members of British society and they have all mostly kept strongly to Polish traditions as we as a family have done. Even extending to the generation of grandchildren and even great grandchildren.

Most of the newly arrived Poles lived in army camps, renamed as re-settlement camps spread throughout England and Wales. They remember their experiences of WW2, the deportation to Russia and relatives dying on the 2,000+km journey. The NKVD coming in the middle of the night, giving them only half an hour to pack. The extreme hunger in the camps and many thousands who died from starvation, typhus and other diseases.

The older refugees had to come to terms with having lost everything they owned, their property confiscated by the Soviets, taken over by 'neighbours' or burned to the ground, their livelihoods lost. They had to realise that although they had gone through terrible hardships they were 'compensated' by living in a free England. Many were never reunited with relatives or knew what had happened to those left in Poland. My Babcia Kazia never found out what had happened to her Mother Sofia, who would have been in her 60's at the outbreak of war.

Their country had been decimated, 20% smaller than in 1939 and the loss of the Kresy was a great blow to many of them. Many Polish refugees were from the 'lost territories', the eastern borderlands and in their eyes they felt they had been as badly treated as Germany and yet they had been on the winning side!

The severing of diplomatic relations between the Polish Govt in exile and the Soviets in 1943, meant that all future discussions regarding Polish matters took place between the representatives of USA, GB and USSR, without Polish representation and Poland was handed over to Stalin

On their discharge from the forces, there was provision of free passage and 56 days pay and allowances plus a war gratuity for the years of service and rank in the Polish forces while under British Command. My Dziadek was registered as being in the Army from 1941-44. Large numbers of Polish servicemen did return to Poland, approximately 105,000, their fate mostly unknown although many were put on 'show trials' in their now Soviet homeland, imprisoned or murdered.

The Polish re-settlement Act of 1947 was passed to meet the needs of the Poles and their dependants, either as a cash allowance or maintenance in the re-settlement camps. Health needs were met and registration was given to Polish Pharmacists and Doctors to practice in Britain. These measures identified the Poles as a special case which caused some ill feeling in the Labour Govt and wider public, in a post war England suffering many shortages and rationing. Ignoring the fact that Poland had more than shared the efforts put into winning the war against the Germans.

Mieczysław was born on 15th September 1923 in Dermanka in the Wołyn region of eastern Poland (now Ukraine) he had 4 sisters and his father was an Osadnik (military settler) who had been appointed a forest ranger. The war put a cruel stop to all his ambitions when the Red Army invaded in September 1939 and occupied the area.

On 10th February the whole family were deported and he remembers the words of the soldiers who came to his home in the deep of the night, 'you've got 20 minutes, get something to eat, get something to keep you warm.' He recalls they were taken to the train station about 22km away and packed into cattle wagons, about 50 people per wagon, they didn't know where they were to be taken. They travelled for about 2 weeks and kept alive by only a bowl of hot soup served once a day. At the end of the train journey they were put onto sledges, some walking at the side, on the journey to the camp which was to the west of the Ural Mountains, Derowetka (my family were also in that camp) in the Arkhangelsk region and here they lived in barracks with a number of families sharing each hut. Living conditions were very crowded, they worked in the forest cutting trees and wood from 7am to 7pm. Each worker received 400gms of bread a day, 200gms for those who stayed in the barracks.

After the 'amnesty' in June 1941 Mieczysław was allowed to leave to join the Polish army. It was a complicated journey, many families were diverted by the NKVD to further forced labour picking cotton for the Uzbeks.   Transport was later arranged taking them to the port of Krasnovodosk on the Caspian Sea and across to Pahlevi in Persia. By February 1942 he had joined the Polish army and much of 1942 and 1943 was spent training in Egypt. Late in 1943 the army embarked for Taranto in southern Italy and he fought throughout the Italian campaign, including Monte Cassino and was with the troops when they took Bologna in 1945.

Only 3 out of 7 of his family survived, his mother and father died in Russia and also two of his sisters. His other 2 sisters spent 5 years in India. He arrived in Liverpool with his army unit in September 1946, 'it was horrible, the terrible rain after the sunshine of Italy and sometimes so foggy.' His sisters soon arrived from India and were located in a resettlement camp in Lancashire. He met his wife when visiting them and got married in Preston. The family moved to Birmingham where job opportunities were better but they experienced some 'hostility and snubs from the locals and landlords.'

The family settled and became productive and enjoyed being members of the Polish community.

Zofia was born in 1928 in a small village near to Drohiczyn in the Polesie region. A child of Osadnicy, military settlers, who were given land on the eastern borderlands in recognition of their participation in WW1 and then the Bolshevik War. Life she remembers was very good on the land and her father had been made mayor of a town close to the farm.

'It all came to an abrupt end when war broke out with the German bombs and then the Russians harassing the Polish population'. The fateful day of 10th February 1940 arrived which severed their connection with their homeland. In the depth of that very cold winter they were only given 20 minutes to pack and told they were to be sent to Siberia. They were taken to the train station and put into cattle wagons. The journey took about 3 weeks and they were only given 1 bowl of weak soup a day. Zofia was just 11.

In the camp people were allocated various jobs in the forest, cutting down trees, cutting logs, loading and transporting them to the railway line. Hard labour, disease and starvation were the norm. One day someone turned up at the camp and asked them 'what are you doing here, don't you know that there's an 'amnesty.' Russia is at war with Germany.'

This was excellent news but logistically, organising the now free Poles scattered all over the vast Russian steppes and getting them to the Polish army, was a formidable task. It was the autumn of 1941 and their journeys in the trains and trucks in the freezing temperatures would be a constant worry as was finding food but they eventually arrived in Bukhara in Uzbekistan. Her grandmother was very ill from lack of food and died from starvation.

The family then became separated, her father left to join the army and typhoid struck her mother and brother and disease and starvation continued. The family somehow made it to Krasnovodsk on the Caspian Sea but were too late for the boat so had to go back to Bukhara and she joined the scouts. They eventually did get onto a boat bound for Pahlevi and then onto Tehran. After recovery they were sent onto a camp in Kampala where food was plentiful and nutritious. Her father had arrived in England in very bad health, it was now 1948 and Zofia and her family were sent to England by plane.

They were in a resettlement camp called Daglingworth near Cirencester then moved onto Northwick camp near Moreton-in-Marsh. They were finally reunited with their father and brother who was in the RAF.'

She ended up as a teacher and like all post war Poles settled and worked, married and had families and became involved in the now growing Polish community. They were well adjusted and fully integrated into their new country, determined to make the most of the opportunities offered to them. Like all Poles new to the country, they made a meaningful contribution.

It was hot in Pahlevi when Paulina and family landed after 3 days, and it was now August 1942 and her father was taken straight to hospital in Tehran. 'We were all washed down and given clothes and then transported to Tehran.' Her mother was also ill and was taken to hospital, Paulina went to look for her father but she was exhausted and collapsed and the medics took her into the hospital. She finally found her father, his face was yellow and he was very ill but he recognised her.

Her father left hospital and joined the army, she, her mother and sister went to Ahwaz and from there to India. 'Once there we were divided into groups and we went to east Africa to Masindu' and in the camp her mother and sister fell ill with malaria, her mother was reduced to 42kg and they received much needed medical help.

When the war had finished they wanted to go back to Poland but her father didn't think it was a good idea as they had nothing to go back to. They went instead to England and to a resettlement camp in Cambridge and her sisters to special schools to learn English and get qualifications quickly.

The family lived and worked in Cambridge for a time and then the Midlands. She and her future husband had 7 children and kept strongly to their Polish traditions taking a very active part in the Polish community.

CHAPTER 11– Personal Recollections

Michalina born 30th November 1926 in Ciepliwoda, her parents had moved there as military settlers after the Polish-Russian war of 1921.

Life was turned upside down in February 1940 when her mother turned up at the school accompanied by a Russian soldier and tearfully told her she had to leave school because the family were being deported. That evening they were told to pack and were taken to the railway station, packed into cattle wagons with many other thousands.

Into the bitterly cold snowy weather they travelled for about 3 weeks, travelling mainly at night stopping in the middle of nowhere. They eventually arrived at a camp at Gorodok Poldniewica in the Vologda region, where my family were also taken to. They were to find out that previously the occupants had been the Tatars, deported there many years ago by the Tsar and had all died. It was winter when everything was frozen and bitterly cold, they were given a bread allowance and the amount depended on how much work they did.

Her father was skilled at making furniture and he organised a group of men with similar skills and they were able to earn some money and also work indoors away from the severe frost. Until illness struck, the family lived as well as they could but her father and mother, 2 brothers and sister-in-law got ill with typhoid which was terribly painful.

At the 'amnesty' in 1941 they were able to leave the camp. Many young men left to join the army but her remaining family needed money for food and found work on a farm and were given meat in exchange. Her mother spent time preparing food and in November 1941 they left travelling south east to Uzbekistan. It took a month travelling only by night. Reaching Uzbekistan they had to work in the cotton fields for 9 months in order to subsist, waiting for transport to the Caspian Sea. Michalina contracted malaria and was very weak and ill for many months. By August 1942 the order came to take them to Persia and they were taken by train to Krasnovodsk on the Caspian Sea. 'We were terribly thirsty and some boys were selling water like gold dust, but we had little money so we only had one small bottle between 4 girls.'

When they landed at Pahlevi, it was beautiful, clean beaches and clear water. They were stripped of their clothes which were burned because of infestation, their heads were shaved and they all had a bath. The men's trousers they were given had to be tied on to them as they were far too big, they had lost so much weight.

They spent time in hospital in Tehran to treat malaria and then moved to a transit camp in Ahwaz. They were there for 2 years until moving to Palestine with the cadets. Here the climate suited her better after suffering for so long with malaria.

They were eventually transported to England, from Egypt to Liverpool and were put in an American ex army camp in Foxley. After education and taking their A levels, finding jobs was the next thing, some found work in factories and some of the girls went to Wales to work as nurses.

Jan, Julian, Jadwiga, Bolesław all born between 1919 and 1927 in central Poland or in the eastern borderlands of Poland. Children of military settlers and living on the Osada's of the Kresy region. Exiled to Siberia by the Russians or to France and Germany by the Germans to work as hard labour. Taken by their oppressors and given very little time to pack before being loaded onto trucks or trains.

After the 'amnesty' they were free to go if they were on Russian soil, as they couldn't go back to Poland they headed south to join up with the Polish army in Tehran. Many spent time there recovering and working for up to 3 years, before being sent onto Lebanon to make room for other refugees.

They eventually came to England and were in resettlement camps before finding work or education. In the case of some of the refugees in earlier arrivals, they had travelled onto Blackpool to join the Polish Air Force base training there before fighting in the Battle of Britain.

There was no returning to their homeland. All property, farmland had been burned to the ground by either the Germans or the Russians. The lands of the Kresy razed into a wilderness. The messages coming from Poland and other Poles was that life under the new regime was not good, although this was not generally known to the wider British public.

I've included some personal recollections more specific to living under the Soviets after they had taken over the eastern borderlands, from those who lived through it. Recollections from individual Sybiraks, who had settled on the Osada's and worked the land after the 1921 Bolshevik War. Single military men in their 20's without a roof over their heads on an empty grassland with no farm buildings, agricultural implements or life-stock, who were faced with farming the land from scratch.

These recollections are mostly in their own words with some amendments for grammar and they give an insight into how the Soviets were 'welcomed' into Poland, who played an active part in the deportation of the settlers, who took over their empty properties and who collaborated with the Germans and the Russians, in the lootings, killings of entire villages, and the genocide by the UPA.

The majority of Byelorussians were quite friendly, benefitting from work on the settlers' Osada's, as did many of the other ethnic communities. The problems occurred from the communists within the Jewish, Ukrainian and Byelorussian communities once the Soviets arrived in the Borderlands.

Helped mainly by these communists, livestock and cereals, potatoes, almost everything from the land, farm buildings and homes were taken by the 'Soviets' from the Polish settlers.

The make up of the communities was reflected in the schools within the Osada's, Polish, Byrlorussian, Tartar, Jewish, Lithuanian and Ukrainian. There were scout groups and many other multinational social gatherings.

Janina from the Osada Krechowiecka, from where my own family lived, says 'there were only 9,000 military settlers and many civilians including their families, up to 4500 and 1 in 5 of those settlers deported were from military families. On 10th February 1940 the number of families taken was 26.790 made up of 139.286 people. Before the war there was much help between the many different groups but then the conflicts began.'

Maria from Osada Budowla, 'the Bolshevik agents under orders of the Soviet command, incited the killing and beating by the Byelorussians and brutal executions, people and children buried alive and Polish soldiers shot.'

Dr Wladysław, from Osada Bortnica, '1941 German units heading eastwards towards Russia on the Dubno-Rowne Road began imposing a new order with the Ukrainian militia with repressions of the Jewish population of Dubno and other nearby towns and repressions against Poles with massacres of 50 people by Ukrainians. By 1944 the Red army had crossed into Dubno with heavy battles through January and February and all Osadas were razed to the ground to hide that Poles had lived there.'

Bronisława from Osada Mackzkowce 'the Ukrainians began to strut about sure of their importance and the Jews were building numerous welcoming triumphal arches without hiding their feelings, they joyfully embraced the units of the Soviet Military as they thanked them for saving them from the Polish capitalists and bourgeoisie'.

Felicja, from Osada Ostrowska from the book, Leaves in the Wind, 'Communist Poland never allowed it to be admitted that the borderlanders were deported, nothing was said about the misery and the many deaths, starvation and abuse.'

Wanda, from Osada Pilsudczyzna 'the population was mixed Polish, German and Ukrainian. After the deportations the Ukrainians who had also assisted in the deportations, became very haughty to the Poles, their brutality was at its height following the Germans heading eastwards towards

Russia in 1941. Gangs of Ukraianian militia robbed and murdered the Poles. Hipolitowka was encircled by them and houses doused with petrol and set alight. All perished, with the escapees mowed down by machine gun fire. One uncle saved relatives but was murdered, mutilated with his eyes put out and his chest slashed. One uncle's body was never found.'

Stanisław, from Osada Ulanowka 'there were many refugees from the west, petrified and in a daze. Explosions were heard from Brzese, from bombs and anti aircraft fire, villages were alight. Soviet army entered and the Germans withdrew. Jews were welcoming the Soviets with arches and the Byelorussians and Ukrainians were 'settling old scores'. Arrests began and many settlers were imprisoned. Agitation had arisen with various groups coming together, stripping their 'liberated country' naked.'

Zofia, from Osada Adampol 'as soon as the Soviets arrived the local population who had seemed well disposed towards us changed. They felt that they had Soviet backing and harassment began as well as robbery and arson attacks. Settlers were shot and it was even worse at night. Food, possessions, many things were taken leaving nothing to feed the family.'

Waclaw from Osada Kuchczyce, '… those perfidious Belorussians and Jews began constructing arches of welcome for the encroaching Soviet army, some Jews put red arm bands on their sleeves and having been assimilated into the NKVD, denounced Polish patriots to the Soviets. They would have the same punishment meted out to them by the NKVD'.

Zygmunt from Osada Chrynow, '…that very next morning Poles were murdered by Ukrainians in the church at Chrynow and in many neighbouring civilian villages such as Kalusow. I can remember a frightened woman running down the country lane calling out to me, 'they are murdering' ……. Among those killed were my uncle Ignacy, his daughter Stefania and my godmother and once the Ukrainians had discovered them in the attic, the neighbour and his children. Also murdered in the church were the priest, Eliza and others….. In July 1943 in the village of Kalusow the Ukrainians herded together all the men and women in the barns where they were killed.'

Halina from Osada Niechniewicze, 'the most worrying concern was weapons, which Mother had hidden away and for which the Soviets constantly searched. With a sudden rattling on the door in the middle of the night which would alert everyone, we children would cry and Mother would be put up against a wall and threatened with a rifle. Very often those involved were not Soviet soldiers but Belorussians. …on 10th February 1940 at 2 o'clock in the morning we were all roused and started crying, in strode two NKVD men and 4

Belorussians, one of them read out something in Russian which none of us could understand. One of the locals asserted that we were an undesirable element in the locality and were to be resettled in some nearby province. It's more than evident that local peasants knew exactly what was in store for us'.

'Soviet troops confiscated everything, horses, cattle, sheep and our supply of food. There were constant checks and searches for arms. What an army they were. Hungry, clad in tatters and with outright threats and petty annoyances from 17th Sept to 10th Feb when we left. Most were Byelorussians to whom my parents had shown great generosity and they took everything they could carry from the house and farm buildings and were involved with the Soviets on 10th Feb to arrest us. Although four of them helped us to take bedding, clothing and footwear and carried them out to the sledges.'

Edward from Osada Kuchczyce, 'In Lachowicze I bumped into a Jew from Kleck who delivered apples to the station and gave him a little money to take me back with him on his cart. In my conversation with him I had to be very careful because a large number of poor Jews were committed to communism and in the towns the majority of commissars were Soviet Jews. Lots of people who had been sympathetic towards communism had the scales taken from their eyes as they realised they had fallen into a trap. There were quite a number of people mainly Belorussians and Jews who had constructed welcoming arches for the invading Red Army and for some their reward was deportation to Siberia and Kazakhstan.'

Władysław from Osada Budowla, '17th September arrived and the road was filled with tanks, lorries pulling trailers, horses being ridden without saddles, in such a manner was the entrance of the Red Army while at the same time Belorussians prowled through the villages. They sported red arm bands on their sleeves and the rifles and boots confiscated from the Polish soldiers who had retreated from the Germans. These peasants claimed to aid in 'the liberation from the Polish masters', in fact anarchy reigned and news broke that 11 settlers from Lerypol had been murdered and buried in the forest by Belorussians from Ogrodniki village…….'. The Byelorussians who stood up for the Poles were threatened with murder and many settlers from Osada Budowla and Osada Lerypol, approx. 25, were also murdered.'

Zofia, from Osada Nowosiolki, 'the military settlers were drawn from a wide disparity of social class yet lived in amity quite well. The relationship between the settlers and the indigenous people was more than acceptable, one must nevertheless admit that among the locals there was an element hostile to the Poles, especially towards the military families. There was destruction of crops and animals, frequent threats of murder which later proved too true, encouraged by Bolshevik propaganda among Byelorussian communists.'

Alicja from Osada Chrynow, 'We reached Poland in 1946 and only two of my mother's brothers Piotr and Julian were awaiting us. My grandparents, her sister Weronika and brother Felix were murdered by the Ukrainian UPA units in July 1943.

And from **Christine**, a personal account of her father Wladyslaw who lived in Hraine with his godparents, wife Janina and two sons, who came home in April 1943 after fighting with the partisans. He had heard the stories of Ukrainians murdering Poles and of villages being burned

'The UPA began their murders in the village of Hraine which was mostly Ukrainian and ¼ Poles. It was brutal. His sons Julian 8 and Roman 5 were beheaded as were all the children in the village. Women were nailed to barn doors, it was horrific and his godmother was tied to a chair and daggers were thrown at her. His godfather with his hands tied behind his back was made to kneel and had his tongue nailed to the table.

Some of the villagers had their hands tied with ropes and the UPA on horseback pulled their limbs apart. People were burned alive, cruelty beyond belief. Wladyslaw had been hidden by a Ukrainian friend and a cousin, from the killers in a pile of manure, he escaped to the woods and never came back.'

All the properties vacated by the deportees were instantly taken over by former 'neighbours' from the Byelorussian, Ukrainian and Jewish groups. My family had barely got onto the sledge taking them to the station when their property was seized.

Zofia, from Osada Chlewiszcze 'the 'Soviets' were constantly searching homes, taking possessions, hay, potatoes, cereal, furniture. They would just arrive and take what they wanted as the Soviet admin had been established so quickly. Arson and raids began on the farms and settlers' houses, with arrests and burning down of farms. A general election was held and all settlers were collected and taken to vote as Soviet citizens,'

The Germans and Soviets incited the UPA, to a point, to murder the Poles although historically the Ukrainian UPA wanted 'their land' back and needed very little encouragement, lauded by the Ukraine to this day.

The common theme throughout these recollections is the way the mostly communist element turned against the Polish settlers, after having lived and worked amongst them for so many years. It seems obvious that the intent of that element was to 'settle old scores' in order to 'get their land, back'.

These many recollections were from the Polish refugees living in England who would eventually become British citizens under the Aliens Registration Act of 1929. Before then they had to register in a Police station every time they moved houses, or visited relatives, or changed jobs and this continued until 1962.

I have detail of the movement of my own Grandparents from 1948 to 1962, logged in their Aliens Pass Books.

They had gone through very similar hardships and made England their home, made an immense contribution to their own and English communities and were also sending parcels to their own families and orphanages in Poland until the 1990's.

They had suffered for Poland, been happy in Poland and helped their homeland whilst living in England. Most of the Poles here after the war have been happy, making new lives for themselves, they are grateful to England. They began here in resettlement camps, and set up Polish schools. The risk of returning to Poland was high, conditions for families were difficult under Soviet rule.

'I felt a stranger there, you could feel the atmosphere of occupation' said relatives upon visiting their sisters who had remained in or gone back to Poland. Family members would be imprisoned by the new Soviet regime for the most spurious of reasons. Many returnees were accused of being spies and arrested, went through sham 'trials' and sent to labour camps or gulags, those who had been Partisans as very many had been, met worse fates.

Kazia and Adam, my Babcia and Dziadek, died in England within a year of each other in 1983 and 1984. It's a long time ago but I will never forget them. Their homeland Poland had been chilled to the marrow by Stalin's invasion and taken over by Communism, they could not go back. They were in Lebanon in 1946 with their son Janusz, waiting for permission to join their daughters Alicja and Jasia who had earlier travelled to England. Alicja with her English husband and Jasia to Teacher Training College.

In England, the Attlee Government was hesitant to allow more dependants into the U.K. and was writing to Polish servicemen asking them to go home! By early 1947 however their prospects looked brighter with the Polish Resettlement Act, the first ever mass immigration legislation of a British Parliament. They would soon be able to make arrangements to join their daughters. They arrived in February 1948 having waited 18 months for permission.

They had heard of the difficulties of returning to their homeland, from relatives of those who had been met with aggression from the Soviets. They would be treated as 'dissidents' as Adam was ex Military (British Army 1941-44 and Polish Cavalry 1915-1921). Being deported by Stalin in 1940 to the USSR would also be a black mark against them, their future in Poland would be dire.

Dissidents, were classified as the Polish' intelligentsia', or what remained of it. Stalin had murdered most of them shortly after he invaded Poland, Teachers, Professors, Lawyers, Doctors, Military, Students, Priests, actors and many others. They would be deprived of their professions, forbidden to study or to travel. If they joined the Communist Party they might survive in the most menial of jobs, porters, railway workers, cleaners in schools and apartment blocks, porters in stations or be left to their own devices. Most likely they would be 're-educated' in another gulag.

They would be treated as criminals for uttering the wrong word, reading the wrong book or newspaper, simply for thinking freely. My grandparents would not have survived under Soviet control, it had been difficult in the labour camps and having fought against the Russians in the Polish-Soviet war (1919-1921) my Dziadek would most likely have been sent to a gulag or worse. My Babcia would probably be sent with him and I would never have known my 'dissident' grandparents.

The Secret Police were in control, even the trees in the parks were bugged, seems ridiculously extreme but this was Stalin's Communism, this was now Poland, ally of the UK and USA, sold out to Stalin. Files were kept on 'dissidents' and those of 'interest' and the NKVD policed the border between what was permitted and what was forbidden they saw enemies everywhere. Any deviance from the 'norm' was quickly dealt with.

People would inform on a person of 'importance' a neighbour even. Friends betrayed friends although the situation was not as brutal as in East Germany where the Stasi, 12 times bigger than the Gestapo and 35 times bigger than the NKVD was in complete charge. With an army of informers at their disposal to keep notes on 6 ml people, files which stretched 125 miles! It seems quite incredulous but that is Communism.

Loss of personal freedoms with no individual liberties, where the government controls everything and where all goods are 'equally' shared by the people, although from conversations with friends of mine who have lived through Communism, the practice is very different. Most goods are shared by the controlling totalitarian government employees and little gets to the ordinary people! When the ordinary people queue for hours at the shops the shelves are bare, cleared by those on the other side of the counter!

It took another war to eventually defeat Communism across Europe, the Cold War instigated by Stalin in 1947 which created tension between democracies of the western world and Communist countries of eastern Europe. It wasn't until post 1989 that ordinary people eventually overcame the unfairness of the regimes, the corruption of the few, the persecution by the few and the growing riches for the few.

The ignorance about Poland in WW2, especially in the media, about her role as an Ally and her Resistance is astonishing. When it comes to the question of Polish conduct under powerful, brutal, German and Russian occupations, it is treated as a sideshow to Jewish suffering, overlooked.

The world of WW2 was one in which it was easier to hide the truth, London and Washington have obscured the facts for very many years, of the Polish citizens exiled to the wastes of Siberia, 'advised' not to talk about it when they were safely in Iran! After so long it is unforgiveable that the truth is still hidden and in many cases misused by revisionists to spread misinformation.

With the children of the Sybiracy becoming more involved in their family history and with the writings of just one prominent historian, Norman Davies; who has written comprehensive books on this maligned and misunderstood country; one by one the planks are being knocked down but it is a battle for the truth.

My Mother Alicja is 97 and suffers from Alzheimers and her moods are unpredictable but she was happy when I last saw her. It took some time to decipher what she said due to her speech as she told me she remembered how 'we survived the camps, we got out, we got out as a family, all of us, safely, we were so lucky, I am so happy, life is wonderful'. You can imagine the impact it had on me, there were much needed tissues to hand.

My family was very lucky to have found refuge in England. They missed their homeland dreadfully but they had survived the labour camps and the long, arduous journeys from the USSR towards the Polish Army, as a unit and they lived out their lives as free people.

Alicja is my darling most loving Mother, together with Kazia, my inspiration for setting pen to paper to record the family story. This is for her, for Babcia and Dziudziu, for Ciocia Jasia and Wujek Janusz, for Wujek Walery, Ciocia Ziuta, Włodek, Zbyszek and Marysia, the Goral's and the Radomski's, my family, they are not forgotten.

Teresa Radomska 2021

Poland 1916–1940

The Radomski Bloodline

Radomski Family 1930

Władysław Radomski – 1917

Adam Góral – 1917

Tolus Radomski – 1917

Adam Góral
& Walery Radomski – 1917

Walery Radomski 1919

Ziuta Radomska – 1919

Tolus, Bronia, Kazia, Walery,
friend – c1917-18

Walery, Kazia, & Bronia
Radomscy – 1918

Ziuta & Kazia – 1919

Kazia & Adam Góral – 1920

Walery Radomski – 1918

Władysław Radomski – 1920

Jasia Góral – Równe 1935

Góralowie – 1936

Parish Church –
Równe

Adam, Gienia, Kazia & Janusz

Ziuta & Marysia
Radomska – 1937

Walery Radomski   Kazia Góral   Adam Góral   Ziuta Radomski

Walery Radomski's house (Osada Krechowiecka 1937)

Osada Krechowiecka – 1937

Janusz – 1938

Równe 1937
Kazia with Ala, Janusz
and Jasia

Ala, Halina, Jasia, Janusz
Osada Krechowiecka 1938

v

Janusz & Adam Góral –
Równe 1936

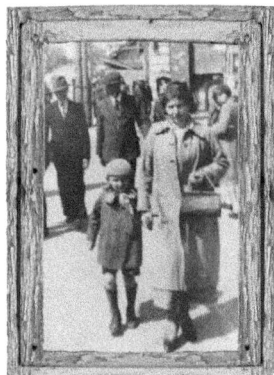

Janusz with Kazia –
Równe 1936

Ala & Janusz Góral –
Równe 1938

Równe 1939
Kazia & Adam with Janusz

Ala Góral – Równe 1938

Ala Góral – Równe 1938

The War Years
1939-1945

Jasia – Palestine 1944

Ala – Teheran 1943

Teheran 1943

Jasia & Adam – Palestine 1943

Ala, Jasia – Pahlevi 1942

Kazia, Ala, Janusz,
Adam – Teheran 1943

Ala at the sick bay – Teheran 1943

Ala & Kazia – Isfahan 1944

Kazia – Isfahan 1944

Mosque – Isfahan

viii

Jasia – Nazareth 1943

Jan, Kazia, Adam, Ala –
Teheran 1943

Janusz – Teheran 1943

Ala, Janusz, Ziuta, Kazia, Marysia –
Teheran 1943

Isfahan 1944

Adam, Włodek & Walery –
Teheran 1943

Ala & Bill – Isfahan 1944

Ala & Kazia – Isfahan 1944

Ala – Teheran 1944

Ala – Teheran 1944

Ala & Bill – Teheran 1944

Ala, Janusz, Kazia – Isfahan 1944

Ala & Jasia – Gazir 1945

Ala & Jasia – Gazir 1945

Ala & Bill – Gazir 1945

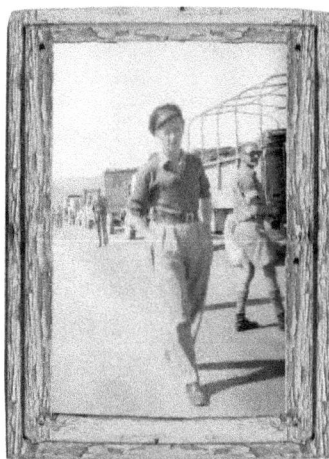

Bill – between Khanaqin, Iraq
and Kermanshah, Persia 1945

1st Xmas together since 1942 – Ghazir, 13 Dec 1945

The Wedding – Ghazir, Lebanon 1946

Passports & Certificates
of Registration
for Adam & Kazia Góral

Alien's Order A128295
& A128294 – 1948

Necessary paperwork
for our grandparents
to enter England

England
1946–1960

Jasia – 1949

Kazia & Adam – 1948

Janusz – 1949

Bolesław, Jasia, Ala, Janusz
– Kew Gardens 1949

Jasia & Bolesław –
Victoria, 1949

Janusz, Jasia, Bolesław –
London 1949

Bill, Ala & Walery – 1951

Bolesław & Jasia –
Wedding, Victoria, 1949

Walery – 1952

Bolesław & Jasia –
Wedding, Victoria, 1949

Marysia, Wiesiek –
Wedding, Brompton, 1950

Lytham St Annes 1952

Alec – Lytham, 1952

Alec & Janusz – Victoria
c1952

Alec & Jasia – Victoria, London 1953

Alec, Tony & Teri –
Victoria, London, 1952

Teri, Alec, Tony, Chris – 1956

xvi

Kazia & Adam with Ala & Grandchildren – 1956

Brixton – 1957

Sisters Kazia & Gienia – Brixton, 1957

Wiesiek, Marysia, Wlodek, Walery, Gienia, Marek, Kazia – 1957

Janusz & Pam Reception – Chelsea, 1956

Janusz & Pam Wedding – Clapham, 1956

Halina & Wiesiek Morawiec – c1959

Jasia & Bruno Wedding 1966

Adam – c1963

Janusz – Bedford Hotel c1965

Jasia & Bruno Wedding 1966

197 s

Alec – Wedding 1972

Adam & Kazia – Streatham c1976

Adam & Kazia – 1976

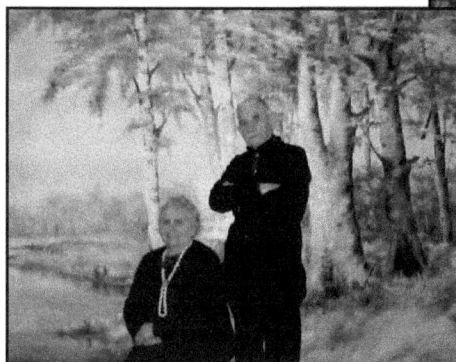

Ala with Adam & Kazia – c1979

Alec & Hazel – Wedding 1972

Ala 1985

Janusz with
Queen Mother –
Savoy Hotel c1982

Pamela, Ala & Jasia 1980

Ala & Bill

Adam & Kazia – c1980

Ala, Janusz, Jasia

Ala & Chris 1992

Anita, Tim, Hazel, Alec

Ala, Stan, Jean, Janusz, Jasia

Jasia & Stan

Anita

Tony & Chris

Ania, Anita, Ewa, Hazel

Wiesiek & Marcin

Jean, Jasia, Ala

Jasia & Ania

Alec, Hazel, Chris

Ania, Wiesiek & Ewa

Ala & Teri

Janina
& Wiesiek

Lynsey

Hazel, Ania, Alec, Anita

Chris & Jana

The 2010s
A social revolution.

Ania & Ewa

Nicola, Ala & Nella

Ania, Alec & Ewa

Alec, Ania, Hazel & Ed

Steve, Ania, Marek, Tony

Ewa, Ania, Anita, Krysia

The 2010s
A social revolution.

Lynsey & Anthony

Tony & Hazel

Anita & Wiesiek

Nicola, Natalie, Margaret

Emma & Daniel

Krysia

Ala & Halina

Chris, Anita & Margaret

Tony with sons Will, Jon & Dan

The 2010s
A social revolution.

Alec & Marek

Margaret & Teri   Tony & Anne

Alec & Anita

Chris & Jana   Natalie & Ala

Alec, Ala & Teri

Ala 95th   Maciej

Will & Trinia

Ania & Alec

Tony & Anne

Alec & Chris

Nicola, Ala & Natalie

Ala

Alec & Teri

Halina & Ala

Chris, Hazel, Ania, Teri, Nicola, Ewa, Natalie – at The Polish Embassy in London 2018

Siberian Exiles Cross Awards

A very proud day for the family

Today we are at *The Polish Embassy in London* for the Presentation Ceremony with family members.

Alicja Góral-Hartley has been awarded the Siberian Exiles Cross. Her sister, Janina Góral-Dyki-Misik, has also been awarded posthumously.

The sisters along with their parents Kazia and Adam and brother Janusz were deported in cattle wagons from Równe to a labour camp (Gulag) in northern Siberia on 10th February 1940 on Stalin's orders.

The cross is awarded in order to recognize and commemorate the sufferings of Polish citizens deported to Siberia, Kazakhstan and Northern Russia from 1939–1956 against their will.

The cross memorializes their devotion to the ideals of freedom and independence against Communism.

The application took over a year to process and we are grateful to Elzunia Gradosielska for locating the forms for us and Rysiek Grzybowski for his assistance in preparing the applications.

Teresa Radomska has documented Alicja's story of events in "Midnight Train to Siberia" – *available from Amazon*

Ala

Ewa & Teri

Teri, Ala 95th & Tony

Jasia

Alec, Chris, Marek & Adam

Halina, Teri & Ala

Chris & Alec

Ewa, Chris, Teri, Ania, Marek, Ewa, Adam,
Alec, Elzunja, Danuta, Ryszard

Marek

xxix

Krysia

Marek, Adam, Izabella, Marcin

Ed, Alec, Marek,
Anita & Ania

Ania

Lynsey

Ivy & Nella

Ed & Anita

The Production Team

| Chris | Alec | Natalie & Ala | Teri |

Family Radomski – formerly Bielawski

Walerian Bielawski was arrested and imprisoned in Częstochowa during 1863 uprisings. Escaped prison and moved to Radzymin 30km NE of Warsaw, changing his name to Radomski. Died age 49 had 2 sons & 4 daughters (eldest Wladyslaw)

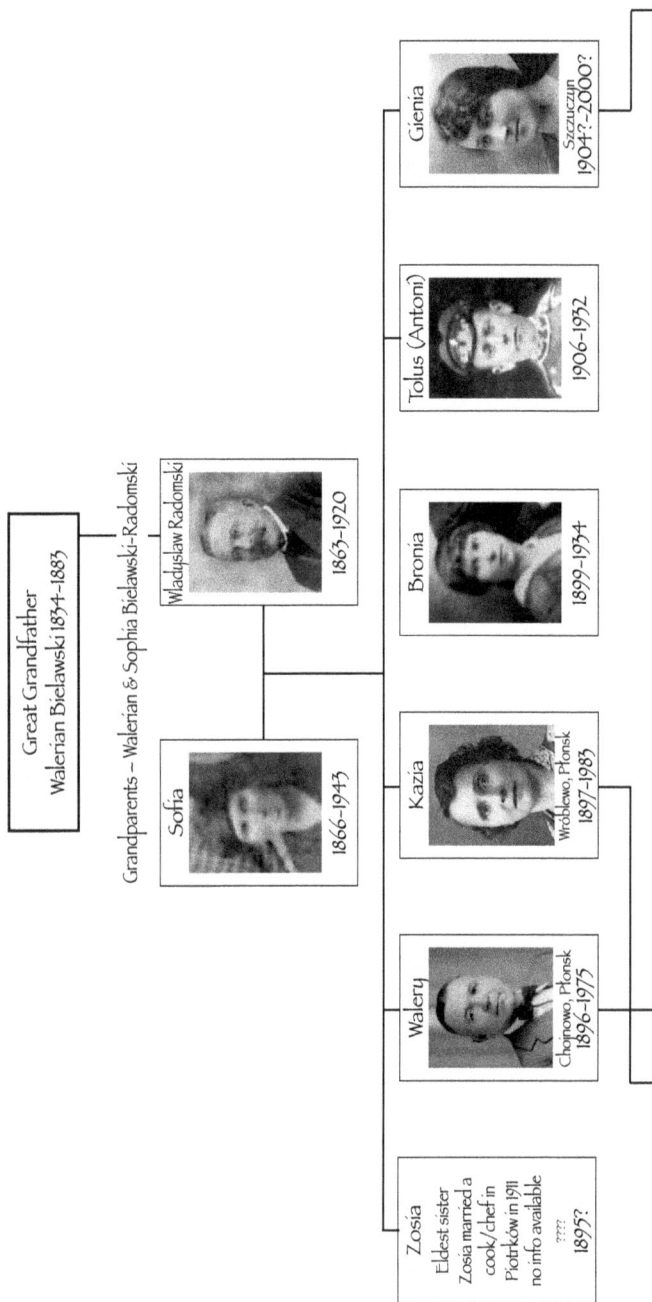

Great Grandfather
Walerian Bielawski 1834-1883

Grandparents – Walerian & Sophia Bielawski-Radomski

Wladyslaw Radomski
1863-1920

Sofia
1866-1943

Zosia
Eldest sister
Zosia married a
cook/chef in
Piotrkow in 1911
no info available
????
1895?

Walery
Chojnowo, Plonsk
1896-1975

Kazia
Wróblewo, Plonsk
1897-1983

Bronia
1899-1934

Tolus (Antoni)
1906-1932

Gienia
Szczuczyn
1904?-2000?

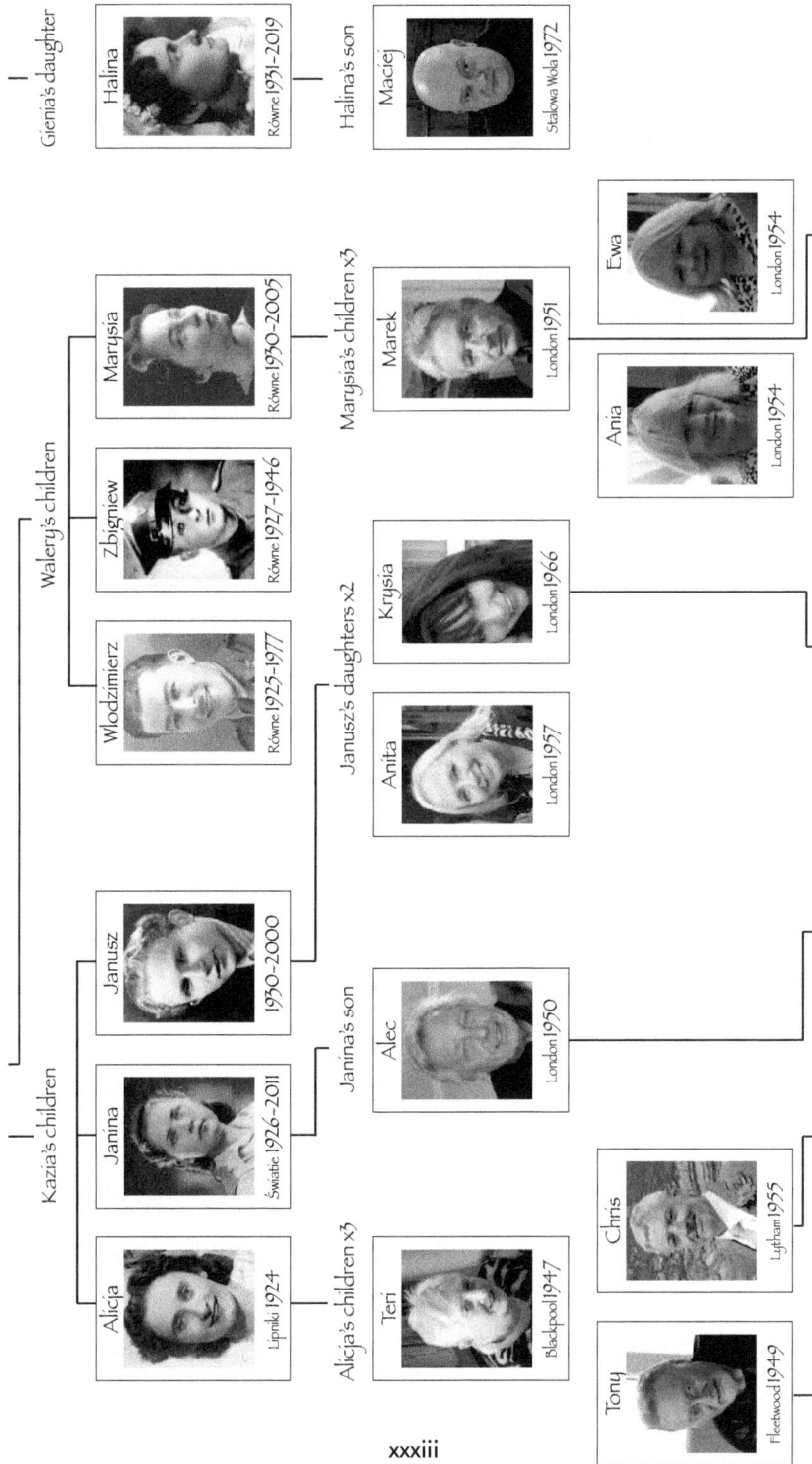

Gienia's daughter

Halina Równe 1931–2019

Halina's son

Maciej Stalowa Wola 1972

Walery's children

Marysia Równe 1930–2005

Zbigniew Równe 1927–1946

Włodzimierz Równe 1925–1977

Marysia's children x3

Marek London 1951

Ewa London 1954

Ania London 1954

Kazia's children

Janusz 1930–2000

Janusz's daughters x2

Krysia London 1966

Anita London 1957

Janina Świątie 1926–2011

Janina's son

Alec London 1950

Alicja Lipniki 1924

Alicja's children x3

Teri Blackpool 1947

Chris Lytham 1955

Tony Fleetwood 1949

xxxiii

Marek's children x3

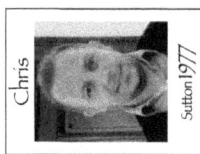

Izabella — Warszawa 1985
Marcin — Warszawa 1983
Adam — Warszawa 1981

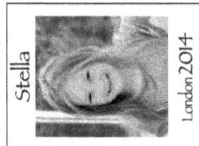

Marcin's daughters x2
Janina — Warszawa 2013
Jadwiga — Warszawa 2017–2022

Adam's daughters x2
Stella — London 2014
Augustyna — London 2015

Krysia's children x2
Jack — 1996
Sophie — 1986

Sophie's sons x2
Damien — 2006
Dean — 2010

Alec's children x2
Lynsey — Sutton 1974
Chris — Sutton 1977

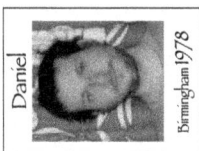

Chris's daughters x2
Natalie — Birmingham 1983
Nicola — Birmingham 1985

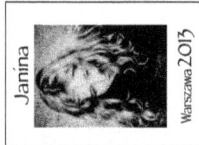

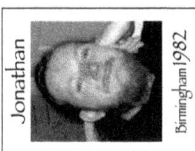

Nicola's daughters x2
Nella — 2014
Ivy — 2016

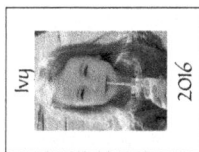

Tony's sons x3
Daniel — Birmingham 1978
William — Birmingham 1980
Jonathan — Birmingham 1982

War is Death to the Truth

My friends know of my Polish heritage and when it has ever come up in conversation I tend to get some quizzical looks and a few questions, amongst them 'how did your parents meet' and I tell them 'in Isfahan, in Persia, my Dad was in the RAF and my Mum and her family were living there.' 'What were they doing in Persia?' 'they had escaped from Russia' I answer 'during the war.' Even today when I am asked about my family and when they came to this country there are those 'looks' or the conversation dries up. I tend not to say much despite being so very proud of my Polish heritage but to those who are interested I give a very brief outline of the Polish deportations by Stalin to the USSR so long ago.

And to explain why this period of WW2 history is not well known of I go on to explain that when my family were newly resident in England after the war, they were reluctant to say very much because of hostility towards the many refugees in the country in the post war years. My Grandparents especially generally kept quiet of why they were in England throughout their lives. The general public knew of the German atrocities, the media comment often and make films to the point of obsession! But of Stalin's atrocities, nothing or very little is known even to this day and Putin the President of Russia is complicating the issue by earnestly rewriting Soviet WW2 history. Implying the war began for Russia in 1941 when she invaded Poland to save its people from the Germans and not that he'd seen an opportunity to spread Communism into Europe through Poland.

I've recently found, via research through the history sites I belong to, some very interesting information which could explain why the world doesn't know or acknowledge the sufferings of the 1.7ml Polish people exiled to Siberia by Stalin. Thousands died on the long journey to Russia and by mistreatment, slave labour and starvation in the camps and on the extremely arduous journey out of Russia to join the Polish army assembling under General Anders in Persia in 1941-1943. Emaciated, ill, barely standing, they headed out to fight with the allies, including the Russians, against the Germans with incredible determination.

The immigrant crisis at the US southern border in 2018 and the US administration's efforts to keep economic migrants in Mexico rather than allowing them into the US is a vivid reminder of a different and completely forgotten episode of WW2 history involving refugee children and the Roosevelt administration's propaganda. It's about the secret censorship by the US government which deceived Americans about Stalin's atrocities.

It is about the collusion with a totalitarian regime that had murdered millions of people in eastern Europe and the USSR and which later forced them to live under communism without freedom until 1989. It is also a reminder of the collusion carried out by the British Government who supported the pro Soviet propaganda campaign.

It is the account of Polish refugee orphans, children who had escaped Siberia, being kept behind barbed wire fences in a former detention centre for Japanese Americans and then being transported in 1943 under US Military guard in locked and sealed trains with blocked out windows, to Mexico, who had offered them asylum for the duration of the war. Roosevelt would not allow Polish refugee children saved from Russia to be given political asylum in the US but helped in transporting them to Mexico. This ensured they would not meet ordinary Americans, especially those of Polish heritage, and they would not be able to tell of their captivity in Russia. It is a story that was never broadcast truthfully, by Voice of America, the US government's official radio station established in 1942 together with the Office of War Information to broadcast WW2 news and propaganda to the world.

The first arrival of Polish refugees on the USS Hermitage in America, consisted of 706 refugees, including 166 children and was a State secret. After disembarking at the San Pedro naval dock near Los Angeles on 25th June 1943, the women and children under 14 years of age were placed in the Griffith Park Internment camp in Burbank, which had been converted to a holding centre after the bombing of Pearl Harbour, for Japanese Americans arrested as 'enemy aliens.' The men were taken to the Alien Camp in Tuna Canyon another detention centre for holding enemy aliens who were considered to be risks to national security!

When the Polish community found out about the arrival of the Polish children they rallied around the exiles and demanded to know why they had been placed in camps. Father Wacław Zajaczkowski even recruited families willing to take in 100 of the orphans. This was not however the plan of the authorities and two days later the refugees were all shipped to Santa Rosa in Mexico. The second group of 726 refugees which included over 400 orphaned children, was also quaranteened to a US army camp near Los Angeles called Santa Anita. After a short stay they too were despatched across the border to Colonia Santa Rosa. The delicate balance of appeasing Stalin, it seems, had to be maintained at any cost.

In March 1943 Senator Danaher inserted into the Congressional Record an appeal from the Polish American community to allow the Polish orphans to stay in the US The Roosevelt administration ignored the appeal. The administration also ignored an appeal from US Democratic Senator Francis T. Maloney. Many Jews, including children trying to find refuge in the US were also refused asylum by Roosevelt, some of them later murdered in German concentration camps.

In 1942 President Roosevelt had created the Office of War Information OWI and this agency joined a host of other wartime agencies including the War and State departments in the dissemination of war information and propaganda. Officials at the OWI used many tools to communicate to the public which included Hollywood movie stars, radio stations and printing presses. The Government was at first reluctant to engage in propaganda, they were not in favour of appeasing Stalin and Roosevelt's close friend and advisor, Under Secretary of State Sumner Welles, warned him about Soviet influence in the OWI and its radio division VOA and in a secret memo to Roosevelt in April 1943, informed him that the VOA Director John Houseman was hiring communists.

Depicting the Soviet Union in propaganda was a difficult task throughout the war as the USSR was an authoritarian regime not a democracy and could not be presented as one. The German attack on the USSR however inspired propaganda in its favour and Hollywood produced pro Soviet movies. Roosevelt promoted the film Mission to Moscow which depicted the Purge trials of Stalin as a just punishment for the Trotskyite conspiracy! The Greta Garbo film Ninotchka however was not released as it ridiculed the Russians. There were other films Why we Fight, The Battle of Russia describing Russia's scorched earth and guerrilla tactics but omitting the reference to the Molotov-Ribbentrop Pact in 1939 between Germany and Russia before they both invaded Poland.

USA led WW2 propaganda was used to increase commitment towards the Allied victory. Using a selection of the media, propagandists instigated hatred for the enemy and encouraged support for America's allies urging greater public support for the war effort and increased production. Patriotism and tradition were the themes of advertising throughout the war as large scale campaigns were launched to sell war bonds, promote efficiency and reduce rumours in an effort to maintain morale.

The U.S produced more propaganda posters than any country fighting in WW2, almost 200,000 designs were printed. These were placed in post offices, stations, schools, restaurants and retail stores and there were smaller ones for private homes. Stories written in the USA or Britain that were critical of the Soviet Union and its policies were often put on hold or not published at all due to the need to maintain friendly relationships with Stalin. George Orwell's anti Soviet Animal Farm, was not published until after the war.

Throughout the war the arrests and forced deportation of Polish families to labour camps in the Soviet Union received no mainstream media coverage at all, the OWI deliberately covered up Stalin's crimes, the deportations and the mass executions of Polish POWs. OWI's Voice of America shortwave radio broadcasts to Europe; which were prepared by Soviet sympathizers and communists hired by the VOA Director John Houseman; repeated Soviet propaganda and disinformation about the Polish deportees who had survived their imprisonment and slave labour in Russia. Later in the war Roosevelt administration propagandists also lied about Polish refugee women and children who were evacuated from Russia in 1942.

One of the most ridiculous lies repeated by the US government propaganda was that the Polish refugees were fleeing from being victims of German occupation when in fact they had been deported on Stalin's orders. Fleeing through the war zone of Poland over 2,000km to safety! The refugees were living witnesses of Stalin's brutality and Roosevelt wanted them isolated and silenced so they would not threaten the military alliance with Russia and his political deals with Stalin for the post war settlement in Europe.

In 1951 the house of Representatives established a Select Committee to conduct the investigation into the Katyn massacre, it was a bi-partisan committee headed by Republican Ray J. Madsen. The committee strongly implied that Roosevelt Administration officials hid, suppressed and censored information about Soviet atrocities. In 1952 the committee blamed it on 'a strange psychosis that military necessity required the sacrifice of loyal allies and our own principles in order to keep Soviet Russia from making a separate peace with the Germans.' The committee pointed out that this psychosis continued even after the war.

There are very many photographs in the public domain of the victims of German persecution, of Jews, Poles, Roma gypsies, Soviet prisoners and many others, in the concentration camps and many scenes of German atrocities.

To find a photograph of a Polish mother and her child as they truly looked after coming out of Siberia, skeletal and in rags, is almost impossible to locate and is an afront to historical truth.

The legacy of silence and disinformation about the Polish orphans and refugees, victims of Stalin's regime, remains to this day, mostly down to the deception of the Roosevelt administration and BBC propaganda and their collusion with a communist regime remaining unchallenged. It is witness to the lasting effects of manipulating public opinion.

To protect Stalin pro Soviet propagandists in Roosevelts administration did not publish photo's of Polish children who were starved, ill or near to death when they were evacuated from the USSR to Persia in 1942. The OWI's VOA broadcasts did not mention the Soviet executions of Polish prisoners of war and the mistreatment of the Polish deportees, including women and children, in the labour camps and gulags. The broadcasts were lies.

There is a US Government photograph of a healthy looking Polish boy, taken by the OWI photographer in Persia in 1943, the boy is well dressed, well nourished, smiling and holding a basket of bread, in complete contrast to the authentic photographs taken by Lieut. Col. Szymański around the same time. British and American authorities throughout the war, assisting in the resettlement of Polish refugees, continued to keep them isolated to prevent them from embarrassing their Soviet ally with the detail of the deportations, executions and other communist atrocities. They were told not to speak of their ordeal and they were certainly not smiling.

Photo of healthy Polish boy carrying basket of loaves

In contrast to the above photograph, those below taken by Polish Army Officer, Lt. Col. Henry I. Szymański, US army liaison officer to the Polish army, of actual refugee Polish children in Persia remained 'classified until 1952' and still are not easily accessed.

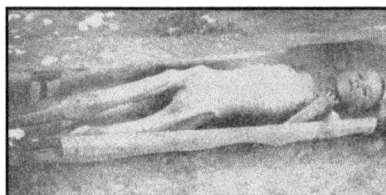

A 10 year old girl, evacuee from Russia August 1942, 3 sisters 7, 8, 9 and 5 boys on the shores of the Caspian Sea.

What was so threatening about these photographs of starving, skeletal, Polish children?

Liet. Col. Henry I. Szymański was a US Army Liaison Officer in the Polish Army, from the class of 1919 under the command of General Władisław Anders, fighting alongside American and British troops in North Africa and Italy. He came from a Polish-American family and was a fluent Polish speaker. On 22nd November 1942 he sent a report on Polish-Russian relations to the Military Intelligence Division, War Department, General Staff (G-2) in Washington D.C. He was awarded the Legion of Merit.

In August 1942 he had seen and taken photographs of many of the starved and dying Polish refugees including children who had been evacuated from Soviet Russia with the Anders' Army. In his lengthy report, which was classified as secret and not published until 1952, he had made his observations on the deplorable condition of these refugees.

The children had very little chance of survival, half of them had already died from malnutrition and unless help could reach the rest they would not

210

survive. Many of the hospitals in Tehran were already inundated with the ill and dying refugees coming in from Port Krasnovodsk by boat to Pahlevi, as my family had done earlier in that year. A visitor at the time to any Tehran hospital would testify to this statement, they were filled with children and adults who had barely survived their ordeal.

The arrests and forced deportation of Polish families to labour camps in the Soviet Union received no mainstream media coverage throughout the war, nor did the murder of Polish intellectuals in 1940, the OWI deliberately covering up Stalin's crimes, especially the mass executions of Polish POWs at Katyn. Soviet guilt denied despite there being significant evidence of the discovery in April 1943 by the Germans. This perhaps the greatest Soviet propaganda lie, the false claim of Soviet innocence of Katyn. OWI director Elmer Davis, wrote and voiced instead propaganda blaming everything on the Germans.

The Congressional Madden committee blamed OWI director Elmer Davis for bearing the responsibility, without full investigation, for accepting the Soviet propaganda version of the Katyn massacre. 'His broadcast reinforcing Soviet propaganda claims was aired repeatedly by the VOA' and the committee also said that 'the VOA had failed to utilize available information concerning the massacre until the creation of this committee.'

Before the war Elmer Davis had been a reporter for the New York Times and a CBS presenter prior to being hired to run the OWI. One of his broadcasts was aired by the VOA on 3rd May 1943, and he was already denying Stalin's guilt over Katyn spreading his propaganda through both VOA and the domestic radio networks of the US 'The easiest way to inject a propaganda idea into most people's minds is to let it go through the medium of an entertainment picture when they do not realise that they are being propagandized.' – Elmer Davis as quoted in Hollywood goes to War c1941.

VOA's shortwave radio broadcasts to Europe prepared by Soviet sympathizers and Communists hired by VOA Director John Houseman, continued to repeat Soviet propaganda and disinformation about the Polish refugees and Poland. The State Department supported by US Army Intelligence eventually refused to issue a U.S passport to Houseman for Government travel abroad and he was forced to resign. He later became an Oscar winning Hollywood actor, a far better stage for his dramatic aspirations.

A former Communist Soviet journalist, Wanda Brońska-Pampuch was a translator and writer and daughter of Mieczysław Broński an activist of the Communist party of Poland. She had accompanied Lenin on his journey from Switzerland to Russia before the October 1917 revolution and worked at the Polish Radio Free Europe radio station telling the truth of the Soviet labour camps. Moscow ordered her assassination in the early years of the Cold War. (Her parents had been executed by the NKVD in 1938).

However the assassination of the journalist wasn't carried out as the assassin, Józef Swiatilo a Polish Security Services Policeman, defected to the West in 1953 and informed the CIA of the orders given to him by Stalin. As well as knowing of the deportations and the Polish refugees, Wanda was well aware of Stalin's crimes and atrocities and the corruption of the 'elite' Communists in the Soviet state. Moscow was especially concerned about the propaganda impact of her accounts of the mistreatment of Polish and Russian children under Stalin's rule.

The US Government institutions who had been responsible for false propaganda about the Polish deportees in the Soviet Union, the Katyn murders and the wartime refugees and so much more misleading information, never ever admitted they had done anything wrong. They insisted that the VOA was created during WW2 to broadcast only truthful news. However, Radio Free Europe, had never lied about Katyn or censored information about the plight of the Polish or other prisoners of the Soviet Gulag which conflicted with VOA's interpretation.

Americans had been lied to and misled by Soviet propaganda from an agency run by active pro Soviet officials in the Roosevelt administration who maintained that not silencing the accounts would undermine the support of the Polish-American community for the war effort! Many American journalists had been deceived by the US government propaganda although very many others had not, including some Polish-radio stations. They saw through the co-ordinated effort of the Soviet and US Governments and tried to expose it.

They reported on the Soviet deportations and Stalin's atrocities despite Roosevelt's officials trying to censor them and shut them down. Some US lawmakers were also not deceived by the propaganda and they and Senator John A Danaher (R. Connecticut) were trying to expose the Soviet influence over the OWI and VOA broadcasts. They were demanding the removal of pro Soviet officials and broadcasters who were deceiving the American people, presenting the Soviet Union and Stalin to the American people as forces for peace, security and democracy.

The Truman administration after the war, stated that releasing such information 'would unleash a bloody uprising in Poland against the communist regime and the Soviet occupiers!' These arguments were rejected by the bipartisan Madden committee, it 'was not impressed with statements that publication of facts concerning this crime prior to 1951 would lead to an ill-fated uprising in Poland' and the committee added, 'neither was it convinced by the statements of OWI officials, that for the Polish-Americans to hear or read about the Katyn massacre in 1943 would have resulted in a lessoning of their co-operation in the Allied War effort,' their more likely allegiance would have increased their cooperation I'm sure.

In later US led attempts to reverse the effects of wartime collusion to protect Stalin the story of the Polish refugees was never fully told. Even as a much needed warning about the evils of Communism, the betrayal of a faithful ally and the deceitful effects of propaganda.

Had they followed the Madden Committee view on this perhaps the US and the rest of the world would have been aware of Stalin's atrocities?

The story of the Polish wartime deportees and refugees and all those who had died in Soviet captivity, has never to this day been properly acknowledged. They were deported by Stalin and then deported from history, their fate never acknowledged as a War Crime, never acknowledged by western historians. At the end of the war Roosevelt, without the knowledge of the Polish Government in exile and the Polish American community betrayed Poland and agreed that Soviet Russia be given the territory of eastern Poland occupied under the Hitler-Stalin pact of 1939.

It was harder for ordinary people to understand what was going on after the war, when for example the NKVD, the People's Commissariat for Internal Affairs, was being described simply as a Police force! The main function of the NKVD was to protect the state security of the Soviet Union and their role was accomplished through massive political repression, the authorized murder of many thousands of politicians and citizens, as well as kidnappings, assassinations and mass deportations.

The rewriting of Poland's WW2 history began almost immediately Stalin took over. School children were taught that Stalin had won the war and saved Poland from Germany. All previous Polish history was ignored and any written detail was destroyed. Only Communism was taught and talking about Poland's WW2 suffering would result in arrest.

Facts had been manipulated during the war to portray Stalin as good old Uncle Joe, airbrushing his public persona rather than portraying him as the tyrant he was. Between 1943 and the end of 1945 more than the sacrifice of Poland at Yalta seemed to be necessary to keep Stalin in good humour and on side. The eyes of the Allies were blind to his acquisition of the smaller nations and one by one Stalin seized them. Estonia, Latvia, Lithuania, some of Finland, Poland, Czechoslovakia, Yugoslavia, Hungary, Albania, Rumania, Bulgaria. The western Allies seeming to ignore the principles they went into the war to protect!

The western Allies ignored that Stalin had committed the most horrendous crimes whilst allied to them, especially in Poland. The cover up of Katyn and the secret deal in Tehran prior to the later meeting at Yalta. Whilst my own family and many Polish refugees were recovering from their ordeal in Pahlevi, Isfahan and Tehran, the Polish borders were moved without the consent of the Polish Government in exile, they were not included in the discussions.

Churchill accused the Polish Government in exile, at a meeting in Moscow of being 'callous people who want to wreck Europe.' Poland who was their ally had fought in the Battle of Britain with the 2nd largest number of pilots, Monte Cassino, Falaise Gap, and Dunkirk. Poland had been fighting for Poland and Europe and had been 'rewarded' by exclusion from the Victory Parade in London in 1946. I didn't learn of this until I was in my teens and then became aware of the disregard my family had for Churchill and Roosevelt. I was chatting to my Ciocia Jasia about the family history, even then collecting information on what the family had gone through, and she expressed her justified anger at the Allies for their treatment of her family and countrymen. I then completely understood. All that anger over the years made complete sense.

Even after Stalin's death the persecution of those who had been deported under his orders continued until the fall of communism in 1989. Their tormentors though continued to prosper. The guards who took part in the deportations and committed the crimes against the deportees all lived very well. They received ranks and privilages, still had power and escaped any punishment. Stalin left this life escaping justice and no Soviets were ever held to account at the Nuremburg Trials.

The anti Communists

Seweryn Bialer was a refugee and ex communist, a Jewish Holocaust survivor born in Berlin who lived in Łódz in Poland before and during the war and was active in the anti German Polish underground. He was arrested and was a prisoner in Auschwitz. He broke with Communism and defected to the West in January 1956. After the war he tried to educate the Americans about the work of the pro Kremlin propagandists in the U.S and he recorded numerous interviews in Polish with Radio Free Europe and Radio Liberty, describing the crimes, corruption and propaganda techniques used by the Communist regime in Poland.

In testimony in June 1956 before a US Senate sub committee, he exposed pro Soviet influence over the early US radio broadcasts to Europe and the Cold War anti American propaganda activities behind the Iron Curtain and in the US He told the committee that 'the communist leaders in Poland are saying to the Western world, very smartly, very cleverly, don't you criticize us in your radios and we will not jam your broadcasts.'

His interpreter was Jan Karski, another refugee and anti communist who fought in the Polish Underground anti German resistance movement. He was awarded the Presidential Medal of Freedom by President Obama in 2012, posthumously, for his efforts to save Jews from the German Holocaust. In 1982 Israel's Yad Vashem recognized him as Righteous Among the Nations. He died in 2000. He unsuccessfully tried to convince British P.M. Churchill and US President Roosevelt to take stronger direct measures to stop Hitler from killing millions of Jews. The world knew but kept silent.

Bialer also revealed in his US Senate committee testimony, that Stefan Arski, a most violently anti western journalist in Communist Poland, was a former WW2 Polish Desk journalist in the OWI. He revealed that the work of Soviet propagandists sent to the US as agents of influence, was to tell lies of life behind the Iron Curtain. Some of which were so outlandish that the Polish Communist Party banned any publishing of their interviews in Poland to avoid being ridiculed by the Poles who actually lived under Communism's collapsing state. This testimony coincided with the June 1956 Polish workers' uprising in protest against the most miserable living conditions, price increases and lack of freedom they were living under.

I'm sure that 'Uncle Joe' was most grateful to his Western Allies for their conspiracy of silence and for preserving the 'good name' of his evil empire. Even more grateful at Yalta when they granted him the right to enslave eastern Europe and half of central Europe!

Why was there a need for this propaganda and the subsequent attempts at the cover up? The concern for the appeasement of Stalin? He had no choice, he was committed to fighting the Germans and he needed the help of the West and from the Poles who had escaped their captivity in the labour camps and gulags to join with the Allies.

A full disclosure of the Soviet atrocities in Eastern Poland, the deportations and Katyn, may have had a completely different outcome of the events at Yalta? Stalin would not have had the upper hand.

Why didn't America open its door to the Polish refugees? The Western Allies knew full well about the deportations, it's clear from their relief efforts in the Soviet Union and in the Middle East as well as from the many reports. They opted to suppress all information, the reports stamped 'confidential' and reserved for the eyes of 'a few persons especially selected for this purpose' who were to be 'confidentially informed of the fate of the Polish citizens under Soviet rule.'

Whilst in Persia's refugee camps in Pahlevi, Isfahan and Tehran, recovering from their ordeal, the Polish refugees were not encouraged to speak about their experiences of imprisonment in the Soviet Union. According to my Mother Alicja they spoke amongst themselves, comparing life in the different labour camps and then slowly opening up to the questioning they faced from the people they met, one such person being my Father William, stationed there with the RAF who met my Mother and listened to her story. Their fate would slowly become known around the camps and a little wider.

Right wing countries who listen to their people and build walls of barbed wire to keep migrants out for economical and affordable reasons are castigated. But what about democracies? The US both during and after the war and even to this day!

The Katyn Lie – Extracts from an article by Ed Warner, Veteran Journalist who worked at VOA as an editor in the 1980's – *16th April 2019*

'War is death to the truth, any plausible lie will do to advance the cause of one side or the other. An example is the Soviet execution of some 22,000 Polish Officers at Katyn forest as it cemented its rule following the 1939 pact with Germany – one after another shot in the back of the head and pushed into a mass grave. 'But we didn't do it' claimed the Communists, 'the Germans did.' And for many years later they were generally believed.'

'The Germans were capable of any sort of atrocity so the lie had a certain standing, but it contributed to a great misunderstanding of the USSR, and the underestimating of Stalin's plans for conquest and occupation. The West was unprepared and suffered the consequennces. The 'good war' that demolished Hitler strengthened Stalin.' He had emerged the victor with a huge empire in Europe and territories in the far

East, then an unexpected Cold War began.

'In their efforts to win WW2 the West's leaders sentimentalized Stalin who was on their side. He became 'Uncle Joe' to Roosevelt and the Americans. He was just a good hearted ex peasant struggling to be a democrat, when in fact he was a tyrant, one of history's coldest mass murderers.

'Hitler's invasion of western Poland followed quickly by Stalin's invasion from the east, launched one of history's most cataclysmic conflicts. No country suffered more than Poland who's people were used brutishly by the two tyrannies as they advanced over its land, reshaping it, moving its borders and killing its people by the millions. The West did nothing for Poland during or after the war!'

'Poland had to help itself, it raged quietly under Communist rule until 1980 when its people inspired by the formation of Solidarność and supported across the world, brought about the collapse of Soviet rule in all of eastern Europe, Russia as well. Poland had led the way, Poland is flourishing with no threat to its existence.'

Ted Lipien – veteran Journalist Cold War Radio
and collegue at VOA – extracts from his article
– *16th April 2019 in response to Ed Warners*

'An excellent article by Ed Warner. During WW2 the US Government-funded Voice of America (VOA), where I was in charge of the Polish Service in the 1980's and where Ed Warner worked as an editor during the same time, was controlled by American Communist sympathisers, admirers of the Soviet union and a number of Communist Party members. These apologists for Stalin blamed the Poles and their democratic Government in exile in London, for asking for an international Red Cross investigation of the Katyn massacre after the mass graves were discovered by the Germans in 1943.'

The State Department took over the VOA in 1945 and censored news about Katyn in an attempt to obscure the Soviet responsibility for the mass murder and VOA was strongly condemned for this in 1952 by the biartisan congressional Madden Committee which investigated the Katyn Massacre. The committee was chaired by Ray Madden, a Democrat from Indiana. It was only then that VOA began to report at greater length on the actual truth about Katyn. VOA did however, revert to limited censorship of any Katyn related news and it was only during the Reagan administration that all restrictions on reporting on the Katyn story were finally removed at Voice of America.'

It was fortunate that Radio Free Europe, who were also funded by the American tax payer, did not restrict its reporting on Soviet crimes and its reports were truthful and comprehensive.

Windrush – Polish refugees collected from Mexico via the US

On 21st June 1948 when the MV Empire Windrush docked at Tilbury Harbour as well as the Jamaicans on board, there were 66 Polish Nationals, the result of a UK Government sponsored scheme to gather Polish nationals scattered across the globe and to reunite them with partners and families in the United Kingdom.

In the summer of 1943 , Poles mostly women and children, amongst the thousands displaced from Poland by Soviet aggressions during WW2 were transported to Colonia Santa Rosa, a refugee village near the city of Leon, Mexico. Four governments, Polish, Mexican, British and American had taken part in the negotiation for their safe haven. The group remained at Santa Maria until the 27th March 1947 when the British Government passed the Polish Resettlement Act. This legislation granted Polish troops who had contributed to the Allied war effort permanent stay and assistance to integrate in Britain.

It was the first mass-immigration legislation designed to enable not restrict foreigners' entry. Arrangements were made to bring their dependents who were in exile throughout the world to join them. In the late 40's and early 50's ships brought thousands of Poles who had qualified, my family was included, my Grandparents and Wujek were stranded in Lebanon waiting to join their daughters in England. They arrived in February 1948.

The Empire Windrush on its route through Kingston docked in Mexico to collect 39 adult women, 26 children and 1 adult male of Polish nationality. Their names and travel details are preserved on the ship's manifest under the heading 'alien passengers' as opposed to 'British passengers,' or even Polish!

Very few people are aware of those Polish citizens on the Windrush despite the controversy in 2018 on the issue of West Indian Windrush passengers with the Home Office in England. Nothing was mentioned of those Polish passengers! Their presence still not acknowledged as it wasn't in 1948 when they disembarked, nothing of them captured on film amongst the cheering Caribbean migrants.

Many of the Poles on board had been separated from their families and were heading to England to rejoin them, or what was left of them. On board the Windrush they travelled in berths below the waterline where it was dark and very musty and they were not allowed to roam freely on board. They could only go out on deck in escorted groups and not allowed to see other passengers!

When they disembarked at Tilbury in Essex on 22nd June 1948 it was cold and damp, in extreme contrast to Mexico. They were quietly moved onto further transport to Resettlement camps, well away from the cameras on the West Indian passengers! Later they would have to register as immigrants and report to the Police if they moved house or got a job or got married, even when they visited their relatives.

I've illustrated my Grandparent's 'Alien's Order' and Certificate of Registration, Passbooks' with detailed information about reporting to Police Stations whenever they left their home address!

Most of the Windrush Poles put down roots in the U.K. and lived out their lives as British Citizens or departed for Canada, Australia or the United States.

Britain designed the Polish resettlement Act after the second world war and it shows how owing to those measures, ethnic and racial groups, in this case, West Indians and Poles, were brought into contact in the immediate post war years aboard the Empire Windrush.

There is another side to this story, at the most, 120,000 of the Poles deported to Siberia managed to escape. Some found themselves in the USA and were a great embarrassment to President Roosevelt who wanted to convince Americans that 'Uncle Joe' Stalin was a nice guy fighting on the same side as America against the Germans and not another monster who had just put millions of people into his own concentration camps. Roosevelt had rung up the President of Mexico and asked whether he could pack these embarrassing Poles to Mexico for the rest of the war, which is what then happened. Which is why in 1948 some of those Poles came on the Windrush to the UK.

British Propaganda

The broadcsts of the BBC Polish Service during the war was a major source of information in occupied Poland although listening to or having a radio was punishable by death under German occupation. For many Poles the BBC was the only contact with the rest of the world and informed the Poles about what was happening in their own country and also on the front as well as internal political matters. The BBC cooperated with the Polish Underground which distributed extracts in newspapers and leaflets and it also worked through the Polish Government in exile,which had taken refuge in London in 1941. The BBC also supported Allied intelligence, sabatoging German action and interrupting work in German factories.

The BBC Polish service was required to follow the official line of the British Government, presenting a positive picture of the USSR, Britain's ally from 1941. Anything considered anti-Soviet was expunged and controversial issues such as the Polish-Soviet border, the deportation of Polish citizens across the USSR, the arrests of members of the Polish Home army, the Armia Krajowa, and the Katyn massacre were all labelled sensitive and withheld from the BBC broadcasts. Many quarters in Poland began to question the impartiality of the BBC as many people in this country do to this day!

The BBC Polish Service was a powerful medium in the Polish-Soviet negotiations due to its large audience in Poland and among the Polish Army fighting all over the world. The BBC European service had been designed as a tool of Britain's foreign policy and the BBC's Polish broadcasts were a significant arm for convincing the Polish people to agree to Stalin's territorial demands.

The acceptance of the Curzon line did not have the support of the Polish population or the leaders of the Armia Krajowa and it would be necessary to sell the policy of Stalin's territorial intentions by way of propaganda. There is an assumption that the British Government, although aware of Soviet political manoeuvring, the arrests and killings of members of the Home Army, concealed this information from the public and the broadcasts to Poland assumed 'an increasingly emotional, anti-German tone' with 'the political questions to be kept in the background' not giving 'an impression that we are concealing anything.'

Coverage of the Warsaw Uprising in 1944 was given a similar treatment when the BBC Polish Service failed to inform Polish listeners about the actual political and military situation. The Political Warfare Executive, PWE, had acknowledged in February 1944 that the Red Army would most probably occupy Poland and up until the end of the war the BBC Polish Service continued to suppress information which would in any way undermine the Soviet Union's position as a friendly neighbouring country and guarantor of Poland's independence.

In 1949 in his dystopian novel 1984 George Orwell painted a terrifying picture of a state machine dedicated to parroting the party line.

It was based on the author's own wartime experience of working for the BBC. The Corporation has changed very little, its prejudices a clear contempt for the British people, it has become a voice only for the Metropolitan middle classes.

Information about the betrayal of the Polish nation and its people is very slowly filtering out to the world, courtesy of the children of Sybyraks who are stubbornly resolute in their endeavour. They are however, up against the rewriting of WW2 history by both Putin and the US Jewish Lobby and Government. Our grandparents and parents did not give up neither shall we in our own venture.

Maharaja Jam Sahib Digvijaysinhji Ranjiysinhji and Polish Refugees

In contrast to Roosevelt's attitude towards the Polish refugees, especially the children, the Maharaja Jam Saheb showed a completely generous and loving nature.

India was the first state to offer shelter to the Polish orphans and the Maharaja offered to provide hundreds of children with a home. As a Hindu delegate to Britain's war cabinet he was aware of the international situation at the time and he didn't hesitste to make his offer. The children were transported to India by members of Anders' Army, the Red cross, the Polish Consulate in Bombay and British officials.

In early 1942 the first group of orphans travelled 1,500km in trucks from Ashgabat to Bombay then onto Balachadi a small seashore town in north western India. It must have seemed like paradise after the hell they had experienced in the USSR. The others were to make the journey shortly afterwards. In total over 600 Polish children found a home in India.

The Maharaja greeted the children with the words 'You are no longer orphans, from now on you are Nawangarians and I am Bapu, father of all Nawangarians, so I am your father as well.'

They were provided with food, clothes and medical care and the Maharaja let the guest house of his palace in Balachadi be used as a school so his proteges could learn to read and write. A library with Polish books was set up so they wouldn't forget their mother tongue and they played volleyball, hockey went camping and staged plays. They were very well looked after and they and the Maharaja were heartbroken at the end of the war when the children had to return to their homeland.

The Maharaja never requested any financial compensation for his gesture his only wish was to have a street named after him in Poland. However, the communist regime did not recognise the orphans' plight since it would have shed light on the atrocities committed by the Red Army.

It was only after Poland became fully independent that a square in Warsaw was named after him, Good Maharaja's Square and a school established, the Jamsaheb Digvijay Singh Jadeja School in recognition of his help to Polish refugees.

A documentary titled 'Little Poland in India' was made in collaboration of both Indian and Polish governments to honour his efforts and those of Kira Banasinska who led the movement in India to rehabilitate Polish refugees.

He was extremely kind hearted and was posthumously given the Commander's Cross of the Order of Merit of the Republic of Poland.

Maharaja Jam Sahib
of Nawanagar

Forgotten Refugees & Silenced Refugees Cold War Radio Museum – helping to generate pro Soviet propaganda through VOA broadcasts
Katyn Forest – Hearings before the US Select Committee to Conduct an investigation on the facts March 14th 1952

CHAPTER 14

Hurtling Bolts of Fury

'we are comrades in life and death.
We shall conquer together, or we shall die together' –
(General Anders 18th June 1941)

On 1st September 1939 Europe was plunged into a second devastating world war barely 21 years after the end of the first war. For Poland it was the beginning of a nightmare that was to last for almost half a century. The Polish nation, its President and Government refused to surrender or accept the occupation of its nation by Germany and Russia and fought to the very end.

The invasion of Poland by Germany and Russia was within the terms of the secret protocol of the Molotov-Ribbentrop Pact signed for the division of Northern and Central Europe into German and Soviet spheres of influence. Hitler needed this pact so that his armies could invade Poland mostly unopposed and he went on to invade Poland on 1st September 1939 and informed Russia shortly afterwards that its forces were nearing the eastern zone in Poland and urged Stalin to move his troops into this Soviet zone of interest.

Ribbentrop was later found guilty at the Nuremberg trials for his role in starting WW2 and was executed on 16th October 1946 by hanging, the first of the German defendants. Molotov meanwhile was removed as Foreign Minister in 1957 and expelled from the Politburo after a failed attempt to have Khrushchev removed as First Secretary. He died of a heart attack in 1962.

The speed of the German advance had taken the Soviets by surprise, they had expected a few weeks rather than a few days to prepare their assault but in the event had to move quickly and on 17th September 1939 the Soviets invaded the eastern borderlands of Poland. The last Polish Army units after a month of fierce fighting capitulated in early October unable to defend against two invading forces, occupying the whole of Poland.

After the invasion, German and Soviet units marched before their commanding officers and held a joint military parade in Bresk-Litovsk on 22nd to celebrate their conquest, it was decorated with swastikas and red stars followed by their national anthems and the changing of their flags. It marked the withdrawal of German troops to the demarcation line secretly agreed between Hitler and Stalin and the handover of the city

223

to Soviet Commander Kombrig Semyon Krivosheim of the Red Army. Other such parades were held across Poland, in Lwów, Grodno and Białystock, Brest and Pinsk to name some. Such celebrations changed dramatically in 1941 when Germany invaded the USSR.

The U.K. and France were obliged under their treaty obligations to declare war on Germany and they did so on 3rd September, World War II had begun in Europe. The contributions of their ally Poland, under siege by two enemie are outlined here.

They fought in the British Navy as well as the RAF and the Army. Polish destroyers Grom, Błyskawica, Burża, Garland and the Krakowiak fought in practically every big battle in the Atlantic, European and Mediterranean waters. Polish airmen contributed heroically to the success of the Battle of Britain in their own squadrons under British command and in RAF units. The Polish 302 and 303 Squadrons were recognised and well documented as the most highly efficient RAF units with the 303 having the highest tally of shot down German aircraft in the Battle of Britain alone.

They made a huge contribution to the Allied effort throughout the war, fighting on land, sea and air. Ground troops were present in the North Africa campaign (Tobruk) the Italian campaign, including the battle for Monte Cassino, the battles following the invasion of France (Falaise Pocket) the airborne brigade parachute drop during Operation Market Garden and in the Allied invasion of Germany. They were considered to be the 4th largest Allied army in Europe after the Soviets, US and Britain.

The Polish intelligence network proved of immense value to Allied Intelligence with pre war and wartime deciphering of German Enigma machine codes by cryptologists Marian Rejewski and his colleagues Jerzy Rozycki and Henryk Zygalski.

Enigma was invented by German Arthur Sheribius at the end of WW1. Codebreaker Lt. Col Jan Kowalski, Polish cryptologist and Intelligence officer, Military commander and creator of the Polish Cipher Bureau, broke Soviet ciphers as early as 1919 and Soviet codes and ciphers during the Polish Russian war in 1920 and as early as 1932 Polish cryptanalyists could decode German ciphers.

Those Polish cryptologists joined the Polish General staff's Cipher Bureau in Warsaw and used mathematics to look for patterns. They had already broken some of the early pre WW2 codes and had built electro mechanical machines which they called 'bomba automova,' the British meanwhile were using linguistic devices.

On the eve of WW2 code breakers Alastair Denniston the Head of the British Government's Code and Cypher School, and Dilly Knox met with members of the Polish Cipher Bureau at a secret facility in a forest in Pyry near Warsaw to share their knowledge. In a later meeting in Warsaw in 1939 between the Polish mathematicians, Gustave Bertrand a French intelligent agent and Alastair Denniston, a 'briefcase of secrets' was given to the British Commander. It included details of the wiring of the Enigma machines and their rotors as well as the design of the 'bomba' the device that helped to tackle machine ciphers.

On 17th January 1940 Polish Cryptologist Marian Rejewski broke the Enigma Code in the presence of Alan Turing during their meeting in Paris, the first time the Enigma Code was broken and the meeting would inspire Turing to develop new ways of code breaking which were later applied at Bletchley Park. The contributions of Rejewski and several other Polish cryptologists to the Enigma Code are other examples of Poland's contribution to the efforts of WW2 being set aside and ignored.

The British in the main treated them sceptically but Turing was able to create a version of the bomba at Bletchley Park which could tackle the sophisticated machines that Germany was then using. 'Pretty much all his breakthroughs were not entirely his own achievement, his insights were brilliant and ground breaking, but he had a serious leg up. All the things associated with his name at Bletchley Park are based on foundation work done by the Poles Marian Rejewski and Henryk Zygalski.' – *Dermot Turing*

Sir Dermot Turing, has recently commented that the 'cult of Alan Turing' has 'been taken to absurd extremes.' He claims in his book, The Real Story, How Enigma Was Broken, that it has 'over shadowed Bletchley Park's debt to the Polish Cryptologists' and that his Uncle's work on the Enigma machines 'was only possible by the work of the group of Polish mathematicians.'

Sir Dermot also states that the 'myth making' has made it difficult to get at the truth, that Britain had 'commandeered' the work done by the Poles and got it grafted into British history.' Sir Dermot in his biography of his uncle's research, has put together the role of the Poles who had been studying Enigma messages before Britain declared war in 1939. He writes that 'without the priceless gift of the theory of the bomba, it is hard to imagine that Alan Turing's crib-checking machine would have been conceived so fast if at all.'

Professor John Ferris in his book Behind the Enigma, an official history of

GCHQ, says that Bletchley Park's contribution to WW2 was overstated and that Turing did not save Britain on his own. 'Bletchley is not the war winner that the British think it is, it did not save Britain although it did help to defeat Germany.' 'The myth is of eccentrics overcoming the odds, the enemy and the establishment and above all of Alan Turing, a mind martyred by his country.'

International amnesia regarding Poland's contribution to the Enigma code and WW2 persists to a great majority to this day! including my brother who looked at me condescendingly when presented with the facts! The allies had been supplied with the secrets of Enigma by the Poles prior to the outbreak of war, but the British desire to appease Stalin, who hated the Polish with a vengeance meant that Polish ingenuity was declared as British!

It remains officially unrecognised to this day and it is hard to overstate the impact the Poles made when they arrived in England in the early part of WW2. A pattern would form with the Polish aces humiliated like the Polish mathematicians were downplayed and an ungrateful Government would want to see the men and women who Hitler feared sent back to Poland!

Rejewski died in 1980 aged 74. He remained silent about his wartime work with the Allies to avoid attention from Poland's Soviet dominated Goverment. He only broke his silence in 1967 when he provided the Polish Military Historical Institute with his memoirs on his work with the Cipher Bureau. Rozycki perished in January 1942, with 222 passengers when the SS Lamoriciere sank in unexplained circumstances. Zygalski remained in exile in the UK and worked until his retirement as a lecturer in mathematics at Surrey University. He was prevented from speaking about his achievements with Enigma/Cryptology by the UK Official Secrets Act. He died in 1978. All three mathematicians putting their efforts into the ongoing development of methods and equipment to exploit Enigma decryption as a source of intelligence.

The remnants of the Polish Air Force had decamped to France early in the war after the Polish Government in exile had been set up there and although heavily outnumbered had fought with distinction above Poland and the Battle of France in 1939. By June 1940 it numbered 7,000 personnel based in France and when that country fell to the Germans, they made their escape to England, to Blackpool their first base.

The Battle of Britain from 10th July to 31st October 1940 was the military campaign in which the RAF defended the UK against large scale attacks by Germany's Luftwaffe. It is believed Hitler's main objective was to compel

Britain to agree a negotiated peace settlement although he intended to invade.

On 11th June 1940 the Polish Government in Exile signed an agreement with the British Government to form a Polish Air Force in the UK. There were to be two Polish fighter squadrons, the 302 Poznański and 303 Kościuszki, made up of 89 Polish pilots with another 50 Polish pilots in RAF squadrons.

There were eventually many Polish squadrons based in Great Britain who fought for the Allies, 300 Masovia, 301 Pomerania, 302 City of Poznań, 303 Kościuszki, 304 Silesia, 305 Greater Poland, 306 City of Toruń, 307 City of Lwów, 308 City of Kraków, 309 Czerwień, 315 City of Dęblin, 316 City of Warsaw, 317 City of Wilno, 318 City of Gdańsk, 663 Polish Artillery Observation squadron. Some 19,400 Polish airmen served in the RAF and PAF and defended British shores and cities.

Their homeland had been crushed by Germany and Russia but they had resisted and although beaten were not quitting, they were exceptional fighters, combat veterans having been through the Polish and French campaigns and had a hatred of the Germans. The stiff upper lip RAF types however, dismissed them as 'hurtling bolts of fury, beyond all reason and authority, they would have to be reeled in and curbed of this suicidal temperament.' A temperament that was to show their exceptional skills in downing the Luftwaffe, putting in place the arrogance of the stiff upper lip Commanders.

They were initially confined to training duties, as if flying 30 death defying sorties against Messerschmitts over Poland counted for nothing! They were humiliated, made to practice on bicycles until they could prove they could wheel left or right in formation! When dispersed among the British squadrons they proved superb flyers, disciplined and popular with their British comrades who were glad to have them on board.

How wrong were these senior Commanders to humiliate them. When the Battle of Britain ratcheted up in August 1940, the skies were full of German planes and there were 142 experienced Polish pilots available, 66 in two special squadrons and the rest scattered amongst other squadrons to back up the hard pressed force of Spitfires and Hurricanes and they were raring to get back at the Germans.

Air Chief Marshall Hugh Dowding AOC Fighter Command of the RAF had this to say about the Polish pilots fighting with the RAF, '…all Polish squadrons swung into the fight with a dash and enthusiasm which is beyond praise… The first Polish squadron 303 during the course of one month shot down more Germans than any other British unit in the same period. Other Poles were used in British squadrons but they were probably most efficiently employed in their own national unit.'

They had been viewed with uncertainty by the British Commanders but the two groups of pilots were soon brothers in arms and the English girls loved these pilots who had been groomed in the old school style by their Officer Corp in Poland. They became a hit with the ladies with their hand kissing gallantry and fearless spirit and young girls were warned to stay away from gin and Polish airmen such was their growing reputation and chivalry. Some English airmen even pretended to be Poles, stitching a 'Poland' label on their uniforms, in order to chat up the girls and I can't say I blame them! The times for enjoyment must have been limited.

When they were ordered into combat on 31st August and let off the leash the Kosciuszki squadron, named after a Polish General, took off from Northolt airfield against an enemy threatening to overwhelm Britain's defences. These 'hurtling bolts of fury' immediately shot down 4 Messerschmittes, bagged a further 6 on 5th September and a further 6 on September 6th. On September 7th the Luftwaffe sent in hundreds of bombers to target London and the Polish squadron shot down 14, a record for any squadron in a day.

It is perhaps in hindsight an appropriate tag, the Poles had to contend with the invasion of their country by the Germans and the Russians whilst also suffering Genocide at the hands of the Ukrainian Nationalists. That they were eager for action against one of their enemies is in no doubt, their resolve was high and these 'hurtling bolts' were extremely accurate, they had more combat experience than most of their British comrades and employed superior tactics, they also wanted revenge.

Despite Churchill's hearty congratulations to the Polish airmen, the RAF bigwigs still turned up their noses as they suspected the excitable Poles must have 'exaggerated their kills' and the next time they went up a Group Captain was sent to shadow them and he witnessed the Poles claim another 14 enemy aircraft destroyed in dog fights and reported back that they had proved their worth 'what they had claimed they did indeed get.' They were super vigilant in their cockpits, they used their eyes scanning every direction rather than rely on instruments and radio, always on the alert, seeing further and acting faster.

By the end of the month the tally of 303 squadron's confirmed kills was over 100, it was to become the highest scoring RAF squadron during the Battle. The methods were simple, swooping down on tight formations of Luftwaffe bombers on collision courses, holding their nerve to fire at the last minute causing the enemy to panic and scatter and to be picked off one by one. The RAF top brass had not expected the Poles to demonstrate better tactics and team work than their own and should have perhaps taken note! They had been embarrassed.

The Poles fought on alongside their British counterparts and ignored the arrogance they had come up against, they were just doing their job and doing it well. One British pilot was killed for every 4.9 enemy planes downed. One Polish pilot was killed for 10.5 enemy planes downed. The newspapers weren't shy about telling of the exploits of the Polish aces in the skies above Britain and King George VI visited them at their Northolt base, signing his name in the squadron diary.

'Britain must never forget how much she owes to the loyalty, indomitable spirit and sacrifice of those Polish fliers. They were our staunchest allies in our darkest days, may they always be remembered as such, I cannot say how proud I am to have been privileged to help form and lead No 303 Squadron and later to lead such a magnificent fighting force as the Polish Wing'. – *John Kent (Canadian) assigned command of Flight A – 303 Squadron.*

The Polish pilots fought on through September and October 1940 alongside their British counterparts and they turned the battle, the Luftwaffe backed off and Hitler's failure to achieve air supremacy led him to postpone Operation Sealion, the invasion of England and instead attack the USSR, ordering his planes to prepare for Operation Barbarossa.

Their job wasn't over, with the Battle of Britain won the Poles continued to fly for their adopted land for the rest of the war. They flew with coastal command, fighter squadrons, bomber squadrons, artillery observation squadrons, engaging in 86,527 combat sorties, destroying 500 enemy aircraft, 190 V1 flying bombs, dropping 14,708 tons of bombs and mines and delivering 12,084 aircraft flying with Transport Command. A special unit delivering supplies to the Resistance forces in occupied France flew 2,747 operations of which 440 were over Poland.

They flew with the Polish 1st Independent Airborne Brigade under General S. Sosabowski, which had been formed in Scotland in 1941, and which participated in Operation Market Garden during 18-26 September, fighting at Arnhem-Driel and covering the British withdrawal across the Lower Rhine. Gen Sosabowski wasn't able to return to Poland and was deprived of his status by the UK and the US in case of upsetting the Soviets which beggars belief but Stalin played both Churchill and Roosevelt throughout the War!

Many of these flights were taken by women pilots, Anna Leska and

Jadwiga Piłsudska daughter of General Piłsudski, being just two of them with several English women pilots, Joan Hughes, Margareet Cunnison, Mona Friedlander and Mary Ellis who flew and delivered Spitfires and who survives at 100. A challenge many women took up but not acknowledged.

In 1945 as the war came to an end and with Poland crushed under Stalin's communism, those Poles who had fought in the hope of returning to their homeland found themselves abandoned. When the incoming Labour Government banned Polish units from the official Victory Parade in London in 1946 for fear of upsetting Stalin, they were devastated, they had fought to defend this land! My family had watched the parade from the side lines, angry and hugely upset. They had all taken risks, made huge sacrifices and were outcasts, the British public had become resentful of their Polish allies who had chosen to stay in England. Although propaganda by the communist supporting papers, the Daily Worker for one, did not help Poland's cause. Not Britain's finest hour!

Labour MPs complained about the cost of resettling the Poles and the Trade Unions turned against them, especially the miners and agricultural workers, despite a huge shortage of labour. Walls near the Polish Air Force bases were daubed with 'England for the English' and 'Poles go home', such was the British public's gratitude, although little was known of Poland's contribution as an ally, hidden by both the UK and the US even to this day.

At RAF Northolt, Polish Airmen, not a grateful Great Britain, erected the monument for those who never returned. It carries the epitaph, 'we gave our souls to God, our hearts to Poland, our bodies to British soil'. Four Polish airmen in the most successful fighter squadron 303 were awarded the Distinguished Flying Cross.

'Had it not been for the magnificent material contributed by the Polish squadrons and their unsurpassed gallantry, I hesitate to say that the outcome of the Battle would have been the same.' – *Air Chief Marshall Sir Hugh Dowding. – It was Poland's finest hour.*

There is a high level move to honour the Polish airmen for what they did for Britain three quarters of a century ago! Lord Norman Tebbit and Lord Michael Ashcroft are campaigning for a monument to be built in Hyde Park. They hope that it will be a reminder of the historic link between the two countries.

One thing I found amusing whilst researching the Polish involvement in the Battle of Britain was their quick thinking when shot down to avoid a lynching as they were often faced with being mistaken for German. They had learned to say in an immaculate English accent, 'eff off old chap' to identify themselves and it worked a treat.

I have mentioned many times throughout this memoir the spirit of the Poles, the spirit my family showed throughout their exile in Siberia, how it was never broken, it was inborn and they also had a most engaging sense of humour, especially my Babcia.

And Winston Churchill said on 1st October 1939 'The soul of Poland is indestructible and she will rise again like a rock which may for a spell be submerged by a tidal wave but which remains a rock.'

And Poland and her people did remain a rock throughout WW2, fighting against tyrants both indifferent to suffering and human rights, completely without mercy in the pursuit of their ideology, Stalin for a class free Communist state and Hitler for a racially pure world, putting people through the most appalling suffering. Two very different men who committed very similar crimes against humanity. Stalin responsible for at least 13 ml deaths through ethnic cleansing, the peoples of the eastern borderlands of Poland, the deliberate famine in Ukraine and his Purges. Hitler's figure is much higher at 20 ml deaths, civilians mostly and many captured Russian soldiers.

Whilst Hitler is consigned to history for his crimes Stalin escaped the censure he so deserved at Nuremburg and is to this day revered in Russia.

The Polish people had much to contend with and they took on their role as ally with incredible energy and ingenuity. The other pilots who fought in the Battle of Britain, making up a total of over 3,000 were British, American, Canadian, Australian, Irish, Belgian, French, New Zealander and Czechoslovakian.

Another device developed by the Poles before the war was the hand held portable mine detector which came into use in 1941. It was designed by Lieutenant Józef Kosacki, a Polish professor and officer in the Polish army, born 21st April 1909 in Łapy, When war broke out he was in France, and after its capitulation he managed to get to England and was transferred to Scotland. Whilst there the Ministry of Supply of Great Britain announced a competition for development of a mine detector due to the very high number of victims of mines. During day time he trained soldiers in the fundamentals of wireless telegraphy and after hours built the mine detector in only 3 months with the help of Sgt. Andrzej Gabros and went on to win the competition beating 6 British designers.

This detector then appeared on all fronts of WW2, it weighed 14kg and could be operated by one person and was extremely effective. Nine sappers with 3 of the Polish mine detectors needed only an hour to clear mines from a 400m long two tank wide passage. He didn't patent his invention but handed it over to the British free of charge, for which he received a letter of thanks from King George VI, though no formal recognition from the British High Command.

It was the first electronic device to become part of a soldier's equipment and was a revolutionary solution on the battlefields of WW2 used extensively in 1942 during the battle of El Alemein in North Africa. Using 500 of these devices the British army passed through German mine fields and within one night soldiers were able to walk through a 4km wide and 10km long minefield by-passing the enemy's position which resulted in a decisive allied victory with the help of this new Polish device. Several thousand were then built and deployed by Allied forces and they were still used up until 1995 by the British Army.

Unlike the Polish Government, in September 1939 the French Government decided that France should lay down her arms and capitulate to Germany and the remnants of the Polish army remaining in France made their way to the Atlantic ports. Of the 84,500 personnel only about 24,000 were saved and evacuated to the UK. The Polish Government and High Command then established their temporary headquarters in London and set about rebuilding the Polish Armed Forces for the second time since WW1.

Polish forces were involved in the organisation of an underground army in occupied France, the Polish Secret Army in France based in cells whose attack on the enemy was to coincide with the Allied landing. It also acted as an intelligence gathering network and among its achievements was the pinpointing of 67 V-1 rocket launch pads which were then bombed by the RAF. In southern France, Polish resistance units took part in the liberation of France either in independent groups or together with the Maquis, the French Resistance.

Apart from breaking the Enigma code it can be argued that the greatest contribution of the Allied victory made by the Polish Forces was in the field of military intelligence. The Polish Intelligence Service formed the backbone of intelligence gathering operations in continental Europe and North Africa, Commander Dunderdale Head of Special Liaison Control noted,

'The Polish Intelligence Service made an invaluable contribution to the planning and successful execution of the invasion and the ultimate victory of the allied forces in Europe'

In 1944 the Service was running 8 stations, 2 independent and 33 cells with 1,666 registered agents. In that year alone it supplied the Secret Intelligence Service with 37,894 reports, US Intelligence with 12,068 and the French with 739 reports. In all they provided information about the invasion of the West, the attack of the USSR, information used by the planners of Operation Torch, on V1 and V2 rockets, German order of battle, warship construction, troop and naval movements, war production and many other aspects of Germany's war effort.

Gen. Kroner Deputy Chief of the US Military Intelligence, said, 'the Polish Army has the best intelligence in the world, its value for us is priceless, unfortunately, we cannot offer much in return.'

The Germans had invaded the USSR in June 1941 and the Allies had encouraged Stalin to establish an army from the Polish citizens and POWs he had deported to Siberia in 1940-1942. After General Ander's release from the Lubyanka prison he was told by the Soviets to make combat ready up to 12,000 men from half starving gulag inmates and after difficult talks with the US and the U.K. Stalin reluctantly agreed and allowed them to leave the USSR with their families and head towards the Western Allies and the Polish Army forming in Persia.

The army had taken on the name of General Władislaw Anders, a former cavalry officer from the Russian Tsarist regiment during WW1. He would command a force which from mid 1941 would make a journey of over 3,500km through Siberia and central Asia, to join him. The journey was exhausting to these weary and starved people, but he would turn this army of malnourished people into a fit and effective fighting force many of whom would eventually confront the Germans in Italy for one of the most crucial battles of the war.

My family had escaped the USSR and were also heading towards the Polish army with many thousands of men, women and children, many of them orphans, who were given as much safe haven along the routes as possible but very many were to die from exhaustion and starvation pressed into further labour in the collective farms along the way by the NKVD. My Dziadek Adam, Wujek Walery and his son Włodek, would become members of Ander's Army and my Mother Alicja, Ciocia Janina, cousin Marysia and Wujek Janusz, enlisted as Polish Cadets.

For the invasion of Italy the Polish forces were to play a large part with the 2nd Polish Corps composed of the 3rd Carpathian Rifles Division, the 5th Kresowa Infantry Division, 2nd Armoured Brigade, Army Group Artillery and units including the Polish Women's Auxiliary Service. The 2nd Corps landed in Italy in December 1943 and January 1944 as part of the British 8th Army and took up defensive positions along the Sangro.

The battle of Monte Cassino, 17th January 1944 to 18th May 1944, at the Monastery founded in 529 AD by St Benedict, would be fought in four stages by many regiments and divisions under the banner of many nations, facing insurmountable obstacles to break the German defences and foremost was the Polish 2nd Corps. The German defences had not been penetrated despite three assaults and heavy bombing and they held fast continuing to block the road to Italy. After previous attempts had failed to take Cassino, General Leese called on General Anders and his chief of staff, General Wiśniowski and offered Anders and the 2nd Polish Corps the mission of taking Monte Cassino, Anders accepted and everything now depended on the Poles.

General Anders' order of the day before the assault read 'Soldiers, the task assigned to us will cover with glory the name of the Polish soldier all over the world. The moment for battle has arrived. At this moment the thoughts and hearts of our whole nation will be with us. We have long awaited the moment for revenge and retribution over our hereditary enemy. For this action let the lion spirit enter your hearts, keep deep in your heart God, honour and our land, Poland. Go and take revenge for all the suffering in our land, for what you have suffered for many years in Russia and for years of separation from your families.'

May 13th the Polish 2nd Corps prepared to launch the fourth assault on the monastery and went into battle. Their task was to isolate the Abbey from the north and north east and take it. The 3rd and 15th Battalions of the 5th Kresowa Infantry Division reached point 517 under heavy fire and lost 20% of its men. The 13th battalion under Col Kamiński was the first to reach Phantom Ridge and were caught in gunfire, mines and traps across both flanks. Casualties were heavy and the units were almost wiped out.

The Polish men of the 15th Battalion who remained on the Phantom Ridge endured the most ferocious enemy fire. They suffered huge casualties and were at total exhaustion, men were lying wounded and in shock. Their sacrifice though was not in vain, they had relieved the British units in the Liri Valley from very heavy enemy fire but by the end of the day the 2nd Polish Corps had to withdraw its troops, the British XIII Corps was not able to achieve half of its objectives and the US II Corps could not penetrate German positions. It had not been a successful day.

The Poles had attacked on that first assault taking heavy casualties. Battalions, Brigades and Infantry divisions were decimated, 'in the valley and on the slope of the ridge lay corpses, twisted human shapes, shattered limbs, bloody bits of bodies.' The Germans had committed a horrific atrocity after the assault, crucifying two young Polish officer cadets with barbed wire and nails. No quarter was given after the barbarity of the Germans.

The Polish 2nd Corps continued to storm the Abbey and the hard fought victory came after 4 long months and 4 assaults and on May 18th Polish troops entered the hill top Monastery, the strategic stronghold of the German defensive position, the Gustav Line, and Lieutenant Gurbiel hoisted the red and white banner of Poland, and the Polish flag flew over the ruins of the ancient Italian Monastery which had been a symbol of German resistance since the beginning of 1944. British troops followed with the raising of the British Union Flag and took control of the town of Cassino and the road to Rome was open to the Allies.

Under constant fire, in terrible conditions and 7 days of fierce struggle to break German defences, it was not just the battle for Monte Cassino, it was a battle for Poland. It is thanks to the efforts of the Poles, the 2nd Corps that Italy was liberated. With victory secured on 18th May 1944, the battle of Monte Cassino, one of the toughest and bloodiest battles of WW2 takes a special place in Polish history and this historic victory is owed to General Władislaw Anders of the 2nd Polish Corps.

The Polish soldiers numbering 51,000 strong, fought with steely courage that paved the way to victory, tragically they had already known that their beloved homeland had been sacrificed to the Soviets at Yalta.

Some of the other Battalions involved in the Battle of Monte Cassino were the 8th Indian and British 4th Divisions, the Moroccan Rifle Division, the French Motorised Division, the 1st Moroccan Infantry, the 3rd Algerian Infantry, the Moroccan 4th Mountain Division, the US II Corps, the British XIII Corps.

The battle was won at huge cost with 55,000 Allied casualties including 4,000 Polish losses, German losses were much fewer at 20,000 killed and wounded. Battle honours were awarded to some units for their roles at Cassino, units which participated in the first part of the campaign were awarded the battle honour 'Cassino I', in addition subsidiary battle honours were given to some units which participated in specific engagements during the first part. These were Monastery Hill, Castle Hill and Hangman's Hill.

Units which participated in the later part of the battle were awarded the honour 'Cassino II.' All members of the Polish units received the Monte Cassino Commemorative Cross, including my Uncle, Bolesław Dyki, father of my cousin Alec who has contributed to this memoir and its prequel.

They had fought with courage and their units are the ones credited with the liberation of the Abbey but the name of the Polish soldier is not known all over the world as is the name of the British, American and others who fought in WW2.

They fought in the 1st Corps of the Polish Army located in Scotland in the summer of 1940 which was to remain its base in the UK until the end of the war. Organised into units it was earmarked for the defence of Fife in the event of an expected German invasion from Norway. The Corps became the base on which the 1st Armoured Division, the 1st Independent Parachute Brigade, the 4th Infantry Division and 16th Armoured Brigade were formed.

Additionally many of the military training, educational and research institutions were located in Scotland. Between 1940 and 1943 the Poles manned 12 armoured trains as part of the defence of the British Isles, stationed in Scotland as well as North East England, East Anglia and Cornwall. After the war many Polish servicemen returned to make their home In Scotland and they were made very welcome, as was Corporal Wojtek with his unit the 2nd Corps.

They fought in Norway and France with many Polish soldiers and civilians making their way to Syria and France via Romania and Hungary, flocking to join the Polish army in the West. By May 1940 there were 84,500 men in France and Syria. In April 1940 the Independent Podhalańska Rifle Brigade was sent to Norway as part of the Allied effort to help that country. The Brigade distinguished itself in the battle of Narvik only to be evacuated on 6/7th June back to France. Meanwhile the 1st Grenadiers Division and 2nd Infantry Rifles Division were sent in to support the French forces on the Maginot Line. The 1st Grenadier Division fought at Lagarde on the Rhine Marne Canal, carrying out a stubborn withdrawal. Surrounded by the enemy its Commander ordered its disbandment and its soldiers were able to escape to Britain.

They had little time to prepare and be ready to fight in the many areas of the War they were to become involved in, not able to form units properly to take on the Germans and under strength but their motivation was revenge and mentally they were ready.

The 2nd Infantry Rifles Division covered the withdrawal of 45 French Corps at Belfort in Alsace. Already cut off by the advancing Germans, the 45 Corps and 2nd Rifles fought at Clos du Doubs with the Polish Division backing onto the Swiss frontier. After heavy fighting on 18th and 19th June the French Commander of 45 Corps decided to withdraw to Switzerland where the French and Polish soldiers were interned. At Montbard the 10th

Armoured Cavalry Brigade briefly repelled the German units which had occupied it on 16th June. In earlier fighting the Brigade had prevented French divisions from being cut off allowing them to withdraw.

Following the taking of Montbard the Germans blew up the bridges on the Brugundy canal, isolated and surrounded Gen Maczek who disbanded the Brigade and ordered troops to try and reach Britain. With France collapsing all around them, the not yet fully organised 3rd and 4th Polish Infantry Divisions were pressed into action taking part in the doomed defence of the Britanny redoubt around Rennes and the evacuation from La Rochelle.

They fought in North Africa with Polish soldiers from the gulags reaching Syria, leading to the formation of the Independent Carpathian Rifle Brigade which in July 1939 after refusing to accept France's capitulation crossed from French Syria (North Africa) to British ruled Palestine. Under its Commander Gen S. Kopański, it took part in the defence of besieged Tobruk in August 1941 to December 1941 defending the heavily attacked western perimeter. After the lifting of the siege the Brigade broke through the enemy positions at El Ghazala enabling the 8th British Army to renew its offensive against Rommel. The Brigade seriously under strength, was withdrawn in March 1942 at the same time as the first evacuation of the Polish Army from the gulags and labour camps in the USSR, was about to begin.

They fought in North West Europe and Dunkirk where Poles were involved in most Allied operations against the Germans, in the Mediterranean and the Middle East and in Western Europe. The size of the Polish armies in the West were estimated at half a million and these included the emaciated Poles from Siberian labour camps. Poland was the only country to combat the Germans from the first day of the invasion of 1939 until the very end of the war.

They fought in France and after landing the Polish 'Black Division' was tasked with breaking the German defence in the Caen-Falaise sector. Polish soldiers entered the battle with the Canadians on 8th August and 10 days later encircled and destroyed the German Panzer Corps in the Chambois area. The 1st Armoured Division continued to chase the withdrawing Germans and liberated towns in France, Belgium and the Netherlands along the way. The battle trail ended in Wilhelmshaven on 5th May 1945 when its commander accepted the surrender of the German naval base.

The 1st Polish Armoured Division commanded by General Stalislaw Maczek had trained intensively in preparation for the battle of Normandy and they played a critical role in the battle of Falaise Pocket from 12th to 21st August 1944. The location of a bloody engagement in the final stages of the Normandy campaign, in the corridor which the Germans sought to maintain to allow their escape. Six weeks later, the German Army was in turmoil with a lack of resources and by late summer of 1944 the bulk of the two German armies were surrounded by the Allies near the town of Falaise and the way to Paris was open. The Poles' dogged stand had ensured the closure of the Falaise pocket and the collapse of the German position in Normandy.

After the battle of Normandy the 1st Polish Armoured Division was sent to Belgium and Holland to push back the German armies. Furious fighting took place in Breda in Holland but the Polish forces valiantly repelled all German counter attacks and obtained the surrender of many Germans, it was one of Maczek's greatest victories, the liberation of Breda. He also went on to liberate the Belgian cities of Ypres, Oostnieuwkerke, Roeselare, Tielt, Ruislede and Ghent.

They fought in the Polish Navy in September 1939, simultaneously in the Baltic and the North Sea, with a Polish destroyer flotilla having arrived from the Baltic in Britain on the day war broke out. At a time when the Royal Navy was desperately short of destroyers, this was a welcome reinforcement. During the war this small but efficient and modern branch of the Armed Forces covered 1,213,000 sea miles, helped cover 787 convoys, carried out 1,162 patrols and operations and sunk 100,000 tons of enemy shipping.

Ships of the Polish Navy took part in most major naval operations, including the defence of the Polish coastline, the sea battle of Narvik, the evacuation from Dunkirk and the raid on the Lofoten Islands. The sinking of the Bismarck after being identified and located by the ORP Piorun, the Dieppe raid, the battle of the Atlantic, Mediterraneum and Arctic convoys and the D-Day landings. The Polish Navy had 2 cruisers, 10 destroyers, 1 minelayer, 6 minesweepers, 2 gun boats, 8 submarines and 10 MGB's.

Poland's Merchant Navy also played a vital role in keeping the lifelines open. It carried 4.8 ml tons of supplies for the Allies and thousands of troops with 58 vessels and 213,903 BRT. It participated in the unsuccessful landing operations in North Africa, Sicily, Normandy and southern France and lost 15 vessels, a total of 60,332 BRT and a loss of over 200 sailors' lives.

There were many individuals who served Poland and the Allies, one of note is Witold Pilecki, the highest example of a hero, who volunteered to be imprisoned in Auschwitz to gather intelligence. When Poland was invaded he volunteered as a soldier, made his way to Warsaw and in a church knelt with others and 'swore to God, the Polish nation and each other' and the resistance movement was born.

Pilecki was a cavalry officer and intelligence officer in the Polish Army in the Polish-Soviet war and also in WW2. He was the co-founder of the Secret Polish Army resistance group and later Armia Krajowa. Pilecki agreed to be captured in the German round ups, he would be the eyes and ears in the camp for the Resistance. Two of his comrades had been included in the first transport to Auschwitz and in August 1940 he intended to find out what had happened to them. There was an awareness that the Germans were intending to use the camp for exterminating the Jews and his intention was to get information for the Allies and the Polish Government.

Auschwitz was initially established by the Germans for Polish political prisoners in 1940 built and operated like all others in Poland by the Germans, the camps were located in far away sparsely populated areas and could be kept secret not only from the German civilian population but also from the West. Such camps, if built in occupied France, Belgium or the Netherlands would have been immediately exposed.

Auschwitz was a hellish place, the SS were in charge but the camp was run day to day by the kapos, inmates with power over their fellow prisoners. Survival would be difficult, Pilecki would witness the barbarity of the kapos and SS, beating several hundred Soviet POWs to death with shovels. Then he witnessed trainloads of people arriving with children and the elderly being gassed almost immediately and the young and healthy being worked to death in nearby labour camps. To get word back to Warsaw would be difficult.

He organised a confidential network which became a resistance movement within Auschwitz which numbered hundreds and was able to secretly send messages about the German atrocities in the camp to the Western Allies. He escaped in 1943 after nearly 2½ years smuggling out reports on what was happening to the Polish and Jewish inmates. How he survived the camp for so long we will never know, it was an incredible achievement.

He worked sorting goods taken from the dead and was close to despair wondering if any of his messages had got through to the Resistance about the crimes he was witnessing. He began to think about breaking out of the camp and one day ran from the bakery he had been sent to work in and with two others got away and found to his horror that his messages had not been believed by the Resistance leaders who thought he was a German spy!

His information about the German atrocities did eventually get through to the Polish Government in exile, the British and US Governments. The Allies were pressed by the Polish Government to take action, bombing the railway lines into Auschwitz being just one option but requests were ignored.

Pilecki later fought in the Warsaw Uprising and remained loyal to the Government in exile after the communist takeover of his country. He was arrested in 1947 on charges of working for 'foreign imperialism' by the secret police who were aware of his work for British Intelligence and he was executed after a show trial in 1948 with a shot in the back of the head in a Warsaw prison on 25th May 1948. His story did not become known until the 1990's after the fall of communism, his fate suppressed by Poland's Soviet controlled communist regime. And it wasn't until then that his children Zofia and Andrzej found out about their father's heroism and that he had been executed. Whilst growing up they were constantly told by the Communists that their father was a traitor, an enemy of the State. They will now know just what a special and brave man he was.

Pilecki is considered 'one of the greatest wartime heroes.' Poland's Chief Rabbi Michael Schudrich wrote in the Auschwitz Volunteer, Beyond Bravery 'when God created the human being God had in mind that we should all be like Captain Witold Pilecki, of blessed memory.' Norman Davies the respected British historian wrote, 'if there was an Allied hero who deserved to be remembered and celebrated, this was a person with few peers.' And in 2013 the Polish Ambassador to the US Ryszard Schnepf described Pilecki as 'a diamond among Poland's heroes' and 'the highest example of Polish patriotism.'

He deserves to be remembered for the first comprehensive intelligence report on the atrocities committed at the German Auschwitz concentration camp alone and his efforts in bringing it to the attention of the Allies.

Another Polish hero is Jan (Kozielewski) Karski who at the outbreak of war joined the Polish army but was soon taken prisoner by the Soviets and sent to Ukraine to a detention camp. He escaped and became a courier for Armia Krajowa conveying secret information between the underground resistance and the Polish Government in exile. From 1940 he too was reporting to the Polish, British and US Governments on the situation in Poland, especially on the extermination of Polish Jews. His eyewitness accounts were like Pilecki's some of the earliest and most accurate on the Holocaust.

In 1942 at the height of the destruction of Poland he was ordered by Cyryl Ratajski, Polish Government Delegate to report on the German atrocities in occupied Poland to Prime Minister Władislaw Sikorski in London. He held meetings with the Jewish Zionist and Jewish Socialist Bund movements and before he left London he met with Jewish leaders who asked him to inform the world of the plight of the Polish Jews.

On his return to Poland, Karski determined to see things with his own eyes in order to make his report and with great risk he was smuggled into the Warsaw Ghetto and a transit camp at Izbica to gather evidence. He witnessed horrors that marked him deeply, mass starvation and the transports of Jews to the Belzec killing centre. In November 1942 he travelled to London where he delivered his full report to the Polish Government and met with Churchill and senior British authorities including Anthony Eden the Foreign Minister, other politicians, journalists and public figures.

The report, by the Republic of Poland, Ministry of Foreign Affairs, The Mass Extermination of Jews in German Occupied Poland, was addressed and sent by the Polish Government in Exile, to the Governments of the United Nations on December 10th 1942.

He then continued onto the US in 1943 where he met with Roosevelt and described what he had seen and warned of Hitler's plans to murder Europe's Jews. He also carried microfilm out of Poland with further proof but Roosevelt asked not one question about the Jews. Allied Governments were focused on the defeat of Germany and his messages did not receive the attention they should have and did not result in any direct action. He met with members of the film industry and artists, with many Government and Civic leaders, Rabbi's and Bishops, the media, a Supreme Court Judge, a Cardinal, with little result. He did however inspire the formation of the War Refugee Board. 'Karski later stated, 'I wanted to save millions and I was not able to save one man'.

He did not return to Communist Poland but remained in Washington working for Polish-Jewish understanding to honour the memory of all victims of Hitler. He received the highest Polish civic and military decorations and was made an honorary citizen of Israel and was awarded the Righteous Among the Nations by Yad Vashem. He died in Washington in 2000.

Karski and Pilecki's cases are exceptional and they deserve to be remembered. They and the Polish Government in exile, were ignored by the Allies. If the Allies had listened and taken action, a very different outcome for the millions of innocents murdered by the Germans may have been achieved

On 16th September 2020 a Blue Plaque was unveiled in London to

Krystyna Skarbek born in Warsaw in 1908 to a Polish aristocrat. Her daring exploits saw her become Churchill's favourite spy and the inspiration for James Bond's lover Vesper Lynd in the 007 film Casino Royale.

She carried a razor sharp 7" commando knife strapped to her thigh and was an expert in the use of hand grenades which she preferred to guns and had a cyanide capsule sewn into the hems of her skirts. When war broke out she escaped to Britain where she offered her services to MI6, was hired and sent back to Poland to gather intelligence and distribute propaganda. When she arrived back in Poland in February 1940 it was the worst winter in living memory with temperatures reaching -30 and my family were by then sitting in a freezing wagon on their way to Siberia. The temperature did not discourage Krystyna who later brought back on microfilm information that Hitler had plans to invade the Soviet Union.

She was arrested by the Gestapo in Budapest and during interrogation bit her tongue so hard it bled and she began coughing to give the impression she was bringing up blood. Her captors terrified that she might have TB released her and unable to continue operating in Budapest she made her way to Cairo and did work for the SOE. She was later sent to France, parachuting in with a mission in 1944 shortly after D Day.

Krystyna was murdered by an ex lover in 1952, who burst into the lobby of her home, the hotel where the plaque is being unveiled and stabbed her. He was hanged 3 months later. She is buried in Kensal Green cemetery under a layer of Polish soil smuggled out of communist Poland.

She was awarded the George Medal an OBE and the Croix de Guerre for her bravery but was treated shabbily by her former employers at SOE after the war and was dismissed with just one month's pay. She eked out a living with a number of ill paid jobs and for all her war time heroics she did not have a glorious end, discarded by the country she served, as were very many Poles who had fought and served the Allies.

Though occupied by two enemies, the citizens of Poland did not accept their fate passively, before the last shots of the 1939 campaign were fired a resistance army was being organised. This was to become the Armia Krajowa, organised in cells it included the whole country and was active under both German and Russian occupiers. The main task was to make life for the occupying forces as difficult as possible, tying down enemy units, intelligence gathering and military and industrial sabotage. The aim was to prepare for a general uprising at the moment of Germany's defeat, it became their absolute intention and drove them on.

Armia Krajowa became occupied Europe's largest and most

professionally organised, efficient Resistance Army. Many operations against enemy transports and industrial production forced Germany to maintain a large occupation force. Due to Armia Krajowa's Intelligence, vital information about the V2 rockets was made available to the Allies as were large parts of the rocket itself. The climax of the operations was the 63 days of the Warsaw Uprising in the summer of 1944, when for the 2nd time during the war Poland's capital fought a bitter and lonely battle in the name of freedom. At its peak Armia Krajowa consisted of 300,000 soldiers, excluding auxiliary civilian aid. In the east, units co-operated with Soviet forces in the liberation of Poland's eastern cities, Lwów and Wilno, only to be forcibly disarmed, deported or murdered by their ally Russia.

Sabotage and covert operations of the AK and the Armed Resistance (ZWZ) from January 1941 to June 1944 involved damaging railway locomotives and wagons, derailing transports and setting them on fire. Blowing up railway bridges, rails and disrupting electricity grids. Damaging aeroplanes, army vehicles, fuel tanks and destroying fuel. Building flaws into aircraft parts, cannon muzzles, artillery projectiles, radio stations and others. There were many thousands of covert operations, many acts of sabotage and the assassination of high ranking German officers.

Between 1941 and 1944 316 Polish officers known as the 'Silent and Unseen' (cichociemni) specially trained in Britain were parachuted into occupied Poland. Their mission was to act as senior specialists either at Armia Krajowa GHQ or at district command level and to carry out special assignments involving intelligence gathering and sabotage.

The most significant operation of Armia Krajowa was the Warsaw Uprising from 1st August – 2nd October 1944, timed to coincide with the retreat of the Germans ahead of the Soviet advance. However the Red Army on direct orders from the Kremlin halted combat operations enabling the Germans to regroup and defeat the Polish Resistance then go on to destroy the city and its people in retaliation. It was fought with little help from the Allies and was the single largest military effort taken by any European resistance movement during the war.

'The city must completely disappear from the surface of the earth and serve only as a transport station for the Wehrmacht, no stone can remain standing, every building must be razed to its foundation'
– *(SS Heinrich Himmler)*

The main Polish objectives were to drive the Germans out of Warsaw while helping the Allies to defeat them. It was also the goal of the

Underground to liberate Poland's capital and assert Polish sovereignty before the Soviet's Committee of National Liberation could take control, they were also looking for justice and revenge for 5 years of German occupation.

The Polish resistance captured the ruins of the Warsaw Ghetto and liberated the Gęsiówka concentration camp freeing 350 Jews but on 7th August the German forces aided by the arrival of tanks and using civilians as human shields, continued pitched battles around the old Town with successful bombardments of heavy artillery. The Resistance counter attacked but were unable to effectively defend without anti aircraft weapons. Even the clearly marked hospitals were dive bombed by Stukas.

SS Police, collaborators and Wehrmacht groups went from house to house shooting inhabitants regardless of age or gender and burning their bodies. Up to 250,000 Polish civilians were systematically killed whilst the Soviets looked on. The main perpetrators were German SS Commander Oskar Dirlewanger who was linked to some of the most notorious war crimes and Russian SS Commander Bronisław Kamiński, whose forces also committed the cruellest atrocities. Dirlewanger was executed on Himmler's orders and Kamiński reportedly died whilst in Allied custody, escaping justice.

German policy was to crush the Polish spirit and bring the Uprising to an end but this didn't succeed, the Poles' spirit prevailed and their resistance only stiffened at the atrocities and they fought on with urban guerrilla tactics. Until September the Germans shot all captured resistance fighters on the spot although later they were treated as POWs. 'this is the fiercest of our battles since the start of the war it compares to the street battles of Stalingrad' – *(SS Heinrich Himmler)*

The Soviets ignored Polish attempts to make radio contact with them and did not advance beyond the city limits and intense fighting between the Germans and Poles continued. By 14th September the eastern bank of the Wistula was taken over by Polish troops and 1,200 men who made it across the river were not reinforced by the Red Army. The lack of air support from the Soviet air base 5 minutes flying time away led to allegations that Stalin tactically halted his forces to let the operation fail, allowing the Polish resistance to be crushed which is most likely, he wanted revenge.

Stalin had not allowed the Western Allies to use Soviet airports for several weeks so the planes had to use bases in the UK and Italy which reduced their carrying weight and number of sorties. He had denied a specific request in August for the use of landing strips in Soviet controlled areas, had referred to the Polish Resistance as a 'handful of criminals' and that the

Uprising was inspired by 'enemies of the Soviet Union.' By denying the Allies landing rights he basically limited the effectiveness of Allied assistance to the Uprising and even fired on Allied planes carrying supplies from Italy who strayed into Soviet air space. The Poles were fighting to rid Warsaw of the Germans and their Russian Ally was doing all he could to stand in their way!

However, without Soviet clearance Churchill sent over 200 low level supply drops by the RAF, the S.African Air Force and the Polish Air Force under British command known as the Warsaw Airlift and after eventually gaining Soviet air clearance the US Air Force sent one high level mass air drop as part of Operation Frantic. US support was limited after Stalin had objected to the Uprising and Roosevelt again did not want to offend him. Churchill telegraphed Roosevelt on 25th August proposing to send planes in defiance of Stalin 'to see what happens' but unwilling to upset Stalin before the Yalta conference, Roosevelt replied 'I do not consider it advantageous to the long range general war prospect for me to join you.'

When the Soviets finally allowed planes to refuel and reload at their controlled airfields it was too little too late and although 100's of tons of supplies were dropped the vast majority fell into German hands and Stalin's permission to land was later withdrawn. The Resistance held the Old Town until the end of August and on successive nights until 2nd September when they withdrew through the sewers which had been a major means of communication and escape for them. Thousands were evacuated and those who remained were either shot or transported to concentration camps.

The highest military authorities in the Western Alliance had been informed of the Uprising and no one had suggested that the preparations be stopped. Historian Max Hastings said 'it was indeed irresponsible of the British to offer neither guidance nor directive to a venture that they knew was doomed to failure.' The Soviets had sat idle for 6 weeks on the banks of the Wistula watching the smoke rise from the devastation of Warsaw. Churchill pleaded with Stalin and Roosevelt to help Poland but to no avail.

'There was no difficulty in finding Warsaw it was visible from 100km away, the city was in flames but with so many huge fires burning it was almost impossible to pick up the target marker flares' – (William Fairly South African Pilot, 1982)

The role of the Red Army during the Uprising remains controversial, it appeared at the outskirts of the city and the Poles were counting on the Soviet front moving into the city in a matter of days, but the Uprising collapsed because of the reluctance of Stalin to help his ally! The city outskirts at the time were defended by the undermanned and under equipped German 73rd Infantry Division and this weak defence was not pressured by the Soviets. On the 11th September when the Uprising was almost over, the Soviets moved into Praga on the right bank of the Wistula and in 3 days gained control of the suburb and the German 73rd Division collapsed.

Stalin had given a direct order from the Kremlin to halt the Soviet advance, seeing a way to rid the Resistance of man power with help from the Germans, there would be far fewer of the Resistance to imprison and execute once he had control of Poland. Could this be Stalin's revenge? Did he cast his mind back to the battle of the Wistula in August 1920 when the Poles had a decisive victory against the Bolshevik forces during the Polish-Soviet war, a victory that had led to Poland's independence and the return of her eastern borderlands. Where Stalin himself had disobeyed a direct order from his Commander in Chief, Hayk Bzhishkyan, leading to the Bolshevik loss. Bzhishkyan who later became a victim of Stalin's Purges, shot in 1937.

'Is all of modern European civilisation a kind of macabre plot against Poland? How many absurdities must one people live through in so short a time, from such a diverse set of sources? Every time Poland makes an ally, said ally becomes unreliable, deceptive and cowardly. Every time a country becomes Poland's enemy, its capacity for heartlessness and ferocity seems redoubled' – *Halik Kochański The Eagle Unbowed (from Michael Dougherty's review)*

The German hatred for Poles and Poland meant that Warsaw had to be destroyed, Polish pride and identity had to be wiped out. The destruction of Warsaw had been planned before the start of WW2, Hitler had decided it was to be turned into a German provincial town and after the Uprising once the remaining population had been expelled, the Germans continued the destruction of the city, burning and demolishing remaining buildings using flamethrowers and explosives to destroy house after house. Polish monuments and national archives were destroyed. By January 1945 the city was 90% destroyed, 250,000 were dead 'it was one of the most atrocious crimes of the 20th century' – Dan Cruickshank – The city was devastated, a smoking ruin with death and destruction everywhere.

Under the chairmanship of Mark Pritchard MP, a debate secured by Daniel Kawczynski MP, was held in Westminster Hall on 2nd July 2019 to debate WW2 and the Polish Contribution, attended by many MPs from all parties to express gratitude and acknowledge the contribution Poland had made as an ally in WW2.

There are too many speeches to illustrate here on the performance of the Poles in the RAF Battle of Britain and protecting the convoys of soldiers moving towards Normandy, the Army at Monte Cassino and Falaise Pocket. The Polish ships that took part in Operation Neptune and the Polish Underground and Home Army, the AK the Intelligence services and very many other operations with the Allies some I've covered in this chapter.

I'll concentrate on just one speech which sums up the debate, and that is from Steven Pound MP. Others' responses can be accessed via Hansard.

'...I turn to the heroism of the Polish Army, those who fought with General Anders, walked, marched and in some cases crawled from Siberia through the whole of Persia to north Africa to turn the tide in El Alamein. As we have heard, they fought from Tobruk up through Sicily and into the impregnable mountain fortress and Benedictine monastery that could not be broken, Monte Cassino, which was occupied by a crack division of German paratroopers, in fact the crack division of the Luftwaffe.

Those paratroopers held out against one of the biggest combined armies that has ever been assembled. There was a New Zealand regiment made up entirely of Maori, as well as people from North Africa, France, UK, Canada, Australia and the US but there was one group of people, the Poles, who fought their way from hilltop to hilltop, up that precipitous mound and planted the red and white flag in the still smoking ruins of Monte Cassino. With the nobility that typifies those people, General Anders' army then planted the Union flag. I have climbed that hill and seen how difficult that must have been, but my memory is not just of the beautiful and newly restored Benedictine monastery, it is of the graveyard at the foot of Monte Cassino. There is an allied graveyard and a Polish graveyard why? There were so many Poles who died that they could not be incorporated into the allied graveyard.

At the base of that graveyard is one grave that stands alone, it is always covered in flowers, either red roses or poppies, poppies for the poppies in the snow. It is the grave of General Anders, one of the great heroes. Like the Hon member for Shrewsbury and Atcham, (Kawczyński) I recently had the honour of meeting Senator Anders (daughter of Gen. Anders) and to briefly discuss those days. There are three sets of headstones in that graveyard, some with the Orthodox cross, some with the Star of David because Jewish Poles fought here and some with the Christian cross.

One of the utter tragedies is that while General Mark Clark was racing towards Rome, where the photographers were waiting for him, General Anders was told by the Supreme Commander of the British Forces that there would be no return to Poland. He was told that for all that the Poles had done, that was it. Because of the pact with the brutal dictator (Stalin) there would not be a British supported return to Poland. As a human being and a hero, General Anders could have done what many of us would have done, he could have said 'In that case we are going home. We are throwing down our rifles, we are taking off our packs and we are leaving' Anders did not do that, he said, 'We fight on' and fight on they did. That typifies the strength and determination of the Polish people.

I want to touch on an area that has not been touched on in any detail, and that is the extraordinary contribution of the Polish naval forces. In 1939 the Polish navy was in quite good condition, a modern navy, with submarines. It managed to escape from Gdańsk and the seaports in north Poland to Leith, the port in Edinburgh where the flagship the Pioruń (thunder) was laid down in the John Brown shipyard. She was renamed and crewed entirely by Poles. These Polish ships which came under the command of the First Sea Lord, Admiral Sir Dudley Pound made an incredible contribution in theatres of war from Narvik, Dunkirk, the Lofoten Islands as well as the Murmansk convoys where the grandfather of my Hon Friend, Paula Sheriff, sailed with them to the Normandy landings.

In two particular areas the Polish navy made an incredible contribution, the first was the awful night of 13th March 1941 when more than 1,000 people in Glasgow were killed. It was called the Clydebank Blitz. I pay tribute to Martin Docherty Hughes who introduced a debate on the floor of the House about that subject. John Brown's shipyard and the Singer factory were bombed ruthlessly and Clydebank and Hardgate and virtually that whole part of Glasgow were destroyed. The opposition to the Luftwaffe was led by the N class destroyer ORP Piorun. (meaning thunderbolt) She was in harbour undergoing repairs. She had six anti-aircraft guns and some old refitted Bofors guns. She fought off the second wave of the Luftwaffe and how many lives she saved I cannot even begin to think. It is extraordinary to think that Piorun was laid down in the very shipyard that she then defended, having sailed from there to Poland and back again. It is almost as if she was born to defend her birthplace, as many a Pole would.

The second thing is the extraordinary occurrences of May 1941 when the hinge of history was turning. The Germans had massive naval superiority, they had the two best ocean raiders in the world, Bismarck and Tirpitz. They also had the best navy cruisers, Gneisenau and Scharnhorst. Had they got out into the north Atlantic our supply routes from Canada and America would have been finished. There would have been no opportunity whatever for us to continue the war at sea. Tirpitz as we know was destroyed in the fjords of Norway by the RAF but Bismarck had earlier that year in the battle of the Denmark strait, not only destroyed the British taskforce but sunk the pride of the Royal Navy, the mighty Hood.

In May Admiral Tovey and task force H were sent under the instructions of Churchill, to the area off the Norway coast to sink the Bismarck. Who was there at the front of that? Not just Rodney and Repulse but Piorun the Polish destroyer that steamed ahead as fast as she could and it is said, did not even wait for embarkation orders. She left Scotland and headed for the battlefield. Then as we know Bismarck had her steering gear crippled by a Faery Swordship torpedo and was slightly reduced in her manoeuvrability but she still had powerful weapons, eight 15 inch guns in four turrets. Piorun was one of the ships in that task force that on 25th May 1941 received probably the most significant message received in the sea war and it came from Bletchley Park. It came from a Polish interpreter who had managed to break the codes and it told precisely what the German Admiral was doing. Even though Piorun was then straddled at 12,000 meters by a complete bombardment from Bismarck she carried on. Some say she delivered the coup de grace, some say she was the last torpedo fired into Bismarck.

I will close by saying two things, Betrayal is an ugly word but I think that in some ways the Poles were betrayed at the end of the war. We compensated with the 1947 legislation but in some ways we let the Poles down. I would say that the Poles never, ever let us down. It is not for me to make an obvious pro European statement but is it not wonderful what we can achieve when we fight together in a common cause? If I ever have to fight anyone anywhere at any time, let it be with the brothers and sisters of the new republic of Poland, some of the bravest and most heroic people it has ever been my honour to know.' – *House of Commons, Hansard 02 July 2019.*

Polish Memorials in the U.K to the fallen Polish allies amongst the few are Alrewas and Northolt. In the post war years commemorative memorials have been erected in towns and cities where Polish military were stationed. One of the best known is that at the Polish Air Force in Northolt, London which was unveiled in 1948. In 1976 the Katyn Memorial was unveiled in Gunnersbury Cemetery, London. In 2000 a statue of the Polish Prime Minister and C in C Gen. Sikorski was unveiled in Great Portland Street, London. There is a plaque to the Polish Air Force in Westminster Cathedral, a Polish Air Force memorial in the RAF Church of St Clement Danes and a plaque in St. Paul's Cathedral. There is also a Polish Navy memorial in Plymouth.

At Alrewas, at the National Memorial Arboretum, there is an official memorial to the Polish forces fighting under British Command, erected in 2009, 70 years after the outbreak of WW2. It only happened due to the lobbying of Marek Stella-Sawicki and Polish Associations. Far too late for our grandparents to appreciate but at least a commemoration to their memory. There is nothing yet, to the memory of the 1.7 ml Polish deportees to Siberia.

The Duke of Kent officially unveiled the large memorial in September 2009, commemorating the sacrifice and contribution of the Polish Armed Forces in WW2. It represents the 3 branches of the Armed Forces and the Resistance Home Army. It is surrounded by 16 tablets giving insight into the role and achievements of the Polish Armed Forces in the struggle against Germany. It was backed by the Polish Ex-Combatants Association which provided most of the funding.

Present at the unveiling ceremony were the last President of the Polish Government in exile, Ryszard Kaczorowski and the Rev Bronisław Gostomski, parish priest of St Bobola and chaplain to the Polish Ex Combatants Association who blessed the foundation stone. Both were killed on 10th April 2010 in the crash of the presidential plane in Smolensk on their way to pay tribute to the 25,000 Polish officers murdered by the NKVD at Katyn and other places in the USSR.

Montormel Hill 262 – The Montormel Monument was built in 1965 and the Memorial in 1994 right in the heart of the Falaise Pocket to commemorate the last battle of Normandy and the sacrifice of the Polish soldiers fighting 'for our freedom and yours'. A Sherman tank that once belonged to the Polish 1st Armoured Division, is on display at the Museum's entrance as well as a bust of General Stanislaw Maczek.

British soldiers acknowledged the fighting spirit of the Poles. An Irish Guards officer in the 78th Division described his encounter with them. 'Their motives were as clear as they were simple, they only wished to kill Germans and they did not bother at all about the usual refinements when taking over our posts, they just walked in with their weapons asked where the Germans were and that was that'. The 78th Division history in an entry states, 'Of their resolve there was no doubt, for whose gallantry the Division soon learnt to feel an awed yet amused admiration. They exposed themselves with the most reckless abandon, they seem to know no fear.'

After nearly 6 years of war in which Poland had played an active role throughout, she emerged as the heaviest loser on the winning side. At Tehran in autumn 1943 Poland was handed over to Soviet rule by her

Western allies. The later Yalta conference only confirmed this act of betrayal for Poland and her people. Poland had been robbed of half of her territory, annexed by the USSR and under Soviet rule another long struggle to regain her independence began. Polish interests had been subordinate to those of Britain, France and America as they had been at the beginning of the war.

The Victory Parade 8th June 1946

'We were the first ally of Britain, fighting with them, side by side, from the very beginning of the war. It was the day of the victory parade and we were not represented.' – *My Ciocia Janina Góral*

In March 1939 Britain and France had pledged to go to war if Hitler attacked Poland. It was a meaningless gesture as in September Britain did declare war on Germany but gave no military assistance to Poland before it was torn apart by the Germans and Russians.

Stalin believed that Russia had paid the heaviest price for the war in Europe and felt it entitled him to do basically what he wanted and so he negotiated at Tehran and Yalta accordingly, brushing both the US and GB aside in his demands.

Churchill and Roosevelt agreed to Stalin's demands over Poland's destiny, his demands were *'right and just'* Churchill had said in the House of Commons. 'Poland's ally was rewarding Poland's deadly enemy with our territory.' – *Janina Góral*

Poland was pushed into communism although Stalin maintained it would be 'sovereign, independent and absolutely democratic, all in his own vision.' On 5th July 1945 Great Britain and the US recognised the communist regime of Poland.

The official London victory celebrations were to celebrate the end of WW2 and were represented by the British Commonwealth forces and Allies and they were a show of strength from Britain and its allies after defeating Nazi Germany and Japan.

These celebrations took place in London on 8th June 1946, consisting of a military parade through the city and a night-time fireworks display. Most Allied countries took part in this parade, but Poland was excluded and the lack of representation of their country caused huge controversy and anger amongst the Polish forces and their families.

Ten MPs signed a letter published in the Daily Telegraph in June 1946, objecting to the treatment of the Poles. It read, 'Polish dead lay in hundreds on Monte Cassino, The Poles fought at Tobruk, Falaise and Arnhem, Polish pilots shot down 772 German planes. The Polish forces who fought under British Command have not been invited to the Victory march on June 8th. Ethiopians will be there, Mexicans will be there, the Fiji Medical Corps and Labuan Police and the Seychelles Pioneer Corps will be there and rightly too. But the Poles will not be there.'

Polish troops were the fourth largest allied group, where were the Poles? The Polish troops felt hugely betrayed for their loyalty to the Allies and those who were stationed in the U.K. were even being asked why they weren't going home! They could not go home, they did not have a choice.

Their absence at the Parade was down to the British Labour Government caving in to Stalin's demands with a whimper. Clement Atlee the Prime Minister, wanted to broker peace with the Soviet Union and the Government had recognised the Communist Politburo in Poland but not the Polish Government in exile, in London, to whom the Polish troops were loyal.

Stalin did not want the Poles included in the celebrations and the Labour Government did not want to anger the new Stalin approved Communist Government in Poland, they were fearful of Russia's reactions if they allowed the Poles to the celebration. Fearful of what I wonder! The Attlee Government also refused to allow the erection of a monument to the Polish Officers murdered by the Russians in Katyn in 1940.

Polish fighters, eastern borderland deportees, in fact, anyone Polish who had fought so valiantly with the Allies was therefore left out because the British Government was more concerned with post-war relations with Stalin than celebrating and acknowledging their ally Poland's considerable War efforts.

Atlee even wrote to the Polish soldiers in March 1946 asking them to return home! My Ciocia and the rest of the family and very many other Poles were extremely angry at this attitude towards them. Those Poles who did return to their homeland were accused by the Stalinist state of 'working against the state' and many were executed. Others were sent to labour camps and this was also extended to those Russian soldiers returning home.

In later years it was claimed with some justification that the Soviets' reach extended to the militants of the trade unions in their determination to cause massive disruption to the British economy during the strikes of the 1970s and 1980s and evidence has emerged regarding key Labour players, of which there was a multitude on the left of British politics, who saw everything through the philosophy of Communism.

252

The best known amongst several Union members in the pay of the Soviets was Jack Jones, according to the KGB, he was cultivated by the Soviets in the aftermath of the Spanish Civil War and given the codename 'Drim' (dream). He enjoyed Soviet contributions towards his 'holiday expenses' and was regarded by the KGB 'as a very disciplined and useful agent.' With the influence of Union members at the very heart of the Labour government, it isn't surprising they carried the wishes of Stalin to Attlee.

The Poles were instrumental to the Allied war effort, having played key roles in the Battle of Britain, especially Squadron 303 made up of fearless, some would say reckless Polish airmen who with air cadets had made their way to England across war-torn Europe to enlist and fight the Germans. They have only recently been acknowledged as the foremost squadron in the RAF during the Battle of Britain, with the most kills. Their major efforts in the conflicts at Monte Cassino, Falaise Gap, Normandy and the Warsaw Uprising, were forgotten.

Those brave Polish servicemen were not invited to participate in the Victory Parade, because of pressure from Stalin on the Labour Government and his warning to those Poles in Poland, not to accept any invitation! It was a final betrayal, a callous act of political duplicity, One of the most shameful acts of the Cold War from a spineless Labour Government.

The anger at the injustice of this never left my Ciocia and this came across quite strongly when she explained to me what had happened.

Hugh Dalton, a former Labour Chancellor of the Exchequer, said in 1940 "On the day of victory, Poland, as the first nation to stand up to Hitler whilst others grovelled to him, should ride in the van of the victory march." Winston Churchill added "Her Majesty's Government will never forget the debt they owe to the Polish troops who have served them so valiantly and for those who have fought under our command."

It was only recently (2002) that the son of a Polish veteran, Michael Moszynski, moved by the injustice of Poland's exclusion, secured an official apology from appropriately, a British Labour PM.

It took however, until 10th July 2005 for the surviving soldiers to march in London and this was down to the lobbying of Michael Moszynski, son of Captain Stefan Moszynski who had raised the issue with PM Tony Blair. He sent a formal apology via his Private Secretary expressing regret that the Poles had not been invited to the Victory Parade.

The plans for the 60th Anniversary were in hand and he promised that the Poles would have a role in this. Michael continued to lobby dignitaries including the Duke of Edinburgh and Sir Michael Jackson, head of the Armed Forces. It was confirmed a few days before the Parade began that the Poles would lead the march down the Mall. A recognition at least but certainly not justice, having ignored their service to the War effort for so long!

The Poles in their thousands, my family amongst a group of Poles from the Kresy, had watched from the streets in tears. They didn't wave flags or rejoice, they were angry and this hurtful insult persists to this day, despite the apology, 60 years too late. For my family and all other Poles it was a question of honour and they were betrayed, they were not treated with the respect and gratitude they deserved.

On the 15th August 1992, The Poles, ignoring the platitudes of the politically-correct English elite, decided to have their own victory parade in Warsaw, the first parade since the end of the war and only after the Communist state had fallen in 1989. The Polish war veterans, deportees and relatives of deportees, walked with pride and honour through the streets of Warsaw.

As Wiesław Wołwowicz, a veteran of the Polish 2nd Corps put it "We were the allies, the allies of the British, and we weren't even invited to take part in the victory parade after the war. We were like people who'd done the hard work and whom nobody wanted any more."

It would seem the Poles were being looked upon as non-persons again, which is how the Soviets had looked upon the deportee Poles, the bourgeoisie! who were in fact ex-military men, farmers and forest workers used to hard labour and Stalin considered them bourgeoisie, but they were dammed in the eyes of the Soviets who hated them thinking them all aristocrats and officers.

The Remembrance Sunday parade in London has only recently begun inviting Polish survivors of the eastern borderlands and other areas to participate. The numbers are few as very many have died and efforts must be made to encourage more survivors and children of survivors to attend.

Many of the stories of the people from the Borderlands who were exiled to the wastes of Russia remain untold. Stalin deported almost two ml Poles to Siberia and other outreaches of Russia and the victims are not honoured in any speeches commemorating WWII.

An important part of history has been little acknowledged by the Allies and the West and had been suppressed by Communism in Poland. How could this be forgotten? My family and up to 1.7 ml Poles were packed into freezing box cars with very little to sustain them, many didn't survive and they died through cold, hunger and disease, left by the side of the rail tracks or in the forests en-route to Siberia.

Another possible reason has emerged for this oversight, the remembrance of WW2 had been seized upon some time ago by various Jewish groups, mainly American and Israeli, who have wrongly blamed Poles for acts committed against them and now claim that Poland was complicit with Germany in the Holocaust. It's a betrayal by the same people the Poles put their lives at risk to save. As acts of humanity by the Poles to their Jewish neighbours were met with instant, brutal retaliation by the Germans, – murder.

The Germans killed them at random. Poland was the only country in Europe that had the death penalty for helping Jews and despite this the Poles saved many thousands of them. Three ml Poles as well as three ml Jews died during the holocaust.

Accounts of the war are incomplete without acknowledging this historical tragedy. The gap is slowly being filled, not by Governments or Associations for Memorials but by ordinary people, survivors and relatives of survivors, the children of Sybiraks. We are writing our own accounts of the deportation of our families and they include Irena Kosakowska, Donna Urbikas, Helen Glindzicz, Irena Rozycki and Beatrice King and also Aileen Orr's beautiful story of Private Wojtek, to name a few.

The account deserves official recognition. The Poles had made a heroic contribution to winning the war in their own country, in the Battle of Britain, in the Middle East, in Italy and Arnhem. The British shamefully failed to give them the recognition they had earned.

Poland not only had to contend with betrayal from its Allies but also Soviet support by the British media who were disgracefully pro Russian, Papers like the Times, one on a long list of Stalin's useful idiots commented that it was 'not difficult to understand Russian unwillingness to supply arms to people who are opposed to friendly relations with Russia'. George Orwell was the lone compassionate voice among the British intelligentsia who denounced Russian behaviour towards Poland and the American Ambassador to Poland Arthur Bliss resigned his post in 1947 in protest against the 'acceptance of illegal action being made legal by Western powers as regards Poland.'

Poland never surrendered, never established a collaborationist government as did France's Petain, who shook hands with Hitler on 24th

October 1940 agreeing collaboration and the deportation of the Jews. As did Norway's Quisling, Hungary's Worthy, Slovakia's Tiso, Croatia's Pavelic, and Romania's Antonescu.

It did not establish a militia to round up and deport Jews to the death camps or kill them outright as did Belgium's Degrelle, Holland's Mussert, France's Petain, Norway's Quisling, Slovakia's Tiso, Croatia's Ustase, Hungary's Arrow Cross and Romania's Iron Guard.

It never established SS units to fight under German command, as did Denmark, Norway, Belgium, Latvia, Hungary, Estonia, Italy, France, Holland, Albania, Ukraine and Croatia.

There were Spanish, Estonian, Finish, Danish, Indian, Latvian, Croatian, Ukrainian, Albanian, Dutch, Belgium, Russian, Belarussian, Hungarian, and French Waffen-SS units but no Polish units. Poles instead formed the largest resistance in Europe and 4th largest allied army after the Big 3.

The Holocaust was planned by senior Nazi Germans and Austrians at the Wannsee Conference in January 1942. No Poles were present. The Allies tried the criminals at Nuremburg, all were Germans and one Austrian. There were no Poles. Poland was NOT complicit with Germany for WW2 as has been inferred by many pro Jewish and pro Soviet revisionists including pro Soviet Academics.

IBM. General Motors and Ford collaborated and profited from investments in Nazi Germany. The French railways transported their Jews to their deaths. No Polish company profited from the Germans.

German, Ukrainian and Jewish collaborators rounded up Jews in the Ghettos. Ethnic Poles instead fought alongside the Jews at the Warsaw Ghetto uprising. The guards in the death camps were Germans, Austrians, Ukrainians and Latvians. Poles were instead victims in the camps.

The Polish Government supported the bombing of Auschwitz but it was vetoed by the UK and USA. The Polish underground developed a plan to liberate Auschwitz but the Allies refused to support it. Poles did liberate some camps, Warsaw's Pawiak prison in August 1944.

The Polish Government in exile issued detailed reports about Auschwitz and others exposing German genocide in Poland, the UK and US Government's suppressed the detail.

Poland was the only country in Europe where aiding Jews meant the death penalty by their German occupier. Poland has more Righteous… those who helped Jews than any other country although very many more are worthy of the noble award.

Yet Poland, as a haven for the Jews of Russia and Europe from the 16th century, compared to her European neighbours, almost destroyed by Germany and Russia, is the target of revisionists. The motives are quite disturbing and no country has come to Poland's defence.

'historical truth cannot be changed, many Poles collaborated with the Germans and took part in the destruction of the Jews during the Holocaust, antisemitism was innate among the Poles before the Holocaust, during it and after it too.' – *Yisrael Katz Israeli politician 2019*

His comment is historically inaccurate and racist.

There are many children of Sybiraks wanting to defend their parents, grand parents and other family members who were victims of either Hitler or Stalin, especially against unsubstantiated comments like that. WW2 Revisionists, have over many years intentionally reinterpreted historical events with contrary 'evidence' to modify historical facts to suit their own agenda.

They specifically blame Poland for many events they were not responsible for and overlook those events for which Poles lost their lives. They look for a different perspective, seeking to learn the truth but in fact distorting it. If they were uncovering new evidence and re-examining it with a truthful interpretation there would be no reason for the children of Sybiraks to voice their concerns.

But they are not, history does change over time because there are more things to discover that can complete the story truthfully. Revisionists decide upon a particular 'fact' and mould their bias to distort it. As for example in Putin's view of Russia invading Poland not because of the Ribbentrop-Molotov pact, but because Russia invaded Poland to 'save it.' A modification and a rejection of what actually happened. Putin also states that Poland was complicit with Germany in starting WW2. If he had facts to support these events they might be freshly judged but there is no new discovery of fact or evidence which can revise his false conclusion.

There are very many others apart from the children of Sybiraks who support and are fighting for the truth, who do not reinterpret historical, factual accounts, manipulate statistical data or deliberately mis-translate texts. There are authors of distinction, I've mentioned some within this text and Members of Parliament who took part in a debate instigated by a Polish MP who's family members died at the hands of the Germans. They gave their support for Poland here in a transcript of a debate I've included above.

Research

Polish Ex-Combatants' Association in Great Britain
Trust Fund and Warfare History Network,
Kresy Family and other history sites,
Forgotten Heroes of WW2,
House of Commons 2019

'Truth does not mind being questioned. A lie does not like being challenged.'

CHAPTER 15

Betrayal & Compassion

Betrayal

During WW2 Jews and Poles alike were persecuted and murdered by the Germans and the Poles later fell victim to the Soviets. There is a strong revisionist lobby that is re-writing WW2 history and my purpose in writing this chapter is to debunk the revisionist claim that the Poles were to blame for the atrocities that were committed against the Jews. The Poles suffered the most appaling retribution for helping Jews in any way, they were murdered together with their familes for even offering a Jew a cup of water. The entire Polish population was at the mercy of the German occupiers.

Members of the Jewish Councils who followed the orders of the German authorities; thinking they had been offered a chance of survival; may have used this as a reason for betraying their fellow Jews, as some desperately hoped to protect their own families whilst others appeared to collaborate with little thought for their own people.

The saddest outcome of all this was, that in exchange for their betrayal, by doing the German's bidding, they were mostly themselves discarded when their job was done and were not spared the gas chambers.

Yisrael Katz said 'historical truth cannot be changed, many Poles collaborated with the Germans and took part in the destruction of the Jews during the Holocaust ....' as did many Jews.

Following on from Katz's rewriting of history, I'll try to balance the argument with the contrast between the many Poles who helped Jews and the many Jews who actively played a role in the destruction of their own countrymen during the Holocaust.

Political theorist Hannah Arendt, a Jew who fled Germany during Hitler's rise to power in her book Eichmann in Jerusalem 1963, wrote that 'without the assistance of the Judenrate.... fewer Jews would have perished...'

I'll repeat what Golda Meir said – *'one cannot and must not try to erase the past merely because it does not fit the present.'*

The Judenrate Hannah Arendt wrote of was a Jewish-German collaborative agency, made up of 12 to 24 members from the Jewish community including Rabbis, other influential members and Ghetto Police. The German's required Jews to form a Judenrate in every community across the occupied territories and each Judenrate was required to ensure German orders and regulations were carried out and that order in the Ghettos was maintained.

They were required to hand over lists of Jews for deportation and that their deportation to the death camps was orderly. They secured money from the Jewish deportees, kept track on vacated apartments and helped police forces to seize Jews to get them on trains to the death camps.

The Germans used threats of terror, beatings and executions to enforce their orders and Jewish council chairmen had to either comply to German demands or pay the penalty, some committed suicide at the prospect of handing lists of fellow Jews to be deported to the death camps, whilst some took to their role more easily.

The organisation and its members remain to this day a controversial subject and one which has to be faced but instead is being overlooked by the revisionist lobby in favour of accusations against supposed Polish collaborators.

Chaim Rumkowski, was the head of the Jewish Council of Elders in the Łódz Ghetto. He had accrued much power transforming the Ghetto into an industrial base manufacturing war supplies for the Wehrmacht and used his power as head of the Judenrat to confiscate property and businesses that were still being run by their rightful Jewish owners. 'He rid himself of those he disliked by sending them to the camps and abused young girls in the ghetto with the threat of death if they did not submit.' – *survivor Lucille Eichengreen*

He is remembered for his speech of 4th September 1942 pleading with Jews in the ghetto to 'Give me your Children' so that others might survive, which was greeted with 'horrible, terrifying wailing among the assembled crowd.' People in the ghetto already in the most appalling situation were faced with this heart rending request to give up their children for deportation to Chełmno extermination camp. There were 20,000 children and also many elderly.

'A grievous blow has struck the ghetto. They are asking us to give up the best we possess, the children and the elderly. I was unworthy of having a child of my own so I gave the best years of my life to children. I've lived and breathed with children. I never imagined I would be forced to deliver this sacrifice to the altar with my own hands. In my old age I must stretch out my hands and beg, brothers and sisters, hand them over to me, fathers and mothers give me your children.' – *Chaim Rumkowski*

He was ruthless, '…an incomparable tyrant who behaved just like a Fuhrer who cast deathly terror to anyone who dared to oppose his lowly ways. Toward the perpetrators he was as tender as a lamb and there was no limit to his base submission to all their demands, even if their purpose was to wipe us out totally …' – *Yehuda Leib Gerst*

He and his Council lived comfortably with their own food rations and special shops whilst his fellow Jews starved. According to an Auschwitz survivor 'had he survived his own tragedy no tribunal would have absolved him nor certainly can we absolve him on the moral plane...' – *Primo Levi*

He is viewed by historians and writers as a 'German collaborationist and traitor' taking an active part in the deportations and abuse of his fellow Jews, fulfilling German demands with the help of the Grune Polizei. He and his family were put on the last transport to Auschwitz and he was murdered there on 28th August 1944 by the Sonderkommando Jews who had preceded him there.

They beat him to death at the gate of Crematorium No2 and disposed of his corpse, seeing justice done, revenge for his crimes. The Ghetto was liquidated in 1944 after the German defeat on the Eastern Front.

Hannah Arendt wrote 'To a Jew, this role of the Jewish leaders in the destruction of their own people is undoubtedly the darkest chapter of the whole dark story. In the matter of cooperation there was no distinction between the highly assimilated Jewish communities of Central and Western Europe and the Yiddish speaking masses of the East. In Amsterdam as in Warsaw, in Berlin as in Budapest, Jewish officials could be trusted to compile lists of persons and of their property, to secure money from the deportees to defray the expenses of their deportation and extermination, to keep track of vacated apartments, to supply police forces to help seize Jews and get them on trains, until, as a last gesture, they handed over the assets of the Jewish community in good order for final confiscation.' – *Hannah Arendt 1963*

GHETTO POLIZEI Badge

'She was a renowned philosopher and today would probably be considered a Holocaust Denier for her moral indictment of the leadership who served in the Jewish Councils. She wrote that 'Jews were sent to their death like sheep to the slaughter.' 'Without the cooperation of the victims' argued Arendt, 'it would hardly have been possible for a few thousand people, most of whom, moreover, worked in offices, to liquidate many hundreds of thousands of other people.' – *Edward Reid - Silent Heroes of the Forgotten Holocaust*

Another Jewish-German collaborationist organisation was Group 13, founded in 1940 and sited in the Warsaw Ghetto, the name taken from its address at 13 Leszno Street in Warsaw. It was led by Abraham Gancwajch and Lejb Skosowski, Dawid Sternfeld and Captain Lontski were also members. Sanctioned by Sicherhheitsdienst (SD) it was also known as the Jewish Gestapo reporting directly to the German Gestapo Office.

The group vied for control of the ghetto with the Junenrate and were the eyes and ears of the Gestapo in the Jewish quarter. 'They knew the complex life in the ghetto, every dive and smuggler, every member of the underworld. It was thanks to '13' that the Germans were able to control what was happening behind the wall.' Gancwajch soon became one of the leading agents of the elite organisation that emerged from '13', which was Zagiew.

Zagiew, founded and sponsored by the Germans and led by Gancwajch was a most ruthless group of Jewish secret agents allowed to own and carry firearms by their Gestapo handlers. They pretended to be Jewish underground fighters but hunted and murdered Poles who were hiding and helping Jews. Their primary goal was to infiltrate Jewish resistance networks and reveal any ties with the Polish underground and it did considerable damage to the Resistance network.

The group's main branch was the Office to Combat Usury and Profiteering in the Jewish Quarter and it was supposed to fight the black market but instead collected large sums from racketeering, blackmail and extortions. The group also ran its own prison and numbered between 300-400 uniformed Jewish Officers wearing caps with green bands and there were also Christian Poles amongst its number. They ran a brothel and had near total control over transportation within the Ghetto.

Its agents organised the Hotel Polski affair in Warsaw, a bait to lure thousands of rich Jews hiding in Warsaw with false promises of evacuation to South America, extorting their money and valuables. Its German and Jewish collaborators led these Jews to believe they could buy foreign passports and leave German occupied territories and some 2,500 Jews fell into this trap, were arrested and moved to concentration camps, others were simply killed.

Both '13' and Zagiew were liquidated by the right wing Jewish Military Union and the left wing Jewish Combat Organisation with shootings and bloody slaughter of Jews killing each other. Skosowski was shot in an assassination attempt in 1943 probably carried out by the ZZW, the Ghetto Resistance, closely linked to the AK. He survived and returned to his activities as a collaborator not sharing the fate of his brother Jews awaiting certain death, but choosing the path of betrayal.

As did the members of the Judenrate and Jewish Police who sent thousands of their countrymen to their deaths. One might perhaps accept that in such horrific circumstances they were hoping to save their own lives but today this is being turned round by Jewish media platforms that it was Poles who were the collaborators and not the Jews!

Emanuel Ringelblum, famous Polish Jewish Chronicler of the Warsaw Ghetto, wrote about the Jewish Police 'which in one sentence was not even mentioned in Gross's 'scientific work.' – *Edward Mosberg, Holocaust survivor.*

'The Jewish Police had a very bad opinion before displacement. Unlike the Polish Police, who did not take part in the labour camps, the Jewish Police were paranoid with this hideous job. It also stood out with terrible corruption and demoralization. However, the bottom of the meanness reached only during displacement. Not a single word of protest against the disgusting function of leading your brothers to slaughter. The Police were spiritually prepared for this dirty work and therefore they did it eagerly. Currently, the brain is strong on solving the puzzle; how did Jews, mostly intelligent, former lawyers [most officers were lawyers before the war] they put their hands on the destruction of their brothers. How did it come to the fact that Jews dragged children and women, old people and sick on cars, knowing that everyone was going to slaughter. The cruelty of the Jewish Police was very often greater than Germans, Ukrainians, Latvians. Many hideouts were 'caught' by the Jewish Police who always wanted to be plus catholique que le pape to please the occupier. Victims that disappeared from the German sight were caught by the Jewish Policeman. The Jewish Police even gave evidence of incomprehensible, wild brutality. Why such rage in our Jews? When did we grow so many hundreds of killers who catch children in the streets, push them on the cars and drag them to Umschlag? Common phenomena were simply that these thugs threw women on cars by arms and legs. Every Warsaw Jew, every woman and child can quote thousands of facts of inhuman cruelty and rage of the Jewish Police.' – *E. Ringelblum – Chronicle of the Warsaw Ghetto Sept 1939 – Jan 1943. 1988 Warsaw.*

In March 1944 Ringelblum was betrayed and his refuge discovered by the Germans. He, his family, the other concealed Jews and the Pole who had hidden them were taken to Pawiak prison. They were all shot amid the ruins of the Warsaw ghetto in March 1944.

The Pole who betrayed them, Jan Lakinski, was later executed by the Polish Underground who did not tolerate betrayal and imposed severe punishment on anyone betraying Jews to the Germans.

Stella Goldschlag Kuber, as a 'Jewish Catcher', identified and sent thousands of Jews to their deaths, she was eventually arrested by the Soviets and sentenced to hard labour. Born on 10th July 1922 in Berlin, with her tall, blond looks and blue eyes she looked almost 'Aryan' in appearance.

She and her family managed to avoid capture in the many round ups of Jews and lived in constant fear. The family were part of the 18,300 Uboats, (Jews living illegally in Berlin), the very group of people she would later betray. To start with everything went well with her Aryan looks and the papers provided by the counterfeiter Guenther Rogoff, but once she was in the crosshairs of one of the Catchers she was arrested, on 2nd July 1943, and then her parents fell into the hands of the Gestapo.

She was submitted to torture by the Gestapo which eventually broke her and she accepted the offer of becoming a 'Catcher.' She was promised that by cooperating she would save her parents. As Roger Moorhouse tells in his book, Berlin at War 1939-45, she quickly became a model 'Catcher' and impressed the officers of the Gestapo with her ingenuity, she did not disappoint. She had an excellent memory for names, dates and addresses and made her mark.

The Resistance circulated her picture as a warning to Jews which was effective because as soon as she entered a café or restaurant they would leave very quickly but she was able to capture 60 Jews in one weekend and received 200 marks for each one.

It is estimated that she sent up to 3000 Jews to certain death. Combing Berlin for Jews hiding as non Jews and even locating her former school mates, handing the information over to the Gestapo. She earned the name 'Blond Poison.'

She was not able to save her parents after all and they were sent to Auschwitz where they died together with her husband. She remained an active 'Catcher' until the end of the war and in 1945 was arrested by the Soviets. She was found guilty in 3 trials, of crimes against humanity and an accessory to murder in a Soviet Military trial in 1946 and German

Criminal trials in 1957 and 1972 and sentenced to 10 years x3 of hard labour. She was never properly held accountable for her crimes, being released early and saw herself merely as a victim.

She committed suicide in 1994 aged 72. Perhaps the burden of denouncing and betraying so many of Berlin's underground Jews became too much to live with or that her crimes were becoming public? Roger Moorhouse's book Berlin at War and Diana Tovar's story of Stella Goldschlag were available for the public to read. The level of betrayal she was capable of is staggering but pressure to survive may have had some impact.

The other side of collaboration with the Germans is becoming known, although at a snails pace and is an important addition to the history books but many authors, media, politicians and others continue to place the blame of collaboration on the Polish WW2 population alone.

And something else from the history books I've found of interest whilst searching through the dusty archives, is Bitter Reckoning 2019, about Israel's trials of Holocaust survivors who were German collaborators. In January 1952 in a 3½ month trial in Tel Aviv a case was brought against Yehezkel Jungster who Judge Pinches Avishar, said 'had made himself a tool in the hands of the barbaric German regime in its plan to annihilate the Jewish people.'

He had served as a Kapo in 1943-1944 and was an inmate at Grodziszcze and Faulbruck camps in western Poland. 'A heavily built man, dressed in a leather jacket and shod in boots, he walked about with a rubber coated metal wire rod in his hand beating at a whim anyone who crossed his path.'

Jungster as a Kapo, was assigned by the SS in a position to supervise other prisoners within the camp. Witnesses testified that he 'beat his victims often aiming for their genitals, even when no German was in sight.' Jungster's case was one of 40 Kapo trials that took place in Israel between 1950-1972.

The Israel state has only in recent years made the transcripts from the archives of some of these trials publicly available. During these trials Jewish functionaries, such as camp supervisors and Ghetto policemen faced indictments for their behaviour during the Holocaust. Prosecutors brought charges against them for collaborating with the Germans, assaulting Jews and inflicting grievous injuries.

They were accused of blackmail and of surrendering Jewish victims to the Germans, of membership of enemy organisations, of the murder of prisoners and even of war crimes and crimes against humanity. In two thirds of these trials all but one of those convicted were sentenced to prison for an average of 26 months behind bars! – *Dan Porat, 2019, Israeli historian.*

Why have these trials been suppressed for so long? kept secret whilst the Jewish lobby bays for the blood of Poland's supposed anti semites and for war reparations long ago paid in financial and military support provided to Israel. Compensation was paid to Jewish Holocaust survivors in hundreds of billions of dollars from the western world, mostly from the US when the sovereign Israeli state was founded in 1948.

'The Germans were the murdering force but someone should have helped' is a question often asked. It was difficult for a Jew to pass themselves off as ethnic Poles as they dressed differently, had hair braids and many spoke Yiddish which made them more identifiable. Perhaps a feeling of guilt amongst Jewish survivors made it easier to blame the Christian Poles rather than admit their own inactions or inability. Ignoring the many Poles who did in fact help their Jewish neighbours, suppressing and manipulating the truth isn't helping to answer that question.

Poland's very location made it difficult to get anyone to safe, neutral or Allied countries, the length of its occupation was greater than in western Europe giving the Germans time to steal their money and property, starve them and work them to death and the level of cruelty drained the strength of the Poles. Those who currently lay blame on the Poles for 'complicity in WW2' may wonder why Poland was the only country where the Germans carried out automatic death penalties for even giving a Jew a drink of water!

The fighting in Poland was some of the worst in the whole of Europe with its leadership and elite deported, imprisoned or murdered by the Germans and the Russians, with many Poles fighting the Germans with the 4th largest Allied army. I wonder what difference that might have made on the Poles' ability to help the Jews even more than they so actively did. The Polish population gave all possible help to the Jews, they had a joint struggle against inhuman occupying powers, a struggle that went on secretly even in the Ghettos under conditions hard to describe or imagine.

The Polish Government continued to be proactive in its efforts to inform the Allies of the extermination camps' existence and pressured the Allies to bomb the camps but the Allies vetoed this, Poland was ignored. Poland set up an organisation specifically to help Jews, Zegota, one of many in Poland and the Polish people saved very many Jewish lives through the AK, other Resistance units and on their own individual initiatives.

Polish collaborators are always presented as anti Semites but Jewish collaborators are presented as desperate people in a desperate situation when in fact both the Jews and Christians faced the same, awful, desperate situation. We cannot possibly imagine.

I hope that time and truthful dialogue will win against the revisionist hate-filled lies targeted against the Polish people who fought the Germans to the very end. Poland as a country has recovered and rebuilt after the onslaught of WW2 but now has to contend with malicious misrepresentation from many fronts. It will take considerable effort to address these falsehoods against well resourced and established revisionists, within a huge, mostly American Jewish lobby.

The Polish people were proactive in saving the lives of their Jewish compatriots, there is evidence and research freely available to all writers of WW2 history which will show this and I'll outline just how they did it. It has not been re-interpreted to fit a pre-conceived theory but to show the extremes, good and bad, that people will go to in times of absolute terror.

Before I do I want to include a poem by Itrzhak Katzenelson, a Polish Jewish teacher, poet and dramatist, born 1886 in Minsk and who lived with his family in Łodz, Poland. His wife and two sons were murdered at Treblinka, he fell victim to the Hotel Polski affair and was murdered with his other son in Auschwitz in 1944. He wrote the following poem from what he had seen in the Warsaw Ghetto, putting the manuscript into bottles and burying them under a tree whilst in a detention camp in France.

The Song of the Murdered Jewish People,
Song 3, Oh Pain of Mine   1943

'I am the one who saw it, who watched closely, when children, wives and husbands and grey haired elders like stones and timber torturer flung onto carts and beaten without pity, abused with atrocious words.

I observed it from the window, I saw the murderers gangs – Oh, God, I've seen those beating and those beaten, walking to their deaths. And I wrung my hands in shame …in shame and disgrace – with Jewish hands death was inflicted on Jews – helpless Jews!

Traitors who ran across the empty street in shining boots, As it with the swastika on the caps – with David's shield, furious they went with mouths, wounded by words alien to them, arrogant and savage, those who thrown us down the stairs, those who dragged us out of the houses.

Those who broken the doors, violently burst into homes, scoundrels, with a club raised to the blow – to homes taken over by fear, they beat us, they rushed elders, they rushed youngsters into the terrified streets and spat straight into God's face.

They found us in wardrobes and pulled us from under the beds and they cursed 'move damn it, to Umschlag, there is your place.' All of us they drove out of apartments, then they searched them long enough, to take the last clothes, 3 piece of bread and groat.

On the street – madness! Look and get numb, because here a dead street that became one cry and terror – empty from the end to the end and full like never before – carts! And from despair, from shouting, it's hard to drive them.

In them, Jews! tearing hair from their heads and wringing hands, some are silent – their silence is louder even than scream. They look, their eyes, is it really? Maybe a bad dream and nothing else? With them the Jewish Police – cruel and savage thugs!

And on the side – the German with a slight smile glances at them. The German stopped at a distance and watches – he doesn't interfere, he is killing my Jews with Jewish hands!'

Compassion

That Jews were being murdered on a massive scale by the Germans was known to the Allies. The many pleas by General Sikorski and the Armia Krajowa leaders to send in the RAF to bomb the railway lines leading to the extermination camps, were refused by Britain despite having a detailed map from the AK of the railway network. Although Armia Krajowa could cause damage by sabotage they did not have the resources to destroy the railway lines.

The Polish Prime Minister Władysław Sikorski, made several visits to London and the Polish Embassy in Washington D.C, sending telegrams between London and Warsaw to document the extent of Polish efforts in pressurizing the Allies for military assistance. In 1941-42 he asked for a U.S declaration condemning German oppression against the Poles and Jews.

The US was unresponsive which only made the situation worse and for Sikorski's appeals for help to become even more frequent and urgent. Britain refused to intervene as 'it was not within the scope of their political objectives.'

However, the Polish Government somehow found it within the scope of its objectives to persist in its efforts to highlight the Jewish situation! The world knew and the world ignored Poland's requests.

Britain and the US also refused to liberate the prisoners in the extermination camps despite the Polish Government's appeals. They

15589059

claimed they could not divert resources allocated to other operations, yet Allied bombers destroyed industrial areas just a few miles from the gas chambers? Their reasoning seems hugely flawed.

Poles did not 'take part in the destruction of the Jews' but continued to be active in reporting German atrocities to the Western Allies. Many despatches were sent and the Polish Government in exile from 1942 provided the Allies with the earliest and most accurate accounts through Foreign Minister Count Edward Raczynski as well as Witold Pilecki and Jan Karski, calling for action from the Allies to stop the atrocities. As we know they were ignored.

'Extermination of the Jewish population is taking place at an unbelievable extent... Mass slaughter of tens of thousands of Jews is being carried out. In the ghettos of Warsaw and Kraków, mass executions are being carried out every day. Jews ill with typhus are being shot. The Jews of Poland are suffering the most terrible persecution in the entire history...'

'The Polish Government informs the governments of the Allied powers of these facts and states that they are in violation of international law and the Hague Convention. The perpetrators of these crimes must be brought to justice and this principle should become the mainstay of the war policy of the Allies....'

'Reprisals on the part of the Allies should be again proclaimed and applied wherever possible... The Germans and their Allies in the Axis... must know that their crimes will not go unpunished otherwise they will intensify the terror in the occupied countries.'

As the massacres spread throughout eastern Poland, the Polish Underground in 1942 reported on the increase of German killings in one of many memo's which read:

'I inform that the news about the murder of several thousand Jews in eastern Galicia is true. Mass murder of Jews was also committed in the Wilno province, in Byelorussia and in the Lublin province. In Wilno alone about 60,000 Jews were murdered.' – *Govt Delegate, 8 April 1942*

On June 9th 1942 General Sikorski made a speech at the BBC warning the Germans of the consequences of their actions. The Polish National Council on 14th June 1942 addressed the Parliaments of the world of the situation in Poland and of the urgency of punishing the Germans.

On 26th July 1942 Stefan Korbonski, head of Directorate of Civil

Resistance in Poland informed London that the Germans had begun the mass deportation of Jews to the death camps at Treblinka, slaughter at the Warsaw Ghetto and the shootings in streets and houses. The US reported this the next day but the BBC waited a month to broadcast it!

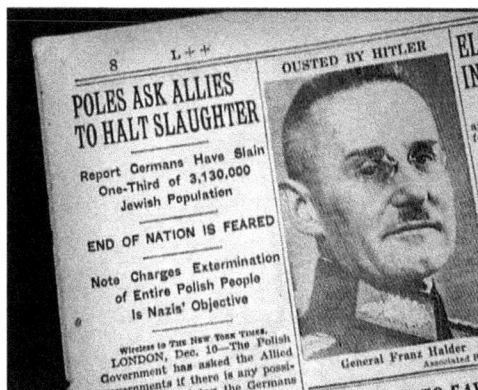

And the world didn't listen!

Count Raczynski sent a note to the Governments of the UN on 10th December 1942, an official denunciation by any government of the mass extermination by the Germans of European Jews. The Polish Government in Exile and the Polish Secret State pleaded to no avail for American and British help to stop the Holocaust. That note and the efforts of the Polish Government triggered the Declaration of the Allied Nations on 17th December 1942.

Jan Karski had embarked on a grueling journey through several occupied countries transporting secret microfilm to the Polish Government in exile in London, with evidence of the crimes committed by the Germans, with photographs, decrees and statistics. The Poles were ignored again and the pattern continues with little acknowledgement of their wartime efforts to this day.

The Polish Government carried out many services to help Jews. It cooperated with international Jewish organisations sending food and medicines through neutral countries such as Portugal and Sweden to the Jews in Poland. When the Jews began to escape the Ghettos in July-August 1942 the Delegatura (Armed Forces Delegation formed by General Anders) granted subsidies to help them and from January 1943 to August 1944 the Polish Government was sending regular endowments to the Polish Council for Aid to Jews, Zegota.

The Poles were greatly frustrated in their rescues by the most stringent conditions in all of German occupied Europe, where any kind of help to

Jews was punishable by death for the rescuer, the rescuer's entire family and neighbours. As many as 50,000 were executed by the Germans solely for helping Jews. They were also hampered by their inability to provide for them which made many Poles unwilling or unable to provide direct help but despite this they sheltered Jews who had escaped from the ghettos for maybe one or two nights or in some cases they assumed full responsibility for the Jews' survival, well aware of the consequences.

The Rescuers

'A Polish Catholic family for 22 months hid my Mother and Grand parents in the village of Lacka Woja east of Przemyśl. They feared they would be betrayed by their neighbours but only the Catholic priest knew about what they were doing. Luckily no one else found out and my family and these Poles survived.' – *Jeffrey Cymbler – Poland's Long War, Sept 2019.*

My Mother's dearest friend of over 60 years, Halina lost her Aunt and Uncle to the German collaborating Ukrainian UPA, who murdered her Uncle, hacking him to death with an axe, raping her aunt many times then throwing them into their home as it was set alight. Murdered not just for being Polish but for harbouring and helping Jews.

They were just two of many in their village who did what they could for their fellow Poles at great risk to themselves, the Germans were suspicious of everyone and brutal in their searches.

Is this the behaviour you expect from a people 'collaborating with the Germans?'

'Tarnow in occupied Poland, the Germans are closing off the Jewish district and turning it into a ghetto. These are the days of murderers running amok, blood covered bodies are lying on the streets, people are trying to escape, some are thrown into a burning synagogue. A few days later a Jewish woman knocks at her Polish friend's door, a young woman answers, what should she do?'

'Giving shelter to Jews means death so says the German law introduced by the occupiers and applicable to Poles. This young Pole's life has just started, was it not for the war she would still be studying physics. She opens the door wider, the Jewish woman (Frieda) enters and stays for over two years'. The young woman who opened the door to safety and eventual liberty for Frieda; they remained friends for life; was the mother of Jan Sliwa. – *Good Samaritans in the Times of the Holocaust – Jan Sliwa*

The Polish people were not 'bystanders' to the murder of their Jewish countrymen, many were involved in helping them despite the persecution and depravation inflicted on them by Hitler. Surviving day to day in a Poland under brutal siege and still helping Jews is only to be hugely respected and acknowledged.

Professor Hans G. Furth, in the Journal of Genocide research estimated that as many as 1.2 ml Polish rescuers helped Jews, Richard C. Lukas historian, estimated upwards of 1 ml Poles were involved in rescue efforts. Far outnumbering any individuals from other countries.

The Eiss Archive that documents the work of Polish diplomats in Switzerland has been obtained by Poland. The Ministry of Culture and National Heritage, the Auschwitz-Birkenau Museum and the Embassy of the Republic of Poland, announced on 6th August 2018 that Poland had reacquired the archive after 75 years and more than a year of negotiations with a private owner in Israel. It is one of the largest collections documenting rescue operations of endangered Jews by the Polish Diplomatic Corps, to get Jews out of Europe by issuing phoney passports from Latin American Countries.

The documents went on display in Bern, Switzerland before becoming part of the collection at the Auschwitz museum a memorial to the victims of the German death camp where some 1.1 ml people were killed. It is estimated that the group of diplomats produced several thousand fake passports between 1941 and 1943.

The collection was found many years after the war and originally belonged to Chaim Eiss (1876-1943) a merchant from Ustrzyki of the Aguda Israel Orthodox movement. He was a member of the Lados group in Bern which forged the Latin American passports, providing Polish diplomats with a list of beneficiaries and smuggled the doctored passports to the General Government. He died of a heart attack in 1943 leaving behind this priceless archive.

'These documents constitute a very important collection showing both the drama of Polish Jewish families as well as attempts to get as many people as possible out of the hell that was the Holocaust.' – *Dr Piotr Cywinski*

The Lados group was led by the Polish Embassy charge d'affairs Aleksander Lados with Polish diplomats Stefan Ryniewicz, Konstanty Rocicki and Julius Kuhl and Jewish activists Abraham Silberscheim and Chaim Eiss who co financed the group. Lados, in his formal capacity was able to give the group diplomatic protection.

In his correspondence with Aguda Israel, Chaim Eiss repeated on many occasions the important role played by the Aleksander Lados group and the role of Konstanty Rokicki a Holocaust rescuer and Vice Consul in Bern. It was on the basis of this relationship that in January 1945 Agudat Israel issued a letter of gratitude to Polish diplomats involved in the negotiations of this most unique operation.

Aleksader Lados died in Warsaw on 29th December 1963, in poverty. Despite saving thousands of Jews he was ignored by the mostly Jewish, Communist Government. There will be no film of his courageous exploits, unlike Schindler's list, where Spielberg (born in Ohio US in 1946) took great creative licence on many issues. Depicting the Poles as not resisting the German occupation and as fanatical anti-Semites, starting with the film's early scenes. The other side of the story can be considered by one of the many books written about Schindler.

When interviewed about 'anything blatantly incorrect' about the film, Leon Leyson said, 'in my opinion those who were depicted as Camp or Ghetto Police were glossed over too lightly. A little bit should have been put in that these were not your casual friends but in some cases they were vicious people.' 'Were those Jews?' the interviewer Stella Eliezre asked, 'yes' replied Leon, 'were they forced to be vicious?' 'well, not really' replied Leon, 'that's the sad part of it of course.'

A comment from another Schindler's Jew, Victor Dortheimer when interviewed, was that 'there were disparities at length' and 'Poldek Pfefferberg's influence on the film was too great considering he was only at the factory for 4 months, only arriving in 1944.' – *Prof. Jeffrey Shandler - Survivors on Schindler's List.*

Roman Polanski's The Pianist, however, is the accurate, true story of a Polish Jew, Wladyslaw Szpilman, who survived through stoicism and incredible good luck. Hiding in various locations, he survived in Warsaw with help from the Polish Resistance, non-Jewish friends, fellow musicians and a friend from the Jewish Police; which he had declined to join; who took him off a train bound for the death camps. He was also helped by a German Captain, Wilm Hosenfeld, a music lover, who gave him food and treated him kindly and would later die in a Soviet prison. Polanski himself was a survivor of the Holocaust, wandering Krakow and Warsaw as a terrified child, cared for by the kindness of the Polish people. Fate and chance played a huge role in the survival of both men. None of Szpilman's family survived the war.

On Tuesday 25th January 2022, a discussion is to be held on the Lados Group; a neglected part of WW2 Polish history; at Clapham Library in London. Poland's purchase of the archive comes as the Polish government is working to emphasise the help Poles gave Jews during Germany's occupation of their country. This is in contrast to the acting Foreign Minister of Israel, Yisrael Katz in 2019 accusing Poland of being complicit in the Holocaust. The archive provides 'irrefutable proof that Poles, the Polish state and its representatives, systematically and institutionally, were proactively involved in saving Jews during WW2.' – *Piotr Glinski*

Culture minister Piotr Glinski said. 'I would ask why this most important document was hidden from view for so long? When it could have resolved so many questions over the years about supposed Polish anti Semitism.'

Poland, more than any other country is recognised by Yad Vashem for Poles saving not only the lives of their Jewish neighbours but so much more. The number does not come anywhere near that officially recognised, it is the tip of the iceberg. For every Jew saved there were up to 10 or more Poles involved in sheltering them which makes the number vastly under estimated and the world will never know the names of those brave people.

The Germans conducted house to house searches and when finding Jews in hiding they shot them along with the Poles who were sheltering them, the family, neighbours and friends, ensuring there were never any witnesses to their murderous campaign.

Teresa Prekerowa a Polish historian and author assumed that 'each Jew who hid amongst the non Jewish populace stayed throughout the war in only one hiding place.'

Hanna Krall a Polish writer and a Holocaust survivor, identified 45 Poles who helped to shelter her from the Germans.

Wladyslaw Szpilma the Jewish Polish musician was rescued by the cooperative efforts of a dozen or more people.
– *Syzmon Datner Jewish Polish historian*

If someone had saved my life from the dire situation that Poland was in, someone who was under threat of death for helping me, who couldn't even feed their own family, when enjoying the safety and freedom they had helped me to achieve, I would be shouting from the rooftops their names and my most heartfelt thanks. The world would know.

The accusation by Yisrael Katz, accusing Poland of collaborating with the Germans in the Holocaust, is historically inaccurate and hugely offensive. The many Jews that survived would not have done so without help from their Polish compatriots.

Poland was not a nation of 'bystanders.' Polish rescuers of Jews are credited with saving up to 450,000 and more, from certain death, aided by the largest Resistance movement in Europe, the Polish Underground State, and its military arm Armia Krajowa. These organisations operated special units dedicated to helping Jews, the most notable was the Zegota Council based in Warsaw, with branches in Kraków, Wilno and Lwów.

Emblem of the Polish Underground State and Home Army – (Armia Krajowa)

One Polish rescuer was Anna Kozminska who at this date, 2020, is still alive and at 101 lives in Warsaw. Together with her step mother Maria Kozminska she hid Abraham Jabłoński at their home in Częstohowa, Southern Poland. With his sister Iza he had escaped from the Częstohowa Ghetto and at the request of his uncle, Maria and Anna gave the 8 year old boy shelter. They attended to his education and took him for walks, telling the neighbours he had lost his family and was under their care. He was with them from 1943-45. They also gave shelter to a man called Rubenstein a relative of the Jabłoński's, his friend Rita and her mother.

After the war Abraham went to Israel where he gave testimony to the humanity and bravery of the women. He located Anna in Warsaw 47 years later and asked her to write her memoirs of the war and at his request on 11th February 1991 Maria and Anna were honoured by Yad Vashem. In 2016 Anna received the Commander's Cross of the order of Polonia Restituta from Poland's President Andrzej Duda. *– thefirstnewswarsaw.com*

He in no doubt showed his gratitude to the women who saved his life and that he was able to find Anna in Warsaw after so many years must have been overwhelming.

The convent walls of the Franciscan Order over looked the Warsaw Ghetto where thousands of Jews were imprisoned, many were children. The Sisters saw at first hand what misery and persecution war could bring and under the leadership of the Order's Superior, the charismatic Sister Matylda Getter, the Sisters began a rescue effort giving refuge to Jewish children they helped escape the ghetto.

Their methods of rescue were varied and grew to involve a giant network from Warsaw which reached as far as the Ukraine. One strategy was to produce counterfeit certificates of baptism. Sister Matylda would work with doctors to expose the certificates to a quartz lamp to make them appear more credible. The children rescued from the ghetto were taken to several orphanages run by the Franciscan Order within Poland with some being taken further afield.

Sister Barbara Król from the Franciscan Congregation in Warsaw, ensured that those children with obvious Semitic features were taken further east as they were safer in the Ukraine. It was a covert operation with the Sisters making calls to the orphanage in Lwów and asking 'would you receive God's blessing?' – *code for a Jewish child.*

The rescue effort was a fraught undertaking. 'It took several people to save just one child' said Sister Barbara and 'a well thought out strategy as the Germans were suspicious during their inspections of the orphanages.' They would order the children to say Christian prayers and listen to the children repeating them and most did, fluently. This was why the sisters taught Jewish children Christian prayers, not to convert them but to help them survive. In this way the lives of about 500 children and 250 adults were saved.

On Wednesday 8th August 2018 the 50th anniversary of the death of Sister Matylda the cornerstone for the construction of the Museum for the Rescue of Jewish Children was laid. Among those present was Lea Balint one of the many children rescued by Sister Matylda, who had travelled to Warsaw from Israel.

Sister Barbara told TFNews 'we are visited every year by people who used to be in our care. They come with their children and grandchildren from the United States and Israel to show that they survived. Matylda was a very strong personality, with decisiveness, a great organiser.' She was one of the first people to be awarded the title of Righteous Among the World's nations by Yad Vashem.

Irena Sendler (nee Krzyzanowska) was another strong Polish woman a Social Worker and humanitarian who served in the Polish Underground in Warsaw and from October 1943 was head of the children's section of Zegota. She was known for her effectiveness when confronted with obstruction or indifference and from her social work encountered many cases of extreme poverty among the Jewish population of Warsaw.

Soon after the German invasion on 1st September 1939 the occupiers ordered Jews removed from the staff of the Social Welfare department where she worked and barred the department from providing any assistance to Warsaw's Jewish citizens.

On her initiative the department's cell became involved in helping wounded and sick Polish soldiers and together with Jadwiga Piotrowska, Jadwiga Salek-Deneko and Irena Schultz, they began generating false medical documents needed to obtain aid that she also extended to her Jewish charges who were now officially served only by the Jewish community organisations, the Judenrate.

She was arrested by the Gestapo on 18th October and as they ransacked her house she tossed the lists of Jewish children to her friend Janina Grabowska who was able to hide the names and locations of the rescued Jewish children in her clothing, preventing it from falling into the hands of the Gestapo. Sendler was taken to the Gestapo headquarters and brutally beaten.

Three hundred thousand Jews were sealed into the Warsaw Ghetto and as employees of the Social Welfare Department, Sendler and a colleague Shultz had access to special permits for entering the Ghetto to check for signs of typhus a disease the Germans feared would spread beyond the Ghetto. She and colleagues would then help Jews to escape and smuggled out babies and small children which became an urgent priority in the summer of 1942.

Jewish children were placed by Sendler's network with Polish families in Warsaw and Orphanages of the Franciscan Sisters, Sister Servants of the Blessed Virgin in Turkowice or the Felician Sisters and other orphanages. A convent offered a Jewish child the best opportunity to survive and be taken care of as almost all of the children's parents had been killed at Treblinka extermination camp or were missing. Most of them were taken out of Poland to safety.

During the Warsaw Uprising a network of emergency shelters was created by Sendler's group in empty private residences where Jews could be temporarily housed while Zegota worked on producing documents and finding long term locations for them. The work was done at extremely high risk but continued with determination of all involved.

In 1965 Sendler was recognised by Yad Vashem as one of the Righteous Among the Nations. In 1991 she was made an honorary citizen of Israel and was awarded the Commander's Cross of the Order of Polonia in 1996, receiving the Cross with Star in 2001. In 2003 Pope John Paul II sent her a personal letter praising her wartime efforts and in 2003 she received the Order of the White Eagle, Poland's highest civilian decoration.

Other awards in recognition of her wartime help for Jews came in 2007 being honoured by the State of Poland and in 2008 by the US Congress, she was twice nominated for the Nobel Peace Prize. It is thought she helped save approximately 2,500 Jewish children, a most courageous woman who helped others in the face of extreme persecution.

Again and again the Polish Government and its representatives informed the Allies of the circumstances of the European Jews and no one listened! – They were aware of what was happening.

Zegota, the Polish Council to Aid Jews was the only organisation in occupied Europe whose express purpose was to rescue Jews. Initiated by two Polish Catholic activists, Zofia Kossak-Szczucka and Wanda Krahelska-Filipowicz it was part of the Polish Underground State and the continuation of an earlier Aid organisation, the provisional Committee to Aid Jews and was active from 1942-45.

It was run by both Jews and non Jews from a wide range of political movements. It is estimated that over 60,000 Jews who survived the Holocaust in Poland were aided in some way by Zegota. Its Operatives were under constant threat of death from German forces and worked in extreme circumstances but showed exceptional bravery and many have been recognised as Righteous Among the Nations.

Zegota was receiving regular endowments from various organisations and in 1943 had received a total of 4.75 ml złotys which by 1944 rose to 12 ml. The Polish Government in exile also allocated £37ml. Other donations from organisations abroad were mostly channelled through Zegota. I haven't been able to establish how much was provided by the WJC although they had 'set up a relief committee for Jewish war refugees and were able to transmit funds for the assistance of persecuted Jews... which helped rescue 1,350 Jewish children to Switzerland and 70 to Spain.' *Reigner*

Other rescue units included the Catholic Front for the Rebirth of Poland led by Zofia Kossak-Szczucka and Witold Bienkowski, also editors of its underground publications. Kossak-Szczucka went on to act in the Social-Help Organisation as a liaison between Zegota and Catholic Convents and Orphanages as well as other public Orphanages which jointly hid many Jewish children.

Zofia Kossak-Szczucka wrote an appeal in August 1942 to Western societies about the murder of Jews in the Warsaw Ghetto. 'The world is viewing this crime, more horrible than anything else in the annals of mankind and is silent, the slaughter of millions of defenceless people is taking place amid ominous general silence... that silence can no longer be tolerated… whoever remains silent in the face of murder becomes the murderer's accomplice, who does not condemn it, condones it' she wrote.

She was ignored by the Western Allies as were Witold Pilecki, Jan Karski and the Polish Government in exile. The world knew and the world was silent.

She would not be silenced and at risk to her own life concealed Jews in her flat, she sought out safe hiding places, smuggled them into convents and monasteries, provided them with falsified identity papers and supplied them with food and clothing. She got hundreds of people involved in these activities, was sent to Auschwitz and the Pawiak prison with a death sentence hanging over her but was later released and fought in the Warsaw Uprising in 1944. She received the title of Righteous Among Nations, posthumously in 1982, an incredibly brave woman.

Jan and Antonia Zabinski a couple from Warsaw, were recognised by Yad Vashen for their heroic rescue of Jews. Jan was a zoologist by profession, a scientist, organiser and director of Warsaw Zoo before and during WW2. The Zoo attracted visitors from all over the country to its large collection of exotic animals and thrived right up until the bombing of Warsaw on 1st September 1939 which hit the zoo killing many of the animals.

He had maintained contact with his pre war Jewish friends and colleagues and helped them to escape, find shelter on the Aryan side of the city which was outside the walls of the Jewish quarter and provided them with personal documents. As many of the cages in the zoo had been emptied of animals during the September air assault he saw an opportunity to turn the cages and pens into a sanctuary for fleeing Jewish friends and strangers.

Over the course of 3 years hundreds of Jews found temporary shelter in these animal cages, until they were able to find permanent places of refuge and several found shelter in Zabinski's private home in the zoo's grounds. He was helped by his wife and young son Ryszard who looked after the needs of the many distraught Jews in their care.

Most of the Zabinski's help went to friends but many were strangers who had sought their help, he paid for all this from his own funds and then with funds received from Zegota. That he was able to continue sheltering Jews for over 3 years is testament to his bravery and commitment to saving his Jewish friends and strangers.

He was also an active member of Armia Krajowa, and participated in the uprising in Warsaw in 1944, was arrested and taken as prisoner to Germany. His wife and son continued his work helping the Jews left behind in the ruins of the city, looking after their needs. On 21st September 1965 Yad Vashem recognised the couple as Righteous Among the Nations.

At the outbreak of war both the Germans and the Soviets rounded up, deported and liquidated teachers, doctors, priests, military men and other leaders, aiming to divide and exacerbate tensions between Catholics and Jews, Poles and Ukrainians, in an attempt to discourage Poles from helping the Jews. To destroy any efforts of the Resistance the Germans applied a ruthless retaliation policy and on 10th November 1941 the death penalty was introduced by Hans Frank, Governor of the General Government.

It was to apply to Poles who helped Jews, 'in any way' by taking them in for the night, giving them a lift, feeding runaway Jews or giving them foodstuffs. 'If a Pole even offered a cup of water to a Jew an entire village would suffer for the humane action of just one Pole.' The law was made public by posters in all cities and towns. It was a policy unique to Poland.

That many Poles had to survive with this type of persecution imposed on them is testament to their character in that many ignored the law and saved thousands of Jews throughout Germany's occupation of their country. Mainstream Polish society was generally sympathetic to the plight of the Jews yet today's revisionists describe them as being antisemitic.

The Poles were not 'anti semites' very many were active in their aid to their Jewish compatriots despite the consequences and Józef Ulma and his wife Wiktonia an ordinary Polish couple and their 6 children were murdered by the Germans for helping and hiding their Jewish neighbours.

They were executed on 24th March 1944 in Markowa near Rzeszów in south east Poland. As a Catholic Józef had underlined in his Bible in red, the story of the Good Samaritan and for defying German dictates the couple and their young family paid the ultimate price, some were only infants, his wife was pregnant.

Dr. Eugeniusz Lazowski a Polish physician saved 8,000 Polish Jews in Rozwadów from deportation to the death camps by simulating a typhus epidemic and Dr. Tadeusz Pankiewicz working in the Kraków Ghetto gave out free medicines saving a great number.

Professor Rudolf Weigl the inventor of the first vaccine against typhus employed and protected Jews in his Weigl institute in Lwów and his vaccines were smuggled into the Lwów and Warsaw Ghettos saving countless lives.

Dr. Tadeusz Kosibowicz the director of Bedzin Hospital was sentenced to death for rescuing Jewish fugitives but he survived the war with his sentence commuted to camp imprisonment.

The Wołyniec family, also ignored the posters put up by the Germans and in Romaszkańce the entire family was massacred for sheltering three Jewish refugees from a Ghetto. The Germans also shot Józef Borowski and eight members of his family for hiding Jews. A huge risk had been taken by very brave people and they and their entire families died.

A number of Polish villages in their entirety provided shelter from the German death squads, offering protection for their Jewish neighbours as well as aid for refugees from other villages and escapees from the ghettos. Post war research has confirmed communal protection in many villages.

German death squads carried out mass executions of entire villages discovered to be aiding Jews, in the villages of Białka near Parczew and Sterdyn near Sokołów Podlaski, 150 villagers were massacred with the Jews they had rescued.

In Sztark in Słonim in December 1942, several hundred Poles were massacred with their priest for sheltering Jewish refugees from the Słonim Ghetto.

In Huta Stara near Buczacz, Polish Christians and the Jewish countrymen they had protected were herded into a church by the Germans and burned alive in March 1944.

In the Kielce region between 1942-1944 200 peasants were shot and then burned as punishment. It was constant, very brave people died at the hands of German brutality for doing their Christian duty.

In the villages of Głuchów, near Lancut, Główne in Ozorków, Borkowo, near Sierpc, Dabrowica near Ułanów, Głupianka near Otwock and Teresin near Chełm, all the villagers were killed with the Jews they had protected.

In Cisie near Warsaw, 25 Poles were caught hiding Jews, all were killed and the village was burned to the ground as punishment as were all the other nearby villages, razed to the ground. The death squads were ruthless, without mercy, covering up the evidence of their brutal murders.

The farm of Jerzy and Irena Krepec in Gołąbki was a hiding place for

30 Jews. The villagers kept quiet and helped with food, some Poles had ration cards but food was scarce for all. The couple even set up home schooling for all the children, Christian and Jewish.

Another farm couple. Alfreda and Bolesław Pietraszek in Ceranów near Sokołów provided shelter for Jewish families and their neighbours brought food to those who they had rescued.

Entire communities were annihilated for helping Jews, Huta Werchobuska near Złoczów, Huta Pieniacka near Brody and Stara Huta near Szumsk, the villagers murdered and their villages raized to the ground and abandoned to this day.

After the war a Jewish partisan named Gustaw Alef-Bolkowiak identified other villages where 'almost the entire population assisted Jews and perished'. They were in the Parczew-Ostrów Lubelski region, Rudka, Jedlanka, Makoszka, Tyśmienica and Bojki.

So many residents in Polish villages provided shelter and protection for their Jewish neighbours from the German death squads.

There were many more Poles across Poland who did their Christian duty and helped those who needed help without thought of the extreme consequences, they were not 'bystanders' to the murder of Jews, nor 'collaborators.'

They were brave Poles helping their Jewish neighbours and they are simply overlooked by politicians Netanyahu and Katz and the revisionist writers Gross, Engelking, Grabowski and the many other revisionists, who appear to have forgotten the vital role that the Poles played in rescuing Polish Jews and the suffering they also endured.

US writer and historian Terese Pencak Schwartz, born in a Displaced Person's camp in Wildecken, Germany, is the author of Holocaust Forgotten and 700 Polish Citizens Killed while helping Jews During the Holocaust. She is a Jewish convert whose Great Uncle Josef Gnidula was shot dead for sheltering his Jewish neighbour in December 1942.

She discovered that there were 5ml non Jewish Victims of the Holocaust and lists in her book 700 Polish Citizens who were killed while helping Jews. There is far too much information relating to her research to include here but it's easily accessible via the internet together with other research on this particular subject on ancestry site, fold3.com.

The Polish population confronted by Germans and Soviets faced the worst conditions humans have ever had to face. Father Maximillian Kolbe was arrested and then released with a warning to lie low but like many other Poles he did not comply, he instead aided 2,000 Jews at his Friary.

He was caught and sent to Auschwitz where Sigmund Gorson a survivor testified that 'he gave away so much of his meagre rations to me that it was a miracle he could live. Now it is easy to be nice, to be charitable, for someone to be as Father Kolbe was in that time and place, is beyond words... *I am of the Jewish faith and very proud of it...* I will love him until the last moments of my life.'

It wasn't just German squads who obliterated entire communities who helped Jews, the Ukrainian UPA death squads supplied and funded by the Germans, executed villagers from Berecz in Wołyn Voivodeship; an area divided into 11 districts; for giving aid to Jewish escapees from the Ghetto in Povorsk in 1942.

Repression of those who helped Jews didn't end in 1945, at the end of the war those Poles became victims of the Communist Security Services, headed by Jewish commanders and were executed, by those they had helped.

Those who took responsibility for the survival of Jews deservedly received the merit of Righteous among the Nations. It is difficult to estimate the number who helped Jews but those who met the criteria of Yad Vashem run into hundreds of thousands. There may have been many who could have offered help, but the threat of the death penalty and inability to provide for them were often the reasons for many Poles unwilling or unable to provide direct help, their safety and that of their own family having to come first.

The people they were hiding would not have had ration cards and food may have been bought for them on the black market at high prices, arousing suspicion. Most of the population lived in poverty but many of the Jewish escapees sheltered by Poles helped towards their upkeep and were grateful for the protection they received.

Poles helping Jews also faced dangers from their own ethnically diverse countrymen, Polish-German and Polish-Ukrainians many of whom were anti Semitic. They blackmailed the hiding Jews and the Poles who hid them, turning them into the Germans for reward. Outside the cities there were peasants of various ethnic backgrounds looking for Jews hiding in the forests to demand money from them. There were Jews turning in Jews and Poles and Poles turning in Jews. Many were starving, others were thieves and rogues and out for whatever they could get. Extreme actions by desperate people and also without doubt a betrayal of their fellow countrymen.

'Estimates of Polish collaborators vary according to the definition of collaboration. ie coerced or voluntary, historians generally agree that when compared to all other German occupied countries, a very small percentage of Poles engaged in what may be described as collaboration. These historians include, Klaus-Peter Friedrich, John Connelly, Tadeusz Piotrowski, Richard Lukas, Norman Davies and Eric Hobsbawn.' Raul Hilberg writes, 'of all the native police forces in occupied Eastern Europe, those of Poland were least involved in anti-Jewish actions.'

'By contrast, a review of the history confirms that the Jewish Councils and Jewish ghetto police 'offered to assist' the Germans in carrying out 'the activities of the Germans' by delivering hundreds of thousands of their own to their occupying executioners.'

'Raul Hilberg and political theorist Hannah Arendt both asked why Jews did not resist and instead force the Germans to do their own heinous work, a question also put forward by historian Isaiah Trunk.' – *Gene Sokolowski PhD*

Historian Norman Davies said, 'elementary justice demands that they (The Poles) are duly honoured and remembered, not because they are Poles but simply because they did their duty as Christians and compassionate human beings.'

Traditional values were wrecked by the wartime terror and lack of food, greed and corruption were the 'only language some understood,' they were up against extreme hardship and the brutality of the occupiers, Germans, Russians and Ukrainians. Living under occupation and privation made people desperate, they were terrified, living on the edge of starvation needing to feed their own family and it pushed people to extreme behaviour which we cannot possibly comprehend.

Communist Betrayers

I'll continue the theme of collaboration with specific attention to the hostility instigated by leading members of the Soviet Politburo towards ethnic Poles post WW2.

A review of Soviet history, 'as substantiated by the Yad Vashem archive, Isaiah Trunk, Norman Davies, Dov Levin, Ben-Cion Pinchuk. Joachim Schoenfeld and many others, confirms that Polish Jews welcomed the Soviets and assisted them by forming militias and revolutionary committees that denounced Polish 'class enemies' for deportation, identified others for execution by the NKVD (Soviet Secret Police) and in some cases, robbed and even murdered Polish officials, priests and land owners. By directly aiding the Soviet Union in its objective to destroy the Polish state, these actions constituted de facto treason.' – *Gene Sokolowski PhD*

Jews had welcomed the arrival of the Red Army into Poland and with the Byelorussians collaborated with them in seizing control of many areas of Poland, Polesie, Dubno, Grodno, Skidel, Jeziory, Horodec amongst them. This has been established by the late historian Thomasz Strzembosz, who identified many locations from accounts of both Polish and Russian sources.

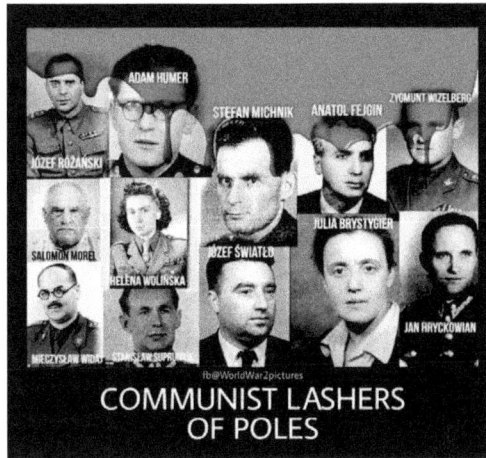

COMMUNIST LASHERS OF POLES

Although this is dismissed by 'historian' and revisionist Jan Gross and his followers, who classified these testimonies as 'anti Semitic,' and expected this argument to absolve any question of collaboration between Jews and Russians! – *Jewish Disloyalty, 1939, review Jan Peczkis 2007*

I'll refer back to Shulamit Aloni, former Israeli Cabinet member and his comment 'anti semitic, it's a trick we use to stifle legitimate criticism of Jews...' now used by the revisionists.

In one of Jan Karski's reports of 1940 to the Allies on how Jews in the east greeted the Soviets, he stated, 'Jews have taken over most of the political and administrative positions but what is worse, they are denouncing Poles and run militia behind the scenes. Unfortunately, these cases are very common and far more frequent than loyalty to Poland and Poles.' No Ally reacted to his statement. – *Wikipedia*

When my family was arrested by the NKVD on 10th February 1940, amongst the several militia who broke into their home, was a Jew who was known to them and who was as aggressive to them as his comrades were. Jews were placed in positions of authority at the Soviet labour camps and were responsible for the deaths of many Poles but once they outlived their usefulness they too became victims of Stalin's tyranny.

The returning ethnic Poles, especially those having undergone deportation and brutality in the Soviet labour camps, had no respect for communism, they had seen it first hand. They returned the brutish hostility they encountered with some antagonism as they saw the Jews who had supported the Soviets as traitors and collaborators and these stereotypes had been strengthened between 1939-41.

'It is only human nature to hold resentment and dislike against someone who terrorized and murdered your people. One may consider it logical and rational, not some sort of unfounded and unnatural hatred.' – justiceforpoland 2020

Many Jews had turned against the Polish nation by becoming actively Communist, making themselves complicit in the Soviet subjugation and oppression of Poland. They had welcomed the Soviets into Poland in the early part of WW2 as their 'saviours' and this was seen by the Poles as being jointly responsible for their suffering, including the loss, once again, of state independence. What also added to resentment between these former neighbours was the encouragement by the Soviets of ethnic and religious differences, using privileges to the Jews and punishment to the Poles. Any anti feeling was most likely down to Jews aligned to the Communist Party.

In July 1944 on the initiative of Polish communists, the Soviet front line was formed called the Polish Committee of National Liberation based in Chełm, its aim was to assume control of Polish territories and was proclaimed by Stalin 'as the only legitimate Polish government,' with full political power and Soviet sponsorship. It was the largest and most powerful institution in post war Poland and had 13 departments, one of these was the Ministry of Public Security.

Known as the UB from 1945 to 1954 and from 1956 to 1990 the SB. it was a most brutal agency combining the Secret Police and the Intelligence and Counter Intelligence Agency It was responsible for the immediate eradication of anti-communist structures, the political base of the Polish Underground State, as well as the persecution of former underground soldiers of the Armia Krajowa.

It was made up of commanders, prosecutors, lawyers, defenders, judges and Secret Police. Operating in the various sections of the UB, the KBW, the Investigative Department, County Public Security Offices, Department IV of the GZI, the Military Board, the Supreme Military Court, the Main Information Board, the Communist Secret Police and other agencies.

'It was under the control of trusted communists, giving many Jews the leadership and they grew into symbols of Stalinist repression. The number of Jews in the UB especially was excessive.' – Michael Chęciński Polish

People's Army & author 1982, Michel Wiewiórka Jewish author, 1984.

Many of those actively involved in the Security Services were of Jewish origin, in prominent roles and engaged in the fabricated political trials and executions of returning members of the Polish Resistance army, Polish Army Officers and Generals. They constructed the most absurd accusations against these 'anti communists' and in the process created an element of fear in the population, generally terrorizing Polish society.

They were Henryk Podlaski, deputy head of the Supreme Military court and head of the Military Board. Oskar Szyja Karliner, who appointed so many Jewish officers to the Board that it became known as the 'Chief Rabbinate of the Polish Army.' Head of the Information Board, prosecutor Col Stefan Kuhl, prosecutor Benjamin Wajsblech. Józef Rozański Goldberg, Director of the Investigative Department at the Ministry of Public Security.

Józef Świato, Dignitary of the Ministry of Public Security, Wiktor Herer, head of the MBP, Lieut Edward Słowik, head of Security office in Siedlce. Head of the Military Prosecutors office, Col. Eugeniusz Lansberg, who was himself saved by Poles who gave him shelter in a Catholic church. He repaid them with numerous death sentences in fabricated political trials. *– justiceforpoland.com*

'There is an over representation of Jews in the UB' and 'denying the importance of the role of Jews in the service of the NKVD is contrary to the basic facts established by historians' *– Prof Andrzej Paczkowski & Dr Jan Zaryn IPN historians and Michael Chęciński 1982 & 2003*

Also part of the system was Judge Stefan Michnik, Lt. Filip Barski, Capt Franciszek Kapczuk, Judge Maria Gurowska, prosecutor Henryk Holder, Judge of the Supreme Military Marcin Danzig, Judge Col. Sygmunt Wizelberg, Judge Aleksander Warecki, prosecutor Col. Kazimierz Graf, Judge Emil Merz, Col. Jósef Feldman, Col Maksymilian Lityński, Col Marian Frenkel and Col Naum Lewandowski

Prosecutors in the General Prosecutors Office Benedykt Jodelis, Paulina Kern, Col Feliks Aspis and Col Eugeniusz Landsberg. Director of the 5th Ministry of Public Security Luna Brystygierowa and Prosecutor Helena Wolińska, for whom an arrest warrant was issued by the Polish Prosecutors office for being responsible for the executions of many detained under her orders.

Only 1% of Poland's post war population was Jewish and that so many were in positions of authority did not sit well with the ethnic

Polish population. Stalinist communism was now rife in Poland, upheld by the terror created by its Security Police. From 1944-1956 over 300,000 Polish citizens had been arrested of whom very many were sentenced to long term imprisonment on bogus charges. There were 6,000 death sentences pronounced, the majority of them carried out 'in the majesty of the law.' Children and young people were sentenced before military tribunals.

The so called 'cursed soldiers' the anti communist resistance who opposed the new occupiers and attacked the Stalinist strongholds, were eventually hunted down by the UB services and assassination squads, murdered or sent to gulags. The 'Cursed Soldiers' continued their armed struggle against the Communist State well into the 1950's.

My grandparents Kazia and Adam both firmly anti-communist, could not return to their homeland. Adam had fought against the Russians in the 1920 War which was why he and many of his military colleagues and their families were exiled to Siberia. He would have met the same fate, instead they joined the rest of the family in England and influenced hugely my Polish heritage.

SB confidants were also active In Kraków including lawyers Maurycy Weiner and Karol Buczyński, the Provincial Prosecutor whose deputies were Golda Jozef Skwiewawski and Krystyna Palkowna. Another lawyer Mieczysław Maślanko, was himself saved from death at Auschwitz by Jan Mosdorf! Other pseudo defenders include Edward Rettinger and Marian Rozenbliy. *– justiceforpolandWikipedia 2020*

The IPN has recently addressed Soviet crimes by Communist Guerillas. 'Especially the pogroms against the Polish civilians by Jews. In 1944 a group of Soviet partisans including Jewish fugitives from the Ghettos in Vilnius and Kaunas, attacked the Polish village of Konivchy in the Wilnius region. At least 38 people including children were killed and many injured.'

'Crimes like these were not unknown. Instead, we hear of events like Jebwabne, where excavation was suddenly halted; reports suggest by the Rabbi's; when German WW2 bullets were discovered at the scene and the barn area was found to be too small to accommodate the 100's of Jews murdered by the Polish villagers. Pogroms were carried out by Jews against the Polish as soon as the Soviets invaded Poland in September 1939. There are very many accounts of these brutalities, of neighbours butchering their neighbours but this has been kept under the covers by the revisionists.' *– Professor Marek Chodakiewicz*

Those responsible for the torture and prosecution of Witold Pilecki were prosecutor Helena Wolińska and Judge Leo Hochberg, Judge Emil Merz, Judge Goldberg, Judge Gustaw Auscaler and prosecutor Paulina Kern and they also approved his death sentence.

Pilecki was posthumously acquitted of all bogus charges in October 1991. Several of these apparatchiks lived out the last years of their lives in Israel, Sweden, US, South America and I believe one married an Oxford Don and died in England in 2008.

Throughout its existence the UB was responsible for imprisoning, torturing and murdering tens of thousands of political opponents and suspects as well as taking part in subversive actions. The HQ was located on Koszykowa Street in central Warsaw and its branches were scattered across the entire country, with each office having 308 full time UB officers and staff monitoring anti state activity, government and civilian communications (wiretapping) and maintaining several concentration camps set up by the NKVD.

Stalin's policy was to put Jews in charge of prison camps as their experience during the German regime would mean that Germans and Poles held there could expect little mercy. One such camp was the Świętochłowice labour camp run by Salomon Morel, wanted by the Polish Prosecutors office for crimes against humanity but whose extradition was refused by Israel. Of the 3,000 prisoners held there more than half were murdered or died there.

In 1947 the Jewish section of the PPR had 7,000 members, even Israel Gutman a historian normally critical of Poles was forced to comment 'it was certainly undeniable that Jews were to be found amongst the Soviet leadership and administrative centres...'

Members of Armia Krajowa and WIN who remained opposed to communism were executed after kangaroo trials staged by Wolińska and Zarakowski among others, or deported to Soviet gulags. People lived in fear, they could see what was happening and had absolutely no control over their own lives. They grew to be afraid and to hate the security services who could arrest them for the slightest, perceived wrongdoing! Political penetration and military control by the Soviet Union was all over the country, the Soviet Northern Group of Forces was stationed in Poland until 1956 and Soviet Intelligence infiltrated everything and everyone, civilian and military.

It was a repressive state, the Polish/Soviet Government and Security Services were made up of hard line brutal Stalinist communists and many of them in the government apparatus were

Jews, they had complete power over all Polish territories. There was no freedom for the people, they were under constant surveillance, they had undergone occupation by the Germans, then the Soviets moved in and the new occupier and its governing apparatus was not welcomed by the Polish population.

For many years public prosecutors and judges as well as functionaries of the Ministry of Public Security, Security Service of the Ministry of the Interior (SB) and the Directorate of Information of the Polish Army (GZI WP) engaged in acts recognised by international law as crimes against humanity and crimes against peace, no one has faced justice.

Extradition has been sought by the IPN, Poland's Institute of National Remembrance, for several of the above mentioned for Stalinist crimes and genocide, for fabricating evidence leading to executions, wrongful arrests, and imprisonment. Claims from those pillars of dictatorship, that a long period of time had elapsed, were considered unfair by the Polish authorities as communism had ended in 1989 when these cases could be brought.

In the case of Wolińska, claims of anti Semitism were expressed but were rebutted by Władysław Bartoszewski. A former Auschwitz survivor, Resistance member, honorary citizen of Israel, one of the Righteous and former Polish Foreign Affairs Minister, who had been prosecuted by her.

He said in an interview with Anne Applebaum in 1998 'I am living example of the fact that the statements made by Wolińska and certain people around her about anti Semitism are nonsense. I witnessed her signature whilst in prison in the 1950's in red pencil on my indictment affidavit and saw many blank arrest warrants with her signature on them...'

I would assume that many of the members mentioned in the communist institutions post WW2 have avoided any charges or extradition requests from the IPN and lived out their lives in well recompensed freedom and like many of the German war criminals, have evaded censure.

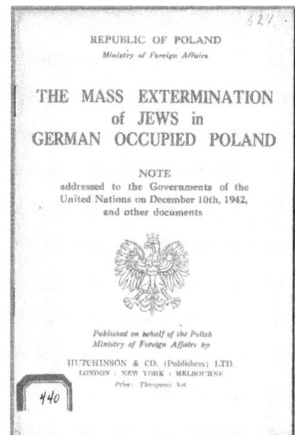

REPUBLIC OF POLAND
Ministry of Foreign Affairs

THE MASS EXTERMINATION
of JEWS in
GERMAN OCCUPIED POLAND

NOTE
addressed to the Governments of the
United Nations on December 10th, 1942,
and other documents

*Published on behalf of the Polish
Ministry of Foreign Affairs by*

HUTCHINSON & CO. (Publishers) LTD.
LONDON : NEW YORK : MELBOURNE
Price : Threepence Net.

440

CHAPTER 16

Erasing The Past

**The Iron lady of Israel, Golda Meir said
'one cannot and must not try to erase the past
merely because it does not fit the present'**

I have included this chapter deliberately as anti Polish propaganda is gathering pace through a false narrative of the Holocaust, unfairly painting the Poles as bystanders and 'collaborators' of even starting WW2. US Jewish groups have power, money and influence and are massaging history about the Polish in WW2, even within the school system.

'The Holocaust was a deeply traumatic wound for the Jewish people but it was not unique in world history, not even in WW2. The Germans engaged in similar Genocides, inflicting similar traumatic wounds against many groups, including gypsies, Bolsheviks, homosexuals and the disabled. The suffering was not unique but the Jewish attitude is that it was unique and that it privileges Jewish suffering, giving Israel and Jewish revisionist groups a cudgel to beat those who criticise it, equating criticism with anti-semitism.' – *Richard Silverstein 2012 – Tikun Olam*

There is an omission in the above quote, Polish Catholics have not been included as victims, yet Hitler's initial command was *'to send to death mercilessly, and without compassion, men, women and children of Polish derivation and language.'*

'The Holocaust of the murdered Polish people is now coming into view after being muzzled for over 50 years and that will upset the apple cart of how some groups view WW2,' – *Joy Zamoyski Koch – January 2019*

From the bottom of that apple cart came the comment from the revisionist Israeli Minister, Yisrael Katz who said in 2019 'historical truth cannot be changed, many Poles collaborated with the Germans and took part in the destruction of the Jews during the Holocaust, antisemitism was innate among the Poles before the Holocaust, during it and after it too.'

Which is historically incorrect and the lack of comment and support from the West for a major ally in WW2 is astonishing! But it seems that western leaders are being led by 'the most preposterous publications of the Holocaust activists. Anti-Polish bigots Jan Gross, Jan Grabowski and Barbara Engelking.' – *Inka Walensa Poland Current Events 2016*

They have built their careers on manipulating the history of Jedwabne, deliberately misconstruing the research of Szymon Datner and proclaiming that the death of a Jew is a transcendental event whilst the death of Poles is '......death like death.....'

Shulamit Aloni a former Israeli cabinet member and winner of the 2,000 Israel Prize said, 'anti semitic, it's a trick we always use to stifle legitimate criticism of Jews and Zionist Israel. When I am in Europe if someone is criticising Israel, we bring up the Holocaust. When in this country (U.S) people are criticising Israel then they are anti semites and the organisation (Jewish) is strong and has a lot of money and the ties between Israel and American Jewish establishment are very strong and they are strong in this country (U.K).'

A quite devious ploy to close debate and frighten anyone against making any critical comment, stifling free speech.

It seems an obvious hatred of the Polish is clouding judgement in favour of their own bias making them blinkered to the facts and it does not apply to just Jewish revisionism, various 'WW2 historians' have added to what can only be called a campaign against Poland and the Poles.

Professor Norman Davies the respected historian revealed in his autobiography how he became aware of how the anti-Polish narrative was initiated. He described how Professor Yehuda Bauer was teaching young British historians to deal with the Holocaust when he met with over 30 professional historians in 1974 in the Israeli Embassy in London, in a closed meeting.

As the top Speaker, Professor Yehuda told them that the 'triad of perpetrators, victims and bystanders' were to be used to describe people involved in the Holocaust. The Poles were to be described as bystanders. Any mention that Polish nationals were also victims during WW2 was denied!'

'The Professor's workshop was clear, there were perpetrators, the Germans (not Nazis) victims, only Jews (not Poles, the Roma gypsies, homosexuals etc the other many millions of victims) and bystanders, the Poles. The meeting was designed to show that Poland was historically the centre of anti semitism and that to say the Poles were anti semites was justifiable' Mr Davies was told to 'sit down Polonfile' when he responded to the comments made.

'Poland had been inscribed in the scheme in a role of bystander and in the 1970's and 1980's it became the dominant narrative and unfortunately it was adopted in the West not just in Universities but as common knowledge and it dominates in the WW2 narrative' – *Norman Davies*

'If you believe a misleading comment, a lie, treating it as fact to disparage Poles, misleading people deliberately and call yourself a responsible newspaper, journalist or an ethical Rabbi, you are wrong and slanderous. You are distorting the memory of the Holocaust victim, rewriting it with the specific aim of wanting people to be anti Polish. Jews and others will believe it because it is continually repeated and it inspires extra belief in their own attitudes which I would define as pure racism and hatred! History is being twisted to fit a preconceived theory.' – *Norman Davies*

This theme continues with accusations from the Israeli Minister Yisrael Katz, who in a TV interview in 2019, quoted a Yitzhak Shamir comment, that 'Poles drink antisemitism with their Mother's milk' accusing all Polish people of 'innate antisemitism.' The Israeli Prime Minister Benjamin Netanyahu had also been quoted by some of the Israeli media as saying 'that Poles collaborated with the German's' but somehow forgot to mention the collaboration of the many Jews with the Germans!

Poland's Foreign Ministry summoned the Israeli Ambassador twice in three days to its offices and the Head of the Prime Minister's office, Michał Dworczyk said 'the Israeli Foreign Minister's comments were 'disgraceful.' Poland's Chief Rabbi Michael Schudrich also released a statement saying Katz's comments had 'offended Polish Jews.'

Poland's Prime Minister, Mateusz Morawiecki said these remarks are 'unacceptable' and 'not only can we not accept such racist comments but with all our strength we want to stress that we will fight for historical truth for the honour of Poles'.

Katz told Israel's Army Radio he wanted to maintain good relations with Poland but his offensive and historically inaccurate comments will not go far towards achieving that. How sad it is that modern day Jewish politicians, Katz and Netanyahu, cannot confront their own prejudices, they seem oblivious to the contradictions and the offence it causes to the Poles of WW2 and their children.

To scapegoat the Polish that such hideous crimes could only be committed by Polish Christians is a huge insult, it's gaining momentum and I am beginning to understand the reasoning behind this aspect of 'WW2 historical truth.' The anti Polish lobby have taken ownership of the Holocaust, encouraging many by giving them freedom to rewrite history and to vilify all others who oppose their 'historical truth in their aim of gaining restitution.

Reflecting on 'historical truth' I'll go back to 1919 to highlight a pattern. Reports of alleged pogroms and mistreatment of Jewish people in Poland, reached US President Woodrow Wilson who sent Senator Henry Morgentham to Poland to investigate and his commission concluded that 'the news had been exaggerated and in many cases had been invented.'

His report identified that none of the pogroms between 1918-1919 were the result of official Polish government policy and the Polish constitution of March 1921 gave Jews full citizenship and the same rights as Poles with the freedom to worship.

The final report dated 3rd October 1919 'denied the authenticity of pogroms' but noted isolated cases of anti semitic nature in which approximately 300 Polish Jews died which they attributed to the chaos of the post war situation and cleared the Polish Government of any role or support for the incidents and noted 'that the incidents had been widely exaggerated.'

The Jadwin-Johnson deposition agreed with the Morgantham report that no pogroms had occurred and blamed 'German propagandists' for spreading the image of Poles as 'barbarous anti Semites' – *Wikipedia, Goodhart, Poland at the Minority Races*

Maybe the anti Polish narrative started from a discussion In April 1996 regarding the restitution of Jewish communal property that had been seized during the Holocaust.

'More than three ml Jews died in Poland and the Polish people are not going to be the heirs of the Polish Jews. We are never going to allow this... they're gonna hear from us until Poland freezes over again' and if Poland did not satisfy Jewish claims it would be 'publicly attacked and humiliated in the international forum' – *World Jewish Congress Secretary General Israel Singer 1996*

The Polish are certainly being attacked with some force! He is a man true to his word who seems to have prompted a hateful campaign of lies and an onslaught of invention, manipulation and exaggeration. Hoaxes designed to attribute to the Poles as many of the crimes committed by the Germans and the Jewish Police as possible.

Most of the assets Singer mentions, properties, art work, jewellery etc were seized by the Germans and the Russians and any properties that were left were destroyed by the intensive bombing. The rubble became shelter to the survivors who rather than looking at an empty shell as a future home saw it as immediate protection from the weather and danger. They too had lost their homes, they had lost everything.

The disregard from the World Jewish Congress for the Poles and the assets seized from them is quite obvious in the quote above from Israel Singer. It continues to this day by Jewish lobby groups intent on 'attacking and humiliating Poland in the international forum' for perceived injustice, when they should be attacking Germany and Russia, the perpetrators of destruction and looting but seem instead to be forging relationships with them.

Hundreds of thousands of Poles exiled to Siberia and those taken to Germany for hard labour, lost absolutely everything, there was no measure of justice for them or the countless other Poles from across Poland. I doubt very much they could prove they owned their properties to make any claim, my grandparents hadn't time to take any legal papers with them when being arrested and forced onto cattle wagons to the USSR! They barely had time to gather food and clothing.

As for the large scale looting of art, from museums and art galleries, carried out by the Germans and Soviets, WJC Art recovery Commission estimates that 110,000 pieces of missing art is worth between $10 and $30 billion. This would take some investigation which I believe is ongoing and the proceeds when found are probably due into the Polish Treasury.

'one cannot and must not try to erase the past merely because it does not fit the present.'

I will continue to repeat this comment because the former Israeli Premier had justice, truth and respect on her side and it has significant meaning today when confronted by the lies of the revisionists.

At the ceremony for the Righteous Among the Nations held in Warsaw in November 2019, 93 year old Holocaust survivor Edward Mosberg stirred controversy by making parallels between Poles and Jews who collaborated with the Germans. 'As a Jew I am ashamed of those Jews who collaborated with the Germans and I ask the Polish nation to be ashamed of the Polish collaborators.'

He was speaking the truth. The Polish PM, Mateusz Morawiecki had made a similar parallel the previous year and also condemned the comments made by the Israeli PM, Benjamin Netanyahu that 'Poles cooperated with the Germans during the Holocaust,' whilst shamefully ignoring the Jewish collaborators!

Edward Mosberg had truth on his side when he called on the Israeli acting Foreign Minister, Yisrael Katz, to apologise to the Polish nation regarding his statement, 'that Poles are genetically predisposed to antisemitism' and 'Poles imbibe anti-semitism with their mother's milk.' He directly attacked Katz for repeating those words, 'this man uttered these shameful words either out of stupidity or out of hatred, I don't know why.

This is an insult not just to Poland, it is an insult to all Christians around the world. I often go to Israel but as long as this man does not apologise or until he is removed from the government I will never go there again. I always come back to Poland with great pleasure.' He later commented that 'I nominate him (Katz) for the Nobel Prize for stupidity.'

Mr Mosberg was born in Kraków and when the war started he was only 13, his whole family was murdered by the Germans. He said 'Poland really doesn't need Israel. Israel needs Poland more.'

He also said of Frank-Walter Steinmeier's (German President) speech 'to say sorry and to ask forgiveness is not enough. The Germans should pay reparations not only to the Jews but to the Polish Christians as well. I will never stop talking about it. ...to forget or forgive would mean to kill the victim a second time.' He is to be greatly admired for his honesty and honour.

'What is the difference between a murdered Jew and a murdered Pole'
– *Edward Mosberg*

Mr Mosberg recently commented on a Court case regarding Barbara Engelking and the article by Mashe Gessen, which contained an item by her blaming the Poles 'for killing 3ml Jews.' 'It is a shame that the editor of the New Yorker allowed it, it lies about Poland's role in WW2......'

'The beginning of the article talks about the author Jan Gross who said that Poles killed more Jews than the Germans did during the war, this is a lie. I was born in Poland and I've survived the Holocaust, the responsibility for all that happened cannot be attributed to Polish society. The Misha Gessen article is nothing less than a manufactured piece of revisionism.'

'The Poles had nothing to do with that. We cannot accuse Poland or its government of collaboration with the Germans because at that time there was no government in Poland. Whereas most European countries collaborated with the Germans.' – *Edward Mosberg polandin.com 2021*

The Jewish narrative seems to overrule any other, it has a powerful media, an industry popularizing 'historical fiction' mixed with a drop of truth! And generally the West doesn't delve very deep to challenge it!

Hitler's intention was to cleanse 'all leading elements of Polish society' and I am quite frankly appalled that the Jewish lobby is ignoring that he murdered so many other millions of people and is twisting history to suit a preconceived theory. The Slav's, Poles, Russians, Ukrainians, Slovenes and Serbs, were the most widely persecuted group by the Germans in the most brutal occupation.

Edward Mosberg – Holocaust survivor

His plan was to exterminate around 85%, over 20 ml of ethnically Polish citizens with the remaining 15% to be used as slaves. At least 1.5ml Polish citizens, mostly women and children, were sent to German territories between 1939 and 1945 to act as slave labour, making room for large numbers of ethnic Germans on the Polish lands emptied by this forced mass deportation. They worked and lived in appalling conditions with little food and very many perished. *– ushmm.org*

I've read Jewish scholars, Raul Hilbrerg and Isiah Trunk who wrote Judenrat the True Account and Hannah Arendt, historians who dig deep for the truth but who are being ignored in favour of modern writers with agendas, seeking popularity but not practising historical accuracy.

Those who 'write truthfully on German-Jewish interaction are being ignored for the modern writers who are lying to the public, it's dishonest and wrong.' *– Historian & Film maker Edward Reid 2020*

Hatred of the Jews was at the centre of German planning but it also included the killing of millions of non Jews, homosexuals, Roma gypsies and the disabled. Hitler had authorised his Commanders to 'kill without pity or mercy all men, women and children of Polish descent or language, only this way can we obtain the lebenstraum we need.' 'It is essential that the great German people should consider it as a major task to destroy all Poles.'

The Jewish community has been successful in raising global awareness of their fate in WW2, it wasn't until the Arab-Israeli war in 1967 when Israel's evident strength brought it into line with US foreign policy, that memory of the Holocaust began to acquire the exceptional prominence it enjoys today.

'Leaders of America's Jewish community exploited the Holocaust to enhance this new found status and their subsequent interpretations of the tragedy are very much at variance with actual historical events and are employed to deflect any criticism of Israel and its supporters.'
– *The Holocaust Industry, Norman Finkelstein*

The Jews have their own free country and Government and whilst promoting awareness of the Genocide they endured they seem to have minimised the Genocide endured by Polish civilians and very many others.

Polish anti-Semitism is being exploited by those ignoring the Polish good carried out in the most awful and dangerous of conditions and despite their heroic sacrifices Jewish and Zionist media and 'historians' perpetuate the myth that Poles are indifferent to Jews. It is a hugely one sided view point, a sweeping generalisation that is not the whole story and should be treated as the propaganda that it is.

'Poland is not a nest of anti Semitism' as the acting Israeli Foreign Minister Yisrael Katz asserts, or ever was. By the 10th century Poland was one of the most tolerant countries in Europe becoming home to one of the largest and vibrant Jewish communities in the world. From 1012 to 1590 Jews had been expelled from most of the countries of Europe, from Switzerland, Italy, England, France, Austria, Spain, Sicily, Lithuania, Portugal, Brandenburg, Russia, Genoa, Venice and the Netherlands.

Bolesław Prince of Great Poland in 1264 proclaimed the Statute of Kalisz, creating legal protections and guaranteed the Jews the freedom of choice of work, commerce and movement. These protections were extended by King Kazimierz in the early 14th century and with these protections the Jewish communities began to thrive. Scholars suggest that by the 16th century 80% of all Jews worldwide lived in Poland. They enjoyed relative autonomy and tolerance and developed a rich social and cultural life.

Poland had offered them a home they called 'Paradisus Judaeorum,' – Paradise for Jews.

Their peaceful existence was threatened after the third partition of Poland in 1795, between Russia, Austria and Prussia with Russia in control of vast areas of its land. They became victims of the anti Semitism encouraged and promoted by the Ochrana, the Czarist Secret Police. Geographic and professional restrictions were imposed confining them to the Pale of Settlement which existed from 1791-1917 in Belarus, Lithuania, Moldova, Ukraine, Latvia and the Kresy in eastern Poland where my family lived.

'The majority of Jews in Poland were poor but for a minority of well off merchants, bankers and factory owners. They made a living as semi skilled craftsmen and traders and lived in small towns known as shtetls but most left the shtetls to live in larger urban centres such as Warsaw, Wilno, Kraków and Łódz and by the 1920's they made up about half of the population of Poland's larger cities. These cities became the cultural, religious and intellectual centres of world Jewry.' – *Richard J Evans – The Third Reich at War*

A comment worth including is from Yisrael Gutman the former chief historian at Yad Vashen and the editor in chief of the Encyclopedia of the Holocaust.

'This feeling of identification of Poles from all social spheres and their anti-German solidarity is previously unheard of in historical achievement and one of Europe's greatest under German occupation'.

'I should like to make two things clear here.'

'First, all accusations against the Poles that they were responsible for what is referred to as the 'Final Solution' are not even worth mentioning'.

'Secondly, there is no validity at all in the contention that Polish attitudes were the reason for the siting of the death camps in Poland. Poland was a completely occupied country. There was a difference in the kind of 'occupation' countries underwent in Europe. Each country experienced a different occupation and almost all had a certain amount of autonomy, limited and defined in certain ways.'

'This autonomy did not exist in Poland. No one asked the Poles how one should treat Jews. Only in Poland did the Germans impose such draconian punishments, death, for helping Jews'.

'Yet despite this the Poles constitute the largest number of Righteous. To a great extent it is the Righteous who have changed the Israeli's perception of Poland, that is what influenced me. I too at first accepted these negative stereotypes as truth. Collaborators, blackmailers, neighbors who wouldn't help.'

'That's what was said in all articles, in books. But when Yad Vashem published its Encyclopedia of the Righteous, I was the editor, I was forced to examine this again through the stories told by Jews who were saved. I don't change my opinions readily but these testimonies brought about a diametrical change in opinion.'

'Gradually they, Israeli's, are learning about this. It enables them to see Poles as real people, made of flesh and blood. The same as Jews. In the archives of Yad Vashem I found testimonies of such deeds, deeds that I myself would not be able to do. And that disturbs my peace. It was a trial, a test of one's humanity. Would we pass this test if placed in that situation? All of us, both Jews and Poles, we are only human. We are not saints. Yes there were blackmailers in Poland, there were also heroes. People like Irena Sendlerowa, of whom you may be very proud.'

He is one of very few who has bravely told the truth! I wonder why it is that so very many Jews saved by Poles cannot also say it out loud? Why Yad Vashem doesn't do more to examine the truth and contest the lies of the revisionists!

Another man of huge influence and a survivor of the Holocaust is the Nazi Hunter, Simon Wiesenthal, liberated by US forces in 1945. He worked with them to search for Germans and their collaborators. He believed in justice not vengeance and did not forget the other minorities who were murdered. He died in 2005, a most honourable man and I salute him.

The history sites I belong to have a membership acutely aware of this misrepresentation and members correct hugely inaccurate information and downright lies promoted by the revisionists in the press, in educational papers, in the media, in posts etc. Just to correct the statement, 'Polish concentration camps in Poland' to 'German concentration camps in occupied Poland,' opens us up to quite a hostile backlash from the revisionists and their supporters.

'Oświęcim is in Poland. In October 1939 Auschwitz as part of the German Reich was annexed. At that time it was a German death camp controlled by the Germans. It is important for me to emphasise this and clearly identify the perpetrators. We owe it to ourselves and to the victims.'
– Angela Merkel, German Chancellor, 6.12.2019

Why has this acknowledgement from a German Chancellor, of the truth, taken so very long?

In January 2018 Professor Szewach Weiss, regarding Poland under the occupation of the Germans, said 'I would like young Jews to hear the truth …in many European countries, Governments collaborated with Germany, France, Norway, Slovakia, Hungary and Croatia. There was no Polish state collaborating with Hitler. Poland was a glorious exception in Europe. There were never any Polish death camps, NEVER.' – Israeli political scientist and Israeli Ambassador in Poland 2001-2003

A recent quote caught my eye, mainly because of the condemnation from the usual 'sources' some expressing their disapproval in the most racist language. The Polish Ambassador to Israel was attacked and many abusive messages sent to him at the Polish Embassy.

'Poland orders Holocaust scholars to apologise in a case that could muzzle research' said a headline in the Times of Israel 12th February 2021 which also appeared in the Canada Times. 'Court rules Barbara Engelking and Jan Grabowski disseminated false information and harmed the honour of a man they said helped kill Jews in WW2, his niece brought the suit.'

Far from muzzling research I would think it would encourage far more scrutiny of the facts before entering questionable research into published essays and books as fact but it's certainly agitated the revisionists!

This article involved 81 year old Polish woman Pani Filomena Leszczyńska who brought a court case for slander against her late uncle Edward Malinowski. A court in Warsaw has ruled that 'two prominent Holocaust researchers, Jan Grabowski and Barbara Engelking, must apologise to Filomena for providing inaccurate information and manipulation of source material which suggested he helped kill Jews during WW2 in the forest in Malinowa in 1943.'

Lawyers had argued that her uncle rather than killing Jews had in fact saved Jews and that the 'scholars' had harmed her good name. This will be very closely watched by relevant historians, authors and the revisionists, as it is expected to set a precedent for independent Holocaust research and I hope it does, by ensuring that there is no 'revisionist' influence in the defendants' future writings and research.

The judge stressed discrepancies in the testimony given for the basis of the case by Estera Siemiatycka in 1996 and also that Filomena's uncle had been acquitted by a communist court in 1950 for the killing by the Germans of 18 Jews.

'Almost the whole village testified on his behalf, said a rescued Jewish woman and three Jews including two eyewitnesses, Lejba Prybut and Chuna Kaplan. All of them stated that they had hidden in Malinkowski's during the war.'

Jewish Rights organisations have expressed dismay at the ruling saying they feared it would 'have a chilling effect' and 'will open the door for other cases.' If it does open the door this will surely be a good way to establish the actual truth and not the view point of manipulators of history, or are they concerned that their own viewpoint is to be finally scrutinised.

A 2019 study on Holocaust Remembrance in Europe argued that the Poles are the 'worst offenders when it comes to efforts to rehabilitate

German collaborators and war criminals' and 'minimizing their own guilt in the extermination of the Jews.' According to the study, by researchers from Yale and Grinnell colleges, the Polish Government has 'engaged in competitive victimisation, emphasising the experience of Polish victims over that of Jewish victims.' 'The Government spends considerable effort on rewriting history rather than acknowledging and learning from it' the study found.

They could have been addressing the revisionist lobby! Studies like the aforementioned on how many Poles aided the German death machine and overlooking the Jews who aided the German death machine, are 'chilling,' exhibiting an obvious agenda of blaming the Poles for Holocaust atrocities, where is truth?

Barbara Engelking was responsible with Jan Grabowski for the paragraph in question before the Polish Court. She is paid by the Polish Government as a leading Holocaust expert and has also proclaimed:- 'this Jewish death was the result of the absolute impossibility to reach an agreement. For Poles it was simply a biological natural question-just death, nothing more, whereas for Jews was a tragedy, a dramatic experience, metaphysics, the encounter with the highest'!

'Her agenda leans in favour of Jews, saying they are special, more important than Poles and guides what she writes! standards that are not upheld are not standards, they're lies.' – *polishtruth.com*

How can a Jewish 'historian' make such a statement? How can she say this without criticism? This type of thinking is similar to what Hitler propagated when he said that 'one people had value while others are worthless'. Or is that too extreme a comparison! This is what she seems to be inferring!

If she is teaching others, she is spreading an awful thinking and should not be working for the Polish Government in a position of historical research. She should not be trusted as an objective source for Holocaust history on that statement alone.

I have yet to read any extensive research by Jan Gross or Jan Grabowski, whose academic integrity has previously been questioned, or Barbara Engelking, on Jewish transgressors, or any acknowledgement from the many Jewish organisations. They themselves continue to 'emphasise the experience of Jewish victims over that of Polish victims.'

Many Poles, including my family, will watch the Engelking case with interest, the weight of Jewish support is gathering and I sincerely hope that truth will prevail, that Poland's wartime generation do not continue to undergo this revisionist hatred and carry the burden of German crimes alone.

This court case may open the way towards other cases and that can only be something positive, concentrating on the truth rather than 'manipulating' it. I have found the language commonly used by the anti Polish lobby not only inaccurate in terms of history but hugely offensive. The abuse suffered by the Polish Ambassador to Israel is similar to the vitriol targeted at anyone standing up for Polish truth and those comments from the Israeli politicians are simply racist.

Monika Brzozowska of PDB Solicitors in Warsaw, on behalf of Pani Filomena Leszczynska, the plaintiff in the civil case, has presented a letter to the New Yorker Magazine, expressing 'grave concerns over the amount of untrue, misleading and inaccurate information' in the article, 'regarding the case of Lezczynska v Engelking and Grabowski.'

She stated that Engelking 'had relied on unproven, unchecked and moot gossip to accuse a man of complicity in murdering Jews ...' 'there were other testimonies, omitted, of other Jews who testified in defence of E. Malinowski after the war, absolutely crucial, was the testimony of Lejba Prybut.'

There is more evidence presented by the solicitor to the New Yorker against the claims the paper made and the outcry against the case, 'restricting and suppressing Holocaust research and to curtail academic freedom' which is not the case but revisionists do seem rattled.

She closes her letter with, 'Readers of academic publications are entitled to assume that a scholar accusing someone of murdering or having been complicit in murder must have absolutely substantive and undisputed evidence. Accusing anybody in complicity of murder is one of the worst accusations. Therefore, any accusation must be supported by undisputed documents, unequivocal eyewitness testimony and indisputable accounts. Every scholar, in any field, needs to carry out their research with due diligence and accuracy.' – *Monik Brzozowska-Pasiek PhD and Jerzy Pasieka, for a full transcript. – monika.brzozowska@pdlegal.pl*

The court's task was 'not to establish historical facts but to scrutinise the scholar's methodology, it ruled that the scholars had failed to exercise due diligence and apply a valid methodology.'

Scrutinising historical facts is something Edward Reid a US film maker and historian, defender of Polish truth has been active with for some time, he has been 'cancelled' from many speaking engagements because his research and views don't fall in line with the necessary mindset. He grew up in the educational system of the US and saw how WW2 history was being manipulated against Poland and took up the cause for truth. – *@justiceforpoland*

He has had death threats, been verbally attacked and those of us on various Polish history sites are also verbally abused by hostile Jewish and Russian 'trolls' for expressing any pro Polish comment or historical fact. It is very deliberately targeted and this court case will either step up the war of words against the Poles or hopefully go some way towards setting the agenda for truthful research.

Those of us who want to record the war time experiences of our families as accurately as possible are up against revisionist and racist comments similar to the one from Elie Wiesel, a Romanian born American and holocaust survivor. A man lauded by the Los Angeles Times as 'the most important Jew in America' winner of a Nobel Peace prize in 1986 and called a 'messenger to mankind' by the Nobel committee.

He said, 'Poles live in this contaminated and cursed land and those who live on contaminated and cursed land are themselves contaminated and cursed. It is not a coincidence that the camps of the greatest annihilation arose from them in Poland and not elsewhere.'

Auschwitz and other death camps were sited in Poland by Hitler because the majority of Europe's Jews lived in Poland. It made his murderous intentions easier to carry out. Perhaps the Jewish lobby could acknowledge the suffering of the ethnic Poles and the very many others, and refrain from calling Auschwitz a Polish death Camp!

Równe where my family lived had a large Jewish community and friends of the family helped Jews to hide. Halina is my Mother's long time friend and her Aunt and Uncle were murdered for hiding Jews, many others hid Jews knowing the consequences and they paid with their lives.

I find it dishonourable of those now spreading lies about the Polish people which is why the other side of the story needs telling. The true story of the bravery of the Polish nation and her people at a time of incredible cruelty by not one but three aggressors.

Wiesel's comments towards a people who were co-victims of unimaginable cruelty, beggars belief. Like the other comments illustrated it exploits Jewish suffering over any others and shows utter contempt for the Polish people and the very many who lost their lives to help and save their Jewish countrymen.

Continuing with the theme of revisionists, let me bring in the Russians, the current Russians who maintain they 'saved Poland from the Germans,' despite their friendly pact with them in 1939!

Putin said, 'it was them, who while pursuing their mercenary and exorbitantly overgrown ambitions, laid their people, the Polish people, open to attack from Germany's military machine and moreover, generally contributed to the beginning of the second world war.' – 20th December 2020 informal summit of the Commonwealth of Independent States – *foreignpolicy.com*

His remarks triggered many angry rebuttals and historian Sergey Radchenko, found Putin's piecing together of a version of events from this statement and other comments, a 'tad bizarre' and 'fact checked him.'

His verdict? – 'Putin the amateur historian would not get a passing grade at any reputable university. Nor would he be able to get his views published in any peer-reviewed journal, he has twisted his evidence to support preconceived notions and is guilty of gross omissions.' – *Sergey Radchenko Jan 21 2020*

Radchenko, like Navalny, an outspoken opponent of Putin, may find himself a target of the Kremlin with such comments, alongside another contender for that title, Dr Anastasia Vasilyeva. A brave medic who has fought to save the life of Navalny; languishing in a penal colony; amid concerns for his life. Inevitably, she's been arrested, beaten and thrown into a cell by the FSK, simply for supporting Navalny's views.

In Tver a Russian city, local 'patriots' have demanded the removal of a plaque commemorating the murders of Polish officers at Katyn, as 'untruthful.' This was removed from the building that once housed the HQ of the secret police, by the leader of the local Nationalist movement.

It's a confusing episode, as Russia had issued a declaration in 2014, from the lower house of the State Duma, condemning the 'horrific tragedy' of the 'Katyn crime that had been carried out on direct orders of Stalin' and expressing hope that this could mark 'the beginning of a new stage in relations with Poland.'

The Jewish revisionist lobby have stated that this was the first mass murder of approximately 500 Jews, without any reference to the 20,000+ Polish Military officers also murdered!

In 2015 Russia's ambassador to Poland Sergey Andreev claimed that 'Poland was partly responsible for being invaded by Nazi Germany because it had repeatedly blocked the formation of a coalition against Hitler' and the 'Soviet Union's occupation of eastern Poland was simply an act of self defence,' he said.

The truth meanwhile, which must have escaped Mr Andreev, was that Poland had refused to allow the transit of Russian troops through its territory. He has also conveniently forgotten the Soviet Union's willing signature on the Ribbentrop-Molotov pact of 1939 with Germany and their subsequent joint celebrations in several Polish cities in September 1939 after their invasion!

One such official military parade was in Brest-Litovsk on 22nd September held by both armies, just one of the celebrations marking the withdrawal of the German troops to the demarcation line and the handover to the Russian troops of the city and its fortress.

In 2019 Poland chose not to invite Russia to the commemoration of the 80th anniversary of the outbreak of WW2. Russia's Foreign Ministry criticised the decision saying it was the Soviet Union which 'liberated Poland from the German aggressors.'

The offensive from Russia continued, other senior officials added their misinterpretation of historical issues with the Duma Speaker Vyacheslav Volodin, accusing Poland of 'collaborating with Nazi Germany 80 years ago' and called on Polish leaders to be 'honest and apologise.'
— Daniel Tilles editor in chief ,Asst Prof of History at Kraków University – historynotesfrompoland.com

It's quite beyond belief! And I'm only thankful that my Babcia and Dziadek are not alive to hear these insane ramblings from the resurgent Stalinists!

There was widespread criticism of Yad Vashem the Israeli Holocaust Memorial, for allowing itself to be used to present Russia's revisionist views of WW2 history. In response Yad Vashem issued a press release saying 'that a Polish speaker was not considered necessary 'as it is especially appropriate that the leaders addressing this event represent the four main powers of the Allied forces which liberated Europe and the world from the murderous tyranny of Germany.' Another lapse of memory!

The four main Allies he categorised were, the US Britain, Russia and France, despite France being occupied by the Germans from 1940-1944! Poland served as a major Ally, with the fourth largest army and is being downplayed to this very day. Poland fought from the very beginning to the very end.

Yad Vashem did later apologise for allowing 'inaccuracies' and 'distortions' at the forum such as 'not including any reference to the partition of Poland between Soviet Russia and Nazi Germany' This was far too little too late, Yad Vashem had legitimised Russia's WW2 narrative, and shown its revisionist hand, Jewish ties are still strong with Russia it seems and what does it say for honesty, Yad Vashem, Russia and Israel?

Reparations

Post WW2, there was a severe shortage of housing right across Europe and throughout Poland, especially in the larger cities, Warsaw and Gdańsk, Poznan, Kraków, Katowice and Lublin. The destruction made it impossible to find shelter and those who had survived lived where they could, occupying the debris left after the bombings. The Communist party exploited the situation by telling Poles if they refused to sign the Communist Manifesto they would 'lose their living quarters and their jobs unless they reconsidered their attitude.'

The provisional Communist State had passed a decree in 1945 which placed 'abandoned and former German properties under state administration' and many of these had been owned by Jews and Poles alike. To reclaim them and provide evidence of ownership, with the relevant papers would have been difficult to impossible, everything having been destroyed in the bombings.

With regard to restitution and the Amendment to the Polish Code of Administrative Procedures, the following can be considered an explanation, 'Imagine a house in Warsaw, burnt out and abandoned in 1945. Before the German occupation six families had lived here, one of them was Jewish. Some of the residents had perished, some had been deported and some had fled the persecution. Shortly after the war the building was nationalised by the Communist Government, two new families moved in, then three more. Some had lost their own properties in eastern Poland now part of the Soviet Union. They never received any compensation. Precarious lives continued under Communist dictatorship, generation after generation.

Then came freedom, in 1990 local authorities offered remaining occupants a deal. You can purchase your flat at a reasonable price and most eagerly agree. New sewage systems are installed, windows are replaced and furniture is updated. Then comes a surprise.

In 2005 a law firm representing pre war properties suddenly pops up. They demand for the premises to be vacated and returned to the 'legitimate' owners, there are lots of similar claims, predominantly in Warsaw. Some are straight forward and transparent but many others dubious to say the least. Some ownership certificates are missing, some documents are forged, fertile ground for egregious real estate scams. The so called 'wild re-privatisation' leads to utter chaos. Mafia like entities control large parts of the real estate market, white collar crime thrives. After 45 years of Communist rule and more than 30 years since democratic transition, people who had never had anything to do with the war and the Holocaust now faced eviction from the properties they legally acquired and invested in. They live in fear and insecurity. Hundreds of pending cases and hundreds of families who do not know whether the apartment or the house they live in is actually theirs.

In 2015 the Polish Constitutional Tribunal issued a ruling which basically put an end to these predatory practices and it is being implemented in the Polish Code of Administration Procedure. A 30 year non discriminatory statute of limitations has been imposed, the longest possible according to the Polish legal system. Nevertheless, all interested parties will still be able to file civil suits and obtain compensation in a fair procedure before the court of law.'

Marek Magierowski – Journalist and Poland Ambassador to Israel 2018

A 'fair procedure' that has raised 'defamation and censorship from the usual sources.'

Any one returning to their abandoned homes would find them taken over by Poles and any of the ethnic minorities whose reluctance to vacate them was simply a fear of homelessness. Up to 2.5 ml Poles had been expelled from their own lands, farms, homes and enterprises had been seized and all traces of Polish culture obliterated. Those who remained were barely surviving.

Any WW2 reparations sought by the Jewish Council are due from Russia and Germany, not Poland. My family lost everything, their Osadas, their homes and livelihoods, all farms across the Kresy were seized without recompense to the owners. Germany and Russia demolished the country and absconded with its treasures, – they owe Poland.

During an event in Pułtusk, in eastern Poland referring to Jewish restitution, PiS leader Jarosław Kaczyński said that while some 'claim Poland has financial obligations relating to WWII, we have no war obligations, not only from the point of view of the law, but also from the point of view of elementary morality and decency. We don't owe anyone anything. It's us who should be paid. Some in the West owe us over US $1 trillion.'

However, the response from the Jerusalem-based World-Jewish Restitution Organisation said that 'Poland is the only major country in the former Soviet bloc that has taken no action to return private property confiscated by the Germans or nationalised by the Communist regime.' A report published in 2017 at a convention hosted by the European Shoah Legacy accused Poland of the 'worst failure to live up to the Terezin declaration, agreeing on the measures to right economic wrongs that accompanied the Holocaust against the Jews and other victims of German persecution in Europe.'

It is neither a treaty nor a legally binding international agreement and I suspect very few if any 'other victims' have claimed for 'economic wrongs,' my grandparents certainly did not. They neither had the intention nor the necessary legal documents of proof, they were exiled to Russia with only the bare essentials!

Current threats to Poland from those seeking reparations (US Senators, the US Jewish lobby) for Jewish properties destroyed during the War, are made by misrepresenting history which is leading to strained relations. Accusing the Poles of anti-semitism with statements 'Poles drink anti-semitism with their Mother's milk' is slanderous and this from an Israeli politician!

'Poles should have the full right to be proud of their history, heritage and culture and celebrate under the white and red flag, we remember the tragic fate of the Polish nation during WW2 so there will be no agreement to paying compensation from our side.' – *Polish PM Morawiecki*

'And we will never agree to any payments for anyone for this reason, any compensation', the PM announced. 'We will find the right legal formulae and as long as we are responsible for governance these regulations, the legislation that we will implement will not be to any claims from any side, we will not allow it' the PM added.

Poland's war damages estimated in 2017 by successive Polish government commissions were $750 – $1,000 billion. Material damages to Warsaw alone which was 85% destroyed, were assessed by a special commission in 2005 at $54.6 billion and $60 billion in 2018, due to the Polish Treasury.

Germany and Russia should pay reparation to Poland for razing the country to the ground and inflicting starvation, death and destitution on its people. Jews seem not to be aware that ethnic Poles had also been imprisoned, experimented on, tortured or gassed in Auschwitz. They seem oblivious to the fact that ethnic Poles and so many others had suffered these fates, or that 140,000 Poles made up 11% of Auschwitz inmates and about half of them died there, the first group targeted.

Poles account for up to 3ml murdered by the Germans, 1.5 ml were enslaved in Germany, 200,000 children were kidnapped and those who could not measure up to their kidnappers' Aryan ideal were murdered. Over 300 Polish villages were destroyed and their inhabitants murdered,

20% of Priests were killed. Many hundreds of thousands were deported and murdered by the Soviets and they have been ignored by the' Holocaust industry.'

Norman Finkenstein a son of Jewish parents who survived the Warsaw Ghetto, writes in his 2000 book, the Holocaust Industry, that 'US Jewish establishments exploit the memory of the German Holocaust for political and financial gain as well as to further the interests of Israel.' 'It has corrupted Jewish culture and the authentic memory of the Holocaust.'

He is a controversial figure, a sharp critic of Israel. 'It was only after the establishment of the Holocaust Industry that outpourings of anguish over the plight of Jews in WW2 began. This ideology served to endow Israel with a status as a 'victim state' despite its horrendous human rights record, backed by the US.' He sees the 'New York Times as the main promotional vehicle of the Holocaust Industry.'

He claims there are 'two known frauds connected to the Holocaust, that of the Painted Bird by Polish writer Jerzy Kisinski and Fragments by Binjamin Wilkomirksi. The authors were defended even after their supposed frauds had been exposed.'

Some of the defenders he identified as 'members of the Holocaust Industry and that they support each other, Elie Weisel supported Kisinski, Israel Gutman and Daniel Goldhagen supported Wilkomirski, Wiesel and Gutman support Goldhagen.'

Authors exposed as Holocaust frauds but defended and supported by those writing the same revisionist fiction.

He was denied entry to Israel in 2008 for 10 years as a result of his standpoint and responded to his critics by saying 'none, so far as I can tell, question my actual findings.'

"Finkelstein has raised some important and uncomfortable issues' – *Jewish Quarterly*

Polish suffering is being silenced by some of the most slanderous revisionists. Polish voices are not being heard and I wonder at the perceived softly, softly approach of the Polish Government to confront them!

This beautiful land that my family was exiled from, was contaminated firstly by the Germans with their murderous campaign of Polish and Jewish citizens and then by the Russians with terror and persecution through their brutal Secret Police, the UB and the Judiciary.

I read a review recently by Michael Brendon Dougherty on Halik Kochanski's book The Eagle Unbowed and I'll quote part of it.

'Is all of modern European civilisation a kind of macabre plot against Poland? How many absurdities must one people live through in so short a time, from such a diverse set of sources? Every time Poland makes an ally, said ally becomes unreliable, deceptive and cowardly. Every time a country becomes Poland's enemy, its capacity for heartlessness and ferocity seems redoubled'

'...The parallel holocaust inflicted on Poland and the Poles started in 1937-8 with the massacre of 200,000 Poles living in the USSR, continued in 1939-41 in the eastern borderlands of Poland and resumed throughout Poland as of 1944 in the course of its 'liberation' by Stalin's troops, the subsequent reign of Soviet terror that lasted to 1955 and then the oppressive tyranny until 1989.'

'There is an ugly subplot of treason here too in which Franklyn Roosevelt and the ruling establishment of Great Britain appear in the role of villains.'

The subplot referred to relates to the Tehran and Yalta conferences in 1943 and 1945 where the two mentioned villains betrayed Poland to Stalin, gifting him the right to Poland and its people to be ruled by the tyranny of communism.

There will soon be no one to bear witness to the atrocities of WW2. My Mother is 97 and I remember when we were children she would sit quietly for periods on end, lost in thought thinking no one would notice. – I noticed. – She would walk up and down the lounge, up and down for ages trying to walk away the memories, and I noticed. – So many of her friends died every day in the labour camp and on their long journey from Siberia to freedom and it 'hurt my head to remember' she said and I noticed her awful headaches.

She would tell me 'I'm crying in my heart every day.' In 2003 she wrote her memoirs but left so much out because she couldn't remember or it was too painful. In the beginning of her Alzheimers she would talk of the labour camp in Russia and tell me 'it hurts my head, but not so much now' bringing the emotion of writing her sequel flooding back to me and I've cried very many tears over the laptop.

How she coped over the years since WW2, with the memories she couldn't put away and which resulted in a nervous breakdown in her late thirties, I cannot comprehend. The whole family suffered post war in different ways and they and the suffering of all survivors of WW2 must not be overlooked.

Children of Polish WW2 survivors must speak for them, as I do for my family because survivors are few and are taking their first hand experiences with them, leaving the deniers' a window of opportunity to rewrite history. Russia's President Putin is doing just that, telling the world that Russia came to Poland's aid against Germany! So why did Stalin exile 1.7ml Poles to Siberia? Why did he murder so many? Polish citizens suffered murder on an unprecedented scale and failing to honour them is disrespectful to all the victims.

I can only concur that the revisionists are hiding Jewish crimes behind the Polish crimes, wiping them from WW2 history in order to maintain that the Holocaust story remains as innocent and respectful as can be! To acknowledge that Jewish crimes were committed would spoil the vision of the Holocaust and take away the sense of victimhood.

The Jewish community in coming to terms with its wartime transgressors must 'cleanse' its own ranks from those who assisted the Germans in the persecution of its own people and stop placing the blame on the Polish. Are they morally and ethically untouchable? Are they above criticism?

'There were two Holocausts, one changed the conscience of the Western World and led it to carve out a sovereign Jewish state, Israel, and provided hundreds of billions of dollars in financial and military support for the State and in individual compensation to Jewish Holocaust survivors, £220 ml in 1999 alone to individual survivors.'

'The other Holocaust, the forgotten one, the most cruel and genocidal outrage that any nation suffered went by like a blip on history's screen. The Holocaust of the Polish people and their country is unrecognised. Neither Germany the main perpetrator nor Russia the secondary one has made any amends or restitutions.'

'The Polish people deserve that their holocaust be spelled with the same capital H that the Jewish holocaust merits, they deserve that Germany takes responsibility for it and makes the proper amends' – *Max Denken June 2018, Ecstacy then Eruption*

Taking into account all the victims of persecution, the Germans systematically murdered an estimated 6 ml Jews and an additional 11 ml during the war. Do we commemorate them all? We regrettably do not.

There were Polish and Jewish transgressors, there is little doubt, some broke the moral code out of greed, some had grudges, some were rogues, some did it to save themselves in incredibly desperate times. There were

Polish and Jewish survivors and so many other survivors of the Holocaust, who must be included in the remembrances but the emphasis is on the Jewish dead and the other victims are an afterthought, with each passing year deleted from memory.

To declare as Yisrael Katz did that 'historical truth cannot be changed, many Poles collaborated with the Germans and took part in the destruction of the Jews during the Holocaust.' is nothing short of propaganda, aimed at gaining restitution, what the Jewish lobby see as being owed to the surviving Jews of WW2 by Poland.

In fact, Israel Singer summed up the general WJC objective in his comments back in 1996.

'more than three ml Jews died in Poland and the Polish people are not going to be the heirs of the Polish Jews. We are never going to allow this... they're gonna hear from us until Poland freezes over again' and 'if Poland did not satisfy Jewish claims it would be publicly attacked and humiliated in the international forum' – *World Jewish Congress Secretary General Israel Singer 1996*

Netanyahu, Katz and Ingelking, Gross, Grabowski, Kisinski, Wilkomirski and many others seem to be following his lead, actively manipulating 'historical truth' turning a blind eye to the Jewish transgressors and dishonouring the memory of the many Poles who saved Jews?

It suits their revisionist narrative and is conducted through many routes including the New York Times, the Canada Times, the Times of Israel, various publications, historical 'authors' the media, teachers' resources and even Holocaust memorial sites, without accurate historical context.

Let me illustrate how easy it is to manipulate the narrative.

Gene Sokołowski PhD, a member of Polish Media Issues, a world wide group whose aim is to fight any anti Polish sentiment, especially in the media, wrote to the North Carolina State Superintendent Catherine Truitt regarding how he had a problem with three statements in a North Carolina teacher's resource on the Holocaust. He then wrote to the Chairman Michael Abramson and two other Council members, Karen Klaich and Juanita Ray.

Mr Sokołowski stressed in his letter that he hopes to 'arrive at a mutually agreeable resolution of each of the above statements so that historical fact and context are accurately presented to North Carolina's students and teachers.'

'In the paragraph titled 'Death Camps in Poland' each of the following derived from the specific statement 'German leaders chose Poland for the killing centers for several reasons.'

'Those statements were, first, '......non Jews, [Poles] in these areas had age-old traditions of anti Semitism and were unlikely to oppose the activities of the Germans, second, 'in fact, many Poles offered assistance' and third, 'the Holocaust would not have been possible without the aid of these local populations (Poles).'

Mr Sokołowski asked Mr Abramson to' cite the historian [s] title of the scholarly work [s] he used as supporting sources and to provide his counter argument for many omissions in the teacher's resource.'

Michael Abramson replied to him by saying, "we have reached out to the United States Holocaust Memorial Museum to ensure that everything in our guide is factually accurate. I will be in further touch with you when we have completed the work Mike Abramson, Chairman, NC Council on the Holocaust.'

Is this where the revisionist narrative starts, in schools? Where historical fact and context are inaccurately presented! There seems to be a huge vacuum of dishonesty at play here, at many levels!

'In a time of universal deceit, telling the truth is a revolutionary act.' – George Orwell

Due to the Allied wartime 'code of silence' our parents' tragic story is largely unknown outside of Polish circles. We children of Sybyraks are endeavouring to bring the truth of WW2 'crimes' to the public domain and have a battle against not only the Soviet revisionists but also the Jewish revisionist lobby. It's a battle we cannot lose against a notoriously abusive industry, much louder than the defenders of the truth. There are many dragons to slay.

I'm finishing this chapter with a tribute to Artur Rubenstein a noble man and a Polish-American classical pianist, possibly the greatest. Born in 1887 in Łódz, Poland then part of Russian Empire, to a Jewish family, the youngest of seven children of Felicja Heiman and Izaak Rubenstein. A child prodigy at the age of 4, he played in many of the world's venues. He last played in Germany in 1914 disgusted by Germany's conduct during WW1. He died in 1982.

Throughout his life he was deeply attached to Poland and at the inauguration of the United Nations in 1945 he showed his Polish patriotism at a concert for the delegates. He began the concert by stating his deep disappointment that the conference did not have a delegation from Poland.

He later described becoming overwhelmed by a blind fury and angrily pointing out to the public the absence of the Polish flag. He stopped playing the piano, told the audience to stand up, including the Soviets and played the Polish national anthem loudly and very slowly, repeating the final part in a great thunderous forte. When he had finished the public gave him a great ovation.

Oh to have been there to see the Soviet expressions! My Babcia and Dziadek would have taken great satisfaction.

Throughout this memoir I have referred to Germans rather than Nazis and only included Nazi from quotes.

The quote from Jan Sliwa will perhaps explain it better than I can.

'As time goes by, the Germans were eliminated from global awareness and replaced by abstract 'Nazis'. The 'Nazis' have no homeland or children. They evaporated in 1945. But as we need the figure of a villain, this role was given to the Poles. Therefore, we can read about 'the Jews murdered by the Nazis in the Polish death camps', because the only national identity mentioned here is the Polish one, the association 'Nazis – Poles' is imprinted into readers' minds. Repeated over and over again, it almost has a long-lasting effect. It leads to such mental acrobatics as the statement made by Andrea Mitchell of MSNBC about the Jews fighting against the Polish and Nazi regime in the Warsaw Ghetto Uprising'

'Regular ignorance, but often intentional manipulation, distorts history. Today the Holocaust reports hardly mention the Germans, apart from saying that they apologised and that the 'matter is closed'. On the other hand, these terrible Poles would 'not accept any responsibility for the crimes of the Third Reich' as France Culture TV said recently.'

'No, we do not want to be blamed for someone else's crimes.
Many people forget that Poland was neither part of the Third Reich,
not its ally but a conquered country under brutal occupation.
Unlike anyone else, the Poles fought Nazi Germany from the first
day of the war until the last one and did this on all fronts,
from Narvik to Tobruk, from Breda to Berlin.'

Truth has it's own power, it just needs to be unleashed at the relevant target. And as Aleksandr Solzhenitsyn said, 'the single step of a corageous individual is not to take part in the lie. One word of truth outweighs the world.'

Alicja Góral – 2019

CHAPTER 17

Casualties of War

'The Germans killed more people in other countries but only in Poland did they implement a comprehensive cultural genocide as well.'
– *Max Denkin 2019*

From the very beginning of the 1939 German Military campaign, about 200,000 Polish civilians were killed in the Luftwaffe's bombing operations, including the bombing of Frampol, Sulejow and Wielun, towns with no military infrastructure. Civilians were strafed from the air with machine gun fire in what became known as a terrror bombing campaign when columns of fleeing people were systematically attacked by the German fighter and dive bomber aircrafts. The siege of Warsaw was a target from the beginning with unrestricted aerial bombardment by the Luftwaffe and there were huge numbers of civilian casualties. Apart from military facilities, German pilots targeted civilian facilities such as water works, hospitals, market places and schools.

So many innocent people were eliminated by the atrocities committed by Hitler who I can only describe as a vengeful lunatic, and Poland had to contend with another tyrant, Stalin, who let his army stand on the banks of the Wistula during the Warsaw Uprising in 1944, allowing the Germans to destroy Warsaw, letting them do his work for him so Poland could more easily fall into his hands. Stalin, Poland's ally would not let any other Allied planes land on Soviet held territory to refuel and then go on to drop much needed supplies to the Poles. He was reluctant to help the Polish Resistance and the Soviet advance had been halted by his direct orders.

The Warsaw Uprising was the last major operation fought by the Poles, led by Armia Krajowa it was the single, largest military effort taken by any European resistance movement during the war, from 1st August to 2nd October 1944, it was timed to coincide with the retreat of the Germans ahead of the Soviet advance but the Soviet's halted their combat operations and the Germans were able to re-group, defeat the Polish Resistance, destroy Warsaw and murder its civilians in retaliation. There was no restraint, no adherence to the rules, the citizens of Warsaw were murdered.

The exact number of casualties is unknown but estimates are 16,000 members of Armia Krajowa killed and about 6,000 badly wounded. Between 150,000 and 200,000 Polish civilians died mostly from mass executions, innocent women, children and the elderly. Jews who had been harboured by the Poles were exposed in German house to house clearances and in systematic evictions of entire neighbourhoods.

The world knows of the crimes committed by the Germans but the war crimes perpetrated by the Soviets are not, those crimes committed by the Red army and the NKVD were carried out under Stalin's policy of Red Terror and there were many crimes committed without his orders, against prisoners of war, mass rapes and executions in territories held by the USSR.

When the Allies established the post war International Military Tribunal to examine war crimes committed by the Germans, the Soviets had taken an active part in the judicial process, being one of the main driving forces behind it's creation. Inevitably there was no examination of their own criminal actions and no charges were ever brought against its troops. Today the Russian government is engaged in 'historical negationism,' its media referring to war crimes as a 'western myth' and in Russian history books the atrocities are either altered or omitted entirely.

President Putin in June 2017 did acknowledge the 'horrors of Stalinism' but he also criticised the 'excessive demonization of Stalin' by 'Russia's enemies.' The Russians have refused to acknowledge their crimes 'because they seem to think that much of it was justified against an enemy who committed far worse and partly because they were writing the victor's history' but this doesn't include all the innocent civilians, Poles, Hungarians, Finns, Lithuanians and others raped and murdered by them. Putin's revisionist view of WW2 includes accusations of Poland being complicit in starting the war, just one way of whitewashing Stalin's crimes.

How does a country come back from almost 5 years of German occupation then lose its fight for justice, freedom and even deserved revenge? Almost too quickly came the end of the war on 8th May 1945 and the weary Poles had yet more hardship to face. It was only the beginning for people left homeless by the fighting, those released from captivity and those who had been exiled as an act of revenge, as in the case of my own family, deported from the eastern borderlands of Poland, their freedom snatched away. People were shocked to discover the atrocities carried out by the Germans but the atrocities waged by the Soviets were as brutal and are to this day blotted out of the history books, with the Russian President Putin, doing his utmost to ensure that Stalin is seen as a hero and not the villain he was, responsible for the deaths of millions.

The economies of many European countries were left in tatters with industrial and agricultural infra structures devastated. Towns and cities had been destroyed by bombing raids with Warsaw being razed to the ground on Hitler's specific orders, means of communication had been damaged and food was short. In response the US in 1947 devised the European Recovery Program allocating $13 billion for the reconstruction of Europe which Stalin declined for Poland.

Russia had suffered huge losses in the war against Germany with 8.7 ml combat deaths and 19 ml by starvation, mass shootings, concentration camp and prison deaths, harsh labour, famine and disease. The economy had been ruined and about a quarter of its capital resources destroyed. To help rebuild the country limited credits were obtained from Britain and Sweden but Russia refused assistance offered by the US under the Marshall Plan. It coerced instead Soviet occupied Central and Eastern Europe to supply machinery and raw materials and Germany and former German satellites made reparations.

There were world shortages of coal, meat, oil, fats and sugar which caused considerable hardship to the people. Europe was worn down and disorganised with those who may have been best able to organise a recovery, killed. Free and democratic organisations had been dissolved and the results of a prolonged lack of food and fatigue resulted in a reduced work force. People were tired of food rationing and they were impatient for an end to war restrictions. In England rationing ended at midnight on 4th July 1954 but compared to Europe life was not as hard. My family were sending food parcels and clothing to our family in Poland until the 1970's and possibly later.

Women did not fare well in wartime or afterwards. When the Red Army swept into Germany, between January and August 1945 there was the largest incidence of mass rape known in history where an estimated 2 ml women and girls were raped by Red Army soldiers. Natalya Gesse was a correspondent at the time said that the Soviet's didn't care about the ages of their victims, 'the Russian soldiers were raping every German female from 8 to 80, it was an army of rapists.' Allied troops also played a significant part in the terror and rape, like the Soviets, feeling it their 'divine right.'

In Poland by 1944 German atrocities were replaced by Soviet oppression, troops were engaged in mass scale looting, and other crimes against the Poles causing the population to fear and hate the regime. There was an orgy of violence, theft of anything they could lay their hands on, random executions and mass rape. The number of rape victims ranged from 150,000 to 200,000. In some cases women were gang raped by as many as several dozen Soviet soldiers during the 'liberation' of Poland. This was happening throughout the major cities taken by the Soviets and they also raped Soviet and Polish women liberated from concentration camps and Embassy staff they had captured from neutral countries.

My great grandmother Sofia Radomska survived most of the war in Poland and would have been in her 70's (1866-1943). It is a great regret that the family has no detail of her wartime circumstances, whether she was able to escape the atrocities or fell victim to them, we do not know, or how and exactly when she died. We can only pray that she had been kept safe from harm.

The family was scattered across parts of Poland and Russia at the time of the German and Russian invasions and contact between family members was very difficult although we do know that she somehow found out where they were and sent them parcels of food and seeds.

My great Aunt Genia, Sofia's daughter, with the help of her brother Walery, was able to escape westward to the Lublin area I believe, with her daughter Halina in 1940. Both survived the war and were able to continue their lives in Poland and eventually able to visit us in England.

My immediate family were at this time recovering in the Middle East having escaped the labour camp in Siberia, arriving in Pahlevi in Persia (Iran) in 1942. In one respect they can be considered to be very fortunate not to be in Poland at the time of the hideous atrocities committed by the German and Soviet troops and the massacres committed by the Ukrainian UPA.

Mass rapes and murders, looting and many other crimes were committed against the innocent Polish population. Violence and oppression, torture and unspeakable savagery, especially to women and girls whatever their age. The barbarity was relentless, the depths of wickedness, unpardonable and no-one has ever been held accountable.

The rapes of Polish women reached a mass scale during the Red Army's Winter offensive of 1945. One of the factors for the escalation of sexual violence against women during the occupation of Poland was the complete sense of impunity on the part of the individual Soviet units left to fend for themselves by their military leaders. Looking for food and provisions the marauding soldiers formed gangs to clear the fields of grain, herded livestock away and looted Polish homes, ready to shoot anyone who got in their way, as in Jędrzejow. They plundered goods from stores and farms and raped farmhands in Zaleśie, Olechów, Feliksin and Huta Szklana, and committed murder-rape in Lagiewniki. Heavily armed they did what they wanted, robbing cars, horse drawn carriages, even trains. – *Dr Janusz Wróbel IPN*

In the county of Leszno Soviet war commanders began to openly claim 'that their soldiers needed to have sex.' The month of June 1945 was the worst, a 52 year old victim of gang rape from Pinczów testified that two Soviet war veterans returning from Berlin told her that 'they fought for Poland for 3 years and had the right to have all Polish females.' I don't think any Polish citizen will agree that Russia 'fought for Poland', it fought to take over their country.

There was no adequate protection from the Polish Militia as they were mostly unarmed and they could only warn women not to walk outside without escort, although this didn't guarantee their safety. For women trains and the stations were especially dangerous in Bydgoszcz, Radom and Legnica. A grave situation in Pomerania was described in a report by one agent of the Delegatura Rządu na Kraj as 'virtual orgies of rape.'

I cannot begin to imagine the terror these women must have gone through, to experience rape not once but many times with the associated violence against them. To know their mothers and daughters would also be vulnerable to sexual abuse from aggressive soldiers intent on their 'spoils of war' is unimaginable. How could they keep themselves safe from the constant harassment and what must this have done to their lives, the trauma, their self esteem, emotional development, confidence and the most awful physical injuries, how could they heal post war with little support available. So many unpleasant memories, flashbacks and nightmares, how would they ever feel safe, the impact on them must have been shattering.

I can understand why so many thousands of women committed suicide as living with the aftermath and stigma of rape must have been almost impossible. I doubt that any single soldier of any country faced the consequences of his actions and lived his life without looking back at his horrendous actions, as the Soviets said, they 'had the right to have all Polish females.' This needs long overdue international attention, there has been an appalling history of impunity for this abuse and humiliation against women. It has been downplayed as an unfortunate but inevitable side effect of sending men to war! Giving them a license to rape and plunder in enemy territory. It goes on to this very day, still being downplayed by the International Tribunal established to try war crimes! If they are not able to carry out their responsibilities for human rights and humanitarian law women are still open to the most grotesque behaviour by men!

With nearly 2ml Russian deserters and former POWs at large in Soviet occupied Europe their banditry became a serious problem for the citizens. It is difficult to estimate the number of rapes and sexual assaults on Polish women, girls and children as their ethnicity was not often stated on Soviet and Polish official reports but according to Joanna Ostrowska and Marcin Zaremba the total may well reach or even exceed 100,000, but it 'remains a matter of guesswork.'

By 1947 the Soviet command began to isolate their troops from the population in an attempt to stop this carnage by their soldiers but rapes also occurred under other occupation forces, the British, American, French, French Moroccan and Australian. Historians Eiji Takemae and Robert Rickets in a letter to the editor of TIME published in September 1945 wrote of an American army Sergeant telling them 'our own army and the British army along with ours have done their fair share of looting and raping, this offensive attitude among our troops is not at all general but the percentage is large enough to have given our Army a pretty black name and we too are considered an army of rapists.'

The Russians were extremely hostile and cruel to those they now had under their control, to those imprisoned they used torture on a wide scale with prisoners scalded with boiling water in Bobrka prison, in Przemyślany prison people had their noses, ears and fingers cut off and their eyes were put out. The breasts of women were cut off in Czortków prison and in Drohobycz prison victims were bound together with barbed wire. Similar barbaric atrocities occurred in Sambor, Stanisławów, Stryj and Zloczow prisons.

The physical destruction of war lay all around, 'By the banks of the Rhine, the beer gardens, hotels and great houses were all smashed to pieces. A burnt out German tank lies among the ruins with ammunition scattered all around in the streets, shells still enclosed in their packaging of straw and on the bridge down by the landing stage stood an AA gun, with part of the bridge lying in the river Bonn. It stank, rubbish hadn't been collected for many months and it lay in stinking heaps. There are green midges that come out of the rubbish and the grass is tall and potato plants are growing out of the grit and debris and there are bodies, remains of people everywhere. There was only bread in the shops and the trams had just started working, and there was a postman, things had started to move.' – *Observer, August 1945.*

In Poland, German owned farms and houses were handed over to Poles and Germans were rounded up by the Polish militia and put in camps before being removed from the country. Many more were expelled from Czechoslovakia with up to 14,000 people being thrown over the border every day. About three quarters went to the US zone in west

Germany and the remainder to the eastern Soviet zone.

Further expulsions followed from Hungary, some were sent to labour camps in the Soviet Union and in Romania tens of thousands of Swabian Germans and long established German peasants loaded their wagons for the long trek to their ancestral homeland. Most of the Germans in Yugoslavia fled or were expelled with many sent to labour camps by the Soviet Communists.

The German presence in eastern Europe was quickly brought to an end with most victims now refugees and according to official West German accounts, by 1950 at least 610,000 Germans were killed in the course of the expulsions, from a total of approximately 11.5ml. Those who returned home were unwelcome, their property now with new occupants who would not vacate the premises which would make them homeless.

Those Poles who returned to the eastern borderlands now under Communist rule found their homes confiscated with mostly Ukrainians having taken over. My Wujek Walery's Osada had been taken over by Ukrainians and much of the old homeland had been deliberately scorched by Stalin.

'nothing but nothing remained, everything had been razed to the ground, even forests and trees had been put to the torch so that no one could ever recognise his roots and wouldn't dare put a claim to it.' – *Jan Wojcik, Journalist, 'Voice of Solidarność'*

My Grandparent's Osada had also been taken over by Ukrainians and the apartment in Równe was no longer theirs, occupied by Byelorussians. My family had barely left their homes before their 'neighbours' had moved in! Any returning Poles were unwelcome, there was much hostility and they realised that there was nothing to go back to! Nearly 2ml Poles were compulsorily transferred from eastern areas of Poland taking the place of Germans expelled from the former German regions of Pomerania and Silesia, now transferred to Poland.

The immediate post war period in Europe, as my family realised in 1945-46, was dominated by the Soviet Union annexing the countries it had invaded. The new states were Poland, Bulgaria, Hungary, Czechoslovakia, Romania, Albania and East Germany. Over 200,000 Soviet ex POWs and civilians repatriated from abroad and suspected of having been German collaborators were sent to forced labour camps after scrutiny by the NKVD.

The integration of millions of refugees in their countries of transfer was not easy. European states were preoccupied with the sufferings of their own people and the huge task of rebuilding their countries to have much compassion for strangers. The response of the Labour Government to the influx of Poles, their ally, into Great Britain was extremely negative as was the attitude of the Trade Unions and my family experienced hostility from many areas, they never forgave the UK Government for the way it had treated Poland. The Commonwealth countries however and Scotland were far more friendly and accommodating.

The international response to the refugee crisis took a legal and organisational format. The Universal Declaration of Human Rights of 1948 guaranteed 'a right to seek and to enjoy in other countries asylum from persecution' and forbade the 'arbitrary deprivation of nationality.' The Geneva Convention on Refugees of 1951 defined refugees, accorded them specific rights and prohibited their refoulement (or forcible return) from countries of refuge. England eventually introduced the 1947 Polish Resettlement Act although it only came after PM Atlee had written to many Polish servicemen requesting they return to their homeland. An added insult which got a mostly angry and negative response.

Polish citizens killed in the war by both the German and Soviet regimes or those expelled to distant parts of Siberia were counted as Russian, Ukrainian, or Byelorussian casualties of war in official Soviet historiography, which makes the correct estimate of Polish citizens forcibly transferred after the war very difficult to estimate. The border change also reversed the result of the 1919-1920 Polish-Soviet war, in which my Dziadek Adam and Wujek Walery had fought and won against the Bolsheviks, regaining the Polish territory lost in 1795.

According to the official 1931 census the number of Polish citizens living in the Kresy before the outbreak of war was about 5.27ml, in Równe the home town of my family there were 40,600 Poles. Both the Polish Communist government and the Soviet government did not divulge, conveniently, the number of Poles they had expelled from the Kresy in 1940-1941 in an effort to keep Stalin's ethnic cleansing to a minimum. After ethnic cleansing by the Germans, the Soviets and the murderous campaign by the Ukrainian Nationalists (UPA), the Kresy was drastically reduced to 1.8 ml inhabitants.

The alliance between the Western Allies and the Soviet Union began to unravel even before the war ended. Stalin, Roosevelt and Churchill exchanged heated correspondence over whether the Polish government in exile backed by Roosevelt and Churchill or the provincial Polish Communist Government backed by Stalin should be recognised and we know the answer to that. Stalin won, again. Tensions were high and it was thought by a number of allied leaders that war between the US and the Soviet Union was likely.

On 5th March 1946 Churchill said in his speech at Westminster College in Missouri, 'a shadow has fallen over Europe.' He said that Stalin had dropped 'an iron curtain between East and West' and Stalin responded by stating that 'the co-existence between communist countries and the West was impossible' and in mid 1948 the Soviet Union imposed a blockade on the Western zone of occupation in Berlin.

Poland had little chance to control its own affairs after the war as the Soviets began to immediately foster communism and control, holding a most likely falsified national referendum by communist officials, approving the nationalisation of Polish industries and creating a single party assembly, which included many Jewish Communists, among them Hilary Minc, Jakub Berman, Salomon Morel, Mieczysław Mietkowski, Józef Rożanski and others. 'it was certainly undeniable that Jews were to be found amongst the Soviet leadership and administrative centres.'
– *Israel Gutman, historian*

Poles had no respect for communism and were distrustful of the Jews and communists in the leadership roles, seeing them as supporters of the Soviets, collaborators and traitors. Many had suffered brutality under the communists in the labour camps and gulags and the new regime did not go down well with ethnic Poles. Any ill feeling towards the Jews was most likely down to their membership and influence in the Communist party.

In 1947 in a mostly contrived election the Soviet backed Władisław Gomułka won a huge majority of the seats and promised to lead Poland to Communism. He was removed by the Soviets from the leadership of the party the following year and replaced by Bolesław Bierut as communisation of Poland wasn't happening quickly enough for Stalin and Bierut's orders were to speed it up.

The soldiers of Armia Krajowa were persecuted by the Soviet forces and imprisoned as a matter of course, most deported to the gulags of the Donetsk region and in 1945 alone, 50,000 were transported there, many were murdered. The Red Army carried out campaigns against Polish partisans and civilians and many were arrested, accused of being fascists to justify their death sentences. Mock trials were organised and at least 6,000 death sentences were issued, the majority of them carried out, and 20,000 partisans died in prison. These Poles had resisted the Germans and the Soviets saw them as being capable of resisting them in the same way, they were seen as a threat and they had to be dealt with.

The war did not end happily for Poland. The heroes of the Resistance were murdered by the Red Army and the NKVD. The country remained under Soviet occupation. The great majority of Polish military veterans were stranded in western Europe with most unable to return to their homeland now part of Ukraine and Byelorussia. These Poles, many of whom had experienced deportation to the Soviet Union, my family amongst them, could not return without fear of retribution and they subsequently formed the nucleus of the post war Polish community in Britain and many countries of the Commonwealth.

Good did not triumph over evil for the Poles, there was no triumphant march in the capital. Justice caught up with the worst German offenders at Nuremberg but the Soviets escaped censure and the Poles were caught up in the worship of Stalin and his Communists with Roosevelt's helping hand, there was no justice for them, only another occupation of their country by a foreign invader.

My family heritage is hugely important to me, it is in my roots and my heart and the more we children of Sybiraks write of our parents' and grandparents' history at the hands of the tyrant Stalin, the more we will recall the anger, emotions and grief felt by them for their betrayal at the hands of their Allies. The true picture of Poland in WW2 must be known and the amnesia of the West must be challenged.

The Rebirth of Poland

Poland has had to fight hard over the centuries for its very existence especially against Russia. Its written history begins in the 10th century when it was ruled by the Piast dynasty, headed by Mieszko Piast I who reigned from about 960-999. In 966 he became a Christian and his people followed his example. Poland's history from then on is one of many struggles, facing threat after threat to her borders by her hostile neighbours from as early as 1241 and through to 1916 from the Mongols, the Teutonic Knights, Ukrainians, Swedes, Turks, the French, Prussians, Austrians, Germans and Russians, all helping themselves to Polish territory, a most beautiful country with plentiful natural resources.

Poland has seen ages of economic prosperity and peace, military success and revivals of learning, but more often than not she has been defeated and weakened by enemies who joined forces with others against her. This story demonstrates the particular antipathy between Poland and Russia.

Poland seems to have been portrayed by Russia as an anarchic, dangerous country, its Catholic faith and democratic ideas requiring suppression by its more 'enlightened' neighbour. The two countries have long histories, dating to the late Middle Ages and relations have always been tense. The Kingdom of Poland and the Grand Duchy of Muscovy have struggled for control of their borderlands and over the centuries there have been several Polish-Russian wars, the catalyst being the Polish union with Lithuania (1386) which brought Catholic Poland and Orthodox Russia into a continuing state of unrest.

There have been other wars, with many other enemies intent on conquering and dividing Poland, but Russia has been the foremost aggressor, her only ambition to keep Poland weak and divided, suppressing Polish culture and imposing her will. This has proved difficult, as Polish culture and political activity have continued to flourish.

The Poles have never been suppressed for long however hard her enemies tried to impose their will. The Poles' strength of human spirit and Catholic faith was unbreakable and saw them through each conflict. In 1794 they were crushed by the Prussians and Russians, who together with Austria in 1795 went on to divide the last part of Poland between them. The Polish King Stanisław August abdicated and the Polish Commonwealth (Rzeczpospolita) ceased to exist, removed from the map of Europe in stages known as 'the partitions' of which there were three. Poland was deprived of its sovereignty for 123 years but never gave up hope of reclaiming its borders.

She regained her freedom in 1918 and became an independent country but faced more unrest and uprisings from neighbouring countries, the Bolshevik Ukraine, Germany, Lithuania and Czechoslovakia and there was another longer war between the two main protagonists, Poland and Russia, from 1919-1920, and in 1920 the Polish army, against massive odds, stopped the advance of the Bolshevik army and gained big territories in the east. A war both my grandfather Adam and great Uncle Walery fought in.

On 11th November 1918 the day WW1 ended General Józef Piłsudski declared Poland's independence and countless men and women had celebrated, especially those who had played a part in Poland's rebirth. Among those would be Adam and Walery and I'm sure they would have raised a glass of Polish Wódka to their win, although they would have to engage in further battles to ensure their county's independence.

Poland's statehood had just been re-established and she now sought to secure territories previously lost to the Russian empire and see the end of 123 years of suppression. The country would be reborn as the Second Polish Republic and look to carve out its borders from the territories of its former hostile neighbours.

When her next war with Russia erupted in the aftermath of WW1 she had few allies and suffered setbacks due to sabotage and delays in deliveries of war supplies. Workers in Austria, Czechoslovakia and Germany refused to transport materials to Poland and in Gdansk British troops were asked to unload ships with military supplies because the German workers refused to do so. Lithuania's stance was mostly anti-Polish and the country eventually joined the Soviet side in July 1919.

Western public opinion was swayed by the press and left wing leaning politicians and was strongly anti-Polish. Many observers expected Poland to be quickly defeated and become the next Soviet republic but Britain proposed negotiations between Poland and Russia to stabilize their border at the Curzon Line which was disregarded by the Russians. They expected a quick victory and total Polish capitulation.

Britain's Liberal Prime Minister Lloyd George was a Soviet sympathizer and authorised the sales of British armaments to Russia and blocked any aid to Poland. On 6th August 1920 the British Labour Party published a pamphlet stating that 'British workers are not Poland's allies' and the French Socialist newspaper L'Humanite declared 'not a man, not a sou, not a shell for reactionary and capitalist Poland. Long live the Russian Revolution, long live the Workman's International.'

France continued countering Bolshevism, despite Socialist propaganda from L'Humanite, and sent a small advisory group to Poland's aid in 1919. It was mostly made up of French officers and British advisors, headed by the British General Adrian Carton De Wiart and French General Paul Henrys. These men were entrusted with training the officer corps and their effort was vital in improving the organisation and logistics of the Polish army.

The Polish cause in Britain was led by the Secretary of State for War, Winston Churchill and a few MPs who urged moving RAF units, formed in 1918, to support Poland and there was also support from the head of the British Military mission to Warsaw, General Sir Adrian Carton de Wiart otherwise support was minimal.

One of the most significant developments in American-Polish relations leading to the rebirth of a sovereign and independent Polish state, was US President Woodrow Wilson's, recognition of Poland's independence after WW1. In 1919 the President was awarded the Nobel Peace prize and the Polish Order of the White Eagle its highest state distinction.

The President's part in securing the moral and material weight of the United States for the cause of Poland's independence and his contribution at the Peace Conference of Paris was, like a lot of meaningful records not recorded in the history books.

In a message to Congress on 8th January 1918 Woodrow Wilson presented a peace programme that set out the principles of a lasting and just world order after the victory of the Allies in WW1. It became known as Wilson's 14 Points and became the truce signed on 11th November 1918 in Compiegne, which ended military operations. His proposals were also enshrined in the provisions of the Treaty of Versailles on 28th June 1919. The programme provided for new rules in international relations and amongst other things it provided for the creation of the League of Nations as an institution whose goal was to ensure lasting peace and international cooperation.

From Poland's point of view, the most important point was 13 which provided for the creation of an independent Polish state with free access to the sea. Pursuant to the plan, the reborn, politically and economically independent republic was to be established 'in territories inhabited by the undeniably Polish population and its territorial integrity should be guaranteed by international conventions'. Wilson had Germany cede territorial control to Poland in Upper Silesia and Danzig giving access to the Baltic Sea. His personal friendship with the composer Ignacy Jan Paderewski may have been partly responsible for his friendly policy towards Poland.

The first clash of arms between the Poles and Bolsheviks took place in Vilnius in January 1919 not long after the defeated Germans had left the city. A short time later the Bolsheviks took the city and Józef Piłsudski Poland's head of state, launched an offensive to recapture it which proved to be a success mainly because the Bolsheviks were also engaged in conflict with the counter revolutionary White Russian troops.

Among those who volunteered to join the Polish army were many young men from the United States who served under Polish colours. Enthusiasm for Poland's independence was rising in the growing Polish community in America, 4 ml strong in 1914. America's neutrality had prevented any action when WW1 broke out but by 1916 the situation had changed.

In April 1919 General Haller and his army of 68,000 well trained troops travelled to Poland and these men were welcomed by Marshall Piłsudski and integrated into the Polish Army. They fought on all fronts to establish Poland's borders and they played a valued role. In all 42 US Officers and 1,892 enlisted men gave their lives to the cause of Poland's independence.

Piłsudski succeeded in forming an alliance with Symyon Petliura, President of the Ukrainian people's Republic, and they started their campaign by attacking Kiev and freeing it from Bolshevik control, although not for long as a counter offensive began shortly afterwards. The Polish front collapsed and in May 1920 the Soviets forced the Polish troops to retreat.

The Polish situation was critical given the intensive pressure at the river Bug and it became necessary to retreat to the Vistula river. The Poles regrouped and formed an assault group on the Soviet advance, determined to defeat the Bolsheviks on the right bank of the Vistula in Warsaw which resulted in very heavy fighting. The Soviets advanced to cross the Vistula north of the Polish capital in an attempt to capture it as they had done in 1831.

The Poles succeeded not only in stopping the advance towards Warsaw but also regrouped in preparation for a massive counter offensive. On 15th August 1920 the Poles attacked the unprepared Soviets who failed to put up any resistance, taken completely by surprise. The Soviets' northern front was crushed and the Battle of the Vistula was won by the Poles.

The last main battle took place on the river Nemen between 20th and 26th September 1920 and despite Soviet counter attacks the Polish troops crushed their resistance. Both sides were exhausted and a truce was signed in October 1920. Peace negotiations were negotiated in Riga, the Latvian capital and since the Poles had been victorious they could have claimed a border well to the west of the River Bug. They were unwilling however to take further territory where the Poles would be a minority and Minsk was left to the Bolsheviks, the new border was drawn to the west of the ceasefire line resembling the old border of 1793-1795.

Poland was still a weak and fragmented country, rural and poor although economic growth had begun to grow in the early 1930's under Józef Piłsudski. American Poles became more conscious of their heritage developing a stronger connection to their nation and turned to US President Woodrow Wilson for his support of Poland, they were growing concerned at Germany's gathering strength and future military capability. Demonstrators met with Wilson's Secretary, Joseph Tumulty, urging the Wilson administration to help Poland maintain peace against a re-arming Germany and Tumulty reported on Germany's aggressive militaristic aggression against Poland and other eastern European nations as early as 1936.

In spite of a non-alignment policy, the Poles realised that an attack by Germany was inevitable, Poland's nightmare was that any agreement between Germany and Russia would destroy Poland, Piłsudski had made a non-aggression agreement with the Soviets in 1932 and a similar pact with Germany in 1934 but neither Stalin nor Hitler had any intention of respecting these agreements and history has confirmed this. Germany and Russia signed the Ribbentrop-Molotov pact in 1939, which included a secret protocol about the abolition of Polish independence and the sharing of its territories.

A more recent war has been fought against the Russians for freedom from the communist tyranny imposed post-WW2, a fight between the workers and the Jaruzelski government which had imposed martial law. The Solidarity movement won this in 1988/89 when the communists gave in and elections were eventually held. In 1991 the Warsaw Pact (signed in 1955 to compete with NATO, comprising USSR, Eastern Germany, Poland, Czechoslavkia, Hungary, Bulgaria and Romania) was dissolved and the Cold War was officially over.

Since the fall of communism Polish and Russian relations have entered a new phase, seeing both improvement and deterioration but frankly there is little change. Putin is now engaged in rewriting WW2 history accusing the Poles of complicity with the Germans in starting WW2. It is beyond reason.

It is difficult to foresee what the future holds for Poland, but it is to be hoped that European Union membership will be beneficial. Poland seems to be safer from Russian colonialism than at any time in its history. However, there are constant issues, one being that Poland is moving towards the West and away from the Russian sphere of influence (joining NATO and the EU) and pursuing an independent political stance. Relations worsen at remembrance of historical events, like the Katyn massacre, which Poland sees as genocide and Russia as a war crime.

Poland supported the democratic Orange revolution in the Ukraine (2004) and Russia then criticised Poland's perceived lack of gratitude to them for its liberation from German occupation. Forgetting their own occupation of Poland in September 1939, ignoring the existence of the Ribbentrop-Molotov pact they co-signed with Hitler and the many deportations and atrocities committed by both Germany and the USSR.

In 2008 there was a dramatic worsening of relations in the South Ossetia war, Poland taking a leading role with the international community on the side of Georgia against Russia. An agreement between Poland allowing the US to install an interceptor defence shield earned the response from Russia that it made Poland 'a legitimate military target'. Russia later announced that it was to set up missiles in Kaliningrad, close to Poland and its Military Exercise, Zapad, in September 2009 involved a simulated nuclear attack against Poland, suppression of an uprising by a Polish minority in Belarus and many other operations of an aggressive nature which continue to the present day.

The recent election results in Russia (March 2018) gave Vladimir Putin enormous majorities for a landslide victory to the presidency and his party to the Duma (council assemblies, governmental institutions created by Tsar Nicholas II) and exposed corruption on a massive scale. Independent monitors declared the election 'hugely unfair and skewed in Putin's favour'. The result was expected, Putin's ceremonial dais was out well before the outcome was known and it resulted in tens of thousands of very brave and very angry young demonstrators and opposition activists (denied by Putin from standing for election) gathering in Moscow's Pushkin Square.

He was openly mocked when he claimed the poll was 'open and honest' but as the opposition leader pointed out, if it had been a free election, why had the streets been flooded with troops? He claimed there were 12,000 police and army personnel who had formed a 'wall of steel' armed with truncheons and dogs.

People had experienced democracy post communism and a good standard of living and freedom under Gorbachev's early leadership and did not want to see a return to the hard line of Putin, advocate of subversion, destabilisation and disinformation, tried and tested Russian methods of domination, Lenin and Stalin methods.

They defied the vast police and army clampdown across Moscow, chanting 'Russia without Putin', there were ugly clashes with many activists detained at Lubyanka Square, in the shadow of the FSB headquarters, site of the notorious prison, (where my Wujek Walery was imprisoned) countless ordinary demonstrators were arrested and there were also many arrests in St Petersburg.

Opposition leaders who were barred from contesting the presidential election sought to spark their own 'Arab spring' in emotional speeches to over 20,000 people gathered in a very icy Moscow. The word 'revolution' had been voiced. 'If we don't want revolution then we want free elections' said Mikhail Kasyanov, Putin's former premier. 'Otherwise revolution is inevitable.' A noble view from desperate people but one which has been subdued by the 'authorities' the FSB (secret police) who run Russia, headed by Putin.

Mikhael Gorbachev had demanded that Mr Putin withdraw from the presidential elections and that local elections already declared should be cancelled and re-held. It was to no avail, Putin 'won' 64% of the vote and independent monitors issued a blistering condemnation of the 'serious problems in the unfair election', having found evidence of widespread vote rigging, voters bussed to voting stations voting several times and votes fed into voting machines many times!

Only the higher tiers of Russia's new democracy are equal, everybody else is just as the Poles were considered to be, 'non-persons'. The Oligarchs, Putin's friends, living in opulence in Russia and London are now finally becoming open to scrutiny since the Skripal poisonings (2018). Many in the Russian Federation know of the victims of political repressions in the USSR, especially the millions of their people deported and murdered en masse in the Purges and the gulags but they know little of the Poles deported to the USSR and the other nations who were also repressed, deported and murdered, a list that is not yet complete.

Even today, Putin's regime increasingly defends what Stalin did and blocks any memorialization of its victims. There are more than 700 memorials to the victims of the Stalinist repressions erected across the country in isolated places, some on the sites of former jails, gulags, camps and mass graves, very few are in Moscow or other major cities for the many to see. *– Elena Meygun of Nazaccent.ru*

Elena Meygun has detail and pictures of some of them which she says show that 'the peoples of our country are united not only by the word Russian but by a common tragedy.' To look at these pictures one thinks of the millions of victims of a system whose collapse Putin has described as 'the greatest geopolitical tragedy of the 20th century'.

Moscow continues to engage in other geopolitical tragedies, the ethnic engineering and genocide when occupying Crimea in 2014, forcing Crimean Tatars out and sending ethnic Russians in! Following in Stalin's footsteps who in 1944 deported 191,000 Tatars in boxcars to mainly Uzbekistan.

In the hands of Putin Russia remains a threat to Albania, Estonia and Latvia, Poland and other countries he seeks to reclaim. His empire, simply as a land mass is the largest in the world, with many natural resources and yet it struggles economically to compete with other nations. Gorbachev started a major regeneration programme but wasn't allowed time to finish the renewal of Russia and in the hands of Putin it seems only the Oligarchs prosper. As did the higher echelons of the Communist party to the cost of its people.

Putin's behaviour will be watched with keen interest by many as he has recently, 2020, assured his presidency until 2030. Russian 'democracy'.

It will be interesting to watch how future political events unfold, especially for the Poles, who also wish to see a Russia without Putin and full democracy. Russia continues to seek suppression of others as well as its own people, albeit by more sophisticated means, the rigged ballot box and offensive military operations on the borders of Poland and the Baltic states and hacking into the computers of various countries to influence elections and referenda.

Poland meanwhile continues to be successful economically as a member of the EU, after losing much of its wealth due to war, looting of its treasures by her invaders and political mishandling by its communist leaders. Its culture continues to flourish and members of my family have visited many times, it's a beautiful country and I hope it continues to be free of any aggressive overtures from its hostile neighbour.

'I have a clear conscience because I have fulfilled my duties as a writer. Nobody can bar the road to truth.

I am prepared to die for its advance'. – Aleksandr Solzhenitsyn

CHAPTER 19

The History of Kresy

The Russian Empire had abandoned the Kresy to decline into a large rural backwater after the original Polish landowners had been disposed of in the wake of the insurrections and the abolition of serfdom in Poland in 1864. The devastation of country estates put a halt to economic activity which had depended on agriculture, forestry, brewing and small-scale industries. The Kresy (now Ukraine) was famous for its fertile soil and was known as the bread basket of Europe.

Its decline was so acute that trade and food supplies became a problem and emigration from towns and villages began as Jewish communities in particular, began heading West to Europe and the US. By the time of the newly resurgent Polish state the provinces had been greatly disadvantaged by having the lowest literacy levels in the country as the Russian state had not encouraged education during its rule. The Kresy had suffered many decades of neglect and was less developed than the western parts of interwar Poland and would have been left to go further into decline had it not been for the Polish-Russian war of 1920.

After Poland regained her independence in 1918 my Dziadek Adam and Wujek Walery fought until 1920 for the return of the eastern borderlands. The treaty of Riga was signed on 18th March 1921 when the borderlands were re-established and shortly after demobbed soldiers qualified to receive lands there.

It is the forest that gives the Kresy its magic and mystery. It formed the eastern borderlands in the days when the country stretched from the Baltic to the Black Sea, from the Oder to the Urals and once stretched from the Baltic to the foothills of the Carpathians, it is the 1st reserve of primeval forest in Europe.

When Poles say they are from the Kresy, they mean the eastern borderlands, it is a word that evokes memories of a land of beauty. The first references to this land appeared in the mid 19th century and the use of Kresy with K first appears in post war literature. The Polish exiles in Siberia displaced by Stalin's annexation and those who escaped from Russia, made the Kresy a synonym for the land of their birth, their country. It is the area of Poland dominated by the great forest of Białowieża where the ethnic diversity was as diverse and as natural to the landscape as the flora and fauna of the forest.

The forest emerged when the glaciers retreated to their original site in the mountains of the north after the last ice age in Europe leaving behind a network of small rivers and subterranean water reserves that nourished this vast land lying 170 metres above sea level. It was not long before this plain gave birth to a forest of indescribable beauty.

The forests and the marshes are home to many animals, lynx, wolf, fox, wild boar, beaver, badger and weasel. Owls, orioles, grouse, woodpeckers, ducks sing through the forests and bison herds run through the trails as well as wild horses. A home to thousands of storks, whose human neighbours eagerly await their return to their same nests. My Mother Alicja grew up in a beautiful land and I've included some early photo's of her and the family taken in the Kresy.

Nobles of the Polish-Lithuanian Commonwealth, with a disregard for nature considered these lands their own hunting grounds and in time destroyed many animals and birds, exploiting the forest for their own ends, the balance of nature completely disregarded. The forests of the eastern borderlands were later razed to the ground by Stalin so that no one could ever make claim to them.

There are 1.5 metre wide 40 metre tall pines, 50 meter high spruces and oaks 3 metres wide and 40 metres high. Ash, Birch and lime trees, fragrant lindens, larch and alders form a canopy for shade loving plants, mosses cling to the trees and violets cover the ground. There are berries, nuts, fruit and mushrooms.

It is the birthplace of Poland's greatest poets from Adam Mickiewicz to nobel prize winner Czesław Miłosz, men of the Kresy. A variety of people lived in the Kresy, Lithuanians, Jews, Ruthenians and Byelorusssians and smaller minorities Armernians, Tatars, Gypsies, Karaites, Germans, Czechs, Greeks, Scots and Russians.

Kresy Wschodnie, the eastern borderlands, the lands of my grand parents' forefathers, a place of legends and of valorous deeds! The places of mystical Pan Wołodyjowski (Fire in the Steppe) and other fictional characters Zagłoba and Kmicic. Battles against the Ukrainians, Swedish, Tatar and Turkish invaders. Legends survive to this day and films are still made about those times.

Tales and legends

You will hear the legend of a Polish Princess who rather than wed a German threw herself into the waves of the Vistula. You will hear the tale of the wise king who slew a terrible dragon. You will hear the tale of the white eagle whose showy feathers were reddened with blood and hearing this tale you will understand why the Poles have in their crest an eagle.

'When the autumn wind howls outside the windows, when the rain beats against the panes, when the logs are crackling in the hearth, you must strain your ears and order everyone to be quiet and wait patiently until a faint delicate knock is heard. It is the knock of a fairy tale from beyond the seven rivers, from beyond the seven mountains. All her kings are valiant, all knights gallant, all princesses lovely, all horses are swift and unsurpassed but the eagle in the fairy tale is as white as snow, on a field as red as blood.

Polish Paganizm

Slav's for many years worshipped the Great Gods and Goddess represented by the Bird, Bee, Snake Goddess and Mother Earth. They celebrated in the open air around trees that were especially old or had a specific significance, with feasts, offerings, celebration and ritual, raising their hand towards the sun when they swore an oath. Their year was divided from Yule to Summer ruled by the White God and Summer to Yule ruled by the Black Goddess.

They held a belief in fairies, changelings and vampires and in re-incarnation and they honoured their ancestors, each home having a shrine to their own ancestors, believing that the soul existed separately from the body. By the year 966 the Polish nobility had embraced Christianity and Poland became officially a state in the eyes of the West. Mieszko I, a member of the Piast dynasty and father of Bolesław the Brave, ascended to the throne. Lithuania a sister Polish territory was the last pagan state in Europe becoming Christian when Duke Jagiełło married into the Polish dynasty in 1374.

The legend of Smok Wawelski – the dragon of Wawel Hill

Some centuries ago there lived in a cave at the foot of Wawel Hill a most horrible fire-belching dragon, a monster that ravaged the nearby meadows by devouring the grazing cattle. In vain the bravest Knights tried to overcome the dragon but before they could draw their swords the fire from the beast's mouth destroyed them and one after another they fell.

The King sent out his heralds to announce that whosoever could slay the dragon would as a reward marry his daughter. Contenders came in droves but they too were destroyed. Then a shoemaker named Krak decided he would conquer the beast and after stuffing a very fat ram with sulphur he placed it at the cave's entrance and waited for the greedy dragon. As anticipated the dragon swallowed the gift in one mouthful and with its burning throat ran to the nearby Wisla river gulping down so much water it burst with a great bang. The countryside was free from its grip of terror. The town now bears the name of the rescuer, Krakow the old capital of Poland and the princess lived happily ever after!

The legend of Wanda

Krakus had 3 children, 2 sons and a daughter, his eldest son should have been a ruler upon his death but was slain by his younger brother who coveted power for himself. This wickedness angered the people and they banished him from their country.

The daughter of Krakus, Wanda, became the ruler of the country instead, she was very beautiful and although very young when she became queen she had wisdom and understanding beyond her years. She loved her country and she ruled wisely over her people who loved and respected her.

With all her qualities, her beauty and wisdom, many princes sought to marry her but Wanda would not accept any of them for she had not found one who was pleasing to her or who would help her to rule wisely. Poland was dear to Wanda and she waged war against aggressors, leading her soldiers herself into battle. Her presence inspired them.

Her fame spread far and wide and a German Prince named Rytigier heard of her beauty, her valour and the fruitful and rich Polish lands. He sent his messengers who were rough and uncivilised men and who looked about them appraising the value of everything around them, seeming to think it would soon be theirs but who were received with the customary courtesy.

Wanda read the letter presented to her and turned deathly pale at the contents, Rytigier was asking for her hand in marriage stipulating as her dowry, the lands of Poland and threatening war in the event of a refusal. He had a very powerful army and was famed all over Europe as the strongest and best equipped of any Prince. Wanda would not subject her country to a German ruler, she looked at the two messengers and shuddered. Cruelty and rapacity were written across their faces and Wanda thought they were typical Germans. To wage war would be fatal with the armies so ill matched.

In a firm voice Wanda refused to surrender herself and her country to the Germans, she had made her decision, Wanda would sacrifice her life for Poland.

She retired to her apartments and there she prayed to the gods that they would grant Poland freedom from the Germans in return for her sacrificing her life. Her prayer was granted and Wanda threw herself into the river Wisła. When her body was recovered she was buried with all honours and a mound was raised to her memory beside that of her father, Krakus.

The legend of Bolesław and his Knights

When King Bolesław died Poland lost a very able and brave ruler, one who had united the country and made her great. But is Bolesław lost to Poland? Some say not. For there is a legend about him and his Knights who went into a mountain called Giewont which forms part of the Tatra mountain range and routed Poland's enemies. Seen from a certain angle it is like the head of a sleeping knight. Within the mountain is a huge and dark cavern and there sleep King Bolesław and his Knights. They are mounted on horses with their swords beside them and their lances couched. And if Poland ever needs them then they must be awoken to ride forth to serve her. But once they have gone forth they will never return.

The Trumpeter of Kraków and the Hejnał Mariacki

In the ancient capital of Kraków there is a market square, one that I have sat in enjoying a cold Polish beer by a tall, charming building of pink brick in a Gothic style. It has two towers with one slightly higher than the other and from this tower a trumpeter plays a fanfare of a hymn, the Hejnał, every hour which is repeated four times ending quite abruptly on a broken note.

Many years ago as the trumpeter was playing his fanfare he saw a cloud of dust in the distance which grew into a large army of Tartars galloping towards the city. The Tartars had previously pillaged and burned, looted and murdered the Kraków residents and had carried off their young to their camps as slaves. The trumpeter was terrified at the sight of the approaching Tartars and wondered how he would warn the city. Rather than run down into the town which would waste time, he decided to play the Hejnał over and over again thinking that this would alert the town of the danger.

The residents were confused, why was the trumpeter playing the Hejnał over and over again? But they quickly realised that he was warning them. The soldiers sprang to arms, the artisans seized their tools and the apprentices gathered their arrows and crossbows and all marched to defend their city. The Tartars had heard the trumpeter and they had seen him in the tower and as soon as they had come into bowshot their leader loosed his bow and the arrow lodged into the trumpeter's throat.

Kraków though was saved, the trumpeter's task was won and thanks to his warning the people were able to defend their city, inflicting a crushing defeat on the Tartars and killing one of their Princes.

Ever since that day the Hejnał has been stopped at the same note on which it was ended by the Tartar arrow, in honour of the trumpeter who gave his life for the city.

At the battle of Monte Cassino in May 1944, when many Polish troops had given their lives, at the raising of the Polish flag on the hill of Monte Cassino a trumpeter played the Hejnal.

I had picked up some tourism papers from Wawel Castle and was reading about the Tales and Legends of Poland over a couple of cold beers in Kraków square and I was especially interested in the detail from Kresy. I haven't been to see the eastern borderlands, although a visit there is on my list and I would love to see the land where my family came from. I've included some of the tales and legends of the borderlands as they were a magical and enchanting place although I'm sure greatly changed now, being part of the Ukraine it'll be very different.

The last tale seems to be a forewarning of the tragedy to befall Poland in 1939. It has had so many hostile neighbours to contend with over the centuries but exists to this day.

In the middle of the 20th century the people of the Kresy with the rest of Poland suffered a tragedy unlike anywhere else in Europe. The simultaneous attack by two of the most vicious totalitarian regimes in history, Nazi Germany and Soviet Russia. The Kresy was the epicentre of the battle between these two giants, wreaking unprecedented destruction on the people, land and the great forests.

The savagery of the onslaught was driven by ideologies aimed at the eradication of all cultures in these lands, whether by race or class, to be replaced by their own, communism and repression. Germany eventually failed but committed crimes of savagery that irreparably altered the ethnic makeup. The Polish nation was all but destroyed, millions of Poles, Jews, Ukrainians and Byelorussians were killed and Stalin deported many millions more to the depths of Siberia and then imposed Communist rule upon Poland in 1940. The losses both material and cultural were heart breaking.

CHAPTER 20

Równe

The first known reference to the town of Równe dates back to 1283 when it was part of Halych-Volhynia. By the 14th century Równe came under the control of the Duchy of Lithuania and by 1569 the city was part of the Polish-Lithuanian Commonwealth. In 1793 Poland was again partitioned and Równe became part of the Russian Empire and in 1797 it was declared a regional town of Volhynian Governorate.

During WW1 it was briefly under German, Ukrainian, Bolshevik and Polish Forces until 1919 when it served as the temporary capital of the Ukrainian People's Republic. At the conclusion of WW1 in accordance with the Treaty of Riga in 1921; which had brought an end to the Polish-Russian War; Poland had regained its eastern borderlands and independence from the Russian Empire. She had not been an independent country since 1795 and in 1940 again lost her freedom to Stalin. Równe, in the Kresy, home of my family was just one small town in eastern Poland overrun by tyrants as would many more such cities across Poland be until 1945.

Her history is interesting, made up of many rebellions against the Russian Empire's strict and repressive regime and anti Polish conflicts and wars by other foreign invaders, the Prussians and Austrians. The list is long. My grandparents had settled in Równe shortly after marrying in 1923 to settle the land which had been abandoned by the Russian Empire.

During the years since the Bolshevik War Polish soldiers who had fought in that war and also in WW1 were allocated land on the regained eastern borderlands of Poland. They would work the land to bring it back to productivity and to also act as a military presence on the border, protection against their old enemy, the Bolsheviks.

There were many ethnic groups living in the Kresy at this time and although initially there was suspicion against the Polish ex military Osadnicy, (settlers) relationships improved over the first few years as there was good work on the Osada's. There had been decades of neglect and under investment compared to the western parts of inter war Poland but a great deal would be established by common effort and the settlements became economically sound and together with the Jewish trades and crafts it continued to grow.

Across the entire Kresy the population amounted to 13.2 ml, the overwhelming majority 75% lived in the countryside, made up of peasants 55%, 27% workers, 1% Bourgeoisie, 5% Intelligentsia, 11% small businessmen and 0.3% landowners. The breakdown of the religious groups were Catholic 11.5%, Russian Orthodox 74.6% Jewish 11.3% other 2.6%.

By the 10th century Poland had been one of the most tolerant countries in Europe becoming home to one of the largest and vibrant Jewish communities in the world. In the mid 1200's Jews had been expelled from most of the countries of Europe and Bolesław Prince of Great Poland in 1264 proclaimed the Statute of Kalisz, creating legal protections and guaranteed the Jews the freedom of choice of work, commerce and movement. These protections were extended by King Kazimierz who in 1349 had invited Jews into Poland from Europe where they had been the victims of violent attacks. With these protections the Jewish communities began to thrive and Scholars suggest that by the 16th century 80% of all Jews worldwide lived in Poland. They enjoyed relative autonomy and tolerance and developed a rich social and cultural life which would come to a dreadful end in September 1939.

The population specific to Równe according to the Polish 1931 Census and Demographic data was made up of 11,173 Poles (26.5%), Yiddish 20,635 (50.8%), Hebrew 1.922(4.7%), German (0.8%) 327, Ukrainian 3,194 (7.9%), Belarussian (0.1%) 58, Russian 2,792 (6.9%), Lithuanian (0% 4), Other (1.2%) 507. An extremely mixed and hardworking population.

By 1921 the population had expanded into various sectors, industry, trade and crafts and there were doctors, lawyers engineers, high schools and a business school as well as the Osadas managed by the ex military Poles providing farm produce, meat, wine, flour, agriculture, forestry, brewing and small industries.

Jews had been living in Równe since the atrocities committed against them by Cossacks and Catholics in 1648-49 in Chmielnicki. They added to the economic growth of the region with merchants involved in farm produce and lumber trades and by the 19th century involved in the importation of porcelain, glass and shoes. Further economic growth was seen in the 20th century with the construction of a brewery as well as a soap factory, flour mills and brick yards. As a result of this growth community services expanded and there were 6 synagogues, a hospital and an aged people's home.

It was here that my family, the Góral's, Grandparents Kazia and Adam lived and worked the Osada Krechowiecka from 1924 until my grandfather realized he wasn't suited to farm work and rented his Osada to a German family then moved into the town with Kazia and the children. Kazia's brother Walery Radomski and his wife Ziuta, lived on the Osada from approximately 1922 until the lives of the families were shattered on Hitler's invasion of their country.

After spending 18 years working on the settlements, the accomplishments of the many military settlers were considerable and the family was settled and happy in Rowne. They had a good social life with friends from all the ethnic groups and the children were doing well at school. It was all to come to an end when rumours circulated around Równe that German troops had been seen on Poland's borders. After such a short time of independence the Osadnicy were afraid, suddenly aware of tensions amongst the locals. Life became very difficult with sudden hostility from a small number of their neighbours which gradually spread and became a huge worry to my grandparents.

When war officially broke out in September 1939 the city was overrun by the Red army and it didn't take long for the Soviets to take action against the inhabitants of the Kresy. In February 1940 the military settlers across the region were deported to Siberia and my family was put into box cars for a journey of over 2,500km to the Russian labour camps. They were leaving Równe and its people to the brutality of the Russians, Germans and the Ukrainians and had they not been exiled they may have fallen victim to the barbarity of the UPA.

Half of the inhabitants of Równe were Jewish and there were about 23,000 in Równe alone prior to the German occupation and between 6th and 8th November 1941, approximately 20,000 were taken to a pine grove in Sosenki and killed by the Einsatzgruppe C and their Ukrainian collaborators. A Ghetto was then established for the remaining Jews and in July 1942 the Jewish population was sent north to Kostopol some 70km away where they were killed.

The Ghetto was subsequently liquidated in July 1942 and only a handful of Jews were able to escape the deportations, joined the partisans and took part in the liberation of Równe with the Red Army in the Battle of Równe. By 1944 there were 1,200 Jews accounted for, from those who lived there prewar and with refugees from western Poland they made up half the population of the town.

The territorial changes in Poland immediately after WW2 were extensive, the Oder-Neisse line became Poland's western border and the Curzon Line its eastern border. In 1945 after the defeat of Germany, Poland's borders were redrawn in accordance with the decisions made at the Tehran conference of 1943 with the Allies. Stalin had demanded recognition of the military outcome of the top secret German-Soviet pact of 1939, the Ribbentrop-Molotov pact he had agreed with Hitler, which 'the West were unaware of' and which I find very hard to believe!

Stalin repeated his stance more forcefully at the Yalta conference with Roosevelt and Churchill in February 1945 in the face of the looming German defeat. These new borders were ratified at the Potsdam Conference in August 1945 exactly as Stalin had proposed, he already controlled eastern Europe, his troops were all across it and he was simply finalizing matters to suit his own ends.

The pre-war eastern territories of Kresy were now annexed by the USSR and most of the remaining Polish inhabitants were expelled. As a result of the Potsdam agreement to which the Polish Government in exile was not invited, Poland lost 179,000 sq km 45% of prewar territories in the east, including over 12 ml citizens of whom 4.3 ml were ethnically Polish. Those territories are today part of sovereign Belarus, Ukraine and Lithuania.

World War two decimated Poland, not only had the Polish Eagle to defend herself against the German and Russian armies but the Ukrainian UPA were rampaging and murdering their way through the eastern borderlands, in Równe and many other villages, brutally killing mostly women and children, innocents. The population of Poles of the entire area of the Kresy by 1939 was around 5.2 ml but after ethnic cleansing between 1939 and 1945 by the Germans, Russians and Ukrainian Nationalists it was down to about 1.8 ml inhabitants.

In Lebanon in 1946, where my family was living as refugees after their escape from the labour camp, they watched the unfolding events across Poland with great sadness. My grandparents Kazia and Adam never returned to Równe it was now under the control of the Soviets and there was no room for those previous inhabitants who despised communism, they would still be regarded as 'enemies of the state' and treated accordingly.

They had lived happily in the eastern borderlands, a land of beauty, of tales and legends until their lives were disrupted forever by their hostile neighbours, the Bolsheviks and the Germans who used terror to destroy the Polish people and their land. Stalin however failed to destroy their spirit and Poland's people have rebuilt.

CHAPTER 21

The Corporal and the Generals

Corporal Wojtek, 'happy warrior'

It was May 11th 1944 the final battle of Monte Cassino and before the attack General Anders addressed his troops, 'For this action let the lion's spirit enter your hearts and keep deep in your heart God, honour and our land, Poland.' He urged his men to take revenge for the suffering of Poland and for what they had endured in the years spent in Russia as deportees.

The story of Wojtek, the wartime bear and hero is a true story of a very special animal, who thought of himself as a soldier. A bear of 6 feet weighing over 30 stone with a liking for beer and wódka, this is Wojtek the bear, adopted by the Polish 2nd Corp in Teheran in 1940. He also had a taste for cigarettes and wrestled with his comrades in the Corps. A bear thrown into a dangerous and frightening world but a world into which he very quickly adapted. And he was a bear who gave his Polish survivors hope and the opportunity to care for another living being. Most had been imprisoned in Siberia and had lost their families and like Wojtek they had no home.

The first wave of Polish troops from Siberia who travelled across the Caspian Sea to Pahlevi arrived in Spring 1942 and amongst them was a young girl Irena Bokiewicz who was with her Mother travelling with the staff of General Boruta Spiechowicz. On route from Pahlevi to Tehran they came across two Persian boys with a bear cub and Irena immediately fell in love with the tiny bear. Lieut. Anatol Tarnowiecki who was in her group bought the cub from the boys and gave him to Irena. They carried on their journey to Tehran and arrived at their civilian camp. The bear grew quickly and caused mischief and became a handful to Irena and after 3 months she could no longer keep the cub in the camp. She gave him to the army as a mascot and this is how Wojtek joined 22nd Artillery Supply Company on 22nd August 1942.

It wasn't long before Wojtek became a central part of life in the Polish camp. He picked up the Polish instructions quite quickly and was taught to salute when greeted by a senior officer. The soldiers enjoyed his company, a distraction of the war that was going on around them, and the bear returned the love and attention given him despite causing some chaos. He treated everything as a game even taking the soldiers clothes off the drying lines. To make up for his behavior he made a very good security guard, terrifying those who broke into the camp.

They fed him, played with him and kept him occupied, he was their child, and the day to day challenges of looking after their 'baby' took their minds off the horrors of the war that had inflicted the most awful atrocities on Poland. Wojtek lifted the hearts of his comrades whose future was very much unsure, they were living in limbo, were homeless, stateless and penniless and Wotjek was the only thing they owned and he gave them reason to live.

The Polish corps was to join the Allies in North Africa prior to their posting to Italy alongside the British 8th Army in 1944 and although pets were forbidden Wojtek it was decided, would go too. To allow him to go with the 2nd Corps he was enlisted officially as a soldier in the 2nd Polish Corps and served with the 22nd Supply Company. He had his own pay book, rank and serial number and lived in tents with his fellow army friends.

Three attempts to break through to Monte Cassino had already failed. For the fourth assault General Anders volunteered his Polish troops to spearhead the attack. In the 3 weeks before the attack it was Wojtek's company's job to supply the artillery positions with the ordnance they needed for the job. It was slow and laborious driving the shells along sheer mountain precipices, along hairpin bends in the dark and without lights as a complete blackout was required so as not to alert the enemy.

It was at the Battle of Monte Cassino in 1944 that Wojtek the bear made an impression on and won the huge affection of his fellow soldiers and achieved legendary status. The role of Wojtek's transport corps was to carry 100lb crates of artillery shells from lorries to a battery position. He worked and copied his comrades, paws outstretched indicting to them he wanted to help, going backwards and forwards with the crates, piling them as high as he could, without ever dropping a single one. It was just another game to him and he enjoyed being with the men.

Monte Cassino was a decisive battle and one of the bloodiest. Allied troops launched 4 assaults against the German and Italian held line and eventually the stronghold was defeated but at huge cost. 55,000 allied soldiers died against 20,000 German casualties. Wojtek's actions were invaluable and from that day a bear carrying an artillery shell became the official emblem of the 2nd company. The Poles wore it either as a cap badge or on their sleeves or lapels of their combat uniforms. The bear had been truly blooded in one of the most historic engagements of WW2 and being exposed to the rigours of intensive warfare hadn't seemed to change his temperament.

Wojtek was quite unique, he had never been trained for the tasks he carried out with his comrades, under heavy fire from shells. He helped them because he wanted to, he was a soldier. He worked with them through heavy artillery, never being acclimatized to the noise of the explosions that shook the ground and he survived all this.

Animals have always been used in warfare, elephants were perhaps the first, with details being found in Sanskrit writings dating back to 1,100 BC. Horses, camels, pigeons, mules, dogs, canaries, dolphins and sea lions have been trained to take part in warfare and millions of them have died in the service of their country. Horses in particular, with 8 ml dying in the first world war, all these animals were incredibly courageous. I read somewhere that even glow worms were used to read maps in the dark trenches.

In 1946 Wojtek arrived in Scotland with the 2nd Polish Army Corps, a seasoned military campaigner. He had spent 2 years in the Middle East with his comrades and almost 3 years in Italy as the allies fought their way through Europe. He had arrived at Winfield Camp for Displaced persons on Sunwick farm in October and it wasn't long before the community became aware of the soldier bear. His Polish servicemen loved him dearly, they were far from home and Wojtek provided entertainment and fun and someone to love.

Following the disbanding of the Polish army in 1947, many Poles were unable to return to their country because of Stalin's communist state and the threat of being shot as traitors or simply 'disappearing' to one of the gulags. Many of them emigrated to the USA, Canada and Australia. What was to be the fate of Wojtek? It was very sadly decided by the Polish unit after many months of wavering that Wojtek would be relocated to Edinburgh Zoo, many of the men in the unit openly cried at this decision.

He was treated well in his new home given tea with milk every day and the odd nip of wódka and beer. He responded better to Polish and his old army comrades used to visit him and jumped into his enclosure to play with him, cuddle him or wrestle with him. The Zoo keepers were not impressed but the Poles were insistent. He was there for 16 years and died on 2nd December 1963 aged 22, he was 35 stone and over 6 feet tall.

There are many memorials to the soldier bear, in addition to the statue in Duns, there is a plaque in his honour at the Imperial War Museum and a bronze statue was unveiled in Princes Street Gardens in Edinburgh in 2013, of him walking proudly at the side of a Polish soldier. Kraków city erected a statue of him in 2013 in Park Jordana, unveiled on the 70th anniversary of Monte Cassino.

In 2011 a film Wojtek the bear that went to War was broadcast on BBC 2 Scotland, on 17th September 2014 a music video called Wojtek was released by Katy Carr, on the 75th anniversary of the Soviet invasion of Poland. He is referenced in Hearts of iron IV as an Easter egg achievement, 'Bearer of Artillery'. In the Scythe board game a fictionalized Poland known as 'Polania Republic' has the characters 'Anna and Wojtek', where Wojtek is Anna's bear companion. There have also been many books written on this remarkable bear cub, amongst the authors are Aileen Orr from Scotland who grew up knowing Wojtek.

The animator Iain Harvey, who was the executor producer on the TV adaption of The Snowman is planning a film called A bear Named Wojtek, and hoping to release it in time for the 75th anniversary of VE day, on May 8th 2020. Not many Sybiraks are alive today and will not see this but their children will and they'll see it in part as a long deserved recognition of the WW2 effort of the Polish people, previously overlooked. That it may have taken a bear cub and his involvement in the War to recognize this is a wonder.

When I was a child I had a huge teddy bear called Wojtek. My Grandparents, Kazia and Adam had bought it for me and my parents sometimes placed it at the foot of the stairs hoping to prevent me from running up and down and hurt myself. I ran everywhere, for my parents it was purely a safety measure but Wojtek and I worked in tandem, I would run for the stairs and he would 'fall' over and make way for me. Later, he was joined by another similarly huge bear called Bartek, for my brother and this also didn't work as a safety measure. They would both somehow leave the way open for us to explore the upper landing. We loved those bears and I still remember them, especially Wojtek, he was my first love and what a lovely memory to have. I was about 3 years old and my Grandparents hadn't been in the country very long, having arrived from Lebanon in February 1948 and spending some time in Resettlement camps.

Wojtek will be remembered as a most exceptional animal who thought of himself as a Polish soldier. He was very special to a group of hardened survivors of the disaster that had befallen Poland. Wojtek had given them hope, the chance to love, protect and care for another living being. They played with him, wrestled and cuddled him, he helped them stay grounded. He was a powerful symbol of freedom and solidarity for all Poles, wherever they were and I believe he continues to be to this day, especially at the many remembrances of WW2.

Baśka

Wojtek wasn't the only bear to serve in the Polish Armed Forces, Wojtek had a predecessor, a polar bear called Baśka from Murmansk in northern Russia and was conscripted into the Polish Murmansk Battalion.

349

In December 1919 she paraded in front of the Chief of State Józef Piłsudski. Unfortunately her life ended tragically.

When soldiers are deprived of family and a normal life a big animal like a bear becomes everything that they have lost. Polar bears have a savage temperament and to tame one is quite an achievement and that Wojtek and Baśka could trust their soldier parents says an awful lot. They had both been found at an early age and had not been exposed to other bears and it had been easier for the bears to take on human attributes. Had the soldiers been cruel to them they would almost certainly have killed them.

The history of Baska's unit begins after the Bolshevik Revolution in 1917 and Russia's withdrawal from the Great War. Polish soldiers who had served in the Tsar's army were scattered across the territory of the fallen Russian empire and when the Bolsheviks seized power in 1917 and Russia dropped out of the war, independent Polish Units were formed only to find themselves in a vicious civil war.

General Józef Haller, who created the Blue Army, decided to find a purpose for these soldiers in the newly reborn Poland and sent them to fight in the armies alongside the Whites, an anti Bolshevik coalition, including British, French, Italian, Serbian, American, Canadian and Australian soldiers against the Reds (Communist supporters). They had to cope with sub zero temperatures and frostbite in the long Russian winter whilst in the summer the thaw turned into a vast swamp, teeming with mosquitoes.

In mid June 1918 General Haller received permission from the allied countries to start recruiting soldiers for the Polish units in Russia. Recruitment commissions were set up in Murmansk and Arkhangelsk and a unit was formed in the town of Kola which became a battalion of around 300 Polish riflemen who went into battle alongside the British against the Bolsheviks near Lake Onega in Karelia. The fighting was brutal.

In early 1919 Arkhangelsk was occupied by the Entente countries under command of the British who intended 'to conquer Russia from the North, hang the Reds of the Kremlin on lampposts and essentially, get rich on the area's natural resources'. – *Eugeniusz Malaczewski – The history of Baśka of Murmansk 1920's.*

One of the Polish soldiers Walenty Karas an officer cadet was competing with an Italian Captain Bersaglieri, for a certain lady's favour, who had a weakness for animals. The Italian had a pet arctic fox with white blue fur and the Pole decided to outclass him with the young bear he had bought at a market in Arkhangelsk. His gesture however failed to spark a romance but it did begin a most remarkable love affair between the Polish army and bears which was to be repeated in WW2 with Wojtek.

After Baśka, although not fully grown, had killed a dog unfortunately belonging to a senior British officer, a Corporal Smorgonski was tasked with taming her because of his methods of training the recruits. The bear was tamed and she became so domesticated she slept curled up at the foot of his bed. She even had her own military rations just like any other soldier and she was made an official member of the army given the military rank of 'daughter of the regiment.' Malaczewski writes that, 'the bear was tamed like a domestic dog' and later accompanied the unit 'like a pet.' The soldiers were crazy about their polar bear.

By the summer of 1919 the British and other allied powers decided to withdraw before another winter took hold and in the autumn the 460 men of the Polish Legion were evacuated, with 6,500 refugees joining them to the West on a ship, Toloa, and the bear sailed into the port of Edinburgh on 2nd October 1919 with them. Marching through Edinburgh to the Dreghorn Barracks the Polish soldiers in their characteristic blue uniforms and the young polar bear caused a sensation.
– *(Account verified by Major Bronislaw Duch 1929 published in The Scotsman on the occasion of the first congress of the soldiers from Murmansk).*

The Poles left Scotland on 1st December 1919 on board the Helena to a newly independent Poland, sailing to Gdansk but for unclear reasons they were diverted to Szczecin on 4th December. From there they took a train to Poznan, crossing the Polish border near Krzyz and reached Modlin their new station on 6th December.

Later that month, Baśka and her unit took part in a military parade being received by Chief of State Józef Piłsudski on Saski Square in Warsaw. The Murmansk battalian was received as heroes and the young bear was admired by the large group of onlookers who had gathered to watch the parade. It is unbelievable that one of the most dangerous animals in the world marched through the street of Warsaw, offering her paw to Sikorski and then also in Edinburgh making such a mark on history.

With her new found celebrity Baśka accompanied her unit to their barracks at the Modlin fortress 20 miles from Warsaw and she had only been there for a short time when tragedy struck. During the summer of 1920 the polar bear was suffering from the heat and the soldiers would take her down to the river to cool her down. However she swam off downstream to a nearby village and maybe seeking some food and trustful of people, approached some peasants working by the river who misunderstood her intentions, attacked and killed her. Her soldier comrades who had been frantically searching for her were said to be distraught when they learned of her death. They took her body to a taxidermist and she was later put on display in a museum in Warsaw.

She survived the Warsaw Uprising and the occupation in good condition in a special display case but later, officers for communist indoctrination from the People's Army, Chief Political and Military Command threw her into a storage room with the rest of the memorabilia that signified the distinguished times of Poland fighting against the Bolsheviks.

It is not known what happened to Baśka, some accounts say she was thrown out when the communists were getting rid of everything associated with the history of Poland's second Republic. Others that she was donated to the Polish Hunting Association.

Not quite the distinguished military record of Corporal Wojtek but another young bear, a daughter of the regiment, who touched the hearts of the Polish Military and became their mascot and a symbol of solidarity. Baśka like Wojtek is remembered in Poland and the link with Scotland is an interesting one. A female Polar bear from the far north, the Arctic Circle representing the Poles and then Wojek another motherless young bear, from the desert of Persia, both visiting Scotland. – *Rzeczpospolita 2017*

The Corporals Baśka and Wojtek gave the military men of Poland something to focus their minds on, to love and to raise their morale. The bears saw them through the days around the warfare they were faced with, the horrors they would see around them. The military aspects of war were left to the Polish Generals of World War 2.

General Władisław Anders

And I'll start with General Władisław Anders perhaps the most well known, born on 11th August 1892 – 12th May 1970 born in the village of Krośniewice, Błonie, west of Warsaw, at that time part of the Russian empire. Poland did not then exist as an independent state as a result of the partitions of Poland at the end of the eighteenth century. He was a Cavalry Officer during WW1 and commanded a force that from 1941-44 made the epic journey through Siberia, central Asia, the Middle East and Africa.

When the Germans attacked the USSR in June 1941 everything changed. Stalin knew that one day he would need the Poles to fight the Germans and when the British and Americans joined Russia as allies, they encouraged Stalin to establish an army of Poles from those he had deported from Poland to the USSR in 1940-41.

Anders had already commanded a tank regiment during the German invasion but defeated, fled to eastern Poland where the Soviets arrested him and took him to the Lubyanka prison in Moscow. He was later hauled from his prison cell and told to raise an army of 120,000 and to make it as combat ready as quickly as possible. Stalin had taken a liking to Anders, after their first meeting he had sent him two thoroughbred horses and a limousine, intended probably as a bribe which didn't work. Anders loathed all Russians as did all his men.

The prisoners and deportees were physical wrecks from their imprisonment in the gulags and prison camps, they were half starved, yet Anders would make them into a fit and effective fighting force. These men desperately wanted to leave the USSR and after negotiations with Britain and the USA they were allowed to leave with their families, towards the Polish army which would be formed under British command in the Middle East. Once word had got to the labour camps across the USSR (word was withheld from many camps) many of the men were eager to join Anders, my Dziadek Adam and Wujek Walery amongst them. Preparations were made for him and the family to leave and a journey of over 5,000 km began in December 1941.

Their road to freedom was very far from smooth, Stalin had been unwilling to allow General Anders to raise the army, however, only after he became an ally of the British and Americans to fight the Germans did he agree. Many attempts were made to prevent the Polish people from reaching the recruitment posts by any means possible. The NKVD hounded them constantly while these families, left to their own devices with little means of subsistence, trudged southwards, flocking to Anders' army. For many it was a death sentence, those that survived the journey from the USSR, were emaciated and gaunt, their health almost destroyed by the hard labour they had endured, and it was doubtful they would be turned into a fighting force.

My family, Dziadek Adam, his bother-in-law Walery and his son Włodek all wore the British army uniform and my Mother Alicja, Ciocia Jasia, Wujek Janusz and their cousin Marysia all wore the uniforms of the Polish Cadets. It was extremely doubtful that those who did not have a relative in the Anders Army, were able to leave the USSR. Many thousands were left behind and would eventually become Russian citizens, having their Polish citizenship revoked.

353

The journey from the USSR would take these starving, ill and barely standing people, the Anders army, through many locations, Samarkand, Kazakhstan, the Caspian Sea, Isfahan, Tehran, Baghdad, Syria, Jerusalem, Sinai, Cairo and Libya. Wives and children were given safe haven although many did perish at the hands of the NKVD. These incredibly long journeys took a huge toll on the escaping Poles.

Anders' goal was to get as many Poles out of the camps and gulags as he could. It wasn't to create a military force initially although he did just that, admitting the elderly and disabled into the service, but it was to take care of the children and the women, as many as he could. At the Polish recruitment posts dotted around the USSR, they were given food and shelter and regained a little confidence.

Anders and his army eventually crossed the Mediterranean with the Allied invasion of Italy in 1944 and when the British suffered huge losses at Monte Cassino it was the Polish Army which forced the Germans back behind the frontiers of the third Reich.

Anders had turned his 'army of beggars' into a military force, his greatest achievement the capture of Monte Cassino on 18th May 1944. After the war Anders lived in exile in London until his death in 1970. He was a remarkable man and leader.

A leader who rescued thousands of Jews from Soviet Gulags and allowed over 3,000 to desert to Palestine; despite desertion being punishable by execution, including Menachem Begin; On 18th September 1950 the Jewish Telegraphic Agency on behalf of Jewish groups urged President Truman to revoke permission given to Anders to visit the US accusing him of being an anti-Semite.

And as he represented the Polish State so does his daughter Anna Maria Anders as Ambassador to Italy and Secretary of State at the Chancellery of the Prime Minister as at 2019.

'There comes a time when one must take a position that is neither safe nor politic, nor popular, but he must take it because conscience tells him it is right' – Dr Martin Luther King Jr

General Józef Klemens Piłsudski

Another General who had an incredible impact on Poland, known for the Miracle of the Vistula was Józef Klemens Piłsudski born on 5th December 1867 – 12th May 1935 in Zułów, Wilno. He was the leader of the second Polish Republic (1918-35) Chief of State, First Marshall of Poland, Minister of Military Affairs. A distinguished figure in Polish politics, viewed as the father of the second republic.

From November 1918 when Poland regained her independence, until 1922 Piłsudski was Poland's Chief of State. In 1919-1921 he commanded the Polish Forces in six wars that redefined the country's borders. He seemed on the brink of defeat against the Soviets in the Polish Soviet war, in which both Adam and Walery fought, when in the Battle of Warsaw 1920 he threw back the invading Russians.

The aftermath of WW1 brought great unrest across all Polish borders, in the east Polish forces had clashed with Ukrainian forces in the Polish Ukrainian war and Piłsudski's first orders as Commander in Chief of the Polish Army was to provide support for the Polish struggle in Lwów, in November 1918. He was also aware that the Bolsheviks were no friends of an independent Poland and that war with them was inevitable. The Bolsheviks were advancing west and it was a major problem to Poland but a lesser one than that of the 'White Russians', the fighters of the old Russian Empire who objected to Polish control of the Ukraine, territories now within the Polish borders.

The decisive battle of the Polish Soviet war was fought from 13th to 25th August 1920 as the Red Army forces commanded by Mikhail Tukhachevsky approached Warsaw. The Soviet strategy was for a massed push towards the Polish capital which would have an enormous propaganda effect for the Soviets. Piłsudski's forces, battle hardened and determined counter attacked from the south forcing the Russian forces into a disorganised withdrawal eastwards behind the Niemen River. Estimated Bolshevik losses were 10,000 killed, 500 missing, 10,000 wounded and 66,000 taken prisoner. Polish losses were 4,500 killed, 10,000 missing and 22,000 wounded.

Before the Polish victory at the Vistula the Bolsheviks and majority of foreign experts considered Poland to be on the verge of defeat. The stunning and unexpected Polish victory crippled the Bolshevik forces and secured Poland's independence and her eastern borders. It also stopped Lenin's ambitions of a communist revolution spreading across central and western Europe through Poland, although Stalin would succeed from 1939 onwards.

Piłsudski had secured Poland's independence, lost in 1795 in the third partition of the Polish-Lithuanian Commonwealth and regained territories from former partitioners, Russia, Germany and Austria-Hungary after 123 years.

General Władislaw Sikorski

Another General playing a prominent part in Poland's bid to establish its independence from Russia was Władislaw Sikorski born on 20th May 1881 – 4th July 1943 in Tuszow Narodowy, Galicia.

Prior to the first world war Sikorski established and participated in many underground movements that promoted the cause of the independence of Poland from the Russian Empire. He fought with distinction in the Polish Legions during WW1 and later in the Polish Army during the Polish Soviet war of 1919 to 1921. Playing a prominent part in the decisive battle of Warsaw (1920). In the early years of the second Polish Republic he held government posts, including Prime Minister and Minister of Military Affairs. Following Józef Piłsudski's May coup of 1926 he fell out of favour with the new regime.

During the second world war he became Prime Minister of the Polish Government in exile, and Commander in Chief of the Polish Armed Forces. He preferred the reestablishment of diplomatic relations between Poland and Russia which had been severed after the invasion of Poland in 1939, but Stalin broke off the diplomatic relations in April 1943 following Sikorski's request that the International Red Cross investigate the Katyn Forest massacres which Russia had been responsible for.

In July 1943 a plane carrying Sikorski plunged into the sea immediately after take off from Gibraltar killing all on board, except the pilot. The circumstances have ever since been disputed and have given rise to many theories. Sikorski had been the most prestigious leader of the Polish exiles and his death was a considerable setback for the Polish cause.

General Stanislaw Maczek

A lesser well known Polish General who fought for the freedom of Poland was Stanislaw Maczek, born in Lwów, Poland 31st March 1892 died Edinburgh, Scotland 11th December 1994. In September 1939 after Poland collapsed under the double pressure of Germany and the Soviet Union, General Maczek and his men after desperate resistance against German forces, reached Hungary and then dispersed before regrouping in France where General Władislaw Sikorski had set up a Polish Government in exile in the spring of 1940. Maczek recreated the 10th Motorised Cavalry Brigade and threw it into battle against the advancing German invasion forces. After being forced to retreat and abandon their tanks they regrouped in England and formed the free Polish Army.

Through Maczek and Sikorski's efforts the 10th Brigade was reborn on 25th February 1942 as the 1st Polish Armoured Division under Maczek's command. The Division landed in Normandy on 1st August 1944 with 16,000 men and 400 tanks. On 5th August Major General Maczek's troops were placed under the command of Lieutenant General Guy Simmonds' Canadian Corps to crush German resistance and reach Falaise Gap in the battle of Normandy. In its attempt to close Falaise Gap the Polish Division found itself cut off from the Canadian troops on 19th August and despite short supplies and heavy casualties the Polish combat units faced the German Army in bloody conflict around Chambois and on Hill 262, Maczuga. They held fast until 21st August when they were finally relieved by the Canadian forces.

The Polish Division joined the Canadians and marched towards the Seine and then onto the Somme, Antwerp and the Scheldt. In September 1944 they were placed under British command and redeployed in the Mass sector. In April 1945 they embarked on the final push towards the

North Sea, through the Netherlands and Germany and reached Wilhemshaven, taking the surrender of the Kriegsmarines Naval base.

In May 1945 Maczek was promoted to Lieutenant General and placed in charge of 1st Polish Corps stationed in Scotland. The end of the war did not bring a happy ending to Maczek and his troops, they had sacrificed their lives for freedom of their homeland and for the allies only for Poland to fall under Soviet domination. Once demobilised Maczek chose Great Britain as his country of adoption and settled in Edinburgh. He published his memoirs in 1961, Od Podwody Do Czołga and died in 1994 at the age of 102 and is buried in the Polish Military cemetery of Breda in the Netherlands.

He has recently been memorialised in bronze in Edinburgh, thanks to a campaign by the late Lord Fraser and his daughter Katie Fraser, 'My Father was determined that a memorial to this exceptional man and all the Polish soldiers whom he led should be realised.' It was designed by Bronisaw Krzysztof. The General fought in Poland and France, commanding the 1st Polish armoured Division in N.W. Europe and fought through Normandy and then the Low Countries before taking the surrender of the German naval base at Wilhelmshaven.

He was stripped of his Polish citizenship and exiled, branded an enemy of the state by the Soviet Union.

CHAPTER 22

Democracy to Communism

By the end of that war Poland had lost 20% of its people, over 6,000,000 were murdered, half of them Poles and half of them Jews. The population of Warsaw alone was reduced to 25,000 from a pre war figure of 1,289,000. Poland also lost 38% of its national assets while Britain lost 0.8% and France 1.5%.

The two great cities of Lwów and Wilno, centres of Polish culture for many centuries were now part of the Soviet Union. Churchill, in a rare statement of clarity confided after the war that 'terrible and even humbling submissions must at times be made in the general aim,' Poland suffered the most among all the warring nations in WW2 and was treated almost as an enemy by her Allies, England and the United States' who more or less handed Poland over to Stalin!

Long live the great invincibles,
Karl Marx, Freidrich Engels, Vladimir Lenin and Joseph Stalin.

ДА ЗДРАВСТВУЕТ ВЕЛИКОЕ, НЕПОБЕДИМОЕ ЗНАМЯ
МАРКСА-ЭНГЕЛЬСА-ЛЕНИНА-СТАЛИНА!

forward to Communism, glory to the party of Lenin and Stalin, work
for peace and for the happiness of the people

The Soviets now had control over the country and the communist party took charge, controlling administration, the economy, media, education and all other domains of social life. Internal and foreign policies of the Polish People's Republic were entirely dependent on the Soviet Union. Stalin's right hand man Jakub Berman a Jewish, Polish Communist, who had joined the Communist party whilst at Warsaw University, was in charge of the Ministry of Public Security, over-looking the persecutions in political trials of former members of the Polish Resistance.

In January 1945 the Soviets arrested 16 Polish Resistance leaders on charges of subversion and espionage and all but 3 were found guilty on those trumped up charges and sent to prison. Four died and the US and Britain did not intervene. Members of the Armia Krajowa, Peasant battalions and National Armed Forces would face the same fate. After 1947 military resistance was diminishing although there were still small guerrilla groups operating, with the last fighter being killed in 1963. The scout movement was abolished but underground youth groups began to emerge on a mass scale to take its place.

Thousands of Polish soldiers still in Europe post war, suddenly found themselves homeless and afraid to return home and those who had dared to return were immediately arrested by the NKVD, executed after a 'trial' or sent to a gulag. Over 100,000 Polish military and civilians were arrested and interned in abandoned concentration camps and more than 10,000 members of the Armia Krajowa, were sent to Soviet prisons and labour camps. Between 1945 and 1947 thousands more Poles disappeared and the true figures will never be known.

To control the population, the successful Soviet tactic of terror and propaganda was used, 'hypnotising the peasants' into believing that they were under the control of the rich landowners and that Communism would save them! And like in East Germany there was a secret Police Force with agents in every street and block of flats. Dissent was heavily punished with show trials, prisoners held in foul prisons and tortured. It is estimated that in the period 1944-56 some 50,000 people were killed and hundreds of thousands were imprisoned and sent to forced labour camps.

In 1947 the first elections were held but they were anything but democratic. Through brutal intimidation the Police arrested and murdered scores of citizens in order to ensure that the Soviet backed Communist Peasant Party won and they received more than '70% of voter support.' The same has happened today, 2020 in Belarus, its people protesting on the streets after the 're-election' of its President!

Following nationalisation of the economy, farmers were the last remaining group of private asset owners and by 1948 the Communists had launched collectivisation schemes forcing them to give up their land which caused great uproar, bringing back memories of Stalin's collectivisation and five year plans which caused massive famines to many millions, especially in Ukraine, which became known as the Holomodor.

Many schools were closed, teachers purged and text books destroyed. Children were taught about the history of the working class, the Russian revolution and the achievements of the Soviet Union. The aim was to turn the young into slaves, who would never, ever consider opposing Communism. They were not told of the suffering of their Grandparents and parents during WW2, under the extremes of German and Soviet, occupation, the murders, deportations, labour camps, and concentration camps, they grew up oblivious to what their country had endured.

Gradually, anti church propaganda and repressions intensified, many priests and nuns, monks and bishops were imprisoned. Anti religious policies escalated in 1953 when the Polish primate Cardinal Stefan Wyszynski was arrested and imprisoned, priests were intimidated to take an oath of allegiance to the new Communist country.

Communist rule began to show its gross fiscal mis-management and its irresponsible use of Poland's many natural resources and despite Poland's economy in absolute ruin, Stalin did not allow Poland to have any aid from the Marshall Plan, the US initiative for the European Recovery Programme, providing aid to Europe following the devastation of WW2. It provided more than $15 billion to help rebuild Europe and would have helped Poland enormously, Stalin refused.

Increasing resistance by the Poles came to a head in Poznań in June of 1956 with 100,000 people taking to the streets demanding an improvement to living standards and for religious freedom. The protest was brutally put down and 58 people died as a result.

In the autumn to appease the social tensions the communists changed the administration of the party. Poles called for a withdrawal of Soviet forces stationed in Poland, wanting independence from Moscow and for the release of Cardinal Wyszynski and in an attempt to quieten society the communist authorities decided to make certain concessions.

Collective farms were allowed to be dissolved, the system had never worked and farmers regained control of their own farms, censorship eased off temporarily and Soviet soldiers returned to Russia, the power of the repressive state apparatus was restricted.

The Catholic Church also felt the change, Priests were released from prisons, Bishops allowed to return to their dioceses and Religion was reintroduced in schools with permission given for the construction of new churches.

Inevitably, to the Soviets there was far too much freedom being allowed and a new wave of repressions started. Crosses were removed from schools, religious education was again abolished and the construction of new churches suspended with the confiscation of church assets. This triggered strong social opposition from the Poles to Stalin's iron fist.

The economic situation had already by that time worsened and in December 1970 the authorities increased prices which sparked a series of strikes in the whole country. The most dramatic events took place in Gdańsk and Gdynia, Elbląg and Szczecin. The army used military type fire arms against the workers killing 45 people with over a 1,000 injured.

The next crisis was just a matter of time and an attempt to increase prices in 1976 sparked another wave of strikes and demonstrations. Prices were put on hold and the protesters were severely punished. This spurred the creation of opposition organisations, the Workers Defence Committee and the Movement for the Defence of Human and Civil Rights.

The whole population was trapped under a dictatorship which claimed to represent all the people, but represented only the worker and peasant classes, which were more easily controlled with promises that could never be kept. All others were 'the enemy', the category that my family were designated in 1940 and the reason given for their deportation to Siberia. Every single aspect of life was controlled under the Kremlin's direction, assisted by the police, militia and the party bureaucrats. Control was by fear, hunger and lies.

The communist way of operating was in three steps: 'Plan an effective deceit, execute a ruthless crime and then justify it with an outrageous lie.' My Mother Alicja's relatives in Poland were brought up in a dark and inaccessible place, where they had to observe the harsh party line. To successfully work as doctors, as both Halina, cousin of Alicja, and her husband Wiesiek did and to not be considered enemies of the state, it was necessary that they toed the party line. It certainly allowed them more freedom, as well as an apartment with two bedrooms!

They were able, with Ciocia Gienia, to visit the family in England in the early 60's and allowed to educate their son to a good standard, which the ordinary Pole found very difficult to access. Education and advancement were denied you, especially if you were a former deportee, or another designated 'enemy of the state' or even a relative of one.

The family in England had little knowledge whatsoever of Halina and Wiesek's political affiliations, or how they had lived through communism, such is the lack of information. Were they relieved at Poland's eventual freedom from the curse of communism? Or were they committed party activists who, having lost their party status, were suddenly on a more equal footing with the rest of the 'democratic' population? However, in order for them to be able to succeed in their chosen field as doctors, membership of the Party was probably a requirement.

What is known is that life was generally very difficult. People queued even for toilet rolls and to obtain the most basic of needs. There were empty shelves in the shops, intermittently supplied by the mostly unproductive collective farms. Shops were owned by the state and run by their favoured party members, 'who stole most of the food for themselves.' The only shops overflowing with goods were the propaganda 'shops,' peddling the state pronouncements! The family in England were sending food parcels and clothing parcels to Ciocia Gienia up to the 1980s.

People did help each other to survive, they had to, if it was only keeping someone's place in one of the many queues! Where possible people paid for items in cash so that transactions could not be traced by the state. People only had short conversations for fear that too much interaction would put them in danger of being arrested and interrogated. It just sounds so implausible but this was the way.

First hand testimony from those who have worked and lived behind the Iron Curtain is enlightening, 'living under the untouchable Marxist hierarchy, is no more than 'a Marxist zoo,' caged up with all signs of humanity and normal reactions banned' *(A N Other October 2019)* 'Those in control ruled with an iron fist, they were a small group of extreme Left-wing Politicians and their card carrying comrades. They all lived in luxury and were only ever seen travelling down the revered centre of the road in their Russian built Zil limos, claiming they were against privilege but then taking it for themselves to be at the top of the privileged tree'.

There were over 100,000 state informants, which is why people were so guarded and felt so isolated. You say too much and the information could be manipulated and used against you, so to avoid arrest and interrogation you become an informant! Criticize the state controlled news programme openly and you were in big trouble.

You were a rebel if you listened to Radio Free Europe and if you had access to American television stations you opened yourself up to harsh consequences, although very few had a T.V. If you were found out, you would be on your way to the gulag! It all sounds ridiculous and far fetched, but this was the ghastly and miserable existence under communism.

It can be assumed that this is perhaps why the family and people generally were so reluctant to divulge any information. In England there is mostly freedom of thought and word and it is taken completely for granted, we can't imagine a life without it, although Left Wing Woke groups are trying their hardest to destroy free speech! Political Correctness has followed the footsteps of Communism! within the universities especially with student unions refusing to allow speakers who they disagree with, attending forums to debate! They seem only to be able to debate with those they agree with and cancel anybody who disagrees with their ideology. A very easily upset group of anarchists who would fit easily into the role of Stalin's useful idiots!

Those Poles who had not returned to their homeland after the war were vilified, and those who had returned were put at a great disadvantage. They were blacklisted and suffered severe deprivation and hostility. Even after communism it was extremely difficult to let go of old habits and adapt to democracy and free speech, chat freely in the street, criticize the news without looking over your shoulder.

In early 1960's Poland there was increasing distrust of the Soviet intelligentsia and university students protested demanding freedom of speech, study and culture and the abolition of censorship. The authorities reacted by applying mass repressions and an anti-Semitic campaign forcing many people of Jewish descent to leave Poland.

In 1968 Poland experienced a political thaw which slowly turned into anti-Russian feeling. Student riots in Warsaw and Kraków were forcibly put down and repression against intellectuals ensued. Food was increased by 60% which led to riots in the Baltic states which were also repressed with great bloodshed.

This gave the authorities the excuse for a change of leadership in the party and as well as offering concessions to the people, Edward Gierek replaced Gomułka as Premier and western loans were to enable living standards to improve, political liberalism was also eased.

The Soviet run economy however was not reformed and crisis followed crisis. In 1978 another attempt to increase prices sparked another wave of strikes and the protestors were severely punished but this only resulted in opposition organisations forming, the Workers' Defence committee and the Movement for the Defence of Human and Civil Rights. The underground press grew in stature and an independent education system began to form.

On 16th October 1978 Cardinal Karol Wojtyla Cardinal of Kraków, was elected as Pope which threw a shock wave through Communists in Poland and Russia and Poland's sense of destiny began to take shape. The authorities were unable to prevent Pope John Paul II from visiting his homeland in June 1979 at a time of huge crisis for the Poles. Any Soviet objections would be seen worldwide.

At a mass attended by hundreds of thousands of rejoicing Poles he gave them hope for the future .... 'let your spirit descend, let your spirit descend and renew the face of the earth, the face of this land.'

These were prophetic words, hope and confidence was settling into the hearts of the Poles.

The Summer of 1980 brought a series of strikes across Poland by the worsening economic situation under Communist rule. The strikes in the Gdansk shipyard in 1980 proved to be ground breaking, they were sparked by the dismissal of Anna Walentynowicz, a resident of Równe, my Mother's home town, who was an opposition activist.

A list of demands was put to the authorities including the right to create independent trade unions, the strike spread to Szczecin, Wrocław and Jastrzębie and the scale of the protests forced the authorities to make some concessions resulting in the formation of the union, Solidarność.

Solidarność had been born under the leadership of Lech Wałesa, was independent and self governing and despite obstacles put up by the authorities began to spread across the country. By 1981 nearly 10 ml Poles were members and farmers and students followed suit creating their own unions.

Solidarność was exceptional in that after a very short time the Poles were engaging in public matters that had been denied them for so long. The Union gave people hope and there were plans to reform all organisational levels of society. The Poles were determined, they were strong in their belief that their spirit would prevail.

This was a massive undertaking and thousands of uncensored magazines and books were circulated telling the truth of Poland's recent history in WW2 which previously had been forbidden, not taught in schools. Literature was now being published and there was an undercurrent of reform against the authorities.

After years of imposed atheism, Solidarność was attracting people with broad views, the common values of truth and justice, solidarity and patriotism and religion. These then all began to emerge from the underground into public life.

The communist authorities had been planning to abolish Solidarnosc and the pressure was coming from Moscow to disband it. General Jaruzelski the Defence Minister, Prime Minister and First secretary of Poland, ordered a massive build up of troops along Poland's borders to emphasise Soviet authority.

Something very similar is happening in Belarus today, people worn down by ruthless dictator Aleksandr Lukashenko in power since 1994 and re-elected after a rigged election with violent suppression of hundreds of thousands of protesters. Police brutality and Secret Police (KGB) monitoring dissidents! The opposition leader Svetlana Tikhanovskaya forced to flee the country to Ukraine with other opposition members and Putin keeping a very close eye on the state of conflict within Belarus. Reminiscent of the Soviet era?

On December 13th 1981, martial law was declared in Poland followed by arrests of Solidarność leaders and of intellectuals. Tanks and armoured vehicles appeared   on the streets of Poland and despite the Soviet crackdown, Solidarność went underground to avoid an invasion by the Red Army. Economic sanctions were quickly imposed by the West against Poland and the Soviet Union.

Telephone lines were cut and travel was restricted with people not being allowed to travel to other towns. All organisations were suspended apart from the Communist party, 3,000 people were interned on the first night and in total 10,000 members of the Union and other organisations were sent to internment camps. Over 10,000 people received prison sentences and tens of thousands were sacked.

This brought about hundreds of strikes over the entire country despite the threat that resistance would be punishable by death. The Poles had ignored the German punishment by death, for any Pole found to be helping their Jewish neighbours in WW2, their children with the same attitude, would do the same and ignore the Soviets.

The strikes were violently put down and protests broken up but the Polish spirit, that had seen the Poles as such strong Allies in WW2, prevailed and Solidarnosc was not destroyed. The Union had been recreated clandestinely in factories and the Polish underground with the Church playing a huge role.

There were worldwide demonstrations in solidarity with Solidarność and there were even protests within the Soviet bloc. Sanctions were imposed against the Communist authorities in Poland and the Soviet Union and Lech Wałesa was awarded the Nobel Peace prize in 1983 which the Soviets saw as an insult to them. The Communists did not give up and although martial law was halted in 1983 the repressions continued and the Poles looked towards the Pope for support and he visited Poland in 1983 and 1987.

In 1988, after another wave of strikes, the Communist Party in Poland agreed to share political power, it was unable to prevent Poland's decline and at the end of the month the Soviets gave recognition to Solidarność and talks began between interior minister Kiszczak and Wałesa but talks broke off by October. By February 1989 further talks produced an agreement allowing for national assembly elections and on April 5th 1989 an agreement was signed in which the party and representatives from the Solidarność movement specified their conditions.

In the elections of 1989 Solidarność thrashed the Communists, winning almost every seat it contested. Lech Wałesa, Solidarność's leader, was elected president of Poland in 1990.

The election of Cardinal Karol Wojtyla as Pope had strengthened the people's resolve in coping with the ruthless realities of Communism, and on one of his early visits to his homeland he had encouraged millions of his countrymen with the words "do not be afraid." He returned to Poland in 1991 to enjoy with his people a free Poland. Full sovereignty was regained in 1992 with the withdrawal of most of the Soviet occupying troops. Poland then returned, officially, to Christianity. The Poles ever resourceful, had followed their faith throughout, although secretly and quietly. The Soviets couldn't arrest an entire country, despite their domination!

The events in Poland, the first country in the eastern bloc to throw off the shackles of Communist tyranny, inspired the collapse of Communism in Europe as a whole. Adapting to a free society and economy has not been as smooth as some Poles might have hoped, but the country has emerged from the captivity of Communism and is now a member of the European Union and NATO.

It would have been wonderful had my grandparents Kazia and Adam lived long enough to see their homeland free again. They at least lived out their days in freedom in England with their family, the family that had survived the ordeal of Stalin's labour camps, the family whose spirit he could not break. I wonder what they would have made of the leader of Poland's Trade Union?

Lech Wałesa, the leader of Solidarność, was he an icon or a Communist? I have recently been made aware by my cousin Maciej Morawiec, son of Halina and Wiesek, living in Poland, of information coming to light about Lech Wałesa, also known as Lejba Kohne, which has long been withheld.

Maciej was born and has lived in Poland all his life, under Communism and now democracy and he has sent my cousin Alec an enormous amount of papers in regard to Wałesa and his role as a puppet of the Communist Government in charge of Poland at the time of Solidarność.

The writers of these papers, Marian Kowalski and Pawel Chojnacki are on record saying that Wałesa was instead controlled by the Communist regime throughout the 'transition of Solidarność to democracy' and that Poland is still run by the communists, or rather the children of the communists.

This is intriguing, and to a point makes a great deal of sense. No one had ever been removed from their positions in the Communist regime, the judiciary, universities, teachers, schools, courts, police, doctors, all had grown up under Communism and most agreed and benefitted from it. Those complicit in this include the Church, Catholic Bishops, the Media and many diplomats in duping the world in maintaining the façade.

Wałesa was arrested several times by the Communists with his fellow Union members, and under Jaruzelski's martial law, he had been put up in 5 star hotels whilst his colleagues were apparently put into internment camps!

It has been maintained that Wałesa was a secret service agent, who as a figure head helped the Communists overthrow the anti-Communist government in 1970!

This does beggar believe, on the one hand, but on the other a point to debate? Of course Poland would have needed a transition period post Communism, but according to my cousin Maciej, the transition is still ongoing, Poland is still under the rule of the children of post war Communists as Poland failed to get rid of the old Communists who continued to occupy positions of importance in the government, judiciary and the secret police for most likely decades after 1989.

The so called 'systematic transformation' in Poland and other post Soviet countries was an orgy of embezzlement by the Communists, its chief beneficiaries. This 'new class' privatised itself and are living well off their pillaging!

This requires more investigation and I am looking into this further, awaiting documentation from cousin Maciej and will most likely require another book on the subject, I'll leave that project to my cousin!

A friend of mine Jadwiga known as Jagoda Gąsior from Grodek in Radom, in south west Poland has given me her personal account of life under Communism, of her upbringing in Poland. She has lived in England since 1976.

She is the daughter of Stanisłowa (born 1925) and Jan (born 1912) who married in 1944 and had three children. Jagoda has a brother Stanisław and sister Krystyna.

Her grandfather Jósef owned land and mills and was a kulak, so called by the Soviets as someone who owns land and considered much richer than the peasants he employed but who worked as hard on the land as did his wife Anna and children.

Jagoda's family were poor, they were not richer than the peasants. They had little to eat with most of the food her grandfather produced going to the Soviets, having to meet the high criteria of his government masters which left them with little for themselves and the peasants who worked their land.

Despite their hardship, her grandparents Anna and Jósef helped their Jewish neighbours, friends of Anna's, who they hid in their barn. Many Poles did help Jews at the risk of the death penalty imposed by the Germans, only in Poland, not on any other German occupied country.

Her Grandmother Marianne told her of seeing Russian soldiers in 1945, in rags, no uniforms, feet wrapped in felt and straw wandering the countryside. Early one morning she went to the stable to find her cow missing and found the group of soldiers eating the cow over a fire and she found that sheep were also missing. The Russians felt entitled and took what they wanted only adding to the great hardship of the post war Polish people. They didn't care.

Jagoda had no childhood to talk of, there were many shortages, nothing in the shops and what there was had rotted and the fruit in the markets was mouldy.

Education was not as high a standard as pre war as all teachers had been deported or killed by the Germans and Russians and those who were left were not highly educated. The country had been completely ruined by war.

No one knew of the tragedies of the war, they were not taught about what had happened, the war was rarely mentioned. All that was said was the Russians freed the Poles from the Germans and they should be grateful. Nothing told about the English or Americans in the war but a lot about the Russians winning the war.

When Stalin died in 1953 enforced vigils were held in schools all over Poland and children kept vigil at his portrait and one child repeated a remark his parents had made about Stalin, overheard by one of the Communist teachers and the parents were hauled to the headmaster and interrogated.

A friend of Jagoda's, an army Captain Charek, wept many tears at Stalin's death, tears running down his face, and she couldn't understand why he had wept like that. Although the brainwashing he had received in the army would have made him believe everything about the Father of the Nation and his expression of sadness would need to be dramatic.

'We were brainwashed but didn't know it, it worked so well we didn't know any different.' Larissa, a Russian friend of Jagoda's has been so brainwashed she is too scared even whilst living in England, to say anything 'inappropriate.'

'We were taught about Lenin, Marx and communism and my father listened to the radio but there was only propaganda no news about what was happening in the country, we were only told how awful the west was.'

Jagoda decided she didn't want to work on the land and after attending the Gymnasium gained a place at a University in Warsaw and worked part time for a tourism company for a chance to work abroad and perhaps study in London.

By the 70's people were allowed to visit other places and the Poles were eager to get away from 'grey Poland'. In 1976 Jagoda accepted an invitation from a friend in England, Krystyna, to come over for 3 weeks but overstayed her Visa. She had met her husband to be Ken, in Poland whilst working for a Tourism company and they married and she stayed in England which upset her family but they realised the consequences of her going back after overstaying her Visa.

Her sister was staying in her flat whilst Jagoda was in England and was spied on by one of the tenants, the Police had her followed and knew her every step and who stayed in the flat. The phone was bugged with any calls recorded and the same had happened to her parents, as well as being summoned to attend the Police station and interrogated.

The family weren't able to let Jagoda know of what they were experiencing as communication wasn't very efficient and any call or letter would be tapped or censored!

In 1978 on a visit home, Jagoda was 'invited' to attend a Police Station, 'would you like to come for a chat,' you didn't refuse, she went. They knew she had a UK passport and wanted to know about her job, her husband, about her and the companies she and her husband worked for, who her colleagues were what they did, who they knew and would she like to work for them? and pass on information for them? and would she send them some information in the future about the West? Anything about the West. Would she like to spy for them? she declined as diplomatically as she could.

Jagoda's mother Stanisława came to visit her in England soon after Jagoda's daughter was born in 1979 and stayed for 3 weeks. There was an unexpected delay at Heathrow airport on her return journey and she wasn't able to arrive back in Poland on schedule, arriving a day later. She was summoned to the Police station and interrogated as to why she was late coming back into Poland. The intimidation of citizens was relentless.

When leaving Poland after a visit with her Mother and reaching the eastern German border, surrounded by barbed wire fences, they were always met with the most stringent of inspections. Guards with dogs would search cars, wheels were removed and tyres inspected, everything removed from the car, baggage sorted and items thrown out. It took considerable time and people were made to feel under huge pressure and afraid, as was intended.

Jagoda's mother had given her a duvet for the baby and a guard spotted it thinking someone was being smuggled in and poked it thoroughly. – Smuggled out maybe, hardly in.

People couldn't buy clothes off the peg as in the West, they had to buy material and make their own. My own family sent parcels of clothing and food to our family into the 1980's and a lot of those clothes ended up in the Warsaw markets which Jagoda used to visit to find clothes of better quality than they could ever make.

Life under communism, imposed on Poland after the end of WW2, was a life marred by Stalinist repressions, social unrest, political strife and severe economic difficulties. My grandparents were right not to go back to the arrests, imprisonments and persecution.

My Cocia Jasia and Mother Alicja were in touch with their cousin Halina by phone over the years and Alec had tracked down Maciej, Halina's son via Google, and we all three now have regular contact via email and through Facebook history sites, Kresy Siberia and Kresy Family. Despite many attempts by the family to find out what happened to Grandmother Sofia, Kazia's Mother, it is still not known what exactly her fate was. There were some reports that she had been shot by the NKVD in eastern Poland, but there is no way of investigating this to confirm it.

The family knew that Halina's husband Wiesiek strongly disapproved of their Catholic faith. Janusz, on one of his visits to Poland, once tackled him about this and asked if he was a Communist which of course Wiesiek brushed aside. He did not however join the family in church for very long before leaving on an 'urgent' matter! He was very critical of the family for not returning to Poland after WW2 and made his views known, he may have had some resentment about this as he was by marriage related to deportees and this would have been known to the Soviet authorities and perhaps be on his record. He also maybe wasn't aware of the retribution suffered by the returning military Poles and their families although I may find this difficult to believe!

The bond between the Radomski's, Kazia and brother Walery and their families was very strong, it had to be to have survived massive upheaval and deprivation. They almost died from starvation and from illnesses they became susceptible to, malaria, typhus, dysentery and typhoid. They weren't heroic, but luck and significant circumstances did play a part in their survival.

They supported each other in freedom and assimilated themselves to a new country despite some initial hostility, working and living happily and productively until retirement and beyond. They had their family and that's all they needed to give them strength. And they became my family and how proud I am of them, their life and history.

Kazia and Adam, Walery and Ziuta are long gone; they died without being able to revisit their old country which was a great regret to them. Zbyszek and Włodek died before their time and Janusz, Marysia and Jasia were lost to us more recently, my Mother Alicja is the only remaining member of this incredible family at 97.

Each and every one remains
forever in our memories,
and we raise a 'Polish measure'
to them at certain times of the year.
Their bond and spirit
were broken not by Stalin
but simply by the passing of time.

'I plead with you, never, ever give up on hope, never doubt, never tire and never become discouraged, be not afraid'. – **Pope John Paul II**

CHAPTER 23

Timeline of events

Lenin and Stalin

1918 The murder of the Tsar and his family took place in Yekaterinburg, overseen by the Ural Regional Soviet, most likely sanctioned by Lenin. My family passed by this town on their escape from the labour camp in 1942.

1918 Treaty of Brest-Litovsk according to which Russia ceded large tracts of land to Germany. Finland, Estonia, Latvia, Lithuania, Georgia, Armenia and Azerbaijan proclaim their independence from Russia.

1918-1920 Civil war between the Bolsheviks (Reds) and anti Bolsheviks (Whites) ravages Russia. In Northern Russia, British, French and US troops capture Murmansk and Arkhangelsk where my family were incarcerated in 1940. In 1919, while in the Russian Far East they occupy Vladivostok, which was held by the Japanese until 1922.

1918-1921 Policy of 'War Communism' with the state taking control of the whole economy, millions of peasants in the Don region starve to death as the army confiscates grain for its own needs and the needs of urban dwellers.

1919 The Cheka were entrusted with the establishment of the gulags across Soviet Russia in 1919, holding about 50,000 prisoners in 84 camps in 1920 and by the end of 1923 there were 315 camps with 70,000 prisoners used as slave labour. Intellectuals deemed to be opposing the Bolshevik government were exiled to the most inhospitable regions, where my own family were to come across them when they were searching for food. Lenin personally scrutinised the lists of those to be deported and ordered the execution of up to 20,000 anti Bolshevik priests.

1920 Poland-Russian war. After the German garrisons were withdrawn from the eastern front following the Armistice, both Polish and Soviet armies moved in seeking to gain territorial expansion in the region, Poland wanting to reclaim territories lost in the last partition. They had first clashed in February 1919 with the conflict developing into the Polish-Russian war. Unlike previous Soviet conflicts this had greater implications for the spread of communism and revolution into the rest of Europe. Polish forces pushed into the Ukraine and by May 1920 had taken Kiev from the Soviets.

After forcing the Polish army back, Lenin urged the Red Army to invade Poland itself, believing the Polish proletariat would rise up to support the Russian troops and spark European revolution. This did not happen, they did not rise up, most had no Communist leanings and the Red Army was defeated at the Battle of the Wistula. The Polish armies pushed the Red Army back into Russia, forcing the Sovnarkom Council to sue for peace, which culminated in the Peace of Riga in which Russia ceded previous Polish territory, the eastern borderlands, Western Ukraine and Western Belarus, back to Poland. My Dziadek Adam and Wujek Walery fought in this battle.

1921 Peace treaty signed with Poland, the Treaty of Riga. Lenin had expected a swift victory confident in the Bolsheviks' ability to organise themselves effectively, however, Poland, by winning this battle had saved Europe from the invasion of Lenin and his Communism and spoilt his aspirations.

1921 New economic policy ushers in a partial return to the market economy and a period of stability. Soviet rule established in Georgia.

1921 Polish France Military Alliance.

1922 Union treaty formally joins Russia, Ukraine, Belarus and the Trans Caucasus with Georgia, Armenia and Azerbaijan, into the Soviet Union. In 1922 it joined its republics to the Union of Soviet Socialist Republics.

1923 Germany recognises the Soviet Union.

1923 Lenin's health declines and will lead to his death

1924 The Uprising in Georgia against the Bolsheviks put down by the Red Army.

1925 The creation of the USSR. Soviet Union adopts constitution on the dictatorship of the proletariat and stipulates the public ownership of land and the means of production. The Sovnarkom becomes a national body. Lenin dies and is replaced by Józef Stalin.

1928 Adoption of Stalin's first 5 year plan, with the state setting goals and priorities for the whole economy. It signifies the end of the New Economic Policy and the battle for grain begins, it proves to be a disaster.

The collectivisation of agriculture begins, mostly because of a mistrust of the peasantry as 'petty bourgeoisie' a relic of the old society. Numerous relatively prosperous peasants, (Kulaks) are killed, millions of peasant households eliminated and their property is confiscated. The Kulaks were a threat as long as they controlled the food supply, they were too keen on free trade, family life and their farms and had to be 'socialised'.

Sinoi-Soviet conflict with the Chinese warlord Zhang Xueliang of China over the Manchurian Chinese Eastern Railway, it is put down by the Red Army.

1932 Poland-Russia non aggressive pact. To allay fears of a war with the Soviet Union.

1933 Roosevelt, President of the United States recognises the Soviet Union.

1934 Poland-Germany non aggression pact, to forgo armed conflict for 10 years.

1934 Soviet invasion of Xinjiang, ends in stalemate.

1934 Soviet Union admitted to the League of Nations, on recommendation of Roosevelt, whose WW2 relationship with Stalin, 'Uncle Joe', would determine Poland's post war fate.

1936-38 Announcement of the discovery of a plot against Stalin's regime headed by Leon Trotsky ushers in a large scale purge in which thousands of alleged dissidents in the armed forces, the Communist Party and the government were sentenced to death or to long term imprisonment in the gulags.

1937 Xinjiang war, Red Army fight Uyghur rebels with Sheng Shical of Xinjiang government.

1938 Battle of Lake Khasan, Soviets repel Japanese incursion.

1939 Battle of Halhin Gol, Soviets defeat Japanese Army retaining existing border with Manchukho.

1939 August, Soviet Union and Germany conclude a non-aggression pact, (Molotov-Ribbentrop) and Germany invades Poland on 1st September, triggering WW2. A Pact now denied by the Russians post war as it would implicate Stalin as colluding with Hitler, as he was for a third of WW2.

1939 Soviet troops invade Poland on 17th September, which is then divided between Germany and the USSR. Russia maintains they went into Poland to save them from the Germans. Their intention however was to take over and spread Communism throughout Europe.

1939-40   Russian-Finnish war which ends with Finland ceding territory to the USSR, the present Russian constituent republic of Karelia.

1940   Soviet troops occupy Poland, Lithuania, Latvia and Estonia which are then incorporated into the USSR. Romania cedes Bessarabia and North Bukuvina to the USSR which declares the Moldovian Soviet Socialist Republic, the present independent republic of Moldovia.

1939-40   Soviets annex 10% of Finnish territory and are expelled from the League of Nations for aggression against Finland and the pact with Germany.

1941   April, Soviet Union and Japan sign a non aggression pact.

1941   June, Germany invades the USSR and by the end of the year occupies Belarus and most of Ukraine, and surrounds Leningrad (now St Petersburg). A Soviet counter offensive saves Moscow but the Germans are at the gates of Stalingrad (now Volgograd) and close to the Caucasus oil fields.

1943   Germans fail to take Stalingrad, Soviet troops launch a counter offensive which culminates in the capture of Berlin in May 1945.

1944   Soviets defeat Finland gaining additional territory and Finland withdraws from the War.

1945   Red Army troops clash with Chinese troops.

1945   Soviet Union and the Allies reach 'understanding' on post war spheres of influence in Europe during the Yalta and Potsdam summit conferences, without Polish or other European representation. Poland's eastern territories, which are still occupied by the Red Army, are ceded to the USSR.

1945   August, Soviet Union declares war on Japan, eventually annexing the southern half of Sakhalin and the Kuril islands.

1945-74   Thousands of Baltic 'Forest Brothers' waged resistance against Soviet administration with major fighting ending in 1950's with their defeat. The last partisan was killed in 1974.

1945   Soviet invasion of Manchuria, evicting the Japanese from the mainland, occupying Manchuria, North Korea and Kuril Islands.

1947   The Cold War begins with Soviets opposing the US and NATO.

1948-49   Berlin blockade, Soviet Union fails to prevent supplies from reaching the sectors of Berlin occupied by Western forces.

1949 Soviet Union explodes its first atomic device and recognises the Communist government in China.

1950 Soviet Union and China sign 30 year alliance treaty. Expires 1960 due to ideological clashes between the two Leaders.

1950-53 Outbreak of Korean War sees relations between Soviet Union and the West deteriorate markedly.

1953 March, Stalin dies and is succeeded by George Malenkov as prime minister and by Nikita Krushchev as first secretary of the Central Committee of the Communist Party.

1953 Soviet Union explodes its first hydrogen bomb.

1955 Nikolay Bulganin replaces Malenkov as prime minister.

1955 Soviets establish Warsaw Pact in 1955 in response to NATO in 1948.

1956 Soviet troops crush uprising in Hungary.

Kruschev

1956 February, Kruschev makes a secret speech to the 20th Communist Party congress denouncing Stalin's dictatorial rule and cult of personality.

1957 First ever artificial satellite, Sputnik orbits the earth.

1958 Kruschev becomes prime minister, in addition to Communist party chief, after dismissing Nikolai Bulganin.

Late 1950's ..China falls out with the Soviet Union over Moscow's policy of peaceful co-existance with the West.

1960 Soviet Union shoots down US spy plane U2 over Soviet Territory.

1961 Yuri Gagarin makes the first manned orbital flight.

1962 Cuban missile crisis erupts over presence of Soviet missiles in Cuba.

1963 Soviet Union joins the US and Britain in signing a treaty banning atmospheric nuclear tests, US-Soviet hotline set up.

Brezhnev

1964 Krushchev is replaced as first secretary of the Communist party by

Leonid Brezhnev, Aleksey Kosygin becomes prime minister.

1968 Soviet and Warsaw Pact troops invade Czechosovakia to stem a trend towards liberalisation. The Brezhnev doctrine officially asserted 'the Soviet Union's right to intervene in other Communist States' internal affairs in order to secure socialism from opposing capitalist forces who threaten the international Communist movement.' It was used to justify the Soviet invasion of Afghanistan in 1979 and the spreading of Communism in Angola, South Africa and Cuba.

1969 Soviet and Chinese troops clash across the border.

1972 Soviet Union and US sign SALT-1 arms control agreement heralding the start of détente.

1974 Soviet Union agrees to ease its emigration policy in return for more favoured nation trade status with the US.

1977 Brezhnev elected President under new constitution.

1979 Soviet Union and the US sign SALT-2 agreement. Soviet troops invade Afghanistan, formerly ending the period of detente with the West.

1980 Kosygin is replaced as prime minister by Nikolay Tikhonov, Kosygin dies.

1982 Brezhnev dies and is replaced by KGB chief Yuri Andropov.

1984 Andropov dies and is replaced by Konstantin Chernenko.

Gorbachev

1985 Chernenko dies and is replaced by Mikhail Gorbachev as general secretary of the Communist Party. Andrey Gromyko becomes president. Gorbachev begins an anti-alcohol campaign and promotes the policies of openness/glasnost and restructuring/perestroika.

1986 Chernobyl nuclear power station explodes showering large areas of Ukraine, Belarus and Europe with radio active material. This was down to the incompetence of employees and a design flaw and was only able to be covered up by the Russians for a very short period due to the spread of radio activity across many parts of Europe.

1987 Soviet Union and US agree to scrap intermediate range nuclear missiles, Boris Yeltsin dismissed as Moscow party chief for criticising slow pace of reforms.

1988 Gorbachev replaces Gromyko as President, he challenges nationalists in Kazakhstan, the Baltic republics, Armenia and Azerbaijan.

1989 Revolutionary events begin in Poland in the toppling of the Soviet imposed Communist regimes in central and eastern Europe. They continue in Hungary, East Germany, Bulgaria, Czechoslovakia and Romania. In East Germany an unprecedented series of mass public rallies leads to the fall of the Berlin Wall on 9th November.

Elsewhere in the USSR Soviet troops leave Afghanistan, nationalist riots are put down in Georgia, the Lithuanian Communist Party declares its independence from the Soviet Communist party and has the first openly contested elections for new Congress of People's Deputies.

Yeltsin

1990 Soviet troops are sent to Azerbaijan following inter ethnic killings. Communist party votes to end one party rule and Gorbachev opposes independence of Baltic states and imposes sanctions on Lithuania. Yeltsin elected President of the Russian Soviet Federative Socialist Republic by the latter's parliament and Gorbachev leaves the Soviet Communist Party.

1991 August, Senior officials, including Defence Minister Dimitry Yazov, vice president Gennadiy Yanayev and the heads of Interior Ministry and the KGB, detain Gorbachev at his holiday villa in Crimea but are themselves arrested three days later. Yeltsin bans the Soviet Communist Party in Russia and seizes its assets. He recognises the independence of the Baltic states and Ukraine, followed by other republics.

1991 September, Congress of People's Deputies votes for the dissolution of the USSR.

1991 8 December, Leaders of Russia, Ukraine and Belarus sign agreement setting up Commonwealth of Independent states.

1991 26 December, Russian Government takes over offices of USSR in Russia and the Hammer and Sickle flies for the last time.

A timeline mostly relevant to my grandparent's Kazia and Adam's generation, who grew up in its beginnings and lived through it. Aware of the Russian Revolution and the likely consequences of Lenin's doctrine on their own country. Followed by Stalin's hatred of the 'Polish filth' suffering the consequences of his revenge.

They watched Russia's performance on the world stage and saw the impact of Communism on their country with great sadness. They also saw the effect his Cold War had on the rest of the world and although missing their old life in the Kresy, were thankful for life in a free country.

Kazia born in 1899 and Adam born in 1894, died within a year of each other in 1983 and 1984. They didn't live to see the end of the Polish people's fight for liberty over Communism and they would have been incredibly proud of their countrymen and women.

As I am incredibly proud to be their wnuczka, to have grown up in the culture of these incredibly strong, funny, loving and brave people.

They did not let Stalin break their spirit, they journeyed from the USSR through dreadful hardship with only one thing in mind, to join the Polish Army in the Middle East and although separated many times, made it there as a family.

'one cannot and **must not** *try to* **erase the past** *merely because it does* **not fit the present**' – **Golda Meir**

Acknowledgements

My most sincere thanks and love go to Alec Dyki, my skilful, lovable and dependable cousin who supported me in many aspects of this and the prequel, the most important parts of our heritage and also to family members for photographs from pre and post WWI Poland, WW2 Persia, Lebanon and England.

Anita de Haan • Janina Misik • Marek, Ania and Ewa Skoczylas

• Kazia and Adam Góral • Alicja Góral Hartley

Book Jacket Design by Alec Dyki & Chris Dyki

Book layout by Alec Dyki

And very special thanks must go to a very dear friend, the late Patricia Murphy, without her input and encouragement I would have found this most emotional task much harder to bear.

I also gratefully acknowledge the permission granted by Ryszard Grzybowski of the Association of the Families of the Eastern Borderlands to use artwork and poems and personal recollections reproduced in this book and also in the prequel, Midnight Train to Siberia.

I am indebted especially to my family, in particular my Babcia Kazia, Dziadek Adam, Mamusia Alicja, and Ciocia Jasia. Their role in providing me with the facts of their ordeal from 1940 to 1946 has been invaluable in piecing this story together.

Sources of research

• The Góral and Radomski families personal recollections and archives
• Children of Sybiraks • Kresy Family • Kresy Siberia.• Stalin's Ethnic
Cleansing • Forgotten Refugees • Silenced Refugees • Silent Heroes of
the Forgotten Holocaust • Becky Little, National Geographic
• Poland Forever • Wikipedia • Wojtek Soldier Bear • Norman Davies
• Max Hastings • Christopher R. Browning • Joanna Ostrowska & Marcin
Zaremba • Polish Academy of Sciences • Dr Janusz Wróbel IPN,
• Michael Checinski, IPN • Prof. Chwalba, Jagielonian Univ.
• Dr Kathrine R. Jolluck, Stanford Univ. • Elie Weisel, Vyacheslav,
Volodin, Prof. Daniel Tiles, Krakow Univ. • Jarosław Kaczynski, Polish
President 2005-2010 • Angela Merkel, German Chancellor • Prof.
Andrzej Paczkowski, Dr Jan Zaryn, IPN • Israel Gutman • Władyslaw
Bartoszewski • Sergey Radchenko • Mateusz Morawiecki, Polish PM
• Prof. Szewach • Michael Weiss • Brendon Dougherty • E. Ringelblum
• Golda Meir, Israeli PM 1969-74 • Edward Mosberg • David Moorhouse
• Lucille Eichengree • Yehudi Lub • Primo Levi • Sergey Andreev
• Hannah Aendt • Jan Silwa • Timothy Snyder • Anne Applebaum
• Norman Finkelstein • Polishmediaissues • Poland.pl/history
• Britishpoles.uk • Polish Truth • Historynotesfrompoland.com
• Justiceforpoland • PolishForums.com

I needed to know about my heritage, what had happened to my Polish family to carefully find a way into my Mother's troubled mind, hoping she would allow her memories to make themselves known to me. I started the delicate task of opening up the past and began by talking with the only two surviving members – my Mother Alicja and my dahlink Ciocia Jasia. I had talked to my Mother many times over the years and we often revisited all that I'd remembered when as a child I had sat with my grandparents, Kazia and Adam, listening intently at what made them cry, or laugh and what sometimes made them take a deep breath and go quiet for minutes on end, their eyes going somewhere I have never been, a distant, private and painful place.

It was usually like this when the family got together and I had over the years made many notes and I had to arrange these and all those memories in my own mind before I started writing the story of my family's deportation to Siberia. After my Father died, I gave my Mother two writing pads and asked her to write everything she remembered, from the moment the NKVD had charged through their door with bayonets fixed and arrested them at their home in Równe. Once my Mother started writing she couldn't stop, she told me she cried each time she went into the memory of that day so deeply etched in her mind. Many memories of the past however were more deeply suppressed than she had realised and she had found it very painful and highly emotional and I wondered if I'd put too much pressure on her but my darling Mother persevered with the strength she had developed in the labour camp.

I sent a draft of what I had written to Ciocia Jasia and she was able to recall more detail of those awful events and would go into her own memory time and again for me, to bring their story to life. My cousin Alec, who had helped in the formation of this and the prequel, found his Mother crying one day over my draft and read it himself. This reawakened his interest in the family history and since then we have been a very close and productive team in exploring our heritage. His son Chris has designed the cover and his daughter Lynsey updates the family archive.

I hadn't wanted to reopen old wounds by revisiting the family past, but I wanted to present as truthful an account as possible of what they had gone through, I didn't want to guess so I needed to tread the road into their war time experience. I too found their ordeal emotional and daunting and tears often flowed down my face in the writing of the account. I didn't think I'd react like this, I had wanted to keep my emotions at a distance but somehow the tears gave me some relief and they've flowed steadily throughout the writing of this painful time. I cannot overestimate how highly charged the emotions still run, especially now with my Mother at 97, overwhelmed by Alzheimers. I must finish this for her.

In the early days of recording my family's account of events I had relied heavily on my memory, notes that I'd made and some research. What I had remembered from the days at my grandparents' side was more than I'd realized and those conversations so long ago had set the pattern for my interest in Poland's WW2 history. I have made many new discoveries on this journey, mainly through history sites and have uncovered many facts and untruths, as so much of what happened to the Polish deportees had been buried. Historical amnesia had affected the Western Allies and the general media, despite many reports of Stalin and Hitler's war crimes from Polish sources, the Polish Underground just one.

No survivor avoided their pain or could ever came to terms with what happened. I've met deportees who buried their feelings, unable to talk about or share them, prisoners of their memories. Some had lost a mother, brother and sister and then their father in the space of 3 months and watching your baby sister starve to death on the deportation train leaves a pain that never goes away. Erasing this from their memories was a means of emotional defence and their lives must have been difficult to bear. You can't walk away from the terror they experienced without scars. Each family carried the thought of those left behind in unmarked graves and of those who hadn't been able to make it to safety and freedom.

'We clashed with the NKVD and the Kommandant with the threat of death several times in the labour camps, living in terror of the Bolsheviks, and on the journey to Tashkent, but we somehow managed to survive, we tried to forget them, to bury them but they still got into our very beings and became a part of us.'

My Mother had flashbacks throughout her life, it was seared into her memory, 'It hurts my head' she would say and she had a nervous breakdown at 39. The physical pain has healed but the mental pain goes on forever. 'It's always there, never goes away, to go without food for days at a time, working in the forests in very difficult conditions it was so very hard to cope with. I've never forgotten the deaths around me, people died from dysentery, typhus and starvation, the body and spirit were sorely tested.'

The suffering did not end with their release from the Soviet camps it continued throughout their lives, affecting their family sometimes drastically. The deportees faced many problems adapting to freedom and a normal life. Family dynamics were thrown into confusion, a Polish mother bringing up her English speaking children when she could barely speak the language herself and when shopping brought scenes of hostility. 'When I came to England I got used to people calling me a bloody foreigner and my children Polish pigs. Yes I was traumatised and sometimes I felt it made me stronger more able to cope but some days it's in my mind and I can't lose it'.

Many refugees, worldwide, were afraid to speak openly for fear of putting their family back in Communist Poland in a difficult position, my own family included. There was fear of retribution and people didn't start talking openly until after the fall of the Berlin War and then the fall of Communism in 1989.

This is the story of a most remarkable family, one of very many, taken at gunpoint from their homeland in the Kresy in 1940 who endured a most appalling experience and who lost absolutely everything except the ability to love. I had absorbed so much from bits of conversations and revelations that I had gathered from my family from a very early age. I inherited an understanding of their loss and grief, and the horror and brutality they lived through never left them and this seeped down to me as it must have done to all children of survivors.

Those tears have fallen against my face again as I on behalf of my family hope to lay to rest the ghosts of Stalin's shadow and through these memoirs, illustrate that he did not, ever, break their spirit and I need to keep the flame of my beloved family burning bright.

I have a strong affinity with Poland,
naturally embracing her culture,
it is in my blood.
I was born to a Polish Mother
who had survived a horrendous journey
to imprisonment in a labour camp
and then a trek to freedom,
over 22,000 kms.
I am proud to be a grand daughter
and daughter of the Radomski-Góral family
and I hope to have honoured them
in the telling of their experience.

Teresa Radomska 2021

Alicja, 1938 & 2018 – Polish Warrior Queen

'If you don't recount your family history it will be lost.
Honour your own stories and tell them too,
they may not seem very important but
they are what binds families and makes
each of us who we are.'

Madelaine L'Engle

Milton Keynes UK
Ingram Content Group UK Ltd.
UKHW021113280923
429463UK00011B/107

9 781915 889058